PENGUIN BOOKS

THOMAS HARD

Claire Tomalin worked in publishing and journalism for many years. She was literary editor first of the *New Statesman* and then the *Sunday Times* before devoting herself to writing full time. She is the author of seven highly acclaimed biographies. Her book *Samuel Pepys: The Unequalled Self* was 2002 Whitbread Book of the Year. She lives in England with her husband, Michael Frayn.

Praise for Claire Tomalin's *Thomas Hardy*

"This new biography makes its subject a fascinating case study in mid-Victorian literary sociology."   —*The New York Times*

"Clearly focused, elegantly written."   —*Chicago Tribune*

"Tomalin brings . . . the skills of an experienced and accomplished biographer . . . and the confidence of a deeply informed literary critic. Her prose is fluid, and she can see her subject's strengths and weaknesses clearly but sympathetically."
                    —Jonathan Yardley, *The Washington Post*

"This will stand as the best-proportioned of his [Hardy's] myriad portraits."   —*Los Angeles Times*

"A sensitive and nuanced portrait of one of the greatest nineteenth-century writers."   —*Newsday*

"Scholarly and entertaining."   —*The Atlantic*

"Tomalin's new biography gets in pretty much everything that matters about Hardy's story and does it with impressive economy, wit, and grace."   —*The New Republic*

"An elegant and incisive account." —*BookPage*

"Her portrait of this complex and conflicted writer and her careful and suggestive readings of both the novels and the poetry represent an original, compelling interpretation of this constantly surprising writer." —Michael Helfand, *Post Gazette* (Pittsburgh)

"Another wonderfully readable life by veteran biographer and journalist Tomalin. . . . A richly introspective biography sure to rekindle interest in Hardy's writing." —*Kirkus Reviews* (starred review)

"An intelligent and thorough examination of Hardy, a worthy read for all curious about the richly imaginative world created by a man for whom, as Tomalin makes clear, the inner life was all." —*The Christian Science Monitor*

"A feat of distillation and mature judgment, Tomalin's biography artfully presents Hardy in his intimate and social world, offering succinct and insightful readings of his work along the way." —*Publishers Weekly* (starred review)

Thomas Hardy

CLAIRE TOMALIN

PENGUIN BOOKS

PENGUIN BOOKS

Published by the Penguin Group

Penguin Group (USA) Inc., 375 Hudson Street, New York, New York 10014, U.S.A.
Penguin Group (Canada), 90 Eglinton Avenue East, Suite 700, Toronto,
Ontario, Canada M4P 2Y3 (a division of Pearson Penguin Canada Inc.)
Penguin Books Ltd, 80 Strand, London WC2R 0RL, England
Penguin Ireland, 25 St Stephen's Green, Dublin 2, Ireland (a division of Penguin Books Ltd)
Penguin Group (Australia), 250 Camberwell Road, Camberwell,
Victoria 3124, Australia (a division of Pearson Australia Group Pty Ltd)
Penguin Books India Pvt Ltd, 11 Community Centre, Panchsheel Park, New Delhi – 110 017, India
Penguin Group (NZ), 67 Apollo Drive, Rosedale, North Shore 0632,
New Zealand (a division of Pearson New Zealand Ltd)
Penguin Books (South Africa) (Pty) Ltd, 24 Sturdee Avenue,
Rosebank, Johannesburg 2196, South Africa

Penguin Books Ltd, Registered Offices:
80 Strand, London WC2R 0RL, England

First published in Great Britain by Penguin Books Ltd 2006
First published in the United States of America by The Penguin Press,
a member of Penguin Group (USA) Inc. 2007
Published in Penguin Books (UK) 2007
Published in Penguin Books (USA) 2007

1 3 5 7 9 10 8 6 4 2

Pages 462–464 constitute an extension of this copyright page.

Map illustrations by Andrew Farmer

ISBN 978-1-59420-118-9 (hc.)
ISBN 978-0-14-311287-7 (pbk.)
CIP data available

Printed in the United States of America

Contents

Acknowledgements

This book goes back a long way. My mother loved Hardy and set his 'Faintheart in a Railway Train' to music, and my sister and I knew by heart 'This is the weather the cuckoo likes' and 'When I set out for Lyonnesse', like most children of our generation, I suppose. When I was fourteen my mother saw me with a library copy of *Jude the Obscure* and told me not to read it, advice I naturally ignored. I began to buy every Hardy volume I could find in second-hand bookshops – novels, poetry, memoirs. At Cambridge in the early 1950s I heard George Rylands read the 'Poems of 1912–13' in a lecture hall, an unforgettable experience. My first husband, Nick, and I were married by chance on the 85th anniversary of Hardy and Emma's wedding day, 17 September 1955, but we realized its significance, and he gave me the *Collected Poems* as a wedding present.

In working on this book, which attempts to discuss Hardy's work in the context of his life, I have relied on the labours of many others. First and foremost is Michael Millgate, the Grand Master of Hardy studies, who has not only edited Hardy's letters and those of both Hardy's wives, but also written two meticulously researched biographies of him and an essay on his testamentary intentions, as well as a study of the novels. His contribution to the study of Hardy is immense and invaluable. I met him for the first time about two weeks after I had finished writing this book and regret that it was not sooner. Like all who are interested in Hardy, I owe Professor Millgate a large debt.

I owe another debt to the late James Gibson, editor of one of the two Variorum editions of Hardy's poetry, scholar, biographer and most generous of men. We first met, appropriately, in a Dorchester bookshop, and he immediately befriended and encouraged me. He and his wife Helen invited me to stay and drove me to some of the places I needed to see in Dorset. Before I left, he offered me the files he had compiled over many years in preparing his book *Thomas Hardy: Interviews and Recollections*. It was an extraordinarily generous gift, and I have used it gratefully. His death was a sad blow to all his friends, and I was fortunate to have known him. The Gibsons also introduced me to Andrew and Marilyn Leah at Max Gate, who gave me a princely welcome and allowed me to explore the whole house thoroughly.

Everyone at the Dorchester County Museum has been patient and helpful with my demands, particularly the Director, Judy Lindsay, and Mrs Lilian Swindall, the Archivist. I am particularly grateful to them, knowing that they work under pressure. Judith Stinton of Maiden Newton has assisted me most kindly. Mrs Barbara Davies was good enough to lend me her precious copy of a privately printed history of Melbury Osmond.

My old friend James Rowlatt has put up with my erratic arrivals in Dorset and entertained me beautifully, finding me books and helping me in many ways, walking and driving with me over wide areas of Dorset.

I have again received guidance and help from Richard Luckett, Pepys Librarian at Magdalene College, Cambridge, where the diaries of Arthur Benson are held. My thanks to him and also to Aude Fitzsimons at the Pepys Library. Also to Duncan Robinson and Stella Panayotova at the Fitzwilliam Museum in Cambridge, for enabling me to study the manuscript of *Jude the Obscure*; and to David McKitterick, Librarian of Trinity College, Cambridge, who sent me photocopies of limericks written by Florence Monckton Milnes as a young woman.

Without the London Library and its ever helpful staff I should not have been able to write this book. The same is true of the British Library, which I have relied on both for its printed books and its archives. Thanks to the Curator of the Berg Collection, Isaac Gewirtz, for his kind assistance; also to Michael Meredith, Librarian of Eton College, and to Robin Harcourt Williams, Archivist at Hatfield House, who once again went out of his way to find and send me documents. Elisabeth Stuart at the offices of the Duchy of Cornwall kindly allowed me to examine the papers relating to the visit of the Prince of Wales to Max Gate and the negotiations over the purchase of extra land from the Duchy there. The Society for the Protection of Ancient Buildings welcomed me to their library, where Cecily Greenhill and Philip Venning showed me their Hardy material.

Thanks also to Timothy Hands, Hardy scholar and writer, who brought me much useful material. Also to Helena Caletta, who lent and found me books. Also to Mark Bostridge for sending me photocopies of interesting material. And to Anthony Barnes, who drew my attention to the reference to Hardy in Henrietta Garnett's *Anny*.

John Antell, great-grandson of Hardy's aunt Mary Antell *née* Hand and sometime mayor of Dorchester, gave up a day to talk to me about family history. Mrs Moles, Archivist at Wiltshire County Record Office, Brian York, Archivist at Brunel, and Kate Perry, Archivist of Girton College, all answered my questions helpfully. Myrrdin Jones gave me information about Hardy's visit to Aberdeen, and Mrs Anne Blandamer talked to me about her husband's uncle Harry Bentley, who admired Hardy and was befriended by him when he delivered post to Max Gate. My thanks to all of them.

Particular thanks to Sally Searle of the Old Rectory, St Juliot, who welcomed me so warmly when I stayed there, and gave up her time to visit places along the coast with me and to answer my questions.

Tony Lacey has been my editor at Viking Penguin for over twenty years and I can't remember a single cross word in all that time; his enthusiasm, loyalty, support and editorial suggestions are greatly appreciated. Zelda Turner has put in many hours of work, especially with the illustrations, for which I am grateful. Dinah Drazin has laid out the illustrations beautifully.

Donna Poppy is the most meticulous of copy editors, on whom I confidently rely, and with her eagle eye she has as usual saved me from blunders, repetitions, misquotations and wrong dates. Once again she has been an indispensable part of the process of getting my book into shape.

My agent David Godwin, ever calm and encouraging, has helped me in every way, backed by a great team of assistants, all of whom I have reason to be grateful to, and to whom I give thanks.

Once again my husband has shown patience and kindness while I worked. His good spirits cheered me and his practical help – buying all the groceries for months – was great. He also took time to read the typescript and gave me such excellent suggestions for improving it that I adopted almost all of them.

Illustrations

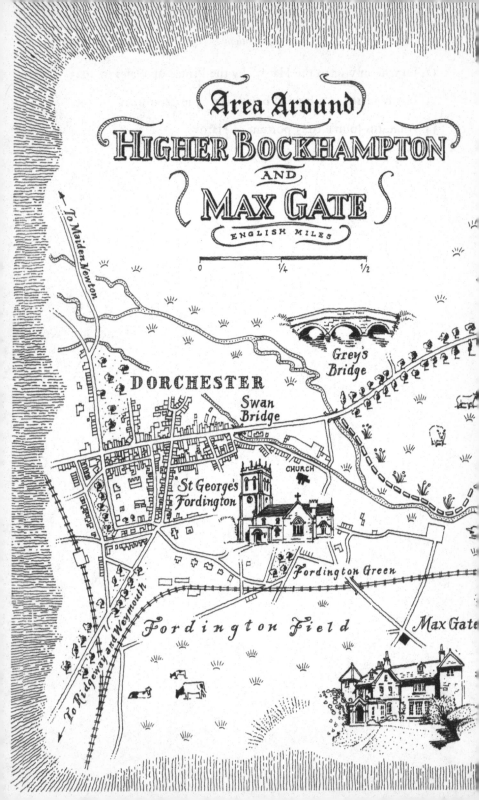

Prologue

In November of 1912 an ageing writer lost his wife. He was not
expecting her to die, but then he had not been taking much notice
of her for some time. They had run out of conversation, he was
in love with another woman, and for some years now she had
withdrawn from him, choosing to sleep alone in a small room in
the attic. She spent much of the day up there too, having her
breakfast and lunch brought up, and reading and writing in a
second attic room. She had just reached her seventy-second birthday. There had been no celebrations. She had seemed unwell, the
doctor had seen her, but she had refused to allow him to examine
her, and he had given no warning that there might be anything
seriously wrong. At about eight in the morning on 27 November
her young maid Dolly went to her as usual and found her alarm-
ingly changed since bedtime the night before, when the girl had
attended her. Now she was 'moaning and terribly ill'. She did not
complain or ask for the doctor to be sent for, but she did ask Dolly
to fetch her husband. Dolly ran down to the master in his study,
where he was making an early start on his day's work. He told her
to straighten her collar – she wore a blue dress with a white collar
when she was working – then he climbed the narrow stairs to his
wife's room and went up to the bed. He spoke her name: 'Em,
Em – don't you know me?' But she was already unconscious,
and within minutes she had stopped breathing. Emma Hardy was
dead.[1]

This is the moment when Thomas Hardy became a great poet.
He was a long-established, admired and popular writer, acknowledged as a great novelist and, more recently, as a poet. His historical
epic-drama had been greeted with interest and respect, and he had
written many fine poems and a few outstanding ones. But it was
the death of Emma that proved to be his best inspiration. Filled
with sorrow and remorse for their estrangement, he had her body

brought down and placed in the coffin at the foot of his bed, where it remained for three days and nights until the funeral.[2] The gesture would have been remarkable in a lover who could not bear to be parted from the body of his mistress, but for an elderly husband who had for years been on bad terms with his wife it seems almost monstrously unconventional, until you realize that he was thinking of his situation quite differently. He had become a lover in mourning.

He began at once to revisit their early love in his mind with an intensity that expressed itself in a series of poems. 'One forgets all the recent years and differences,' he wrote to a friend, 'and the mind goes back to the early times when each was much to the other – in her case and mine intensely much.'[3] The dry old man was 'in flower' as a poet – these were his own words – although the flower was sad-coloured; and he wrote more poems than he had ever done before in the same space of time.[4]

They are among the most original elegies ever written, in feeling and in the handling of language and verse forms. They are both conversational and lyrical. They do not spare the truth about the unhappiness suffered by wife and husband, but they move into the past with an expansiveness and panache he had never found before. In them he speaks to her, he gives her a voice, he conjures her up: sometimes she appears as a ghost, sometimes as the elderly woman who liked parties and hats; more often as the girl of long ago, wearing an 'air-blue gown', or with her 'bright hair flapping free'. And he recalls how she seemed to him once a sublime, almost Homeric woman, 'Fair-eyed and white shouldered, broad-browed and brown-tressed'.

He talks to her about her past self, 'With your nut-coloured hair, / And gray eyes, and rose-flush coming and going'. He remembers how the light of the sunset over the sea, with its 'dipping blaze / Dyed her face fire-red'. He relives a moment when he walked with her on a rainy road, and they exchanged the words that changed their lives, calling up her image and then letting it go:

> I look and see it there, shrinking, shrinking,
>   I look back at it amid the rain
> For the very last time; for my sand is sinking,
>   And I shall traverse old love's domain
>   Never again.[5]

At the same time he knows that she is 'past love, praise, indifference, blame'. She is shut in her grave, 'the clodded shell / Of her tiny cell'. She is wrapped in her shroud, with the rain that she hates – or hated – beating down on her.[6] She is not there where he expects to see her working in the garden in the evening, and when he returns from his walk the house where she should be is empty of her. He needs to speak to her and see her, although he knows he cannot. The poetry allows him to. It keeps him balanced between the possible and the impossible, as the bereaved need to be, so that he can sorrow, and then rejoice, and then admit that the rejoicing cannot change how things are now.

There were times when he thought of the poems as a way of making amends to Emma, 'the only amends I can make', he wrote to another woman he had loved.[7] He was seeing her again in the place where he first knew her, and with which he always identified her, the remote coast of north Cornwall, where the untamed landscape and the young woman on horseback with her hair blowing behind her had seemed almost exotic to him in 1870. Away from Cornwall her exoticism faded, and after they were married they never returned there, for which Hardy blamed himself. More than anything, though, he was re-creating his great romance, writing for the first time openly and boldly of 'The woman whom I loved so, and who loyally loved me', restoring her to the Cornish cliffs where she had seemed to him to embody the spirit of landscape:

> I found her out there
> On a slope few see,
> That falls westwardly
> To the salt-edged air,
> Where the ocean breaks

> On the purple strand,
> And the hurricane shakes
> The solid land.

The sequence, which he called 'Poems of 1912–13', adding the words *Veteris vestigia flammae* ('traces of old flames'), makes up one of the finest and strangest celebrations of the dead in English poetry.[8] It is cast in a different mould from *Lycidas*, *Adonais* or *In Memoriam*, fragmented, less marmoreal, but it still stands beside them. The metrical patterns and shapes of each poem are ambitious, complicated, surprising. The more risks he takes the less he falters, and what he gets away with is astonishing. No two use the same structure. There is a bow to Shakespeare when he reminds Emma's ghost that night is ending, and 'Soon you will have, Dear, to vanish from me, / For the stars close their shutters'.[9] But the voice is purely his own.

'The Voice' was written within weeks of Emma's death, in December 1912. Its first words go straight to the point: 'Woman much missed'. You might think he had written down what was in his heart immediately, but the manuscript shows that his first draft suggested something more complicated and even sinister: 'O woman weird'. We can look over his shoulder and see how second thoughts brought simplicity:

> Woman much missed, how you call to me, call to me,
> Saying that now you are not as you were
> When you had changed from the one who was all to me,
> But as at first, when our day was fair.

The 'call to me, call to me' is made into a wail of grief by the 'Woman much missed' before it. The woman is trying to reach him and explain something complicated: that her death means she is no longer as she was in the later years of their marriage, 'when you had changed', but as she had been 'at first, when our day was fair'. Hardy is looking at three different bits of time: the long-ago past, when he and Emma had been true lovers, the recent past, when they were estranged, and 'now', when he imagines her to be again as she was in the distant past. (This explains the force of the 'woman weird' he began with – she can time-travel inside her grave.)

He goes on to picture her as she used to be, waiting for him to arrive at Launceston Railway Station. Again, he made a change to the second stanza, from a dull 'Even to the original hat and gown' to the marvellous 'original air-blue gown' that lifts and lights the whole poem. It tells us it was summer, and how she stood out luminously in the drab railway station.

> Can it be you that I hear? Let me view you, then,
> Standing as when I drew near to the town
> Where you would wait for me: yes, as I knew you then,
> Even to the original air-blue gown!

Then, to close the poem, he changes the shape and rhythm, reducing the lines as he finds himself reduced, unable to keep his imagination working, brought to his lowest ebb: 'Thus I'. No air-blue to lift him now; he is merely an old man who can hardly move forward among a few skeletal autumn trees, and faltering. In this bleakness the woman's voice is still heard but with no possibility of an answer or an exchange.

> Thus I; faltering forward,
> Leaves around me falling,
> Wind oozing thin through the thorn from norward,
> And the woman calling.

☙

'The Phantom Horsewoman' is as odd and bold as any of his poems, rising from one of Hardy's awkward starts to a conclusion that feels triumphant instead of sorrowful, as though this time the poetry has actually worked magic. It starts with an unnamed 'I' who seems to be observing another anonymous person, 'a man I know', this one old, half mad and obsessed with something only he can see as he gazes out over the ocean:

> Queer are the ways of a man I know:
> > He comes and stands
> > In a careworn craze,
> > And looks at the sands
> > And the seaward haze
> > With moveless hands
> > And face and gaze,
> > Then turns to go . . .
> And what does he see when he gazes so?

Two anonymous men make an impersonal start to the poem, even if both are aspects of Hardy himself. What one is looking at, and seeing continually in his mind, is explained in the last part of the poem, when it changes from the impersonal to the intensely personal. He is seeing

> A ghost-girl-rider. And though, toil-tried,
> > He withers daily,
> > Time touches her not,
> > But still she rides gaily
> > In his rapt thought
> > On that shagged and shaly
> > Atlantic spot,
> > And as when first eyed
> Draws rein and sings to the swing of the tide.

The 'ghost-girl-rider' and 'toil-tried' give a spring to the rhythm, so that the short lines canter away after them like the girl on her horse – and like time that has run away with their happiness, and with her life. Only the poem allows her to pause. This is Hardy's magic. He makes her draw rein, she sings, she is there again, and now that he has written the poem, she will always be there.

Hardy was a writer who made many of his best effects out of incidents and stories he had collected and put aside, sights stored up, feelings he had kept to himself, anger he had not shown to the world. In these poems about Emma he is rediscovering repressed sorrow and forgotten love. He is like an archaeologist uncovering objects that have not been seen for many decades, bringing them out into the light, examining them, some small pieces, some curious bones and broken bits, and some shining treasures. There is a rising excitement in the writing as of someone making discoveries. He has found the most perfect subject he has ever had, and he has the skills to work on it. 'There *is* the harvest of having written twenty novels first,' wrote Ezra Pound in praise of Hardy's poetry.[10]

Are the poems true? His second wife, Florence, indignantly rejected the notion: 'All the poems about her are a fiction, but a fiction in which their author has now come to believe.'[11] She was too angry and jealous to accept that there had been another Hardy and another Emma before she knew them, or to understand that poems have their own internal truth to which both fact and dream may contribute. Maybe it does not matter whether they are true or not, although Hardy himself evidently thought they were. A year after Emma's death, in November 1913, he had a conversation about them with Arthur Benson in Cambridge in which 'He told me he had enough verses for a book, but he didn't know whether he ought to include in it some verses he wrote when his wife died "very intimate, of course – but the verses came; it was quite natural; one looked back through the years and saw some pictures."'[12] Benson's account suggests that Hardy felt the poems showed his past, and that they had come to him almost unbidden: 'one looked back through the years and saw some pictures.' It may be how he preferred to remember and simplify the work that had gone into them, packing fluid feeling into solid shapes, making patterns with words and rhyme, exploring the tension between idea and form. The manuscripts are effectively fair copies with just a few emendations, and, although there were rough drafts, which he always destroyed, it may be that they were composed almost like music in his head even before he put anything down on paper.

Benson added, 'I have forgotten to put down by far the most interesting thing Hardy said. He was talking about his wife's death, and wondering if it was *indecent* to write poetry, and he said "It's natural to me to write poetry – I was never intended to be a

prose-writer, still less a teller of tales – still, one had got to live."'
The question about whether it was proper to publish the poems
did not worry him for long. The volume containing them appeared
in November 1914, three months after the outbreak of the First
World War, which partly explains the small attention given to
them. He wrote to a friend in December, 'My own favourites,
that include all those in memory of Emma, have been mentioned
little . . . I am so glad you like "When I set out for Lyonnesse." It
is exactly what happened 44 years ago.'[13] In that week a review of
the poems appeared in the *New Statesman*, by Lytton Strachey,
who wrote: 'They are, in fact, modern as no other poems are. The
author of *Jude the Obscure* speaks in them, but with the concentration, the intensity, the subtle disturbing force of poetry . . . He
is incorrect; but then how unreal and artificial a thing is correctness!
He fumbles; but it is that very fumbling that brings him so near
to ourselves.'[14] Hardy would not have liked the accusations of
incorrectness and fumbling, but Strachey did see that his poetry is
the real thing, able 'to touch our marrow-bones'.

Hardy went on writing poems about Emma, returning again
and again to incidents in their life together, to the end of his own
life fifteen years later. Some, by no means all, of the later verses
rise to the heights of the 'Poems of 1912–13', and at least eighty
poems belong to her. Inspiration came to him all the time, from a
curl of her hair that she had cut for him once to console him on
parting, which had stayed a bright brown; from the memory of a
walk when her long skirts gathered 'Winged thistle-seeds' which

> . . . rose at the brush of your petticoat-seam . . .
> And sailed on the breeze in a nebulous stream
> Like a comet's tail behind you . . .[15]

Also from the sight of the keys of the piano she had played when
he refused to listen – in the poem 'Penance' he finds the grimmest
of images to stand for his guilt in his own failure in love:

I would not join. I would not stay,
  But drew away,
Though the winter fire beamed brightly . . . Aye!
  I do to-day
What I would not then; and the chill old keys,
  Like a skull's brown teeth
  Loose in their sheath,
  Freeze my touch; yes, freeze.[16]

He said he was prouder of his poetry than of any of his prose, even of his great novels, because he felt that in all the novels there was an element of compromise. His professional life, which appears from most aspects as a triumphal progress, always seemed to him to be a struggle against publishers determined to censor what he wrote, and the wilful misunderstanding and lofty disapproval of the critics. When he talked to Benson of having to write novels because 'one had got to live', he was still showing his sensitivity to criticism, remembering the hard labour of writing against time for serial publication and the many struggles with editors and publishers to be allowed to say what he wanted. He was often despondent even once he had become successful and rich. Only in poetry was there no compromising, and in the 'Poems of 1912–13' he bared his heart as he had never fully allowed himself to do before. It gives them their immediacy and power, allowing us to eavesdrop on his train of thought and feeling as he moves between an old man's sorrow and a young man's bliss.

This book is about how Hardy became a writer, poet and novelist. It starts with his mother, from whom he took a way of thinking and many of his ideas and ambitions. Her story sets the background to his life.

PART ONE
1840–1867

1. Mother

Hardy's life began like this. His mother went into labour on 1 June 1840. She sent for the midwife, a neighbour. The short hours of darkness passed, the sun rose and filled the bedroom with its light, she had a bad time, and at eight o'clock the child was born, apparently lifeless. He was put aside while his mother was seen to. Then the midwife, turning back to the small scrap of humanity, looked closely at him and exclaimed, 'Dead! Stop a minute, he's alive enough, sure!'[1] And so he was: tiny, weak, hardly expected to survive for long, but not dead yet.[2]

He was so feeble that his future remained doubtful. For five weeks he was kept at home, and then on 5 July he was taken to be christened in church. And, although, as Hardy himself put it later, 'he showed not the physique of his father', he was named Thomas Hardy after his father and his grandfather.[3] Three Thomas Hardys in three generations, and not one of them allowed the luxury of a second given name to distinguish one from another: you can understand why he said he wished he had been called something different, such as Christopher, the name his mother wanted to give him.[4] But Thomas Hardy he was and remained.

There was nothing idyllic about his start in life. Jemima was a reluctant mother, and his parents had married unwillingly under pressure from her family, less than six months before his birth. Both were Dorset country people, his father a builder in a very small way, living with his widowed mother in a hamlet a few miles from Dorchester. His newly acquired wife, born Jemima Hand, had earned her own living as a servant since the age of thirteen and had hoped to make a career as a cook. She was twenty-six when she found herself trapped by pregnancy. She came from the village of Melbury Osmond in the north-west of the county, close to Somerset, among the apple orchards. To this day it is idyllically pretty, with a church, a green, thatched cottages set at different

angles to the road and a watersplash where two streams meet. Both
rise in the parkland of the lords of the manor, the Fox-Strangways.
In Jemima's day the third Earl of Ilchester ruled over the estate
and lived in the great house, Melbury Sampford, a sprawling
mixture of styles crowned by a hexagonal Tudor tower with
magnificent windows looking out in five directions. The park had
been enclosed by the builder of the tower and was stocked with
deer. There was a private church for the family, and lions on the
gates. Here they sometimes entertained royalty; from here their
younger sons went to the university and into the Church, assured
of good livings in local parishes; and from here the family set off
for London every spring with the object of making good matches
for their children in the aristocratic marriage market. One daughter
had defied them: in 1764 Lady Susan Fox-Strangways married
herself to an actor, William O'Brien. Although O'Brien was a
friend of Garrick, gentlemanly and gifted, the scandal was great,
but the O'Briens made a happy couple and were in time forgiven.
They were allowed to live in one of the houses belonging to the
Fox-Strangways, at Stinsford near Dorchester, and the Earl fixed a
gentlemanly job for O'Brien, who became Receiver General of
the taxes of the county. He died in 1815; Lady Susan lived on until
1827. She chose to be buried with her husband in a vault beneath
Stinsford Church. It was made by a local builder named Thomas
Hardy. So the Fox-Strangways played their part, remote and heed-
less forces of destiny, in the meeting of Hardy's parents.

None of this was known to the young Jemima Hand. Her
own family's problems took all her attention. She was her parents'
fifth child, and there were two more after her, but it was not a
happy family. Her father, George Hand, had married her mother,
Elizabeth – or Betty – Swetman, with small enthusiasm and against
her father's wishes. That was in 1804. The young couple reached
the altar in the last month of Betty's pregnancy. Both had grown
up in Melbury Osmond, but otherwise they had little in common.
The Swetmans were an old-established family, steady yeomen
farmers with a bit of land; there is still a 'Sweatman orchard' in the
village. Although the village census of 1801 describes her as working as a 'spinner', she is said to have enjoyed enough leisure and

money to indulge her taste for reading Richardson, Fielding and *Paradise Lost*, to have dispensed to the village from Culpepper's *Herbal* and to have worn pretty clothes.⁵ She could expect to inherit her father's savings, whereas George had nothing to offer but dark good looks, defiant intelligence and, presumably, charm. His mother was a Melbury woman, his father had come from Puddletown in south Dorset, he was the eldest of nine, now in his thirties, and he was a drinker. In 1801 he appears to have been a servant in the household of the village clergyman.⁶ Betty paid a high price for whatever she found romantic about him when her father washed his hands of her and his grandchildren. Her mother, Maria Swetman, who might have smoothed things over, had died two years before. Betty gave her name, Maria, to her firstborn.

George picked up work as a shepherd or a gardener, but it never amounted to much. Times got worse as the war with France went on year after year. Things were especially bad for rural workers, and George suffered with the others. Betty may have kept up her spinning, and they seem to have crammed themselves into a small house, part of what had been an ancient monastic building known as Barton Hill Cottages. Drink made him violent. He despised the Church – perhaps a result of being employed by the rector – and refused to allow his children to be baptized. Betty contrived secret baptisms. He had another woman. His lungs were attacked by tuberculosis. Still, the marriage lasted for eighteen years, and children kept arriving. When Jemima was nine, in 1822, he died. Whether she felt more relief than sorrow we don't know, because whatever memories she had of her father she did not talk about him. The family story is that Betty buried him beside his mistress, as Hardy shows Bathsheba burying Troy in Fanny's grave in *Far from the Madding Crowd*.

As a couple, the Hands were originals, thinking for themselves and refusing to follow the paths expected of people in their situation so low down in the social heap. They were also desperately unfortunate. After George's death his parents, who had moved back to Puddletown, took in the eldest girl, Maria, and there drew the line. Betty's father died, stubbornly unforgiving to the end, and she was left with seven children and no income. She considered herself cheated of her rights, and continued to complain 'I should not have been poor if right had took its place' throughout her life; but she had to apply for support to the Poor Law Overseers of the parish.[7] Some help was forthcoming, but in the 1820s it was administered with chill harshness. The parish grudged every penny spent on a child, requiring that at the age of thirteen he or she should become self-supporting and cutting the mother's money accordingly.

Jemima's childhood was the bleakest period of her life. She told her son she had endured 'some very distressful experiences of which she could never speak . . . without pain'. She also recalled to him seeing 'a child whipped at the cart-tail round Yeovil for stealing a book from a stall' when she was herself a girl.[8] Yeovil was the nearest town to Melbury likely to have a book stall in the market, and the question occurs as to whether she herself was the savagely punished book stealer. She and her brothers and sisters experienced all the deprivations of penniless village children: they knew what it was to be hungry and thought themselves lucky if they were warm and dry in rough weather. They wore other people's cast-off clothes and often went shoeless. There were worse things, no doubt, but they survived. Two of her brothers went off to work as bricklayers in Puddletown, partly drawn by the presence of grandparents and an elder sister; also because it was a more thriving place than Melbury, with a market and close to Dorchester. The Hand boys became drinkers like their father; the girls showed a finer spirit. Jemima learnt to sew, to cook and to clean, and that was almost the sum of her education, but not quite, because she could read, and she loved books with the same passion as her mother.[9] There is even a tradition that the family made up verses to entertain themselves.[10] The streak of originality and defiance persisted under the hardship.

At thirteen, in 1826, she went to work. Her first job, as a live-in domestic servant, took her away from home. The biggest local employers were the Fox-Strangways, who required a great many servants for themselves and their relations around the county. The village of Melbury Osmond provided them with a good supply.

Jemima went to the household of an uncle of the third Earl, an elderly clergyman, the Hon. Revd Charles Redlynch Fox-Strangways. His parish was seven miles south of Melbury Osmond, in the village of Maiden Newton in the valley of the River Frome. The vicarage was the largest house in the place, standing next to the church with gardens along the river bank, a very pleasant place where he had lived for forty years. Maiden Newton was bigger and livelier than Melbury, with busy corn mills on the river and several inns for travellers, being on the main road between Yeovil and Dorchester. It was also near enough for her to get home and back when she had a whole free day, on foot, walking being the only means of transport for the poor. She had the satisfaction of earning a few pounds a year, and could rely on regular meals and keep herself dressed to the standard expected of a maid in the vicarage. Entering a different world, with habits and tastes quite new to her, she had much to take in, and since she was quick and interested she learnt fast.

At Maiden Newton she grew from a child into a young woman. She gave satisfaction to her employers, and was promoted from the lowest levels of domestic service to work in the kitchen and then to cook for the family. They took her with them when they went to Weymouth, the most fashionable of coastal resorts and the largest town in Dorset. Weymouth had a broad sandy beach and a port, bathing machines and boats, strolling crowds and bands to entertain them. Army and naval officers were much in evidence. There was a theatre, and dancing in the summer. A statue of George III presided, demonstrating the gratitude of the citizens to the King, whose affection for the place had made it famous. The sea front was lined with handsome houses. In the basement of one of these she no doubt did her cooking, but in her free moments she could slip out to join the crowds, breathe the sea air, admire the view of the bay and listen to the bands.

She never grew tall, and she was not as pretty as her sisters, her head rather big for her body, but she was neat, lively and handsome, with good grey eyes and a bold Roman nose. She had an air of intelligence and humour, and looked like a person who could assert herself and who noticed what was going on around her.

And, while she may have picked up standard English from her employers, she usually spoke like the Dorset countrywoman she was, using 'thee' and 'thou', ''tis', ''twas' and ''twould', 'voot' for 'foot', 'zee' for 'see', 'juties' for 'duties', ''ee' for 'you'. Towards the end of her life her daughter Kate, planning a trip to Bristol with friends, reported her as asking, 'Be 'ee all Bristol crazy?'[11] Although Jemima was a reader, and her mother and two of her younger sisters could write reasonably well, nothing in her handwriting survives except for her name on her own marriage register and on her sister's, as witness. There is not even an inscription in a book, and her son wrote letters for her.[12] You can learn to read without ever getting far with writing, and this may have been her situation.

With or without letters, she kept in touch with her family, divided between Melbury and Puddletown, where her sister Maria married a cabinet maker, James Sparks, in 1828, and began a family. The sisters were fond of one another, and Maria kept an eye on Jemima as well as she could. One of her memories is of how her Puddletown brothers, Christopher and Henry, arranged a treat for her in 1830, when she was seventeen. She had been given a free Sunday, and they got permission for her to be present at the Sunday morning 'barrack-service' for the soldiers in Dorchester, which was a garrison town. She needed to set off early to cover the eight miles from Maiden Newton to be in time, because the soldiers assembled in the riding school at nine in the morning; and she must have been a serious young woman for whom a special religious service was known to be a treat. The clergyman in charge, 'a fine, noble-looking young man' called Henry Moule, was newly arrived in the district and based in Fordington, an outlying district of Dorchester, with a rough population. She never forgot how he preached standing with the great regimental drum as a table in front of him, the soldiers also standing on the sawdust-covered ground throughout his sermon. 'A guinea lay on the drum-head through the service, at the end of which the preacher took it up and hastened away to his parish service at the Church.'[13]

Another memory was from the summer of 1833, when she had a sight of the young Princess Victoria touring the west of England with her mother, the Duchess of Kent. Jemima observed with amusement that when the crowd cheered and the Princess stood up in the carriage to acknowledge their cheers and respond to them, the Duchess 'promptly pulled her down into her seat by her skirts'.[14] The royal ladies were visiting Weymouth and the Ilchesters at Melbury House. Victoria was fourteen, Jemima twenty.

The years she was in service covered the last four years of George IV, the seven years William IV was on the throne and the beginning of Victoria's reign in 1837. When Charles Fox-Strangways died in 1836, she was moved on to a younger family connection, another clergyman. The Revd Edward Murray was vicar of Stinsford, living with his wife and children not in the vicarage but in Stinsford House, which had been Lady Susan O'Brien's. He was extremely well connected: his sister Caroline had married Lord Ilchester, and he was a grandson of the Duke of Atholl.[15] He was also chaplain to the Bishop of Rochester, who happened to be his own elder brother; his mother had been a lady-in-waiting to the Princesses Augusta and Elizabeth, and his clever younger sister Amelia knew everyone at Court, had sat on George III's lap as a child and would be appointed a maid of honour to Queen Victoria at her accession in 1837.[16] That year the Murrays took Jemima with them to London for the Season.[17] She attended the church of St James's, Piccadilly, with the family and, from below stairs, witnessed urban privilege and luxury on a grand scale. On fine afternoons family parties set off in open carriages for the park, and in the evening there were balls in the mansions of Mayfair and Park Lane: servants could get glimpses of the splendours – extravagant feathers, jewels, satins and velvets – from the back stairs or the area steps. She decided she wanted to stay in London and work as a cook in a gentlemen's club.[18]

There was something else that she got from her time in service: the experience of living in a learned household, even if below stairs. Murray was a scholar, and in the year she went to him he published a commentary on the apocryphal Book of Enoch, with much Greek and Hebrew and many references to Hermes Trismegistus, Zoroaster and the Sybilline prophecies. He was also the author of a study of Ezekiel, and published a volume of Calvin's prayers and collects, translated into English and printed in Dorchester. Since Jemima liked to read, it may be that Murray became aware of this unusual trait in a servant and allowed her to look at books in his library.[19] Where else would she have been introduced to Dante's *Divine Comedy*, later said to be her favourite work?[20] According to her son, she also read Johnson's *Rasselas*, Scott and Byron. Being a servant in a rich household made you a spectator of another world, and reading allowed you to look even further, to travel in time and space.

By now Jemima knew her way about Dorset pretty well: from Maiden Newton north over rolling hills, through Cattistock and Evershot to Melbury; south-east to Dorchester along the straight main road, all this part watered by the River Frome; and from Dorchester further south over the downs to Weymouth, Portland and the sea, or else north-east to Puddletown. These were the routes her son would make his people walk in her footsteps: Gabriel and Fanny, Henchard, Giles and Tess. Jemima's employers opened up the landscape of the county for her in other ways. Physically, they owned much of it; spiritually, they exerted authority through the churches, and they and their fellow landowners also ruled over the judicial and political life of the county. In the early 1830s the labouring people were suffering hardship so intense that it led them to break machines and burn ricks, putting the fear of revolution into their masters' heads. A few men were hanged, and indeed the soldiers whose Sunday-morning service Jemima attended in Dorchester in 1830 were ready to put down riots among the starving agricultural workers, and the Revd Henry Moule, who preached to them, organized and served on patrols prepared to oppose any violence.[21] At the Dorchester Assizes in January 1831 twelve men were sentenced to be transported to Australia and forty-four imprisoned. Some then tried to form unions to protect themselves, but in 1834, the year after Princess Victoria's progress through the county, six men from Tolpuddle, a village close to Puddletown, were sentenced to transportation to Australia solely for having attempted to form a union; and, although, as a result of nationwide agitation, they were 'pardoned' and returned to England in 1838, no agricultural trades union was set up in Dorset, and there was no improvement in the subhuman conditions in which labourers were obliged to live.[22] Dorset remained a county in which those who owned the land and those who worked it were hardly thought of as belonging to the same species.

Whatever Jemima expected of life, she did not nurse unrealistic hopes and dreams. She had worked out an idea – or possibly got it from her angry, unfortunate father – which she handed on to her son: 'Mother's notion, and also mine: That a figure stands in our van with an arm uplifted, to knock us back from any pleasant prospect we indulge in as probable.'[23] Her ambition was to find work in London, but instead her employer, Murray, himself left Dorset permanently for London to become a prebendary of St Paul's and vicar of Northolt, Middlesex.[24] He did not take her with him.[25]

During his time at Stinsford, Murray had taken a particular interest in the church music. He encouraged the group of players he found already working there, invited them to come to practise in his study and approved the results. At other churches there were larger groups – nine players at Maiden Newton and eight in the Puddletown gallery, both mixing wind and string – but at Stinsford there were just four string players, who prided themselves on producing better music, and easier to sing by. They were the builder Thomas Hardy the elder on his cello, with his sons James and Thomas and neighbour James Dart on violins. The older man occupied the middle seat of the gallery of Stinsford Church for thirty-five years, and trained the choir; and he went on making music until he died, playing at his last service a few days before his death.

It was towards the end of his life that Jemima Hand began to observe him arriving at Stinsford Church on Sunday morning with his sons. The youngest son, Thomas, was a tall, strong, good-looking young man with engaging manners, blue eyes and a short-cut beard. This is her description of the three Hardys, given many years later and written down by her son:

They were always hurrying, being rather late, their fiddles and violoncello in green-baize bags under their left arms. They wore top hats, stick-up shirt collars, dark blue coats with great collars and gilt buttons, deep cuffs and black silk 'stocks' or neckerchiefs. Had curly hair, and carried their heads to one side as they walked . . . [He] wore drab cloth breeches and buckled shoes, but his sons wore trousers and Wellington boots.[26]

These impressions must date from the months in 1836 and 1837 when Jemima was living in Stinsford House and attending the church there, and this is the likely beginning of her wooing by Thomas Hardy the younger.

The courtship between this Thomas Hardy and Jemima Hand became the subject of a sonnet by their son years later. He dated their first meeting to 1835 and decorously set the scene inside the church, with pew and gallery, window and music:

> She turned in the high pew, until her sight
> Swept the west gallery, and caught its row
> Of music-men with viol, book, and bow
> Against the sinking sad tower-window light.
>
> She turned again; and in her pride's despite
> One strenuous viol's inspirer seemed to throw
> A message from his string to her below,
> Which said: 'I claim thee as my own forthright!'
>
> Thus their hearts' bond began, in due time signed.
> And long years hence, when Age had scared Romance,
> At some old attitude of his or glance
> That gallery-scene would break upon her mind,
> With him as minstrel, ardent, young, and trim,
> Bowing 'New Sabbath' or 'Mount Ephraim'.

This is one of the poems in which he mythologizes his life, moving through time to have his mother looking back at herself from old age. The last lines, with the names of the tunes, once so popular, now archaic sounding, are the most memorable, specific, odd and strong. How much truth there is in this account of his parents' wooing is something else again. The most perfunctory lines are at the start of the sestet, when he speaks of 'their hearts' bond' and Age scaring Romance, conventional and lacklustre words. The problem is that he is glossing over what he did not know. True, they were married in December 1839, but there is a gap in the record for Jemima from the end of 1837 until the marriage. Where she went after the Murrays' departure is not known: his successor, the Revd Arthur Shirley, a bachelor, did not take over Stinsford House but moved into the vicarage.[27] One story is that she worked at Kingston Maurward House; another that she returned to cook at the Maiden Newton vicarage.[28] She may have gone to help her sister Maria Sparks with her four children in Puddletown, or continued at Stinsford House, now the home of a banker who kept seven servants.[29]

What is certain is that her plan to go to London again to work as a cook came to nothing; and in the autumn of 1839 she found herself pregnant. She was twenty-six, repeating her mother's experience at the same age, and she went back to her mother in Melbury Osmond: she must have walked home, as Hardy made Tess walk home to her mother, up and down hill through the autumn landscape, uncertain of her future. It is possible that Jemima hoped to hand the baby to her mother, or even get rid of it, and to return to work of some kind: the coming child became the figure before her, knocking her back from any pleasant prospect she had imagined for herself. But in Puddletown her sister Maria mobilized her husband, James Sparks, to put pressure on Hardy to do the right thing.[30] The marriage was arranged by her family, Sparks marched the reluctant bridegroom across Dorset on the night of 21 December and on the 22nd Jemima was married to Thomas Hardy in Melbury Osmond Church, in the presence of her brother-in-law Sparks and her younger sister Mary.

She had got herself a fine-looking, musical husband with a kind heart, and once married he accepted the situation with good grace. He was nearly thirty, he had the business from his father, who had died in 1837, and he ran it in an easy-going way. He also had a lifetime lease on his cottage and had been looked after at home by his mother all his life. Jemima was to live there for over half a century, yet she never felt it was hers. When her husband died, fifty-two years later, she said she looked at the furniture and declared she did not relate to it. 'All those belonging to it, and the place, are gone, and it is left in her hands, a stranger.'[31] She never ceased to find her country neighbours 'a little rustic and quaint'.[32] She may have spoken like a countrywoman, but she had after all lived in the houses of gentlemen for seventeen years, the largest part of her life, and in London too. She told her son that she had known a governor of Christ's Hospital School, and that he could have been sent there had the man not died.[33] She is said to have continued to hanker after the idea of working in London herself even after the marriage. She proved a loyal wife, but she was against the condition of marriage itself, and she advised all her own children not to repeat her mistake and admonished them to remain single. Such was the force of her words and character that three out of four obeyed her.

Her new life was to be lived in an isolated hamlet of the parish of Stinsford, Higher Bockhampton. A map made for the Ilchester Estate in 1838 shows where the cottage stood, at the top of two rows of irregularly placed small buildings, each with a little land, on both sides of a lane. On the other side from the Thomas Hardys are the cottages of William Keats and James Hardy, his elder brother, a bricklayer, like Jemima's brothers, with three sons. Lower down the lane, land and buildings on both sides belong to Charles Keats. The Keats brothers – they pronounced their name Kaytes – were tranters, or carriers, running horse-drawn carts about the county, and both had large families. Between Charles Keats and James Hardy is the house of Lieutenant Drane, a retired naval officer. There is woodland to the east and heath to the north, belonging to Farmer James Cake, and at the bottom of the lane there are some empty buildings and plots of land. Stinsford lacks shops, a school and a proper road, the nearest one being some way off, but there is a sense of community. Hardy himself reported that there were once dancing parties during the Christmas season, something he must have learnt from his grandmother Hardy: 'This kind of party was called a Jacob's Join, in which every guest contributed a certain sum to pay the expenses of the entertainment

– it was mostly half a crown in this village.'[34] Puddletown, where Jemima's sister Maria Sparks and brothers Christopher and Henry lived, is three miles away across the heath, but Maria and her children would become her closest family. Dorchester was nearer, but she had nobody to visit there; her husband's eldest brother, John, was sunk into poverty and squalor in Fordington, and they were not even in touch.

Three years later the census will show that John Cox, the local Relieving Officer, in charge of poor relief in the parish, has moved into one of the empty houses with his wife and six children: although he was the best-educated man in Higher Bockhampton, Jemima's memories of parish relief in Melbury may not have endeared him to her. The census also reveals that the lieutenant was Thomas Draine, aged fifty, with no wife but two servants, one male, John Downton, and a female, Jemima Paul, with a three-year-old child, Charles Paul. There were now also two families of agricultural workers, the Kindales with five children and the Downtons with two adult working sons; Mrs Downton does not appear on the census, no doubt because she was away from home delivering a baby – she was the midwife. A picture of the world Jemima's children were born into begins to emerge. The self-employed Hardys and the Keatses looked down on the labourers but were in turn looked down on by farmers and professional men; the divisions were clear. Away from the village and above them all were the landowners.

During the months in which she awaited the birth of her first child, she had time to hear the history of the house from her mother-in-law, Mary Head Hardy. It had been built in 1799 as a wedding present by Mary's father-in-law for her and his son. Being a Dorset builder, he knew how to build a cottage using very little more than materials that lay at hand. The outside was of cob, a mixture of sand, clay, chalk, flint, straw and water made into a pudding which hardened into thick, weatherproof walls. The rafters were tree branches, the thatch of wheat straw and the upstairs floors of chestnut wood; only the ground floor was grandly flagged with stone brought from the quarries at Portland. There were small leaded windows, most of them at the front, facing west, but the main bedroom upstairs had an east window. At first there were only two rooms above and one below; it was enlarged later, more than once. Mary Head explained that when they arrived in 1800 the cottage stood quite alone and there were no human neighbours, their only company the birds nesting in the trees, the wild ponies known as heathcroppers, the bats flying in and out of their bedroom at night and the many snakes and lizards – she called them 'efts' – living on the heath behind the cottage. She may also have told Jemima that they had allowed it to be used by smugglers as a depot for their goods, mostly brandy brought over in French boats and carried up from the coast in barrels at night, to be sent on to London later. There was still a pit in the heath near by in which the casks had been hidden.[35] Smuggling was a crime, but it was an accepted activity in south Dorset in the early part of the nineteenth century, carried on almost as much for the excitement as for the profits. The Hardys had no guilty feelings about helping out, or accepting brandy for themselves to eke out the cider they made. Hardy's account of the excitement of defying the law and customs men was given in his story 'The Distracted Preacher', in which a charmingly bold heroine is unwilling to give up smuggling.[36]

The original Bockhampton was down the hill on the river, and when the Hardys settled up the hill their place was at first named New Bockhampton; some time after 1811 it became 'Higher' and the old settlement 'Lower'. Time brought more families who built alongside them. The plots of land were leased from the local landowner and MP, William Morton Pitt, of nearby Kingston Maurward, a grandiose modern mansion. Pitt was the cousin of the Prime Minister William Pitt, at the zenith of his power as the chief opponent of Napoleon and the revolutionary French. While the wars against France raged on, year after year, Thomas and Mary Hardy reared their family of six children – a seventh died young. Lady Pitt's benevolence extended to giving books of psalms to deserving boys, and the youngest Hardy son, Thomas, received one. This was Jemima's future husband, born in 1811. He learnt the building trade from his father and was his mother's favourite, remaining with her when she was widowed and becoming titular head of the family business. But she was now nearing seventy and must have been glad to have a daughter-in-law to help out at home. She would not have held Jemima's pregnancy against her, since she had been in the same condition when she married her husband, and six years older than him too, having already borne one illegitimate child in Berkshire, from which she came. She had been orphaned early and suffered much unhappiness. There were several 'lost' years of her early life which she never spoke about, and her own mother had also given birth to an illegitimate child in her youth.[37] Being pregnant before marriage was usual enough among country people to be no great cause for shame if the man went reasonably willingly to the altar. All the same, the record of this group of women is strikingly consistent. Jemima, her mother, her mother-in-law and her great-grandmother, all strong-minded and intelligent women, had all flouted the rules on sexual behaviour laid down by the Church and gentry.

As a boy, Hardy naturally knew nothing of this history. In time he became aware of it, but he never alluded to it directly. There was no reason why he should, and many reasons not to. You have to wonder how much he brooded on the discovery that he had been an unwanted child who had prevented his mother from living the life she had hoped to set up for herself, and how much this may have contributed to the moods of black depression that came over him at times, both as a boy and as a man, and even when he was well established. It is noticeable that when he wrote fictional accounts of country girls seduced and pregnant, he made Fanny Robin and Tess into romantic figures and victims, betrayed by men of higher social standing and driven to unhappiness and death.[38] He sympathized with them and defended them, but he showed them punished with the severity his society regarded as appropriate. He made their babies die too. In no way did they reflect anything that is known of the lives of the women of his family.

When Hardy was nearly eighty and women were entering the professions and given the vote, he wrote, on hearing of the birth of a baby to his wife's married sister, 'If I were a woman I should think twice before entering into matrimony in these days of emancipation, when everything is open to the sex.'[39] He had come to see the point of his mother's unfavourable view of marriage.

2. Child

The first drama of his infancy was his mother's discovery, one hot afternoon when she came in to the cottage from the garden, of a companionable snake curled up on his chest as he lay sleeping in his cradle. For Hardy, who all his life delighted in contact with wild creatures, this was a good story.[1] He remembered himself as a solitary child, although he was only eighteen months old when his sister Mary was born in December 1841. Fond as he was of her, she hardly figures in his childhood recollections. Nor do his cousins, although there were three older Hardy boys living opposite, George, Walter and Augustus. There were also something like twenty other children scattered about the cottages in the lane, yet in Hardy's memory it was 'a lonely and silent spot'.[2] 'There was my playground when I was a child,' he said later – not 'our playground' – pointing out a flat patch under the beech trees behind the house.[3] All this suggests that he was by nature unsociable, preferring his private world to any companionship. His parents' protectiveness, and fear that he would not survive childhood – they once said so in his hearing – may have encouraged his taste for solitude.[4] Animals pleased him, but he did not like to be touched by people, a trait he kept all his life. An early memory was of getting on to his hands and knees in the pasture to see how the sheep would react. Looking up, 'he found them gathered around in a close ring, gazing at him with astonished faces.'[5] His father showed him how to fold a handkerchief to look like a rabbit, something he remembered how to do seventy-five years later.[6] From the start he felt a sense of kinship with animals, and pity for their sufferings. When his father threw a stone at a fieldfare in the garden, killing it, the child picked it up, and to the end of his life remembered the lightness of the half-starved frozen bird in his hand. This capacity to store up particular experiences and draw on them imaginatively in his writing years later was as strong in Hardy as in Wordsworth.

The close family circle in the cottage was headed by his grandmother, the elder Mrs Hardy, who had been in charge of the family business since the death of her husband, looking after the accounts while her sons went out to the building sites. Much of their work was done nearby on Kingston Maurward, the thousand-acre estate of their landlords, and some for Stinsford Church.[7] They had only two men to help them and took their time over their jobs, partly because this was Thomas's way, also because there was a good deal to be done at home. He was in charge of the garden, growing fruit and vegetables – carrots, onions, parsnips, peas, broad beans and potatoes; in the autumn there would be Gascoyne Scarlets, Golden Pippins and Bockhampton Sweets on their apple trees, and cider to be made.[8] They kept a pig, hens and a few hives of bees, and got milk and butter from the dairy of the Kingston Maurward Estate. Water was hard work, as it had to be brought up from the well. The two women baked bread in an oven fuelled with furze cuttings. Jemima's fine cooking was superfluous here. There must have been days when the change in her circumstances irked her, and she still sometimes dreamt of escaping to a working life in London. But she was bred to stoicism, and when she had enough of Bockhampton she could walk over to Maria's for a sisterly talk, and see her three nieces, Rebecca, Emma and pretty Martha, and the baby James.

Whatever their doubts about his future, Hardy's parents were loving and attentive, and soon aware that his physical frailty went with unusual abilities. By the time he could walk he could also read. One of his earliest distinct memories is of being given a small toy concertina when he was four by his father, eager to infuse his son's life with what he himself loved best, music.[9] He played his fiddle at home in the evening, encouraged the boy to sing and dance, and taught him to play the fiddle alongside him, so that music became a perpetual theme, a perpetual pleasure and an inspiration. Looking back at the end of his life, Hardy wrote his own account of his early response to music, in the third person:

He was of ecstatic temperament, extraordinarily sensitive to music, and among the endless jigs, hornpipes, reels, waltzes, and country-dances that his father played of an evening in his early married years, and to which the boy danced a *pas seul* in the middle of the room, there were three or four that always moved the child to tears, though he strenuously tried to hide them . . . This peculiarity in himself troubled the mind of 'Tommy' as he was called, and set him wondering at a phenomenon to which he ventured not to confess.[10]

If the combination of an ecstatic temperament and a frail body helped to make him into a poet, his father's vast repertoire of tunes sharpened his ear and inspired his rhythmical inventiveness.

His mother made her contribution to the family music by singing traditional songs she had learnt from her mother, Granny Melbury, and by buying an old square 'table piano'. She could not play it herself, but she wanted her children to learn, and as he got old enough he enjoyed tinkering with it, and got on well enough to be able to play simple tunes. The neighbours also had musical parties, and his Hardy grandmother said that 'when she was sitting at home at Bockhampton she had heard the tranter "beat out the tune" on the floor with his feet when dancing at a party in his own house, which was a hundred yards or more away from hers.' The Hardy brothers gave up playing at church when he was three – the choir was disbanded by the modernizing vicar and churchwardens – but there was still psalm singing in which every-one joined, and his uncle James turned the barrel organ that accompanied their singing. The Hardy children were brought up to be strict churchgoers.[11] Church meant psalms but also gazing up out of the windows at clouds and passing rooks, or examining with mixed feelings the gap-toothed skull carved on a monument; and it meant drama.[12] The boy understood that the clergyman in charge was dressed up for the occasion and was giving a perform-ance. One Sunday when he was kept at home in bad weather he wrapped himself in a tablecloth, invited his grandmother to be his congregation, stood on a chair and read his version of Morning Prayer. An older cousin who happened to be in the house was coopted to play his clerk and say the Amens – James Sparks, perhaps, or Augustus Hardy. Tommy then gave a sermon made up of a patchwork of the sort of sentences he was accustomed to hearing from the vicar. The family hardly knew what to think: 'Everybody said that Tommy would have to be a parson, being obviously no good for any practical pursuit; which remark caused his mother many misgivings.'[13] Still in frocks, still delicate and small for his age, he imposed himself by his imagination. He also began to think that the life of a parson might suit him better than other alternatives.

Looking in a cupboard one day, he discovered an old periodical called *A History of the Wars*, full of pictures of soldiers, 'melodramatic prints of serried ranks, crossed bayonets, huge knapsacks, and dead bodies'. He was enthralled, the more so on being told his grandfather Hardy had subscribed to it thirty years ago when he was a volunteer, at the time it was feared the French were likely to land on the Dorset coast. Hardy was stirred by tales of soldiers and battles, and this was the start of his interest in the Napoleonic Wars. His grandmother delighted him by remarking, one particularly hot and thundery day, 'It was like this in the French Revolution, I remember.' She had been a young woman in the 1790s; and she also described how she had been ironing her best muslin dress when news came of the beheading of the Queen of France. She had put down the iron and stood still on hearing of such a momentous event, she said, and she could still call up the exact pattern of the muslin in her mind's eye.[14]

There were also discussions of modern politics in the house, talk of the Corn Laws, for instance, which taxed imported wheat to protect British farmers and sent up the price of bread cruelly for the poor. The struggle to repeal them and allow free trade was eventually successful in 1846. When Tom was five or six, on the day the pig was killed – a regular occurrence in the household – he got out the wooden sword made for him by his father, dipped it into the blood of the pig, and proceeded to parade round the garden waving it and shouting 'Free Trade or blood!' His next political memory was from a few years later, in 1850, when there was a frenzied outburst of anti-Catholic feeling throughout the country, as the Pope instructed Cardinal Wiseman to restore the

Catholic hierarchy in England. On 5 November – Guy Fawkes Day – his father took him to the great ancient Roman amphitheatre outside Dorchester, Maumbury Rings, to see an anti-Catholic demonstration at which a torchlit procession culminated in the burning of effigies of the Pope and Wiseman. He found it grimly exciting without understanding what was going on, and was puzzled by the discovery that one of the evil monks in the procession had the features of a man who worked for his father.[15] Much worse was something he did not witness but was told to him by his father, a story that must have gone back to the troubled times of the 1830s: he said he had seen four men hanged only for *being with* some others who set fire to a rick, one of them a half-starved boy who had run up to see the blaze and who weighed so little that they had to put weights on his feet to break his neck.[16]

Both his parents talked freely, if sometimes sombrely, to him and enjoyed taking him out with them. He had a memory of being in a pub in Dorchester – this must have been another outing with his father – where the tall soldiers of the Scots Greys were drinking, filling the bar with the fumes of alcohol so strong that they actually made him drunk.[17] His mother took him regularly across the heath to Puddletown to see his Aunt Maria and her children; these were cheerful expeditions, and on one occasion they disguised themselves by putting cabbage nets over their faces to spring a surprise on the cousins.[18] Once in Puddletown on a hot day Tom saw a man in the stocks, sitting with his blue-stockinged legs through the holes, the nails in his boots shining; the child thought the man rather a hero and said good-day to him.[19] The dark heath with its stretch of Roman road could be threatening but was friendly enough as long as he was with his mother, with whom he always associated it. 'They were excellent companions, having each a keen sense of humour and a love of adventure,' he wrote.[20] Mrs Yeobright in *The Return of the Native* has something of her character, and his poem 'The Roman Road' raises her ghost tenderly: 'Guiding my infant steps, as when / We walked that ancient thoroughfare'.[21]

From very early he began to make life into art, by seeing the special quality of natural occurrences and by dramatizing and embellishing them. There was a staircase in the front part of the house, which his father had painted vermilion red. On fine evenings the rays of the setting sun lit up the red paint, making a splendid effect. He would watch for this, and developed a ritual response in which he recited an evening hymn by Dr Isaac Watts to accompany it:

> And now another day is gone,
> I'll sing my Maker's praise!
> My comforts every hour make known
> His providence and grace.
>
> But how my childhood runs to waste
> My sins how great their sum!
> Lord, give me pardon for the past,
> And strength for days to come.

The hymn goes on to invoke angels around the sinful child's bed with evangelical fervour, but in his recollection the enjoyment was purely aesthetic, the sunset, the red stairs and the recitation combining to produce a richly pleasurable feeling. He was creating a Hardyesque experience.

His parents followed the forms of religion, and he was brought up to believe in God, and in the Devil and his pitchfork as the destination for sinners, but it was never a gloomy, conscience-searching family. His grandmother was gentle, his father even-tempered, and his mother an able and energetic woman; but he was aware of the divisions between his father and mother. She often pressed him to move the family to a bigger house, either in or near Dorchester, and one more accessible to potential clients of the building business, which would allow him to expand it, make money and become a thriving member of the community. The matter was 'always arising', but her persistence was stubbornly resisted by his father, attached to his birthplace and unwilling to lose the freedoms it gave him. His son observed that he had a taste for lying in the sun 'on a bank of thyme or camomile with the grasshoppers leaping over him' and for solitary walks on the heath

with his telescope; Tom shared his tastes enough to sympathize
with him.²² Formidable as Jemima's willpower and energy were,
her husband won the battle, and they remained at Bockhampton.

This suited Tom as well as his father. One of his best-known
poems about his childhood describes him sitting under some ferns
and deciding he has no wish to grow up or change his way of life:
'Why should I have to grow to man's estate . . . ?'²³ The poem was
written late, but it can be taken in association with something
similar described in the *Life*: lying on his back, looking through
his straw hat at the sun and thinking that he did not want to grow
up. 'Other boys were always talking of when they would be men;
he did not want at all to be a man, or to possess things, but to
remain as he was, in the same spot, and to know no more people
than he already knew . . . Afterwards he told his mother of his
conclusions on existence, thinking that she would enter into his
views. But to his great surprise she was very much hurt.'²⁴ Perhaps
she was more worried than hurt that her son seemed to be showing
the same unwillingness to take on the world as his father.

Two years or so after the birth of Mary, Jemima became ill.
It was a serious episode following a miscarriage and kept her
incapacitated for some months. By then her younger sister –
confusingly, another Mary – had come from Melbury to help out
with the care of the children. There were now three of the Hand
sisters living close to one another: Maria Sparks, Jemima Hardy
and Mary Hand. The ties between them were always strong. The
Sparks family said their mother, Maria, helped to nurse Jemima
through her illness, that it lasted for several months, that she
suffered from 'brain fever', and that she emerged from the sickroom
a noticeably sterner woman.²⁵ An anxious time for the children,
even with their aunts and Granny Hardy caring for them.

In 1846 their other granny left Melbury to join her two sons
and three daughters in Puddletown and Bockhampton. Most of
the Hand family was now reassembled, although they were missing
the youngest sister, Martha. Like Maria she was a beauty, and she
had been married in 1841 in Puddletown to an ardent and rather
dashing suitor, John Sharpe, and gone to live with him in Hertford-

shire; a man of some education, he had been in the army, and now worked as a farm bailiff for Lord Salisbury. In December 1846, when their mother was installed among them, Mary Hand determined to go and see Martha, who had just given birth to her third child. It was a bold plan for a country girl, involving a complicated journey alone and a new system of transport, the railway. She had to take the coach to Andover, the nearest point then reached by the railway, stop overnight in London and go on by coach to Hitchin. A letter to her mother, reassuring her that she had arrived safely, describes the bitter cold on the coach, where she sat outside until the driver took pity on her and took her inside near Blandford; and how she found herself at the London station surrounded by 'a great quantity of men and not one woman – I thought on what Chris [her brother] told me to keep a good look out for the Coachman but no Coachman could I see – so I searched for a Policeman.' The Sharpes had, in fact, arranged for her to be met by a friend, Mr Trask, and deposited at a hotel. Mary found the price of breakfast 'rather too Grand for my Pocket', but at one o'clock Trask reappeared and escorted her to the Hitchin coach. 'I found John and Freddy [Sharpe and his four-year-old son] waiting for me at the coach office. He led me home where I found Martha waiting for me – poor Maid she could not think it possible for me to be at Hitchin – They were all very kind to me . . . their kind love to you Mama, Jemima, Chris and Brothers you will let them see this.'[26] She must have travelled third class in the train, packed into ill-lit box cars on wooden benches where body warmth hopefully made up for the lack of heating; her sister's surprise at seeing her shows what an extraordinary novelty train travel was.

Six months later, in June 1847, the railway reached Dorchester. That year Granny Hand from Melbury died, and Mary married a Puddletown cobbler, John Antell, a man with radical views who had also taught himself Latin, Greek and Hebrew but could not put them to any use or organize his life in any satisfactory way.[27] The wedding celebrations were held at Bockhampton, and Thomas and James Hardy naturally played for the dancing, supported by seven-year-old Tommy. He was still small for his age, but the family were no longer fearful for his life and had begun to treat him more like an ordinary boy.

The Hardys had a change of landlord when William Grey Pitt sold Kingston Maurward and its estate in 1844. The new owner, Francis Martin, paid £15,000 and set himself up as a country squire, and his devout and charitable wife, Julia Augusta, proceeded to do good among the tenants. Within a few years, encouraged by the vicar of Stinsford, Mr Shirley, and with his collaboration, she embarked on the building of a Church of England school in Lower Bockhampton, and also paid for two schoolteachers.[28] When Tommy reached the age of eight, it was decided that he was strong enough to go to school, and the decision was made easier by the opening of Mrs Martin's establishment.

He had been a reader for years, but his writing skills lagged behind, perhaps because no one had encouraged this at home, and quill pens are refractory instruments.[29] Now he worked at his writing, took readily to arithmetic and geography, and proved himself to be a good pupil; but the most powerful effect of the school was not academic. As patron of the school, and with no children of her own, Julia Martin took an intense interest in what went on there and spent many hours acting almost as a supplementary teacher. Tommy became her favourite, and her feelings were reciprocated. That he was small for his age and unlike the other village boys in his ways, being gentle, quick and responsive, made it easy for her to take him on her lap, to pet him and kiss him. She was thirty-eight. She was the first lady – in the social sense – he had ever known. She spoke differently, she smelt differently, she dressed differently. Years later he remembered the four grey silk flounces on her dress and the thrilling 'frou-frou' they made when she moved about. He expressed his devotion by making drawings of animals for her and singing songs to please her, but his feeling for her became 'almost that of a lover' – these are his own words. The erotic excitements of school were extended to Sundays, when the same 'frou-frou' might be produced as her dress brushed against the font when she came into church. There is no doubt that this was an overpowering experience for him, and one he never forgot. Late in life he was still speculating on whether they might have resumed their love and made more of it when she became a widow and he a young man: 'though their eyes never met again after his call on her in London, nor their lips from the time when she had held him in her arms, who can say that both occurrences might not have been in the order of things, if he had developed their reacquaintance *earlier*.'[30] It is a powerful piece of fantasy. For her part, she may not have been fully aware of the effect her kisses and caresses produced on the boy, and would have seen her own enjoyment as innocently maternal. In truth, she was giving him his first love affair.

The love affair was interrupted by his mother. Encouraged by Mary's successful railway journey, she made up her mind to travel to Hertfordshire to visit Martha and to help her over the birth of her fifth baby, due in the winter of 1849. It was also an adventure, a chance to give herself a change from life at Bockhampton, with the bonus that she was escaping any danger of another pregnancy herself for a few months. She announced that she was taking her son with her – 'for protection' she explained; 'being then an attractive and still young woman', he commented afterwards.[31] It meant removing him from school, which may have been a further contributory reason if she had any inkling of his obsession with Mrs Martin.

They set off in the autumn and did not return until well into the new year of 1850. The journey from Dorchester to Waterloo now took only four hours, but the remainder still had to be made by coach.[32] They put up at a coaching inn in London, the Cross Keys, St John Street, Clerkenwell, taking a cheap room on an upper floor. Smithfield was close by – St John Street was the old drovers' road – and he was horrified by the brutality, filth and noise of the cattle market. He had prepared for the trip by acquiring a map of the City and marking out the streets described by Harrison Ainsworth in *Old St Paul's*, a favourite book at the time, and he went out and traced the steps of the hero.[33] He remembered also his mother taking him to see the Pantheon in Regent's Park, and Hyde Park at Cumberland Gate. Then it was time to board the coach, which stopped in the Finchley Road, from which they looked back across the fields at the expanding edge of the city with its new terraces, new roads and building sites.

The Sharpes were now living in Hatfield, twenty miles from London. They had a house near the church in Fore Street, where there was also a day school to which Tom could go. John's position as a farm manager for Lord Salisbury seemed to be a very good one, and they gave the Hardys a warm welcome. Uncle John was a different creature from the Puddletown uncles, possessed of some social grace, his sister a governess and his brother going into the Church. Freddy and Louisa were old enough to be companionable, and, although Aunt Martha had too many children already – one of her babies had died, she was occupied with the youngest and now expecting yet another – she was still a lovely, spirited woman. Many years later Hardy said he modelled Bathsheba, the heroine of *Far from the Madding Crowd*, on his Aunt Martha, so he must have treasured the impression of her physical beauty and charming manners, and perhaps too the spectacle of a more courtly and romantic relationship between husband and wife than he had seen at home.[34]

The Hatfield school was 'somewhat on the Squeers model', and he was bullied by the bigger boys, who resented his superior skills, but as it was a day school he did not suffer too badly.[35] That Christmas he was given *The Boys' Book of Science*, inscribing it 'Thomas Hardy / Dec. 24th 1849'. He also wrote in *The Tutor's Assistant; Being a Compendium of Arithmetic*, 'Thomas Hardys / Book / 1849'. He was kept well supplied with reading matter. His mother had already supplied him with Dryden's Virgil, Dr Johnson's novel *Rasselas* and a translation of *Paul et Virginie*, the French novel that told the tale of innocent child lovers on a tropical island, popular in the 1790s, and all undoubtedly from his Melbury grandmother's collection. Ainsworth he knew already, and he was soon reading cheap editions of other recent historical novels by Bulwer-Lytton and Alexander Dumas.

They never saw the Sharpes again. Even Lord Salisbury's estates felt the pinch of the hard times, and his manager was laid off. No other work could be found, and in desperation John Sharpe applied to emigrate to Canada. Lord Salisbury put up some of the money, and in 1851 the family crossed the Atlantic and settled in Ontario. It was not much easier to find the right sort of work there, and there were no sisters to cheer them. More babies kept coming, and with the tenth, in 1859, Martha died, aged only forty-three. It was a bleak conclusion for Bathsheba's model. John Sharpe became a schoolmaster. Louisa, who preserved a dreamlike memory of the visit of her aunt Hardy and cousin Thomas, wrote to them once, a tiny letter in the neatest hand, in 1870.[36] She lived to be ninety-seven, dying in 1941.

When Jemima and her son got home she did not send him back to Mrs Martin's school. He suffered and said nothing: 'he had grown more attached than he cared to own' is how he put it. To whom could a child of nine complain of losing his love? His mother, determined that he should be given the best education available, had decided to send him to a more serious school in Dorchester, under a Nonconformist headmaster with a high reputation, Isaac Last, who offered Latin lessons. Tom was pronounced fit enough to do the much longer daily walk, three miles each way. There was now no way of being with Mrs Martin, yet he longed to see her so painfully that he worked out a way. He learnt from the village girls that there was to be a harvest supper held at the old manor house on the estate, now tenanted by a farmer, which she would attend; and he persuaded one of the girls to let him go with her, although he had no invitation. They set off together, contriving to leave while his mother was out, and found a lively party in progress, soldiers from the Dorchester barracks having been invited by Mr Martin to be dancing partners for the girls. Presently Mrs Martin arrived. She saw him and came up to speak: 'Oh Tommy, how is this? I thought you had deserted me!'[37] He burst into tears and told her he had not and never would desert her. As a good hostess, she provided him with a dancing partner, her little niece, but after a few dances the party from the great house left, having done its duty. By now the girl who had brought him was taken up with her own partners. He was afraid to go home without her, and too shy to ask for anything to eat or drink, and there he stayed until three in the morning, miserable, hungry and tired.

The one thing that cheered him was hearing the farm women sing together sitting on a long bench under the barn. They chose the popular ballad 'The Outlandish Knight', a villain who came wooing a girl at the great house, getting her to steal away from her parents at night with two horses and stolen gold. When they come to a river the knight tries to drown her as he has drowned many girls before, but she tricks him, pushes him into the water instead and rides home alone, arriving at dawn, seen only by a parrot in the window:

> The parrot being up in the window so high
> And hearing the lady did say
> 'I'm afraid some ruffian has led you astray
> That you've tarried so long away.'

> Don't prittle, don't prattle, my Pretty Polly
> Nor tell any tales on me
> And your cage shall be made of the finest beaten gold
> And the doors of the best ivory.

The parrot agrees not to tell on the girl, and she gets away with her escapade. Not so Thomas, who was scolded by both his parents when he finally arrived home. For him it was the end of the affair. Whatever Mrs Martin's affection for him, she was very much put out when she found his mother had chosen a school for her son with a headmaster known to be a Nonconformist. This is the likely reason why his father was no longer given jobs on the estate, removing at a stroke a good part of his regular and easily accessible work. The Martins did not spend the summer of 1851 at Kingston Maurward, and in 1853 Mr Martin sold the estate and moved with his wife to London.[38]

3. The Bookish Boy

His serious schooldays began in 1850. Tom was ten that year, and his enrolment at Mr Last's school in Dorchester was a sign from his parents that he was being set on a different course from that of his father, his grandfather or any of his uncles.[1] It was obvious that he lacked the physical strength to become a builder. His luck was first that his parents saw he had gifts and capacities of another kind, then that they were in a position to do something to encourage and develop them, and that they lived close to a town which could boast several good schools. Few country boys with his sort of background got more than a few years of schooling, and it was common to start work in the fields at the age of nine.[2] For Hardy, his mother's determination was crucial, the more so because 1850 was not a prosperous year for his father. He and his brother James had divided the business and gone their separate ways professionally, and the 1851 census puts Thomas Hardy down as a mere bricklayer with two assistants. Yet, even if Jemima was the driving force behind the decision to buy Tom a good education, his father supported the plan and paid for it.

So a new phase of his life started when, instead of being escorted to the little Church of England school in Lower Bockhampton, he set off alone on the three-mile walk to school in Greyhound Yard in the centre of Dorchester. It was his first real, regular freedom from parental control, and the daily routine, there and back in all weathers, gave him time and solitude in which to think, to observe and to dream. His route can still be followed across a landscape that has remained relatively unchanged since the 1850s: down the lane to the road, left and on to a diagonal path across the fields for half a mile, joining the road again close to Stinsford; then west down the long stretch of Stinsford Hill into the valley of the Frome. The river was crossed at Grey's Bridge with its three stone arches. In the 1850s there were water meadows from Grey's

Bridge to Swan Bridge, which was brick-built and spanned a small branch of the wandering Frome. This was the edge of town, with its pavements and steeply rising high street, its old churches and newly built town hall, its shops and inns and busy street life.

There were market days twice a week, and four annual fairs for sheep, cattle, wool and leather. The London post and newspapers arrived daily, and there was also a local paper, the *Dorset County Chronicle*.[3] There were circulating libraries and a small theatre in which travelling groups of players made irregular appearances.[4] There was the railway station, a modern gaol and, just out of town to the north, the big barracks. With a population under 5,000 the arrival and departure of soldiers and their horses were always important events, because they brought colour and life to the town; some regiments had their own band to entertain everyone, and they kept the inns busy, and the girls. Apart from the barracks and the workhouse, not much had been built outside the Roman walls, planted with avenues of trees and known as the Walks: Chestnut Walk, Bowling Walk, West Walk and North Walk. Here the citizens promenaded for their pleasure when the weather was fair. And the town boasted one suburb, the village of Fordington, with its own church and green, so close that it was effectively part of Dorchester. Below it the vast green area of Fordington Field stretched away to the south, still unenclosed meadow, farmed in strips as it had been since the Middle Ages.

An army officer posted to Dorchester in 1830 dismissed the place condescendingly as 'three streets and one or two lanes'.[5] Still, it was the County Town, with a mayor and six aldermen. The assizes were held there, and elections, and they sent two MPs to Westminster. In the summer of 1852, at the end of Tom's second year at Mr Last's, the successful Liberal candidate was drawn triumphantly round the town in his carriage by his supporters, and Tom was among them, the Hardys being Liberals, even though his father had no vote.[6] A boy could learn almost as much as he needed to know about life by keeping his eyes open in Dorchester.

If school started at eight, it meant being out of the house shortly after seven. Going home could be more leisurely, giving him time to wander in the water meadows, the woods and other roads.

These long daily walks became his own special territory; their details engraved themselves on his mind and stayed there. When he was an old man, he could point out the place in a hedge where he had put down an umbrella while he cut a stick for himself and then went on home, forgetting the umbrella until his mother asked for it and retrieving it on his way to school in the morning.[7] He learnt to read the noises of the fields and the woods, the bark of the fox, 'its three hollow notes' sounding at precise intervals of a minute, and the sound of game birds rising to their roosts at dusk, 'crack-voiced cock-pheasants' "cu-uck, cuck", and the wheezy whistle of the hens'.[8] He noticed how the hares came out in the fields at dusk and observed the stars as they appeared. He feared nothing in nature, but once frightened himself by reading the story of Apollyon in *Pilgrim's Progress* as he went along and began to imagine that the foul fiend might jump on him out of a tree.[9] In winter he often had to walk in the dark, and one incident was so mysterious that even reading about it raises a shiver. As he went up Stinsford Hill, not a single dwelling in sight, and no street lights, 'he came upon two men sitting on chairs, one on either side of the road. By the moonlight he saw that they were strangers to him; terrified, he took to his heels; he never heard who they were or anything to explain the incident.'[10] What makes it sinister is the silence, because on a country road you expect friends and strangers alike to exchange a word as you pass, and their being seated, as though taking part in some arcane ritual.

Walking the roads, meeting others on the road, exchanging news with travellers, being overtaken by riders, carts and carriers, or offered lifts, were all part of his daily experience throughout his boyhood, so that it is not surprising that the road became a theatre for action in his imagination and walking a central activity in his writing, used dramatically and to establish or underline character. Most of his characters are prodigious walkers. Tess and Jude both walk themselves through the crises in their lives, and Jude effectively kills himself by walking in the rain. Gabriel Oak walks to find work, and Fanny Robin walks through the snow to plead with her lover, and then drags herself along the road to the workhouse, leaning on an obliging dog, to die. Elfride in *A Pair of Blue*

Eyes runs 'through the pelting rain like a hare; or more like a pheasant when, scampering away with a lowered tail, it has a mind to fly, but does not'.[11] The newly-wed lovers in *Two on a Tower* walk nine miles across country to a railway station to avoid being noticed. *The Hand of Ethelberta* opens with Ethelberta, a young widow, taking a solitary walk on a heath, where she sees a wild duck being pursued by a hawk, runs after the birds to see what will happen and loses her way. At the beginning of *The Mayor of Casterbridge*, Henchard is shown on the road, his character to be read not in his words but his walk: 'his measured springless walk was the walk of the skilled country man as distinct from the desultory shamble of the general labourer; while in the turn and plant of each foot there was, further, a dogged and cynical indifference, personal to himself.' And at the end of the book he leaves Casterbridge on foot, a diminishing figure going into the distance, and observed in fine detail: 'the yellow straw basket at his back moving up and down with each tread, and the creases behind his knees coming and going alternately'. In *The Return of the Native*, Mrs Yeobright recognizes a distant, anonymous furze-cutter simply by his walk: 'a gait she had seen somewhere before; and the gait revealed the man to her . . . "His walk is exactly as my husband's used to be," she said; and then the thought burst upon her that the furze-cutter was her son.'[12]

The daily walk in the open air made Tom into a sturdy child. He was still small for his age, but his family forgot that he was meant to be delicate. As an old man, he once said he did not like going to school, and remembered being sent when he was ill and could hardly walk to Dorchester, but this can't have happened often.[13] One who claimed to remember him as a fellow schoolboy spoke of his bright eyes and fair hair, rather curly – like his father's and grandfather's, although it darkened later – and said he used to wear a brown knickerbocker suit. He had a cap and carried his satchel of books swinging on his arm; and his mother sometimes waited for him at her garden gate in the afternoon. 'They thought the world of each other, Tom and his mother.'[14] Another schoolmate, the son of a small farmer, formed a good opinion of Mrs Hardy after she gave him 'two slices of bread and butter and one with sugar on't' after he had helped to deliver a pig to the Hardy cottage; kindly people, this man thought the Hardys, but 'in a paltry way' as to the family business.[15] The descendants of the Revd Reginald Smith at West Stafford, whose son Bosworth was the same age as Hardy and later became a close friend, have a tradition that he once stopped for a glass of milk at the vicarage between home and school.[16] To the daughter of a rich neighbouring farmer, Tom was an 'odd looking little boy with a big head', and her brother Ernest Harding explained that 'the Hardings regarded the Hardys as socially inferior . . . Hardy was just a village boy, although it was recognised that he was an unusual type . . . he never played games, and was a quiet, studious child of a retiring disposition.'[17] Not always, according to Hardy's own account. Passing a cottage one day where a raffle was being organized, the prize a live hen to be awarded on the throw of dice, he put in twopence, threw luckily and won the hen. His parents, instead of being pleased, were angry with him for gambling and forbade him ever to do so again; no doubt they disapproved of the family that set up the raffle.[18] Then some of the village girls, illiterate themselves and seeing Tom was a scholar, got together and persuaded him to read their letters from soldier sweethearts stationed in India, and to write down replies for them. He obliged but said he took no interest in the task, perhaps because he considered their affairs too remote from what he felt love to be – an unexpected disclaimer for a future novelist.[19]

The gulf between gentry and village was a fact of life from the start, and as he grew he observed many further gradations within village life, and understood how safe and sheltered his home was, and how privileged his education. Among the labouring families round about there was real hardship, sometimes leading to grim scenes and tragedy. When he was nine or ten a boy he knew who looked after the sheep near Bockhampton died and was found to have starved to death. He had been trying to sustain himself on raw turnips.[20] That was an extreme case, but there was steady, grinding poverty and deprivation for many others. One of the biggest buildings outside Dorchester was the workhouse, and it may be that the shepherd boy preferred starvation at home to what he knew of the workhouse. The system of poor relief that had helped Hardy's Melbury grandmother, stingy as it was, had been replaced by something crueller when the Poor Law Amendment Act decreed in 1834 that workhouses should be punitive, separating man and wife, parent and child, setting the poor 'apart like wild beasts in a cage, staked off from their fellow men, and regarded as beings of a different caste', as even the conservative local newspaper complained.[21]

The Hardys were never in danger of the workhouse and never short of food, and, although they had no luxuries, there was usually a bit of money in hand, whether to buy train tickets or to pay for schooling. So the gap between Tom's experience and the lives of most of the other children living round about stretched wider. Given his opportunity, he seized it, and among the dull sons of better-off farmers and shopkeepers at Mr Last's school he became a prize pupil. He was quick to learn, with a great fund of curiosity and an exceptional memory. He had no trouble mastering arithmetic, geometry and algebra; he enjoyed drawing and was good at it. He was always reading, whether Dumas or Harrison Ainsworth's historical novels, Bunyan's *Pilgrim's Progress* or *The Boys' Book of Science*. He paid attention to what he read and arrived at his own judgements, deciding, for example, that Shakespeare would have done better to have made more of the ghost in *Hamlet*.[22]

He knew what he wanted too – for instance, he was eager to study languages. Although he did not seek friends or popularity, and shrank from physical contact, he was always ready to help other boys with their lessons. School did not provide a midday meal, and it was too far to go home, so he sometimes carried his lunch-box with him and ate it wherever he chose to in town; and at other times went to his uncle James Sparks's sisters, Amelia and Rebecca, who lived in Dorchester, doing piecework as shoebinders, fixing leather or ribbons to newly made shoes. According to his Sparks cousins, he disconcerted the good maiden ladies by performing 'conjuring tricks' in their house, flicking bread and butter to the ceiling to see if it would stick there.[23] If this is a true story, it is rather a relief to hear of some ordinary naughtiness away from the eye of both controlling mother and disciplinarian schoolmaster, who had a reputation as a beater of bad boys. As far as we know, Hardy was never beaten.

In May 1851, just before his eleventh birthday, the Great Exhibition was opened in London by the Queen. It was the first big tourist attraction in England and succeeded beyond its organizers' dreams, drawing unprecedented numbers of visitors. Special excursion trains were run from the provinces, and the railway companies slashed their fares. Good fathers took their children, and whole parishes went in groups, led by their vicar.[24] Parties set off from Dorchester during the summer at special cheap rates, with third-class carriages open to the skies, and excitement ran so high that spectators gathered by the railway track just to see the long trains packed with people passing through the countryside. The travellers sometimes arrived in London chilled and rain-soaked, but they hurried on to be amazed by Paxton's glass palace and stunned by the range of exhibits gathered from all over the world.[25] Six million people managed to pass through its doors between May and October. It was just the thing a clever schoolboy would long to see: why did Hardy fail to get to the Exhibition?

Money may have been short, but there was another reason: his mother was expecting a baby that summer. Not only that: her elder sister Maria Sparks also gave birth to a daughter in March, at the advanced age of forty-six. Neither woman can have been pleased. Maria had enjoyed eight years without a baby, Jemima ten. When little Tryphena Sparks made her appearance in Puddletown her eldest sister, Rebecca, was already twenty-two.[26] At the same time there was cause for sorrow among the sisters when they heard that Martha Sharpe was leaving for Canada with her husband and five children. Emigrants went with no expectation of returning, believing they were seeing the last of England and of those they loved and left behind; the Sharpes had fallen on such hard times that they were not even in a position to make last farewells. They had been forced to beg money for their passage.[27] So Martha, who had seemed to make the best marriage of the four Hand sisters, was now the poorest, and lost to them. They left England in July.

After this, in August, Jemima's baby was born. He was a large boy, named Henry after his maternal uncle Henry Hand, and he proved to be a solid son with no ambition to break out of the world he was born into and ready to follow his father into the building trade. If Tom was disconcerted to find his mother at the mercy of nature and the physical processes of childbearing and nurture, and sorry to miss the Great Exhibition, he had a busy life of his own to pursue as he started on his second year at Mr Last's; and over the years he became attached to his large, practical, unintellectual brother. Although they had nothing in common beyond family, they remained companionable to the end of their lives, even going on holiday together from time to time.[28]

When Tom was twelve, he bought himself *An Introduction to the Latin Tongue* and began to learn the genders of Latin nouns, devising his own system of colour coding to help his memory. Soon his parents were paying for private Latin lessons with Mr Last, and Tom was reading Caesar. It was a clear signal of his ambitions, since the ability to read the classics was the badge of an educated man and the path towards higher education. There were other schools where he could have learnt Latin and Greek in Dorchester, notably the grammar school, which taught 'by the Eton method', and another run by the clergyman-poet William Barnes, but neither seems to have been considered for Tom. Nor was what was undoubtedly the most efficient educational establishment in the district, run by the vicar of Fordington, the Revd Henry Moule, whose sermon to the soldiers had so impressed Jemima years before. Moule taught all his seven sons up to university level at home, with a group of paying pupils alongside, sons of gentlemen destined for the professions. This was above Tom's social level, and he had small prospects of higher education; and, although Moule was known to the Hardys as a prominent local clergyman with whom they had occasional contact, Tom had yet to be befriended by the Moule sons. So when Mr Last expanded his teaching arrangements in 1853 and became head of an 'Academy', Tom continued his education with him. Last's Academy was backed by local Nonconformists, but its religious bias hardly impinged on Tom.[29] He read the Bible regularly and took himself to church every Sunday, if not always at Stinsford. None of the

Hardys were religious zealots, but they respected the conventions in which they had been reared, and if churchgoing had been more fun when the men made the music, it remained part of the essential order of country life. Mr Shirley kept his eye on Tom and in due course enrolled him in his confirmation class. Hardy's only account of a confirmation suggests that the service did not impress him, but Shirley saw that he was bright and got him to join his own sons as a teacher in the Sunday School.[30]

There Tom found himself instructing girls several years older than himself, something he enjoyed. One was a dairymaid, 'pink and plump', with a gift for memorizing whole chapters of the Bible. Years later he based Tess's kindly friend Marian on her, one of 'the few portraits from life' in his work, he wrote.[31] She amused him, but he fell 'madly in love' (in his own phrase) with another girl, a stranger, seen riding near the South Walk in Dorchester. Horseback riding was a pastime for the rich, which may have added to her appeal; he could not ride himself, but he looked for her for several days and enlisted his school friends in the search, with no luck. Then he met a girl from Windsor and was attracted to her because he had been reading Harrison Ainsworth's novel *Windsor Castle*, but when he found she took no interest in either the historical or the ghostly parts of Ainsworth's plot, he lost interest in her. A red-haired gamekeeper's daughter Elizabeth – Lizbie – was another of his loves, and a more long-lasting attachment was to Louisa Harding, daughter of a local farmer. He once managed to say 'Good evening' to her in the Bockhampton lane on his afternoon walk home from Dorchester, and when he heard she had been sent to boarding school in Weymouth he started going there on Sundays to get a glimpse of her in church. A shy smile was all his reward: the Hardings, as we have seen, did not want to know the Hardys. The teens are for falling in love indiscriminately, and there seems to have been none of the painful intensity of his feeling for Mrs Martin. Louisa and Lizbie are given light-hearted poems, and even when Louisa appears as a ghost in one it is only mildly wistful.[32]

By 1853 Mr Hardy had plenty of work again, and a horse and
trap of his own in which he drove about on his business. Hardy
remembered being taken to Weymouth in the trap as a treat that
year.[33] He got on well with his father and in the holidays would
go with him to one of his building sites, an old house or a church
that was being restored, and listen to him discussing the job in
hand with the architect. Both enjoyed their fiddle playing and kept
up the family tradition, still sometimes joined by uncle James, now
playing the cello, when they went out to make music for the
dancing at weddings and other celebrations. There is a story of
young Tom playing without a break for forty-five minutes for the
country dancers and being stopped by his hostess for fear he should
break a blood vessel; another of a bride so delighted with the music
that she kissed him in her white dress as a sign of her pleasure.
There were occasions too when songs and behaviour became
bawdy, and some of the revellers fell over and ended up in tangled
heaps on the floor. These were evening gatherings, and father and
son might find themselves walking home at three in the morning;
if that meant he was tired the next day, it also gave him a view of
the festive life of the farms and cottages round about, and a contrast
with the quiet, studious hours in the classroom. His mother told
him he must not accept payment, since he was offering a neigh-
bourly service, but one night, seeing that the assembled revellers
had collected several shillings in a hat, he made up his mind to
accept it. There was a good reason. He had seen and coveted *The
Boys' Own Book* in the window of a Dorchester shop, and the
money was enough to buy it. For such a prize it was worth facing
his mother's disapproval. He was a haunter of bookshops, and was
remembered for it by the son of a Dorchester bookseller, who
used to watch Tom at the shop's counter, reading his way through
one volume after another. The boy welcomed Hardy, because he
brought him some particularly good eating apples, the Bockhampton Sweets from his parents' garden, and the bookseller was
too good-natured to complain, knowing that a reader will one day
turn into a buyer.[34]

He called himself 'a born bookworm'.[35] At Christmas 1854 he
won a school prize for his diligence and good behaviour – a book,

naturally, *Scenes and Adventures at Home and Abroad* – and the next summer a Latin testament. But Last, knowing he was unlikely to go to a university, had him work on specimen commercial letters and accounts, set out in the copperplate hand required of clerks. He did not confine himself to it but developed another free, handsome and beautifully legible hand of his own, easily recognizable in the manuscripts of his letters, novels and poems. When he heard that his sister Mary's school boasted a French *mademoiselle*, he went to her for lessons, buying himself *A Stepping Stone to the French Language* for good measure. Then he started on German, using a course provided in a magazine called *The Popular Educator*, given to him by his mother. Self-help was the spirit of the age, enshrined in Samuel Smiles's book, published in 1859.

When he thought of the future, he remembered the family joke that had destined him for the Church as a small boy parroting the vicar's words, and thought it might suit him.[36] His mother's years in service had let her see a particularly agreeable aspect of clerical life, well-born clergymen in charge of small parishes and living in large houses, with leisure to read, take holidays and spend months in London as they chose. Not all had such an easy time. Mr Moule of Fordington gave his considerable energy and talents to improving the physical and spiritual condition of his wretchedly poor parishioners as well as educating the large band of boys in his care. William Barnes, orphaned young, had left school at thirteen, educated himself, become a schoolmaster and struggled to get the degree which would allow him to enter the Church; by then he was fifty, and over sixty before he settled down to the quiet life of a country parsonage. He was an example of someone who had worked hard to break out of the constraints of his life to achieve his ambition and succeeded, but the usual route to a career in the Church depended on family money. No one in Tom's family had ever attended a university, and neither his father's imagination nor his income would stretch to having a son prepared for a university education that would make him financially dependent well into his twenties. He had his mother and his wife to keep, a fluctuating income and other children to consider; when Tom was fifteen Jemima became pregnant again. She was known to believe that large families were a mistake, but the mistake was made, and there would now be a fourth child to bring up at Bockhampton.[37]

In spite of this, Tom was not sent out to earn his living at sixteen. Father, mother and grandmother must have agreed that he could not be put to work in the family firm. They came up with an ingenious side-step, and a step up too: if he was not to be a builder, he might become an architect. Architects took pupils, who paid something towards their training; they helped out with whatever needed to be done in the office or on site at the same time. John Hicks was an architect for whom his father had done a good deal of work, mostly restoring churches; Tom had met him when accompanying his father, and Hicks had formed a good opinion of the boy and was happy to take him as a working pupil. Mrs Hardy bargained briskly for a reduction in the usual premium of £100, payable halfway through the three years, and got it reduced to £40 in cash, paid at the start. In this way Tom was articled for three years, with the prospect of a further three years which might culminate in his becoming an architect himself in 1862. It was not his own choice, but he accepted it without repining.

Hicks's office was in the centre of Dorchester, at 39 South Street, and Hardy began there just after his sixteenth birthday, in June 1856. In many ways his life continued as before. He had the same daily walks in and out of Dorchester. He was still entirely dependent on his parents for pocket money. He was able to go on with his private studies by giving himself three hours' reading from five to eight in the morning; and Hicks allowed all his pupils time of their own during the day. His good sense and humanity contrasted with the reaction of the vicar of Stinsford to Hardy's venture. One Sunday morning that summer Mr Shirley delivered a sermon attacking the presumption of members of the lower classes who aspired to join the professions. The boy took it as a direct reproach and held it against the vicar ever afterwards. He also found it so humiliating that he did not talk about it until the last years of his life, and Shirley's name is never mentioned in any letters or recollections, although the clergyman remained at Stinsford until his death in 1891.[38] This looks like the first awakening of hostility towards the Church, the beginning of his dislike of the narrow-mindedness, snobbery and cant of many of the clergy. He continued to practise as a Christian, although often preferring to attend other churches, and he did not lose his belief yet, but he was surely set on the path of questioning the authority of the Church and thinking for himself.

While he was still at school, in March 1854, Britain declared war on Russia after forty years of peace, and the Dorchester barracks emptied as the troops set off to fight in the Crimea. The excitement was great, but, since they were armed with exactly the same weapons as had been used at Waterloo, incompetently led and ill provided with clothes, food or medicine, the results were not impressive. The war lasted for two years, and in June 1856, as Tom finished his schooldays, Dorchester put on joint celebrations for the peace and the anniversary of the Queen's accession, with sports, flags and Chinese lanterns in the town Walks. In July the circus came to town, and there were horseback representations of the Battle of Alma. This was followed by another diversion, the hanging in Dorchester of a woman found guilty of murder.

Hangings were carried out in public to give a salutary warning to other potential offenders – that was the idea, anyway – but also generally accepted as a form of popular entertainment, and Dorchester Gaol, rebuilt in white stone in the centre of town early in the nineteenth century, had a specially constructed area of flat roof for the gallows, intended to allow them to be observed from below by as many people as possible.[39] So there was nothing surprising about the sixteen-year-old Hardy, who had read of a great many grisly murders and hangings in Ainsworth's novels, joining the crowd of thousands that gathered in August 1856 to watch the unfortunate Martha Browne suffer her punishment.

He took away a vivid impression of what he saw, and it remained in his mind for the rest of his life. 'I am ashamed to say I saw her hanged,' he wrote to an elderly lady who lived near the village from which Mrs Browne came and asked him about it in his old age, 'my only excuse being that I was but a youth, and had to be in the town at the time for other reasons.' He went on: 'I remember what a fine figure she showed against the sky as she hung in the misty rain, and how the tight black silk gown set off her shape as she wheeled half-round and back.'[40] The words 'fine figure' and 'tight black silk gown set off her shape' have been found objectionable, because they suggest he thought of her as an attractive woman in the moment of her death. Only too likely, surely, but hardly culpable. The horrible fact of the helplessness of a dead hanging body is made worse when it is that of a young woman dressed incongruously in her best clothes, which she has chosen for the occasion. It was her last brave piece of vanity, and in its way it was effective.

As it happens, Dickens produced an almost identical reaction to a similar scene. He detested public hangings and campaigned against them but felt obliged to attend at least two and paid large sums of money to hire rooms with a good view. At the first, in 1840, he noticed Thackeray standing in the crowd: also an opponent of public hangings and also feeling obliged to witness one. The second seen by Dickens was in 1849, when a man and a woman, Mrs Mannings, were hanged. Three years later Dickens wrote about it in his family magazine *Household Words*:

having beheld that execution, and having left those two forms dangling on the top of the gateway – the man's, a limp, loose suit of clothes as if the man had gone out of them; the woman's, a fine shape, so elaborately corseted and artfully dressed, that it was quite unchanged in its trim appearance as it slowly swung from side to side – I never could, by my uttermost efforts, for some weeks, present the outside of that prison to myself (which the terrible impression I had received continually obliged me to do) without presenting it with the two figures still hanging in the morning air.[41]

Dickens, like Hardy, found the shape of the dead woman, with all the other associations it brought, particularly appalling, and as far as I know no one has suggested there is anything unhealthy in his mentioning the fact that Mrs Mannings was elaborately corseted and artfully dressed. I don't think we should be surprised that Hardy kept the memory of what he saw of the death of Martha Browne. The hanging of a human being cannot be an easily forgotten sight. There is another letter, from 1926, in which he gave a different account of how Martha Browne's death had struck him: 'I did as a boy see a woman hanged at Dorchester, and, it rather shocks me now to remember, without much emotion – I suppose because boys are like it.'[42] The lack of emotion did not stop him observing precisely what he saw and storing it in his mind. When he was eighteen, he took his father's telescope out onto the heath on the morning a man was due to be hanged at the prison, three miles away, to test out if it could be seen at such a distance. This time he was horrified to catch the very moment the body dropped, regretted his intention instantly and took himself 'creeping homeward wishing he had not been so curious'.[43] He never watched a hanging again, and when he came to write *Tess of the D'Urbervilles* gave no description of her time in prison or of her end.

4. Friends and Brothers

Hardy described himself as being still a child at sixteen. The one extant photograph from 1856 shows a slim youngster intent on making himself look as much like a man as he can: longish dark hair, a faint suggestion about the upper lip that he is trying to grow a moustache, a wide, artistic cravat and broad collar to his shirt, and over this a single-breasted cotton coat, simple but neatly cut. There is something of an unfledged dandy about him. He is after all the son of a handsome father, and he is making an effort to present himself well. You can see why Hicks decided it was a good idea to take him into the office, and why he got on with the other young men there. They were agreeable and relaxed, and enjoyed themselves together. One was Henry Bastow, who had studied the classics at his London school and was soon reading Latin and Greek with Hardy for pleasure, arguing points of grammar and vocabulary. Bastow became his first real friend. When they read in the office, Tom made a habit of running into the Revd William Barnes's school, which happened to be next door, to ask his opinion, and in this way also began a friendship with the poet.[1] Another pupil was Herbert Fippard, a man of the world, already in his twenties and a touch condescending, since he had lived in London and knew the famous dance halls, the Argyle Rooms and the Cremorne Gardens, and the girls to be met there. He impressed Hardy by gliding round the office with an imaginary partner in his arms, whistling a quadrille. Dancing in London was seen to be a different thing from the dancing of the Dorset villages, for which he was still providing much music with his father, playing for parties and weddings, as they did on Christmas Day 1856 when Sarah Keats, the Bockhampton carrier's daughter, a girl he had known all his life, was married.

His life was dividing into three quite separate strands. There was the office, where he was entering the professional world, which no member of his family had attempted to join until now. There was, mostly inside his head, the world of books and scholarship, so intensely experienced that he sometimes talked to himself in Latin on his daily walks; and it held the hope, still vague, of another life altogether, which might be peacefully devoted to books, the reading and even the writing of words. Then there was home and family, and everything that went with them: Bockhampton, Puddletown and the countryside around. Here he was familiar with shepherds, carriers and ploughmen; his uncles were bricklayers, his aunts and cousins dressmakers and carpenters. Just about all of them, including his parents, his grandmother and most of the girls he knew, spoke a different, rustic version of the language he used at the office and was familiar with from his reading.[2] He knew what his father meant when he said, 'She zid a lot of others be gone afore', but he was not sure that Bastow or Fippard would understand him. His mother, for all her love of reading, was not confident enough to write a letter, and she asked Tom to write for her to her sister Martha Sharpe in Canada. He could not help seeing that his most deeply rooted attachments were to people who were hardly taken seriously in the world he aspired to enter. At best they were seen as quaint and picturesque, at worst as simpletons or clowns. True, his parents were a cut above the shepherds and labourers, and were urging him on and proud of his progress; it did not make it any less awkward for him as he advanced away from them in speech and habits.

Just now his home was dominated by women and children, his mother, in her forties, again preoccupied with the process of giving birth. Another sister, Katharine, known as Kate or Katie, appeared in September. Seven people living in the few small rooms meant there was little privacy or quiet, and as the winter came on it was clear that his grandmother Mary Hardy had not long to live. She was eighty-four, and in January 1857 she died. She had been a central and beloved figure in his home life, a teller of stories of the past and of the cottage over which she had presided for nearly sixty years. His novel *Two on a Tower* has what seem to be scraps of a portrait of her in her last years. In one scene the hero's grandmother, who, like old Mrs Hardy, has come from another county and recalls it as she sits by the fire, tells her grandson how she had been dreaming of 'my old country again, as usual. The place was as natural as when I left it, – e'en just three score years ago! All the folks and my old aunt were there . . . yet I suppose if I were really to set out and go there, hardly a soul would be left alive to say to me, dog how art!' That 'dog how art' is so odd it sounds like a bit of Granny Hardy's speech, stored up by a grandson peculiarly attentive to words. He adds a charming story of the old woman scraping off and eating the outside of the pudding she has made for her grandson while she waits for him to come home. He is disgusted by her greed and the scraped-down pudding, refuses it and goes upstairs, then relents, comes down and eats it up in a show of magnanimity. The story is as odd as the speech, and suggests another memory of Granny Hardy, especially as their only purpose in the novel is to underline the grandson's divided situation: he has been to the grammar school and aspires to an academic or professional life, yet his home is a village cottage, shared with an old woman with a funny way of talking and behaving. Hardy knew everything there was to know about these things.[3]

While he mourned his grandmother at home, he liked to think of his other world outside as his student life. He and Bastow took to meeting in Kingston Maurward fields to pursue their classical studies in the open air when the weather allowed, like college chums. Bastow had a strongly religious side too, as a Baptist preparing for adult baptism. Like other converts, he wanted to pass on his beliefs to his friends and get them to join his team, and he set out to win Tom over to the doctrine of adult baptism. Tom first consulted his own team – Mr Shirley, the Church of England vicar of Bockhampton – and found him baffled and unable to advise. Then Bastow introduced him to the local Baptist minister, a Scot as poor as he was learned, with three sons, two of them graduates of Aberdeen University, the youngest already ill with tuberculosis. The sick boy was the one Tom liked best, but all were clever and congenial, and they enjoyed fierce, cheerful bouts arguing over the merits of adult baptism, with much urgent and aggressive citing of biblical texts. In the end Hardy was not convinced, although it took some time, and he absorbed the intricate arguments based on Bible texts so well that he was able to present them years later.[4]

When not reading or arguing with Bastow, he gave his attention to copying plans and tracing drawings at the office. He was a meticulous draughtsman. Hicks was pleased with him and took him along when he went to examine old churches. This was the period of indiscriminate church restoration which made architecture into a booming profession and was carried out with much misplaced enthusiasm. Hardy, who greatly regretted it later, was soon making surveys. He also took up sketching and painting for pure pleasure, going out alone in the open air in his free time. He made studies of animals and landscapes as well as of houses and churches. One day when he was drawing in the fields the eldest son of the vicar of Fordington looked over his shoulder, offering some advice, and they began to talk. Although Hardy knew the name of Moule and had heard his sermons, this was the first time he had got into conversation with one of his sons. Henry Joseph Moule was in his thirties, a Cambridge graduate, currently earning his living in Scotland as a land agent, although his talents and interests were artistic and antiquarian.[5] He must have been holidaying at home when he spoke to Hardy, and through him Hardy soon met his younger brothers, among them Charles and Horace, both at college in Cambridge but enjoying long vacations at home, and Handley, still a schoolboy. Here was a brave new world, and the start of an intense and enchanted friendship.

The Moules were a formidable family. The father was a strenuous, practical, proselytizing, multi-talented man. He had reintroduced Christian worship into near-pagan Fordington after his arrival there in 1828. He was kept busy by the huge expansion in the population of his parish, as the poorest class of people drifted from the land to the town. Moule helped them all as best he could, if not always in ways that best pleased them. For instance, he got the Dorchester races abolished on the grounds that horse racing encouraged vice; it had also been very popular.[6] Later he became a hero when cholera broke out in his parish in 1854, and he risked his own life working with the sick, and also pursued those he thought most responsible.[7] Convinced that housing conditions bore most of the blame for the spread of the disease, he wrote to the landlord to ask for improvements. Fordington lay in the Duchy of Cornwall, and the committee responsible for its administration was headed by Prince Albert, consort to the Queen. Moule wrote him a personal letter, blaming the officials who managed the estate, urging him to action and saying he intended to make this into a public matter: 'I shall publish what I write.'

The answers he got from gentlemen on the Duchy of Cornwall's committee denied responsibility. Moule's anger grew. He asked the Prince himself to look at a map showing the layout of the pitiful housing where the cholera raged. He asserted that 'no inconsiderable portion [of blame for the cholera epidemic] lies at the door of those who, for the last sixty or seventy years, have managed this estate of HRH Duke of Cornwall.' Moule's courage was only partly rewarded. He and his family survived, and he kept the cholera confined to Fordington and out of Dorchester proper, but his letters to the Prince changed nothing. He published the correspondence, his publishers being Bradbury & Evans. Evans was Mrs Moule's brother, and Bradbury & Evans were Charles Dickens's publishers, which might seem promising, but the end of the epidemic also brought an end to any interest in the behaviour of the Duchy officials.[8]

This was only one of Mr Moule's efforts to change and improve the world. He built a second church, raising the money himself, and set up Sunday schools. He enlarged the vicarage as his family grew. Constantly active and alert, he uncovered an ancient burial ground in the parish while getting a new road cut, finding bodies with Roman coins in their mouths, inscribed with the names of the god Apollo and emperors Constantine and Posthumus, and celebrated these discoveries in verse. He published his poems, his sermons and his views on education. He wrote letters to *The Times* about the potato. He invented a sanitary system using earth closets and published extensively on its advantages. He chaired regular meetings of Dorset evangelical churchmen in his house. He gave much and expected much of his parishioners. He fathered eight sons – one died in infancy – and required the seven survivors to live unswervingly by the highest standards, intellectual and moral.

One of his poems warns an infant waking in his mother's arms not to turn to 'impurity' or 'the joy will quit thy breast, / And thou through all eternity, / Wilt never, never rest.' Another predicts 'The End of the Worldling' under 'the dire unmitigated rod'. You sense that these are not idle warnings.

An awe-inspiring father, then, of the same generation as Dr Arnold of Rugby School, and possessed of the same educational and moral confidence. In the words of his youngest son, Handley, he was the 'object of such reverence as perhaps to check a little, on both sides, the easy demonstration of affection'.[9] His wife was remarkable too, the well-educated daughter of a London Unitarian family with literary tastes. She had converted to Anglicanism for her marriage and was as fervent as her husband. Her brother Frederick Evans became a printer and publisher in partnership with William Bradbury, and in 1846 they published Mr Moule's *Scraps of Sacred Verse*, the same year in which they began to issue *Dombey and Son*. Mrs Moule gave her husband wholehearted support in the parish and in the home education of their sons. The results were astounding when you consider that Charles would become President of Corpus Christi in Cambridge, Handley Bishop of Durham, Henry director of the Dorset County Museum; that three more brothers went into the Church, two as China missionaries, one to be elevated to Bishop of Mid China; and all but one wrote and published books in their spare time – about religion, about China, about Dorset antiquities, about Ancient Rome, about their parents and their upbringing.

The Hardys' cottage would have fitted several times into the Fordington vicarage, and the aspirations of the Moule parents for their sons were far beyond anything imaginable by the Hardy parents. The long, low house full of books and young men was always buzzing with activity, with its great dining room that doubled as a classroom. Dinner was at 2.30 and tea, the last meal of the day, at 6.30. Father presided from his study, mother had her own 'Little Parlour'. The garden adjoined a big field where games were played, cricket especially, and the views extended over the water meadows of the Frome and the Purbeck Hills in the distance. In summer the boys went fishing and bathing in the gravelly pools of the Frome, or sometimes they all piled into an old stagecoach and set off for the coast at Lulworth, or swam in the green waters off the long beach at Weymouth. Handley set up a telescope and studied the stars.[10]

Handley was a year younger than Hardy – exactly the same age as his sister Mary – but it was Horace, eight years older, who became Tom's special friend. Horace was the charmer, handsome and gifted. He was a tender-hearted son to his mother, writing to her almost every year on the anniversary of the death of the baby brother who had died before he was two.[11] At the age of twelve he was already playing the organ in his father's church. He was a natural scholar, a born teacher and knew how to organize things. When he and Hardy met, in 1856, he was just setting up a literary club at home, the 'Fordington Times Society', with himself as President. Among its members were his parents, all their pupils, the resident curates and three of his Evans cousins. They held weekly meetings during the school term time, at which original papers, short plays and poems were read. Sometimes there was a debate – 'Is coach or railway travel better?' – or a visitor was invited. One was William Barnes, who sent them a poem, 'Grief or Gladness', and who was complimented by Henry for his use of 'Words of Wessex' in his work. Horace produced an appreciation of Tennyson's *Idylls of the King* and wrote his own poetry too.[12] A pupil called Bridges offered a comedy in two acts, 'The Cow and the Choir', in which a Revd Briggs appeared, determined to abolish the choir in his church, with its squeaking violins, and replace it with his daughter's up-to-date harmonium. Everyone contributed in his own way, and you ask yourself if Hardy sometimes heard about what went on.[13]

Horace taught Handley Roman history by making a plan of Rome with pebbles on the lawn. He read him Macaulay's *Lays of Ancient Rome* and translated Hesiod with him as they walked through the cornfields. He wrote a crammers' guide, *The Roman Republic: Designed for the Use of Examination Candidates*, published by Bradbury & Evans in 1860. But, whereas all his brothers made their way steadily, something went awry for Horace. He was an outstanding student both at Oxford, to which he won an open scholarship, and at Cambridge, where he carried off the Hulsean Prize for an essay on Christian oratory; and yet he contrived to come away without a degree from either university. Officially he was still at Cambridge during the period of the Fordington Times Society and his early friendship with Hardy, yet he seems to have been at home even when he should have been away at college.

The family protected him, lovingly no doubt, but you could not be a member of the Moule family without feeling you must do your best at all times and believing in the power of God to help you. Horace asked himself too many questions to be secure in that belief. And he had other problems: he lived on an emotional switchback. There were times when he shone and dazzled, others when he descended into an inexplicable blackness. To deal with the bad times he began to take opium, and to drink. Hardy was not aware of Horace's problems in the early years of their friendship and saw him simply as an admired and overwhelmingly attractive friend – the best he could ever hope to have. They quickly became close, going for long rambles in the fields, talking and talking as new friends do, Horace taking the role of teacher and patron, eager to give guidance and encouragement and to discuss books and ideas, whether the Greek dramatists or modern developments in science and how they bore on religion. No one had ever talked with Tom like this before, and Horace gave him time, attention and affection. He did not mind his immaturity and woeful lack of polish, but enjoyed having a disciple as much as Tom enjoyed learning from him. This was the second passion of Hardy's life. Mrs Martin had given him an *éducation sentimentale*; Horace Moule enrolled him with what seemed like princely grace into the fellowship of those who live by the written word, whether as readers or writers, and into an intellectual world wider than Tom had yet encountered. Here was a scholar who read Greek as fluently as English and who had attended two universities, a gentleman, easy and graceful, who knew about the world. He knew where to stay when he was in London; who was writing the most significant new books; the correct way of referring to a titled person; and how to lecture to working men, as he did in November 1858, speaking about Oxford to the Dorchester Working Men's Mutual

Improvement Society. Were any of Hardy's cousins in the audience? Probably not.

Horace introduced Hardy to the newest and cleverest of the weekly magazines, the *Saturday Review*, London based naturally, in which social issues were discussed and religion treated with small respect. He even began to write for it occasionally himself. He bought himself books on geology and science that alarmed his father, because they cast doubt on accepted religious ideas, and handed them on to Hardy. Horace's upbringing had been more robustly Christian than Tom's, but, making his way in metropolitan literary journalism, he could not miss the spread of scepticism, and he was too quick and intelligent to ignore it. Just one example he must have been aware of: two German philosophers, David Strauss in his *Life of Jesus* and Feuerbach in his *Essence of Christianity*, had presented the Christian religion as a purely human invention with no divine element. Both were translated into English, in 1846 and 1854 respectively, and made their mark. The translator went on in 1857 to start publishing novels of rural and clerical life under the name George Eliot. In the Moule household the ideas of Strauss and Feuerbach would be anathema if they were ever mentioned. This in itself made a problem for Horace, who wanted to talk about ideas.

Tom's situation was different and easier. Christianity was something he had taken for granted as part of the fabric of his daily life, and Christian theory was not discussed in the family. He read the Bible, he knew all the church services and most of the psalms by heart; indeed, the year was a sequence of church festivals quite as much as it was a sequence of the natural seasons for him. And he remained a fully practising Christian into the 1860s, but his mind was on the move, and with Horace he began to see that there were questions to be asked and lines of thought to be followed that eroded the old faith. As their friendship ripened, they read the notorious *Essays and Reviews* of 1860, religious pieces that offended the orthodox by their attacks on doctrine and by their textual criticism of the Bible. Hardy also claimed to have been an early admirer of Darwin's *On the Origin of Species*, published in 1859, though it is not clear exactly when he read it, or how much it influenced his thinking at that time. He could well have found his own way along the path towards free thought, but Horace was an encouraging companion on the journey and, with his access to books, guided his steps at many points. By 1865 he was introducing him to the work of Auguste Comte, whose Positivist philosophy replaces the worship of God with that of humanity.

The discovery of Comte still lay ahead. In 1860 the Christian side of the argument was bolstered for Tom by his other friend Bastow, who gave him a parting present of a Bible when he finished his term with Hicks, and kept up a correspondence for some time, urging 'dear old Tom' to piety.[14] There was also a brief religious revival in Dorchester in the same year, when Mr Moule put his energies into a mighty Christian putsch and for some heady months filled the churches with revitalized congregations. Hardy appears to have been receptive to this and took to annotating his Bible, marking what has been interpreted as a moment of spiritual significance on 'Wednesday night April 17th / 61, ¼ to 11'.[15] He had nothing to say about his youthful spiritual enthusiasm when he wrote his memoirs in old age, but in 1861 he bought himself another Bible, a prayerbook and a volume of John Keble's popular religious poetry, *The Christian Year*, clear indications of piety.

Keble is the first English poet whose work he records buying for himself. He had read Horace, Ovid and Virgil in the original, and some of the *Iliad*. Scott's ballads and narrative poems were favourites, and his interest in English poetry grew as he had access to more. In the Moule household Cowper, Milton, Longfellow and Tennyson were read, and the fact that poetry was written in the family was important too. Some time between 1857 and 1860 Hardy wrote the earliest of his poems to survive. It is about place, time and change, which were destined to become steady Hardy themes. Not many poets have made such a good start.[16] He writes about what he knows and goes straight for his subject, the cottage at Bockhampton:

> It faces west, and round the back and sides
> High beeches, bending, hang a veil of boughs,
> And sweep against the roof . . .

The simplicity is Wordsworthian, and there is already the characteristic Hardy layering of time. The oak tree outside is 'from a
seed / Dropped by some bird a hundred years ago'. The poet
speaks both as observer and as the child putting a question to his
grandmother about her memories, making three distinct blocks of
time. She gives her answer, quite formally, ending with a lovely
evocative phrase, 'So wild it was when first we settled here.' It is
a confident poem, and it makes you like the poet. There is one
oddity, in his giving it the dignity of a Latin title, '*Domicilium*'
(meaning 'Home'). Latin would have been meaningless to Granny
Hardy. It is here as an offering from one side of his divided self to
the other.

We don't know what Horace said about '*Domicilium*'. It should
have been praise, but he was not always encouraging. Tom was
not Horace's only protégé, and he gave extremely effective advice
to another, a Dorchester boy from a shopkeeping family whom he
encouraged to sit for the Oxford Local examinations and later for
the Indian Civil Service: Hooper Tolbort came first in the whole
of England in both and was embarked on what promised to be a
glorious career. Hardy knew Tolbort well, was pleased for him
and hoped for the same magical encouragement from Horace. The
dream that he might get to a university had become strong in him,
but when he asked Horace for his opinion on the matter, he did
not get the answer he wanted. The disappointment, painful and
with an edge of humiliation, can be felt even in the account Hardy
wrote in old age. Horace advised him to stick at architecture, since
his father expected him to start earning by the age of twenty-one.
He also advised him to give up his Greek, a clear indication that he
did not consider his scholarship good enough. Hardy still thought it
might be, but he took the advice. 'He felt bound to listen to reason
and prudence' is how he puts it.[17] He did not let this spoil their
friendship. It was much more important to him than his pride.

Horace had now given up Cambridge himself and was acting as
tutor to two boys, preparing them for university entrance, staying
in a house in the cathedral close at Salisbury. Tom, reaching his
twentieth birthday, had proved his worth to Mr Hicks, who began
paying him 15 *s.* a week – a modest amount, but the change from

total dependency to being able to rattle a few coins of your own in your pocket is a tremendous one. He always insisted that he was a late developer, but this was a step forward into adult life, allowing him to make his own decisions. He was able to get himself a room in Dorchester, going home at weekends yet free to spend his weekday evenings as he liked, unobserved by his family. His interest in girls had not gone away. He is said to have flirted with his pretty older cousin Martha Sparks, and even to have proposed marriage to a Dorchester shopgirl, Mary Waight, but Martha left for London, and Mary turned him down.[18]

Another young woman, hovering like a pale shadow behind him, was his sister Mary, so close to him in age and so little mentioned in his own accounts of his life. As small children they necessarily shared a room in the small cottage and ran about together in the garden, and he spoke of her once as his 'earliest playmate – a kind little sister, sharing with him, gladly, all she had, proud of him beyond words'. There was no doubt of his importance in her life, while his affection was more occasional, fading when he was busy with other people, with his work, with his dreams and ambitions.[19] After her death he remarked that she had come into the world and left it without leaving a ripple, and it is abundantly clear that she was self-effacing and too modest to make claims on him.[20] Still, in April 1860 he escorted her to Salisbury, where she was to have a higher education at a teacher training college. It was a surprising turn of events for the daughter of modest country people.

Her parents had observed that she, like Tom, was an intelligent child and paid for her to go to a private school run by two ladies in Dorchester. She acquired the accomplishments expected of a well-brought-up early-Victorian girl, learning to paint and to play the piano – no violin for her. She wrote correctly and read widely, Wordsworth her favourite poet. She could sew, and absorbed domestic skills as she was bound to, growing up in a household without servants. All this would have been enough to launch her into the marriage market, the proper culmination of girlhood. But she was not brought up to think of her life in those terms. Jemima had no marital ambitions for her children, as we have seen, but was actively opposed to the idea of their marrying. The reason for her objection was never explained and seems to have been a theoretical one against the institution itself. Whatever she thought of her own marriage, she accepted or endured its limitations, but her daughter was to have a different sort of life. Hence the unexpected spectacle of the Hardy parents applying for a place at the Church of England teacher training college in Salisbury for their daughter. They asked Mr Shirley to recommend her, and they paid for her board and tuition: £4 a quarter, £12 a year. She was there for nearly three years, becoming a Queen's Scholar in her second year, which meant her parents did not have to go on paying.[21]

The Salisbury Teacher Training College, founded in 1841, was installed in a notably beautiful old house, known as the King's House, in the cathedral close. In other respects it left a good deal to be desired. The young women were taught history, geography, arithmetic, grammar, drawing and music, with the emphasis on religious instruction – '8¾ hours a week', with an extra hour for Church history. A student of the 1850s left an account of her experiences there: 'I can only compare my first sensations on taking up my abode there to a shock produced by a sudden plunge into a cold bath . . . The rules were strict, the fare Spartan in its simplicity, and the amount of household work required to be done by the Students seemed to new-comers simply appalling . . . As for the education of that time, attainments were not high.'[22] The object of the training was not to open the minds of the students or to encourage them to think for themselves but to turn out efficient Christian teachers with basic skills, no more. Much of their time was spent doing the domestic work they were required to contribute at the King's House – in effect, they were household servants as well as students. The good was that those who passed through the system and gained a certificate were rewarded by the knowledge that they would be able to find regular work and support themselves.

Hardy was interested enough to think back on Mary's experience when he decided to write about a women's training college in *Jude the Obscure* thirty years later. He made Jude urge his cousin to go to the college, because it would give her a qualification as 'first-class certificated mistress', enabling her to earn a reasonable income and even allowing her a certain freedom of choice about where she worked – more than he felt he had as a stonemason. There was no doubt similar reasoning behind Mary's going, whether she or her parents initiated the plan; the most likely originator, Jemima, had determined that her daughter should never go into service.

Hardy also listed the backgrounds of the students at the college: they were 'the daughters of mechanics, curates, surgeons, shop-keepers, farmers, dairymen, soldiers, sailors, and villagers'.[23] The social level is clear: curates not clergymen, surgeons not physicians, soldiers not officers. Mary's best friend at the college was an orphan, Annie Lanham, brought up by a relative, a miller at Affpuddle, near Bockhampton. Annie had no real home to go back to and earned her own living for years, until she married Mary's cousin Nathaniel Sparks. Hardy wrote of the students as being 'clipped and pruned by severe discipline', and on top of that they were half starved. He makes Jude's cousin Sue tell him, when he offers her a present, that she is 'dreadfully hungry. They were kept on very short allowances in the College, and a dinner, tea and supper all in one was the present she most desired in the world.'[24]

Hungry and inadequately taught as they were, these young women were pioneers. They probably didn't know they were, any more than Hardy knew how curious it was that a college should have been set up for the daughters of the poor at a date when almost nothing was on offer in the way of higher education for girls of the higher classes. Queen's and Bedford College had been established in London in 1848 and 1849 for female students, but one of their male founders felt obliged to declare publicly that the intention was not 'to educate ladies for the kind of tasks which belong to *our* profession'.[25] Florence Nightingale's School of Nursing was not founded until 1861. Oxford and Cambridge were still closed to women. John Stuart Mill's *On the Subjection of Women* was not yet written, and middle-class families had not begun to imagine that they might educate their daughters for careers.[26] Women might set up schools on the principle of Mrs Micawber, without any preparation beyond putting up a brass plate, and young women might become governesses, but a governess was a wretched creature with no standing in the world. If she had been born a lady and down on her luck, her luck was unlikely to change again for the better. Whereas a teacher from a training college could get a certificate and a career without being a lady. Jemima Hardy wanted her daughters to make more of their lives than she or her sisters or her nieces were able to. The year before Mary went to college was the year her aunt Martha Sharpe died giving birth to her tenth child in Canada. Her aunt Maria Sparks brought up six children and of her daughters, the eldest, Rebecca, was still at home working as a dressmaker; Emma had gone into service until she married, in 1860, a poor carpenter from Somerset with no prospects, and started a family; Tryphena was still a child; Martha, the most enterprising, had taken herself to London and gone into service as a lady's maid. Mary would be nobody's servant, and she would have a qualification.

Hardy, who wasted no scrap of experience, also used the college in an early novel, *Under the Greenwood Tree*, written in 1871. He made Fancy Day a Queen's Scholar at her 'training-school', and her father explains to a suitor his reasons for making her 'work as a schoolmistress': 'that if any gentleman, who sees her to be his equal in polish, should want to marry her, and she want to marry him, he shan't be her superior in pocket'.[27] Mr Day is a game-keeper, and on the whole a figure of comedy, but this is not just a comic explanation, because he has given thought to his daughter's situation and done his best for her. Mr Day is more of a feminist than one would expect, and so it appears were Mr and Mrs Hardy. This is why in April 1860 their elder son escorted their eighteen-year-old daughter to college in Salisbury to qualify for a career. There he had his first look at a female 'college', a third-class version of his own dream of a university education.

Since Horace Moule happened to be in Salisbury at the same time with his two pupils, it would have been natural for Hardy to visit him. No visit was mentioned, then or later. There may have been good reason for Hardy to remain silent, because it is likely that Horace was in a poor state to receive him. Whatever Hardy saw or failed to see, one of his pupils kept a diary in which he wrote that his tutor was a 'Dypsmaniac' [*sic*] and had DTs when they were in Salisbury. He did his best to persuade him to stop drinking, successfully for a short time. After this the party left Salisbury and presently moved to Saint-Germain, outside Paris, for the summer, and here Horace went missing. His unfortunate pupils searched for him in Paris, in the morgue among other places, finally sending for help from the Moule family.[28] Henry and Charles went over to France, and at this point Horace turned up in England again. What this meant to the rest of the Moule family can be imagined. Hardy was in Fordington Church on 5 August to hear Mr Moule preach from a text in the Book of Job, 'All the days of my appointed time will I wait, until my change come.' It was now clear to him how bad things could be for Horace; the princely friend was all too liable to fall into the gutter. While it must have changed the nature of their friendship, it did not bring it to an end or lessen Hardy's affection and dependence on him.

A veil was drawn by the family – and by Hardy – over what went wrong for Horace. Drinking can be part of the upward swing into mania; the depression that follows is worse for the sufferer but may be easier for others to deal with. Horace continued to swing between periods of equilibrium – when he could write reviews, play the organ for the inauguration of a new church in Fordington, even preach a sermon against intemperance – and flare-ups of drinking and bad behaviour followed by moods of suicidal depression. The suggestion of homosexuality has been raised and found plausible by some, although there is no evidence to support it. Manic depression seems enough to explain Horace's drinking bouts, his inability to keep jobs, his increasing dependence on the protection of his successful brothers, his guilty feelings towards his family and his spiralling moods, up and down. Doubts about his religious faith would make things more difficult with his parents and add to his guilt.

In April 1862 it was Hardy's turn to behave unpredictably. Giving little notice to anyone, he made up his mind to leave Mr Hicks's office. He said goodbye to Dorchester and Bockhampton, and announced that he was going to find work in London. He had been there only once in his life, as a child with his mother. Now he was shaking off mother, home, all the web of experiences and associations that had formed him but also cramped him in the country. It was a brave move.

5. The Londoner

Hardy arrived in London in April 1862 and remained for five years, until July 1867. He went home every Christmas, and had a visit from his father in the first year, and another from his sister Mary; three of his Sparks cousins were working in London. Otherwise he was on his own. He set out to become a Londoner, and he felt that he succeeded. He walked till he knew 'every street and alley west of St Paul's like a born Londoner', and he always insisted on his familiarity with London life.[1] His own account of these years makes him sound like the most determined and conscientious of cultural tourists. He took in exhibitions, galleries, churches, libraries, museums, dance halls, theatres and opera houses. He haunted second-hand bookstalls in Holywell Street, east of Bunhill Fields.[2] He went several times to hear Dickens read – he must have heard *David Copperfield*, which taught him a good deal about London – and to hear John Stuart Mill speak on the hustings, and to the House of Commons to listen to Lord Palmerston. When Palmerston died, he got tickets for the funeral in Westminster Abbey, very conscious of the fact that the great man had entered the house only a year after the deaths of Fox and Pitt, and while Sheridan still lived.

He went out to see the illuminations for the wedding of the Prince of Wales, and had his waistcoat buttons torn off and his ribs 'bent in' as he struggled to get out of the crush. He enrolled for French classes at King's College. He took himself to a phrenologist in the Strand to have his bumps surveyed and came away no wiser. He travelled on the earliest underground railway line at the first opportunity. He offered himself as an extra in a professional stage production, being interested in trying to write a play himself, and appeared on stage at the Haymarket. He stood in Rotten Row to watch the rich being driven round in their open carriages during the Season. He noticed the tired clerks walking in Oxford Street, and the shop women, and the girls who hired themselves out in the dance halls. By his own account he saw 'the first load of rubbish shot for the making of the Embankment and the first train go over Hungerford Bridge'.[3]

His plan was to make his mark in London and to work his way to success, and he was ready to give every bit of his energy to achieving his ambitions. The difficulty that arose was that he was not sure quite what sort of success he aspired to. The most striking thing about these five packed years is that when he left London he had the germ of his first novel in him, 440 pages drawn from 'the life of an isolated student cast upon the billows of London with no protection but his brains' and meant as a 'dramatic satire of the squirearchy and nobility, London society, the vulgarity of the middle class, modern Christianity, church restoration, and political and domestic morals in general, the author's views, in fact, being obviously those of a young man with a passion for reforming the world . . . the tendency of the writing being socialistic, not to say revolutionary'.[4]

How did the young architectural assistant turn into the socialistic novelist and satirist? He set off for London knowing almost nothing of life in the capital beyond the fact that his mother had worked there and liked it so much that she wanted to leave the country and earn her living there. She failed, as we know, but he surely went with her approval. He seems all the same to have set off with small preparation; but they both knew that he was breaking the ties that might have kept him, as assistant to a Dorchester architect, in working contact with his builder father and demonstrating his ambition to become a different sort of person. He was going to London to find out what he might do or discover there. That being said, he understood that his training in Hicks's office was the only solid qualification he had to offer, and equipped himself with two letters of recommendation to London architects who might be willing to start him off in a job, one from his father, and a return ticket.

This seems to have been the sum of his practical preparations. The train journey was the same as the one he had made with his mother eleven years before, and he is unlikely to have wasted his money on anything better than a bench in the unheated third class. He had a few pounds saved up, but neither work nor lodgings fixed. He knew Horace Moule's other Dorset protégé, Hooper Tolbort, who was already there, preparing for the Indian Civil Service examination, and his Sparks cousins. James had been learning carpentry and the building trade from a London uncle for some time, Nat had joined him, and Martha was in service as a lady's maid.[5] None was in a position to give him much support, since working men put in long hours and a steady six-day week, and female servants were not encouraged to invite male guests to call on them at the area door.

The train still took the best part of four hours to get to Waterloo. When, later, he described the arrival in London of a poor country traveller, he wrote of the walk across Westminster Bridge, preferred to Waterloo Bridge, for which a toll of a halfpenny was charged; and how everyone held handkerchiefs to their mouths to strain off the river mist from their lungs.[6] The river and the air above it were bad for you. It was only four years since the stink rising from the Thames had been so foul that Parliament had been forced to abandon its sittings. Sewage works were now in hand, but they took time, and there would be another cholera epidemic in 1866.

London was a filthy city. There were too many people, too many horses, too much smoke and coal dust, not enough light. There was dirt in the river, in the streets, in the air, dirt that got into your clothes. A foggy day turned white linen brown in a few hours. Tom described one in February when it was 'almost pitch dark in the middle of the day, and everything visible appeared of the colour of brown paper or pea-soup.'[7] He noticed that the trees were sooty and how 'swarthy columns of smoke' rose from the massed kitchen chimneys every morning, spreading out to form a haze that darkened the sun and gave the air its city smell.[8] 'To me London gardens *always* seem faded & dirty,' he wrote later.[9] Even a privileged traveller such as the young Henry James, arriving in London like Hardy in the 1860s, with a credit note for £1,000 in his wallet, was oppressed by London at first. Opulent, yes, but vast, hideous, vicious, neither cheerful nor charming, he wrote home; he saw a 'huge general blackness' and streets of low black houses like 'so many rows of coal scuttles'.[10]

James was quickly installed in Mayfair in a comfortable set of rooms for gentlemen, and he had introductions to the right people. Within days he was dining with Leslie Stephen, Ruskin, William Morris, meeting Frederic Harrison, Rossetti, Burne-Jones and Charles Dickens's daughter Mamey, and feeling that London was not so bad after all; then he set off for Oxford with more introductions. What Hardy faced was the poor man's tramp looking for lodgings. London was a city of lodgers and lodging houses, mostly mean places where slops and ashes were carried up and down narrow stairs all day and hovering landladies' daughters were best avoided; being a lodger provided a dismal *rite de passage* and a good story for nineteenth-century novelists from Trollope to Wells. Hardy has a rueful account of calling at one lodging house where the cousin of a Dorset acquaintance turned him away and added a stern warning of the difficulties he was likely to face. 'Wait till you have walked the streets a few weeks, and your elbows begin to shine, and the hems of your trousers get frayed, as if nibbled by rats! Only practical men are wanted here.'[11] Somehow he found a temporary bed.

The next morning he was out with his letters of recommendation. The first, to Benjamin Ferrey, an architect his father had worked for in Dorset, met with kind words and a promise of help – but then nothing. The disappointment was more than made up for by a piece of astounding luck. A pupil of Ferrey and friend of Hicks, John Norton, with no work to offer, took pity on Hardy and suggested he should come in and do some drawings in his office for token payment, allowing him to look around for something better. Within a week Arthur Blomfield, one of the most successful architects in London, asked Norton if he knew anyone who could do Gothic ecclesiastical drawing, and, on 5 May, Hardy started work for Blomfield at a salary of £110 a year.[12] This was something to write home about, although the sad fact is that not a single letter exists to tell us what he communicated to his parents or how often he wrote to them.

A second piece of luck was that another trainee architect in

Blomfield's office suggested they share lodgings, since he had found some which would do for two. His name was Philip Shaw; he was a gentleman and had his own silver to prove it: Hardy noticed the landlady rattling it about, resentfully he thought. Since Hardy had no possessions at all beyond a bag of clothes and books, the lodgings suited him well enough. They were in Kilburn, at 3 Clarence Place, a small terrace of houses where Quex Road meets the Edgware Road; in those days, there were still fields and farms all about, and the driver of the local omnibus asked, as he set off, 'Any more passengers for London?' Shaw had intellectual tastes and sometimes read aloud to his fellow lodger in the evening. Hardy remembered him choosing Ruskin's *Modern Painters*, and it may have been this reading that first encouraged him to go to the National Gallery and look at paintings. Soon he was making daily visits and keeping a notebook on schools of painting. Shaw was a good fellow, ready to lend Hardy his dress coat when the occasion demanded – Hardy was invited to an architectural *conversazione* – and he even thought of inviting him to Bockhampton, intending to show him off. He wrote to his sister Mary, saying that Shaw would be 'considered a great gun' in the parish and explaining to her how to pronounce 'kon-ver-sat-zi-on-e'.[13]

His letters to Mary are few and not expansive, but they do give a glimpse of a young man eager to learn and to get on, and to pass on his discoveries. 'Do not send back the Sat. Revs [*Saturday Reviews*] but take care of them and put them in your box, so that I may have them when I want them.' Thackeray 'is considered to be the greatest novelist of the day'. *Barchester Towers* 'is considered the best of Trollope's.' Here are the first indications that he was thinking critically about novel writing. 'I tried the Underground Railway one day – Everything is excellently arranged.' The Metropolitan Line opened in January 1863, running from Paddington to Farringdon Street, the trains divided into three classes, third class at 3 *d.*, half the price of first. It was an instant and overwhelming success, and by the middle of the next decade was carrying 48 million passengers a year.[14]

Hardy often described his five years in London as his student years, and with good reason. Some of his activities have already been listed, but, not content with his busy cultural programme, he kept up his own music, buying a second-hand violin and playing in the evenings, tunes from the Italian operas, accompanied on the piano by his fellow lodger. He also taught himself shorthand. He bought himself books: a pronouncing dictionary, a rhyming dictionary, a guide to English literature and many volumes of poetry. He wrote poetry of his own with increasing vigour and confidence. Most of it he destroyed; much of what has survived is curious rather than achieved, but some is good by any standards, and all proof of a passionate commitment to words.

During his first months in London the International Exhibition was an attraction, so powerful that he gave it as one of his reasons for moving to London. He had after all missed the 1851 Great Exhibition, and it was planned as an attempt to revive the glories of its predecessor. It opened just after he arrived, near Hyde Park Gate in South Kensington, covering twenty-four acres with its glass-domed buildings, and remained open for six months. There were photography galleries and machinery galleries; William Morris showed his wallpapers and tapestries; a statue of Shakespeare presided. Hardy often went after his day's work, going on to the Kensington Museum reading room, where he had access to a free library. He managed to escort his cousin Martha to the exhibition at least once, and went with Moule when he turned up in London in August. Moule stayed at his bachelor hotel, the Old Hummums in Covent Garden, and gave Hardy dinner there after taking him to a Jesuit service in Farm Street; whether this was simply open-minded or whether he was actively curious about Catholicism, it also looks like a gesture of defiance of his father. He was in town partly to see Tolbort, who had just achieved his examination triumph in the Indian Civil Service examinations, and also because he was currently planning to study law and was, in fact, admitted to the Middle Temple later in the year. This turned out to be another false start. A few months later he wrote to Hardy from Dorchester saying, 'I am quite right again', indicating that he was recovering from being not 'right' at all and knowing that Hardy would understand what he meant.[15] Hardy may or may not have seen him in Dorset at Christmas. When Horace went down into his black places, he was out of anyone's reach; when he came up, he was still the same charming and energetic person – the best friend.

Blomfield's offices were just off Trafalgar Square, at 9 St Martin's Place. Either architects were particularly agreeable employers or Hardy was twice lucky, because here he was again spending his working hours in a relaxed and cheerful atmosphere among colleagues disposed to be friendly, on a superficial level at any rate. There were six articled pupils and two or three assistants, no formal instruction and not usually very much work to be done. His new boss was as musical as Hardy himself, and encouraged the young men to sing glees and part songs with him; and since Hardy could sight read, he made a useful addition to the office choir. Blomfield himself had a powerful bass voice, and Hardy described him as 'a lithe, brisk man'. At thirty-three he was in the prime of life, a quintessential figure of the establishment, the fourth son of the Bishop of London, born at Fulham Palace, educated at Rugby School and at Cambridge, good at sport, especially on the river, good-natured and good-looking. He was kindly too, and within months of Hardy joining the office Blomfield put his name forward to become a member of the Architectural Association, of which he was the current President; and he was responsible for the invitation to the *conversazione*. There were many occasions on which he took his young assistant out with him professionally, and they got on well enough to form a friendship later in their lives; on the other hand there is no record of Hardy being invited to Blomfield's house to meet his young wife.

Blomfield may not have known that Hardy's cousins were carpenters and a lady's maid, but he did know Hardy was the son of a country builder. Blomfield, son of one bishop and brother of another, moved in exalted circles. Hardy's contemporary Eliza Lynn Linton, making her way as a writer in London, found doors opened to her because her grandfather was a bishop and her uncle a dean. 'What humiliating snobs we are!' she lamented, divided between shame and gratitude for the advantages they conferred on her.[16] Hardy was on the wrong side of this sort of snobbery, and within a year of working for Blomfield he had understood how things lay. Although he won two Architectural Association prizes, one for the design of a country mansion, the other for an essay on the use of coloured bricks in modern architecture, he thought the judges condescending in their attitude to him. He also found architectural drawing where he was merely copying and not originating designs 'monotonous and mechanical', and he decided quite early in his time with Blomfield that he had no hope of succeeding as an architect because it meant 'pushing his way into influential sets which would help him to start a practice of his own.'[17]

He had come armed with one grand address that might have helped him into an 'influential set', that of his old love, Julia Martin, and before he had been in London for long he nerved himself to go to Bruton Street in Mayfair where the Martins were living. The door was opened by the butler he remembered from Kingston Maurward, looking much the same. The lady did not. She was now in her fifties, and whatever dreams Hardy had cherished of a revival of any kind of tender intimacy ended on the spot. He thought Mrs Martin was also disconcerted by his more or less adult appearance – a young man was a very different creature from a small boy, and there was no question of taking *this* Tommy on her lap – and their conversation was awkward. Graciously, she invited him to call again, but once was enough for him, and he did not return to Bruton Street. Yet neither put the other quite out of mind.

In October of this first year his father came to see him, accompanied by a family friend, 'Miss A.', who was looking for a 'situation' in London. Hardy wrote to Mary that the visit 'went off all right', that he took them to the opera at Covent Garden – *Lurline* by the Irish composer William Wallace – and that Mr Hardy, showing a natural interest in building works, inspected the Thames Tunnel and climbed to the top of the Monument. It does not sound as though Tom took his father into the office. 'Miss A.' or 'H.A.' remains one of the unidentified young women in Hardy's life, but, since he was asking Mary three years later 'will it be awkward for you if H.A. & I come down for Xmas day & the next . . . ?', it sounds as though she did find a situation in London and was friendly enough with Hardy for them to travel together at Christmas. It also looks as though he was interested in more than one girl, because he had another involvement with a lady's maid working in Westbourne Park Villas, Eliza Nicholls. She too had a Dorset connection, although he seems to have met her in London, and he began to see something of her in 1862. In a letter of November 1862 he asks Mary, 'Do you ever write to Eliza?', just before mentioning Miss A. He may have been hoping that his sister would not mention either girl to the other.

In May 1863 he left his Kilburn lodgings for Paddington, where he took a single second-floor room at the back of a house in Westbourne Park Villas, No. 16.[18] Perhaps he had discovered that he was not a sharer. He may also have wanted to be more central and liked the idea of being close to Eliza. In fact, Eliza left London in the year he moved, but she is said to have considered herself engaged to Hardy until 1867, when the engagement was broken off after he flirted with her sister – or so it was alleged by her niece many years later.[19] Like the Mary Waight story, the entanglement with Eliza Nicholls is not much more than a family tradition.[20] If we accept that there may be some truth in the stories, they suggest he was a susceptible young man who found himself dealing with more than he could handle. A note from April 1865 indicates general gloom about women and his chances of finding the right one: 'There is not that regular gradation among womankind that there is among men. You may meet with 999 exactly alike, and then the thousandth – not a little better, but far above them. Practically therefore it is useless for a man to seek after this thousandth to make her his.'[21] Two months later, on his twenty-fifth birthday, he wrote, 'Not very cheerful. Feel as if I had lived a long time and done very little . . . Wondered what woman, if any, I should be thinking about in five years' time.' This suggests he was not in a settled relationship with any woman, even though in 1865 he was perhaps engaged to Eliza and also preparing to spend Christmas with Miss A. He wrote some sonnets, 'She, to Him', in the voice of a woman addressing a man who has let her down, dated 1866. They are notable as an early attempt to present a woman's view of things, and they indicate that this is a writer at work rather than a lover, and that he is more interested in finding the right words for the injured speaker than in any feelings of his own.[22]

Hardy took himself to the dance halls whose names he remembered from the worldly Fippard's talk: Willis's Rooms, also known as Almack's, in King Street; St James's, with its painted and gilded walls and blue-cushioned sofas; the Argyle off Regent Street; and, further afield, Cremorne Gardens, now buried beneath the Lots Road Power Station. He had played enough for others to dance to have dancing in his blood, and at these places there was no difficulty in finding a partner, and many of the girls were prepared to sell more than their dance-floor skills. The blatancy and scale of the sexual arrangements in London were impressive. Dorchester had its poor little houses of ill fame, tucked away in the back streets of Fordington, but in London you could hardly miss the prostitutes. Hardy's relative poverty and fastidiousness may or may not have made him resistant to the possibilities on offer, but he did take some turns on the dance floor, and was interested enough in the girls to listen to them talking. 'The Ruined Maid' is one of the best of the poems he wrote in London and may have originated in what he observed at the dance halls. It is not a subtle poem – it does not need to be – but makes its point by its directness, and gives a slap in the face to middle-class Christian morality. At the office, his colleagues joked about famous courtesans who served the rich, Cora Pearl and 'Skittles'; Hardy's poem shows a young countrywoman explaining her new-found prosperity to a friend who chances to run into her in London:

> – 'At home in the barton you said "thee" and "thou",
> And "thik oon", and "theäs oon", and "t'other"; but now
> Your talking quite fits 'ee for high compa-ny!' –
> 'Some polish is gained with one's ruin,' said she . . .

> – 'I wish I had feathers, a fine sweeping gown,
> And a delicate face, and could strut about Town!' –
> 'My dear – a raw country girl, such as you be,
> Cannot quite expect that. You ain't ruined,' said she.[23]

The rhythm bounces along, and the irony makes its point. The language is effective too, or rather the two languages, since this ruined maid is bilingual, like Hardy himself. 'At home in the barton' – a barton is a cow yard – suggests that she may have been a milkmaid, an occupation he would give to Tess of the D'Urbervilles, who also had two languages.

Hardy fell more deeply in love with poetry than with any of the girls he met in London and gave more of his attention to it. He studied Palgrave's anthology *The Golden Treasury*, an inspired gift from Moule; this newly published collection of lyrical poetry, from the Elizabethans to the Romantics, set up Shakespeare, Milton, Gray and Wordsworth as the great models. He imitated Shakespeare in two of the 'She, to Him' sonnets. Palgrave also crammed his book with the sweet, elaborate verse forms of the Elizabethan and Stuart poets that delighted Hardy, although he did not begin to imitate them until later. He included the two greatest odes of Keats – 'To Autumn' and 'To a Nightingale' – 'La Belle Dame sans Merci' and a good deal of the unpolitical Shelley. This was when Hardy first read Shelley's 'Lament' with its tremendous first line, 'O World! O Life! O Time!' It became one of his most admired lyrics, with its message of joy taking flight, of grief taking the place of delight and its tolling 'No more – O never more!' As an anthology should, it led him to read more of these poets. He also bought himself Swinburne's newly published *Poems and Ballads* and was so excited by them that even when he had to go out he could not resist reading as he walked along the street.

He kept many notebooks, in one of which he jotted down words and phrases that pleased him, some listed from dictionaries, e.g., 'gadder to emborder sworder (solr) to plush to tiddle, to slidder, a dallier tid (nice) a noier (an-) to pucker holder tucker dandler fondler philter live in clover'. Also 'to call for, call in, call up (past days) call off, call together (the difft happy hours) . . . carry high, carry me away, carry back to, carry me down to future years, carry forth (her eyes carried f. the tale of her heart), carry on, carry out'. There were quotations from poets he was reading, like his

friend William Barnes with his 'the *leanen* apple tree', 'her shade
a-whiv'ren black'. You can watch Hardy accumulating words,
entranced by their shapes, their sounds and richness, stacking them
up like a bee storing pollen. The shorthand he was learning was
put to use in the notebook to cloak any mention of improper parts
of the body like the breast, or of sexual desire or activity, and also
for the word 'imitate', which he set beside some of the quotations.
Poor Hardy, suffering pangs of guilt for even thinking of imitating
great writers. He needed someone to tell him it is what writers
have always done, teaching themselves by imitating what they
most admire.

He sometimes delivered impromptu talks of his own on poets
and poetry to his fellow architectural students. He also began to
submit his poems to magazines. Everything he sent was rejected.
He felt his solitary situation. For him there was none of the support
that sustained other young aspirant writers and artists, nurtured by
educated families, public school and university, so that they had
an established body of knowledge, a critical audience and a network
of friends before they were in their twenties. Tennyson, William
Morris, Burne-Jones, Swinburne, Gerard Manley Hopkins and
Leslie Stephen all had such support. Rossetti missed the university
but had educated parents and rapidly made friends with Morris
and his group.[24] Hardy had neither the background nor the temperament that would allow him to become part of a group. Moule
was the only friend whose advice he could call on, and he had
distracting problems of his own. The single piece of work Hardy
succeeded in getting published was a short comic essay printed in
Chambers's Journal in 1865, 'How I Built Myself a House', written
in the first place to amuse his colleagues. It is entertaining, but
humorous journalism was not going to be his path to fame.

If he had come to London to escape from a divided life, he soon
saw that he had failed. The divisions were if anything sharper than
ever. His office colleagues were from middle-class families with
backgrounds utterly unlike his. His women friends were servants
in households in which the divisions of class were absolute. His
Sparks cousins were workmen, and, what's more, James, the elder,
seems to have been a radical, possibly even a republican. When

Hardy wrote a fictional portrait of him, he made him speak with a true revolutionary ring of the 'useless lumber of our nation that'll be the first to burn if there comes a flare'.[25] Talk of burning, a fire and a flare sounds more like a Continental revolutionary than an English carpenter. Whether James and Nat belonged to the Carpenters' Union or not, they would have known that its leader, Robert Applegarth, was prominent within the Reform League, founded in 1865 to press for an extension of the vote to working men. It happened that the offices of the Reform League were on the ground floor of 8 Adelphi Terrace, which was also the house to which Blomfield moved his offices in 1863. The reformers were much despised by Blomfield's 'Tory and Churchy young men' – this is Hardy's description of his colleagues. They amused themselves by letting down 'ironical bits of paper on the heads of members', and once nearly came to 'loggerheads' with the resident Secretary of the League. Although this semi-jocular reference is all Hardy had to say about London politics in the 1860s in his memoirs, it must be remembered that he wrote them long after he had resolved to abstain from political comment. At the time he must have had at the very least mixed feelings about the question of reform, and his years in London coincided with a period of dramatic political struggle, fiercely fought. There were demonstrations and near-riots, and the Reform League supported John Stuart Mill when he stood for Westminster in the 1865 election.

Mill was an intellectual hero to Hardy by his own account, and he went to hear him speak at Covent Garden during the campaign. This is his careful description of the occasion, written forty years afterwards:

The appearance of the author of the treatise *On Liberty* (which we students of that date knew almost by heart) was so different from the look of persons who usually address crowds in the open air that it held the attention of people for whom such a gathering in itself had little interest ... He stood bareheaded, and his vast pale brow, so thin-skinned as to show the blue veins, sloped back like a stretching upland, and conveyed to the observer a curious sense of perilous exposure ... the cameo clearness of his face chanced to be in relief against the

blue shadow of a church which, on its transcendental side, his doctrines
antagonized.[26]

Hardy had of course no vote himself, any more than his father.[27]
Mill was returned in the election and gave his support in Parliament
to Gladstone's Reform Bill, which was defeated in the following
year, to considerable anger among reformers and working men. A
cholera epidemic, a bad harvest and a rise in the price of bread led
to riots in the East End. Applegarth and his union and Reform
League friends offered to restore order, if they were listened to on
the subject of electoral reform. The government fell, and the
Conservatives came in, headed by Lord Derby as Prime Minister,
which seemed unpromising.

On 2 July the Reform League held a rally in Trafalgar Square
that drew 80,000 men. A second rally was planned in Hyde Park
for 23 July. To prevent it, the Prime Minister had the park gates
locked, but the crowds were so great that park railings bent and
may either have burst under the pressure or been deliberately
broken. This was surely the day that prompted Hardy to write
the words 'Hyde Park – morning' around the title of Shelley's
revolutionary poem *The Revolt of Islam* in his own recently acquired
copy.[28] Here is an indication of quite another Hardy than the mild,
polite assistant to Blomfield: instead, a young man reading about
revolution and going out to look sympathetically at a great body
of workers protesting against injustice. There was some stone-
throwing, but when troops were called most of the men dispersed.
That evening, however, some went into Chester Square and threw
more stones through the windows of the Police Commissioner,
watched by Matthew Arnold and his wife from their adjacent
balcony. Arnold went to the House of Commons to find out what
was being done about this outrage and came home furious at what
he perceived as the weakness of the police.[29]

Reform meetings continued. In December there were two
more, the first held in the grounds of Beaufort House, Kensington,
at which the speakers acknowledged the help of Gladstone and
Mill. The following evening there was another at St James's Hall,
to which many MPs came. In May (1867) the League called

another rally. This one was formally prohibited by the government. No notice was taken by organizers or men, and 100,000 of them gathered defiantly, to be met by 10,000 police and troops. Despite this there was no violence and the crowds again went home quietly, but the Prime Minister admitted that the government had 'suffered some slight humiliation in the public mind'. The Home Secretary resigned, and the reformers felt they had won the moral victory. After this even the Conservatives and Lord Derby felt that a degree of reform was a safer option than a continuation of demonstrations and possible riots nationwide, and a second Reform Act, adroitly steered by Disraeli, was presented and passed. London's electorate was increased by 41 per cent. Male householders and lodgers in rooms worth ten pounds a year got the vote. Hardy should have qualified, the first man in his family to do so, but by August, when the Act went through, he had left London.

Hardy's comprehensive silence on the subject of politics in his memoir also meant he said nothing of the American Civil War, or of the visit of Garibaldi to London in April 1864, when he was given the freedom of the city and an enthusiastic welcome. No one in London could have missed that, any more than the demonstrations of the 1860s, just as no one who took the trouble to go to hear Mill speak could have been unaware of the struggle for the extension of the vote. Hardy tells us that his first novel was written in a spirit of derision towards the 'Tory and Churchy' people he had been working among at Blomfield's. He himself was no Tory, coming from a Liberal family and with a father who took an interest in politics. Could he be described as 'Churchy'?

In the mid sixties he was reading and annotating French radical philosophers and reformers, introduced to him by Moule: Fourier, who planned ideal cooperative communities without religion, and Comte, the first sociologist, the founder of Positivism, a humanist philosophy which held that man should rule his life on scientific, not metaphysical, principles, and that the worship of God should give way to that of humanity. Whatever Hardy made of all this – he was certainly interested – Mill's arguments against religion in *On Liberty*, where he pointed to the failure of modern Christians to take their rules of behaviour from the New Testament, and protested against the Christian claim to know the whole truth, must have had a still stronger effect. Mill's indictment was clearly reasoned and devastating, because it was applied to the contemporary practice of religion in England, suggesting it encouraged a 'low, abject, servile type of character' and showing it as morally damaging to the whole community. By whatever accumulation of reading and thinking it came about, by 1866 Hardy was no longer writing in his prayerbook or going to church regularly. Yet he found it hard to abandon religion altogether. For a while he had a fantasy of giving up architecture and devoting himself to writing poetry, supporting himself by becoming a country clergyman on the model of William Barnes. The problem was that it would make it necessary for him to obtain a university degree. As late as 1866 he wrote to Moule, who sent him a students' guide to Cambridge; only then, after thinking it through carefully yet again, did he realize that he could not prepare to enter the Church 'while holding the views which on examination he found himself to hold'.[30] In other words, the arguments against religion had prevailed, and he was no more 'Churchy' than he was Tory. And with that decision, he also gave up any further thought of getting to a university.

Losing faith in Christianity was like shedding a protective skin: intellectually necessary but also a melancholy process. The melancholy was perfectly expressed in the 1860s by Matthew Arnold in his poem 'Dover Beach', with its description of the world without faith as having 'neither joy, nor love, nor light, / Nor certitude, nor peace, nor help for pain'. Hardy arrived at his own conclusion with many fits, starts and meanders, reluctant to let go of something that had absorbed so much of his imaginative life at the same time that he was eager to join the ranks of the enlightened. He felt the draining away of the old joyous certitudes as well as pride in the new clear thinking. This ambivalence made him into a poet who, in his later years, still sometimes celebrated belief alongside disbelief. He could no longer believe, but he cherished the memory of belief, and especially the centrality and beauty of Christian ritual in country life, and what it had meant to earlier generations and still meant to some. So he could write about the wish that he might still be able to believe, as in his famous poem 'The Oxen'; and about his memories of being a believer himself.[31]

If Horace Moule was experiencing similar doubts, which seems likely, he was fiercely defended against them by his family. In one way it was fortunate that his brothers, all as pious as their parents, were there to help him back from whatever dangerous journeys he took into unbelief, depression or alcoholism. In the summer of 1864 he went to Switzerland with two of his brothers, much loved companions but also guardians. He was often in brilliant spirits, as when he sent Hardy some good advice on writing: 'the grand object of all in *learning to write well* is to gain or generate *something to say*.'[32] Again, he commented on a piece of prose Hardy sent him early in 1864: 'a bright thought strikes me,' he wrote, going on to suggest that Hardy might try to become London correspondent for a country paper. 'Your chatty description of the Law Courts and their denizens is *just* in the style that would go down.' This may not have been what Hardy hoped to hear, but at least Moule was giving him his attention. He also asked politely about Mary, 'your sister . . . and your plans for her'.[33] By then Mary was teaching in a village school at Denchworth, near Oxford. Hardy visited her there once, but she was so miserably lonely that she begged her mother to let her have her six-year-old sister to live with her. Jemima agreed, and Kate was sent to be Mary's companion.

On New Year's Day 1865, when both Hardy and Moule were in Dorchester, he gave Hardy a copy of Marcus Aurelius, inscribed, 'This is the chief thing: Be not perturbed: for all things are according to the nature of the universal.' In the summer Moule spoke of his interest in Cardinal Newman, whom Hardy found attractive for his poetic writing but not for his views.[34] At about the same time Moule also gave him Auguste Comte's *Positivism*, as far from Newman's thinking as it would be possible to go. With family encouragement and no doubt some special negotiation with the school authorities, Moule became an assistant master at Marlborough in 1865. His brothers Charles and Handley had both been teaching there, and both moved on to fellowships at Cambridge, but Horace remained at Marlborough with no prospect of advancement. He did not like the work. When he talked to Hardy about his unhappiness in 1866, Hardy's sympathy wavered, and he thought momentarily of giving up the friendship.[35] He may well have felt it was impossible for him, who had so little and whose life was going nowhere, to comfort Moule, who was sinking and failing despite having had so many talents and chances in life. Another of Moule's offerings to Hardy was a translation of Goethe's *Faust*, which suggests a grim parallel with his condition as he struggled with fiends he could not control. There was a story that he made a backstreet Dorchester girl pregnant, and that she was bundled off to Australia; and another of an engagement to a 'splendid girl', who broke it off.[36] These crises seemed to pass, and Hardy's friendship endured.

Blomfield gave him a grim architectural task in the autumn and winter of 1866. The building of the new Midland railway line into St Pancras meant that the graves around old St Pancras Church had to be moved. 'Many hundreds of coffins, and bones in huge quantities' were to be dealt with, as well as monuments to some of the famous dead. Mary Shelley had already removed the bodies of her mother and father, Mary Wollstonecraft and William Godwin, but their monument remained, with Godwin's second wife still beneath. The public was alerted to the possibility of mishandling of the dead, and the Bishop charged Blomfield with responsibility for making sure everything was done decently. It meant constant supervision of the work, which was done at night behind a hoarding with flare lamps as the coffins were dug up. Hardy's job was to keep an eye on things in the evening and sometimes into the night. Many coffins fell apart as they were brought out, and Hardy and Blomfield were both there when a collapsed coffin gave up one skeleton and two skulls. Old St Pancras churchyard had become a gloomy spot since the open fields once surrounding it had been built over, and it was now overlooked by a workhouse and hemmed in by cheaply thrown-up terraced housing. In these circumstances even the thought that Shelley had wooed his Mary at her mother's grave there half a century earlier could not do much to cheer Hardy. He got through the job, but it was to be his last winter in London for several years.

The spring of 1867 was cold, with snow falling in mid March. There are no letters from Hardy for the year, only a cheerful half-sheet from Moule to him, announcing he was 'passing through' Marlborough and had heard that Hardy was planning to return to Dorset:

Dear Tom I am delighted to hear of your intended move in our direction. / I shan't trouble *very hard* now to effect a meeting in Town, spite of Patti & Titiens [two celebrated sopranos performing at the opera in London]. However if you *like* to call at the New Humm about 6.30 (I won't engage a bed there) you may very likely find me, dress coat and all – But don't swear if you don't find me Yrs ever affly.[37]

Now Moule was up and Hardy was down. Of the few poems he dates 1867, one is a bitter epigram on existence:

> A senseless school, where we must give
> Our lives that we may learn to live!
> A dolt is he who memorizes
> Lessons that leave no time for prizes.[38]

Another ends elegantly, expressing a truth he grasped but could not yet act on:

> If I have seen one thing
> It is the passing preciousness of dreams;
> That aspects are within us; and who seems
> Most kingly is the King.[39]

The best of his London poems is also from this year. It describes a scene of parting between a woman and the man who is recalling it. He lets us see that the woman is suffering, that he is emotionally spent and that the colourless wintry surroundings – pale sun, bare earth, grey fallen leaves, the 'Neutral Tones' of the title – reinforce and represent his refusal to share grief or even to allow it.[40]

We stood by a pond that winter day,
And the sun was white, as though chidden of God,
And a few leaves lay on the starving sod;
    – They had fallen from an ash, and were gray.

Your eyes on me were as eyes that rove
Over tedious riddles of years ago;
And some words played between us to and fro
    On which lost the more by our love.

The smile on your mouth was the deadest thing
Alive enough to have strength to die;
And a grin of bitterness swept thereby
    Like an ominous bird a-wing . . .

Since then, keen lessons that love deceives,
And wrings with wrong, have shaped to me
Your face, and the God-curst sun, and a tree,
    And a pond edged with grayish leaves.

With this poem Hardy establishes himself as a poet with a voice of his own, to be taken seriously. It was not published for another thirty years.[41]

In five years he had succeeded in becoming a Londoner. Or had he? During the cold spring of 1867 he began to feel ill. His colleagues told him he had lost the ruddy look of a countryman, and he suspected he was suffering from the London atmosphere, sitting in the office at a first-floor window above the stinking river, and reading and working in his room from six to midnight every evening. He was, in fact, embarking on something new, a plan for a novel, but for a time he felt so weak that he could hardly lift his pencil. In July, Blomfield urged him to take the summer off and return in October. So when Hardy had a letter from his old master, Hicks, who was looking for an assistant, he decided to offer himself, and in July he returned to Dorchester. He left most of his books and papers in his London lodging but took with him the plan of his novel.

It was not a glorious homecoming, and his mother did not disguise her disappointment that the son for whom she had such hopes was returning apparently with nothing to show for his years in London. But once he was at Bockhampton his strength began to return. He resumed his old daily walks, and within a few weeks he was well again. Working part time for Hicks left him the hours and the energy to get down to the novel. The manuscript grew and grew, becoming an attack on just about everything he had seen and heard during the past five years. He called it *The Poor Man and the Lady*, and gave it a social and political message, intending it as an onslaught on the callousness and hypocrisy of the middle and upper classes and their indifference to the poor, workers and servants and any who aspired to better themselves by getting an education. By October he had made up his mind to finish it at all costs, dashed to London to collect what he had left in Westbourne Park Villas and told Blomfield he would not be returning to Adelphi Terrace. The first draft of the novel was finished in January 1868, and he immediately began on a fair copy.

Only some innocuous fragments of the novel survive, and they are without the sarcasm, aggression and mischief that publishers' readers found in it; there is nothing to tell us about Hardy's politics or anger.[42] As the next chapter will show, he was persuaded to set aside both the manuscript and any display of the political opinions that inspired it. But the anger remained. The wounds inflicted by life never quite healed over in Hardy. Humiliation, rejection, condescension, failure and loss of love remained so close to the skin that the scars bled again at the slightest occasion. This is why many of his poems return to the griefs of the past. It is also why the rage that appears in his last novel, *Jude the Obscure*, was fuelled in the 1890s by the anger he felt in the 1860s. In a sense, *The Poor Man and the Lady* was a dry-run for *Jude*.

PART TWO
1867–1874

6. The Clever Lad's Dream

Hardy produced a rough first draft of his 'striking socialistic novel' in five months, averaging three pages a day – he was a speedy writer from the first – and finishing on 16 January 1868. Over the next five months he revised and wrote out a fair copy.[1] He could have no idea of his future prospects, and he knew the novel was a gamble, but he was determined to get it done.

Even if he had disappointed his mother, there was comfort in being at home again with her familiar cooking and care, the resumed routine of the walk in and out of Dorchester, and the rediscovery of the natural world. He had not heard a nightingale for six years, and when they congregated yards from the cottage windows in the spring he set about transcribing their song.[2] John Hicks was his usual amiable self, glad to have him back and undemanding; Hardy could just about make a living as a part-time assistant in his office without needing to push himself. But not everything was easy. He believed the locals laughed at him for his failure to achieve anything in London, all too likely in a community where everyone knew everyone else's business and any pretensions to be different were viewed with suspicion; and here he was back on his parents' hands with nothing to show for his five years away. Tradition has it that at Bockhampton he had his own little room in which he slept and worked, but you wonder how this was possible with six people squashed into a three-bedroom cottage. Henry, a tall young man of sixteen, was learning the building trade with their father; Kate, ten years old, was now at day school in Dorchester; and Mary, teaching at Minterne in north-west Dorset, was still too far away to live at home in term time, but during the school holidays she joined the family. So perhaps Tom had to share a room with his brother.

For advice about his novel he went to Horace Moule, who may have read the first manuscript when he was home from

Marlborough for the Christmas holidays and encouraged Hardy to
make the fair copy. A note of recommendation from Moule went
with this second version when it was posted off to the highly
respectable publishing house of Macmillan in the summer holidays,
on 25 July 1868. Since Horace was quite capable of giving Tom
unwelcome advice, he must have thought it good enough to
submit.[3] Hardy also put in a letter of his own explaining that his
intention was to attack the manners of the upper classes by seeing
them through the eyes of an outsider. He then fell into the state
of apprehension and despondency usual to writers as they wait for
a verdict on their work. He read Mill, Carlyle and Wordsworth
to steady himself. Moule, suffering his own recurring miseries, was
on the point of giving up his teaching post at Marlborough, his
future cloudy too.

The publishing history of Hardy's first novel turned into a
nightmare: not because there was a lack of interest in it, but because
his hopes were alternately raised and dashed, month after month.
The first response was an encouraging rejection, if such a thing
can be, in the shape of a letter from Alexander Macmillan, dated
10 August: 'If this is your first book I think you ought to go on.
May I ask if it is? and – you are not a lady so perhaps you will
forgive the question – are you young?' Macmillan wrote of 'real
power and insight' and praised the scenes of country life among
working men, but he said the upper-class Londoners were presented with too much hostility, suggesting that, whereas Thackeray
attacked the upper classes fairly, 'you "*mean mischief.*"'

The utter heartlessness of *all* the conversation you give in drawing-rooms
and ballrooms about the working-classes has some grounds of truth I
fear, and might justly be scourged as you aim at doing . . . Will's speech
to the working men is full of wisdom . . . Much of the writing seems to
me admirable. The scene in Rotten Row is full of power and insight
. . . You see I am writing to you as a writer who seems to me, at least
potentially, of considerable mark, of power and purpose.[4]

He said he was seeking further advice on whether and how the
book might be modified, and he also sent Hardy his reader's report:

A very curious and original performance … much of the writing is strong and fresh. But there crops up in parts a certain rawness of absurdity that is very displeasing and makes it read like some clever lad's dream … There is real feeling in the writing … If the man is young, there is stuff and promise in him: but he must study form and composition, in such writers as Balzac and Thackeray, who would I think come as natural masters to him.

Macmillan did not at this point name his reader, John Morley, although he could hardly have chosen one more likely to find something congenial in Hardy's work. Morley was a journalist only two years older than Hardy, liberal in his politics, a freethinker who had fallen out with his father while at Oxford and so started his professional life in London without a penny. He worked for the *Saturday Review*, had defied convention by marrying a woman with two illegitimate children, taken up Positivism and become a friend of Mill. It is impossible to judge how apt his comments on Hardy's work were, since the manuscript no longer exists, but it is obvious that, for all his reservations, he took it seriously.

Hardy wrote back to Macmillan, waited some time for a response and wrote again in September: 'I almost feel that I don't care what happens to the book, so long as something happens.'[5] He added that he had been 'hunting up matter for another tale, which would consist entirely of rural scenes and humble life; but I have not courage enough to go on with it till something comes of the first.' A postscript asked for suggestions about what sort of story or other literary work Macmillan thought he might take on. The manuscript of *The Poor Man and the Lady* was then returned. He revised it and sent it back in November. In December he went to see Macmillan in London, only to be told that, while he was not prepared to publish it, he would give Hardy an introduction to Frederick Chapman of Chapman & Hall, the publishers of Carlyle. Hardy spent a few days in town and met Chapman at his office in Sackville Street, noting afterwards 'I fear the interview was an unfortunate one.' He does not say why, or tell us where he stayed or whether he saw any friends or family, only that he went home, returned to work and filled up the difficult waiting time reading voraciously: Shakespeare and Walt Whitman, Thackeray and Macaulay, the worldly letters of Horace Walpole and Virgil's epic poem about the foundation of Rome, the *Aeneid*. Absorbed in them, he kept his fear of failure down.

In January 1869 he took himself to London yet again, this time intending to stay for a few weeks. Stoic and sceptical as he was, he still found consolation, or magic, in religious texts, and he marked the date, 17 January, in his prayerbook, beside the psalm that begins 'Bow down thine ear, O Lord, and hear me: for I am poor, and in misery.' It reveals how bad his anxiety was. Macmillan saw him again and this time suggested he might try to find work as a reviewer. After this, Hardy had his first meeting with Morley, who offered to introduce him to the editor of the *Saturday Review*. Although this kind of literary life was not what he wanted, it was at least a sign of their confidence in him, and even of friendly feelings. They liked him, saw his promise and wanted to do something to help him.

Chapman summoned him, and said he *would* publish the novel if Hardy was prepared to put up a £20 guarantee against loss. Hardy agreed, having saved a good deal of his salary from his London years. This time he travelled back to Dorset confident that his book was being prepared for press. Just as well, because before setting off he heard of the sudden death of John Hicks. It was sad news, because he had been a friend as well as an employer; it also looked as though he had lost his job in Dorchester.

At home, he waited for his proofs. They did not arrive. Hardy wrote to Chapman, who replied with an invitation to come and meet 'the gentleman who read your manuscript'. Hardy returned to London, the fifth trip in five months, in March. The gentleman was George Meredith, a handsome man of forty in a frock coat, with wavy hair, moustache and brown beard. At first Hardy did not realize he was the novelist, but he listened to his advice, which was that he would do better not to publish this book: it would certainly bring down attacks from reviewers and damage his future chances as a novelist. He might rewrite it, softening the bitterness of his satire on the rich, or better still put it aside and write another novel 'with a purely artistic purpose' and more of a plot. Even when Hardy realized who his reader was, he did not know that he was another freethinker, also from a modest background – Meredith's father was a tailor, which he found embarrassing – and that ten years before he had been fiercely attacked for his first big novel, *The Ordeal of Richard Feverel*, judged so shocking that the powerful circulating library Mudie's cancelled its order of 300 copies. Meredith lectured him, clearly, kindly and at length, and Hardy took his manuscript away.

Still, he could not bear to give up altogether the idea of finding a willing publisher, and in April he submitted it to Smith, Elder, who had published Thackeray. They took only two weeks to turn it down, and he asked them to post it to Dorchester Station rather than to his home address: there was no need for the family to follow all his humiliations. He had one more try in June, sending it to Tinsley Brothers, a much less prestigious firm. They appear to have communicated to Moule, who must have been in London then, that they would publish it if Hardy would guarantee them financially against loss. Hardy answered that their terms were 'rather beyond me just now'.

So he accepted final defeat in the matter of publishing *The Poor Man and the Lady* in September 1869, after trying for fourteen months.[6] It was an agonizing experience, but his determination was such that he made up his mind to learn from it. He would take all the advice he got and write a different sort of novel, using the country life he knew, dreaming up a thrilling plot – whatever they recommended. Hardy's readiness to follow the dictates of publishers may seem too humble, but it was a practical response. Only by getting himself published, by whatever means, could he test out whether he might go on to make a career as a writer. Later in life he insisted that he was primarily a poet and that his novels were merely his craft, taken up as a means to a livelihood, but this is not the whole truth. He did want to become a serious novelist, and his best novels are great works of imagination, each with its own seam of poetry sewn into the narrative. Even his minor novels are wonderful oddities, amusing, disquieting, distinctive. The point was that he had to get started as best he could, and for years he had to sell what he wrote to earn his bread, which forced him to work too fast. He went on taking advice from publishers, accepted cuts and changes imposed by editors who serialized his novels, snipped, filleted and padded them, sometimes damagingly, into the shapes required by the serial market, and tried to keep to the subject preferred by the circulating libraries and thought suitable for family reading – which was, roughly, romance without sex. This is what he meant when he talked of craft, not art. He was not a Flaubert or a Henry James, who had the luxury of taking time and polishing. He sometimes apologized to friends for the shortcomings of his books, saying he knew he had failed to render what his imagination had first suggested to him. But in 1869 the one thing he knew was that he must get something written that Macmillan, or Chapman & Hall, or Tinsley Brothers, would actually set up in proof, publish and put into the bookshops; and to bring that about he was prepared to write whatever they asked for.

Another effect of his encounter with Meredith, with his perfect air of a man of letters, may have been that Hardy decided to improve his own appearance. He could not produce anything to rival Meredith's poetic locks, but by the end of 1869 he had grown a respectable beard of his own, in colour a yellowish brown.[7] A hairy face was required of writers in the mid nineteenth century, and in appearance at any rate he could now take his place alongside Dickens, Tennyson, Trollope, Arnold and Browning.

While *The Poor Man and the Lady* was still being considered in London, he was offered work by a Weymouth architect, George Crickmay. He had bought Hicks's practice and needed an assistant who understood something about church restoration. Hardy decided to take this on for a few months at least and to move into lodgings in Weymouth. Living under the scrutiny of even the most sympathetic family makes waiting to hear from publishers doubly painful, and he says his spirits lifted once he had made the decision. He stood on the Esplanade facing the sunlit sea, the town band doing its best with some Strauss waltzes close by, and after all the strain was suddenly glad that he would not have to make any decisions about his own affairs for the next three months.

Weymouth was booming and expanding, but it had kept some of the glamour bestowed on it by George III's visits, and still had its handsome houses along the sea front looking out over the dazzling, unspoilable bay. He found himself lodgings in a small street near the harbour, at 3 Wooperton Street, and resumed his bachelor life. In the evening he liked to take out a rowing boat as dusk fell and lights began to shine out along the sea wall, 'seeming to send long tap-roots of fire quivering down deep into the sea'.[8] He was a good swimmer and took early-morning dips, floating on his back to enjoy the lift and fall of the waves and the warmth of the sun.

When a new assistant arrived in Crickmay's office, he turned out to be another dancing enthusiast, and he talked Hardy into enrolling for dancing lessons, where they met Weymouth girls. Hardy found them heavier on the arm than London ones, but dancing led to summer flirtations. He was as hungry for women as any other man of his age, but he fell in and out of love helplessly and often, and distrusted his own impulses. On a boat trip to Lulworth with his sister Mary in the summer of 1868, he had noticed a pretty woman and written a note about her afterwards: 'Saw her for the last time standing on deck as the boat moved off. White feather in hat, brown dress, Dorset dialect, Classic features, short upper lip. A woman I wd have married offhand, with prob- ably disastrous results.' He carried on a half-hearted romance with another local girl, Cassie Pole, lady's maid to one of the daughters of the current owners of Kingston Maurward House and daughter of the butler at another house near by.[9] He must have appreciated the irony of making the hero of his novel fall in love with the squire's daughter while in his own life he was making do with ladies' maids.

Or with cousins. There are stories that suggest he was involved at different times with three of his aunt Maria Sparks's daughters. They need to be taken with caution, because they rest mostly on what their brother Nat Sparks's son (another Nat) alleged years later. Not surprisingly, Hardy himself had nothing to say about any of it, but there may well be some truth in Nat's account, which claimed that Hardy was attracted first to Rebecca, the eldest, on whom he was accused of crudely launching himself at a party

as a boy; then to Martha, whom he was said to have wanted to
marry; and finally to the youngest, Tryphena.[10] Cousins could be
a heaven-sent answer to the need for emotional experiment and
sexual adventure in Victorian England. They were accessible,
flirtable with, almost sisters, part of the family, and, indeed, in
many families marriages took place between cousins. So it is likely
that Tom thoroughly enjoyed the company of all his girl cousins,
flirted with them and made as much love to them as he could get
away with when he had the chance. Tryphena, who had been a
child when he went to London, was sixteen when he returned.
She was clever and pretty, like her sister Martha, and it seems that
a warm cousinly affection developed as they got to know one
another better. She was now working as a pupil teacher in the
Puddletown school. The Sparkses had learnt from the Hardys and
resolved that she should aim higher than her sisters and apply to a
teacher training college when she reached the right age. Tryphena
got into trouble for neglecting her duties at the school in January
1868 and was formally reproved, but she continued with her plans.

The death of her mother in the autumn of 1868 was a blow to
all the family, Maria Sparks and Jemima Hardy being close sisters,
and Maria a good and careful mother to her daughters, now left
to run their own lives, their father being very old and reduced to
poverty. Tom was at his aunt's funeral. He gave Tryphena some
French lessons, passing on what he had learnt at King's College.
She knew about London from Martha, and no doubt he talked of
his London experiences, and when she came to apply for her
training in 1869 she chose the Nonconformist Stockwell Training
College in south London. She was awarded a scholarship and
studied there for two years. But there is no evidence she and Hardy
met in London, and the friendship or flirtation between them
cannot have lasted long.[11]

At the end of her training Tryphena was offered a post as
headmistress of an elementary school in Plymouth. London did
not turn out so well for Martha. Within months of her mother's
death she became pregnant. It was a classic Victorian servant's
story, the father of her child being another servant, the butler in
the same household. She was dismissed at once, and her lover,

William Duffield, was also sent packing. At least he did the right thing by Martha and married her, and they tried to make a go of running a coffee shop in Kensington Park Road. The baby proved to be twins, a boy and a girl, the little girl dying during her first year. Martha had another daughter two years later, and then no more children. The coffee shop was not a success. They struggled on until 1876, when they made up their minds to leave England, not for Canada, as Martha's aunt had done, but further away still, for Queensland, Australia.[12] The fourth Sparks sister, Emma, whom Hardy had visited in Somerset in 1861, also by then living in poverty with her carpenter husband and more children than they could afford, left for Australia too. They were driven by the fear of sinking into still worse misery and destitution than they already suffered. The workhouse loomed brutally in the imagination of the poor, as it was meant to, and Australia seemed a better bet. Hardy must have known of the difficulties and then the emigration of these once dearly loved cousins and been unable to intervene. It was another grim thing to keep at the back of his mind while he pursued his own ambitions through doubts, setbacks and discouragement.

In the autumn of 1869 he started on another novel. He followed Meredith's advice about plot and structured it around a melodramatic and intricate story that included wife murder, a lady of high position with a secret illegitimate child, the result of a rape, and a crop of preposterous coincidences. His title, a good one, told the reader roughly what to expect: *Desperate Remedies*. What had he in mind? The example of Wilkie Collins's recent hit *The Moonstone*, perhaps, and Dickens's use of mystery plots, as in *Our Mutual Friend*.[13] George Eliot's *Felix Holt the Radical*, which also came out when he was in London, in 1866, was another novel that made use of mysteries involving birth, parentage and inheritance. Some of Hardy's book reads as though he had said to himself, if this is what the publishers and the public want, I'll give it to them. On top of the lurid plot points he threw in everything that came to hand, the experience of struggling architects, life in Weymouth

lodgings, a boat trip to Lulworth, the two big houses on the
Kingston Maurward Estate, the trials of a lady's maid, the harsh
treatment meted out to tenants by country landowners, a glimpse
of the London poor and another of apple picking in the West
Country, quotations from English and Latin poets, some picturesquely spoken rustics and a midnight disposal of a body,
supposedly secret, actually witnessed by three separate observers.
If the story sometimes seems in danger of flying apart, he just
manages to tie it up prettily at the end with the sudden deaths of
the two most delinquent characters.

His heroine, Cytherea, is pretty, graceful and submissive. She is
given a striking moment at the start of the book when, attending
a public Shakespeare reading, she looks through the windows of
the town hall at the spire of the local church which her architect
father is restoring, and, as she watches, sees him lose his footing
on the scaffolding and drop to his death. It should be a terrible
experience for her, but it has no point except to mark the beginning
of her and her brother's adventures as orphans who must earn their
livings. By the end of the book she has been through further
ordeals, remaining pretty and graceful throughout, but without
ever managing to become interesting. She is wooed by a young
architect and by a murderous villain, her heart flutters and her tears
flow; she thinks she may end her days in the workhouse and agrees
to marry to escape poverty, the reason that leads 'many thousands
of women' into marriage every year, Hardy tells us. The charm of
Desperate Remedies – and it has its charms, particularly in the early
chapters – lies not in the plot but in Hardy's incidental comments
and descriptions. He describes the dullness of provincial towns
where the citizens are given to watching newcomers, 'silently criti-
cising their dress – questioning the genuineness of their teeth and
hair – estimating their private means'. He tells us that the county
hospital 'is only another name for slaughter-house'. A man in love
looks at the girl he wants to walk home 'as a waiter looks at the
change he brings back', whereas a young single woman tells how
much she enjoys living alone: 'If you knew the pleasure of locking
up your own door, with the sensation that you reigned supreme
inside it, you would say it was worth the risk of being called odd.'

One night, Cytherea, lying awake, hears 'a very soft gurgle or rattle' followed by the low whining of a dog, taken up by other dogs that start to howl. It is the dying breath of the old master of the house, alone in his bedroom, and Hardy says she had heard it before, when her mother died. He is so confident and precise in his description that you wonder if he had heard it himself at the death of his grandmother.

There is also a famous scene in which Cytherea, working as a lady's maid, has her bed invaded by her employer Miss Aldclyffe, an ageing unmarried lady. Miss Aldclyffe presses Cytherea to her heart, kisses her lips with 'a warm motherly salute', asks for her love and questions her jealously about her relations with men. Cytherea is not particularly worried by her physical proximity – beds were often shared – so much as embarrassed by Miss Aldclyffe's bullying insistence on being given the name of the young man she is in love with. Lesbianism was little mentioned in Victorian England, but the episode may well have been based on something told Hardy by one of the lady's maids he knew. At the same time the frisson in this scene is social as much as sexual, distaste for a demonstration of the arrogant behaviour of the upper classes in intruding and prying even into the private feelings and experiences of their servants.[14] No modern reader can be unaware of the sexual element, but the line between physically demonstrative displays of innocent affection and conscious eroticism was not easily drawn in the mid nineteenth century. Even men sometimes had difficulty with it, as Henry James found. Hardy is not describing a rape or an erotic conquest here, although he is showing how Miss Aldclyffe, starved of affection and charmed by Cytherea (as everyone is), wants to make her into her 'pet', something between a companion and a daughter who will devote herself exclusively to her. She describes herself as 'your mamma', and she knows that Cytherea is the daughter of the man she once loved. Her behaviour in the bedroom is imperious, ill mannered and coercive, both physically and emotionally, but not seductive. She continues to bully Cytherea into doing what she wants, including marrying against her own inclinations, but there is no repetition of the bedroom scene. John Morley, who read the book for Macmillan, was horrified by the early episode of the rape of the young Miss Aldclyffe (a 'disgusting and absurd outrage'), which Hardy removed. The scene 'between Miss Aldclyffe and her new maid in bed' he called merely 'highly extravagant'. It is powerful and unpleasant, but there is nothing lewd or titillating about it.

To speed up completion of this book Hardy left Weymouth in February 1870 and returned to Bockhampton and his mother's care. A message came from Crickmay inviting him to travel to Cornwall to look at a church in need of restoration in a remote spot on the north coast. Hardy delayed his departure until March in order to be able to post off his nearly finished manuscript to Macmillan before he went, on 5 March. Then, in the starlit small hours of 7 March, he got up to walk to Dorchester Station and set off on what proved to be the most momentous journey of his life.

7. Lyonnesse

The journey west into an unknown county marked the beginning of a new epoch in his life. The next four years were to be dominated by two enterprises: a personal adventure in which he met, courted and married Emma Gifford; and a gruelling professional ordeal which finally transformed him from an architect's clerk with dim prospects and uncertain literary ambitions into a successful novelist. The two processes were tightly twisted together; they demanded energy, resilience and determination, and neither proceeded easily or straightforwardly. When he and Emma met, he was no more than an aspiring writer, unpublished and with small grounds for confidence. Neither of their families approved of their decision to be married when they heard of it, but they married anyway, and by that time his fourth novel was being serialized in the *Cornhill*, the most widely read and respected magazine in England, and Hardy had arrived on the literary scene. He had already been hailed as another George Eliot and credited with 'the intense minuteness and vivid concentration of the most powerful among French writers of fiction'.[1] All four of his novels had been published in America and three of them also serialized there.[2] The gods had smiled on him: he had a secure reputation, and he was bankable. He could keep a wife.

In March 1870 none of this could have been imagined. His starlit walk in the small hours was the prelude to a long day's travel, because north Cornwall was not easily accessible. From Dorset he had to take four different trains: Dorchester to Yeovil, Yeovil to Exeter, Exeter to Plymouth and Plymouth north again to Launceston; and after this came another sixteen miles in a hired trap before he arrived in front of the rectory in St Juliot, a hamlet so remote and insignificant it is still not marked on road maps in 2005. Once inside the door he found himself face to face with a young lady wearing a brown dress. She was of unmistakable gentility, graceful, with a mass of hair shading from corn-gold to bright brown, dark eyes and a pink complexion.³ She introduced herself and explained that the rector, her brother-in-law, was suffering from an attack of gout – the classic complaint of the Victorian rectory – and could not come downstairs; nor, just yet, could her sister, who was tending the invalid.

Miss Gifford greeted Hardy with the respect accorded to a professional visitor. She knew he came on architectural business, and he spoke as an educated man with just a touch of the soft West Country in his voice; and at first sight he seemed quite old, with his beard and well-worn greatcoat. To him, her social standing was obvious: she was a lady. This was the first time he had met one of her class and age on equal terms. Class mattered to them both. When Emma declared that the nearest neighbours were nine miles away, she meant the people of her own class, because the labouring families she visited in their scattered cottages round about simply did not count as 'neighbours'. And when Hardy spoke of his work to her he did not add anything about his background, parents or home life in a Dorset cottage. He was not going to be the poor man. They conversed, as they had met, as equals.

A maid showed him to his room upstairs, with a window looking over the steep valley and hills rising beyond, not another building in sight. The house was comfortable. Emma presided over their evening meal. He explained his train journey with its four changes, a knight's move, she called it, which is indeed what it looks like on the railway map. Her description pleased him, and he did not forget it. After the meal her sister Helen, Mrs Holder, came down to meet him and took him to speak to the rector in his room. Later the two sisters entertained him at the piano, both singing popular songs. It was what they did on most evenings, although Emma was also a reader, and had ambitions as a writer too.

They had grown up in Devon in a conventional, provincial, respectable world. Their father was a lawyer and a keen Tory; they had an uncle in the Church and another who was a bank manager; other men in the family were schoolmasters. Emma looked with interest at Hardy, because he had lived in London, where she had never been, although they had a brother there now, Walter, who worked for the Post Office. She had passed her first twenty years happily in Plymouth, with an affectionate mother who allowed all her children freedom to run about and clamber on the rocky seashore, even Emma, who was born with a condition that made her slightly lame, though it did not greatly trouble her.[4] She was sent to a school run by two maiden ladies, daughters of an army officer; lessons were in the mornings only and French was well taught. Partly from school, more perhaps from her father, who had literary tastes, she acquired a taste for poetry and for writing herself. Like most well-brought-up young ladies she also learnt to draw and to paint watercolour landscapes and to play the piano. There was much music at home, her father being a violinist – like Hardy's, although Hardy probably kept that to himself – and the children were encouraged to sing part songs. There were dancing lessons too, and parties and dances, Plymouth being full of young naval and army officers; whether Emma danced is not clear. It was a city well endowed with libraries, concerts and a theatre, and she enjoyed her life there and had many friends. A girl with pink cheeks, a generous amount of curly hair and a look of being in full bloom, she was known to her friends, who liked to give one another flower names, as 'the peony'.

Emma's father, being the eldest in his family and his mother's favourite, persuaded her to support him and his family out of her income so that he could give up his work as a solicitor and live a life of leisure. So far he is a figure who could have appeared in one of Jane Austen's later novels. Unfortunately his leisure was enlivened by spectacular drinking bouts. During one of these he put on a marathon Shakespearean performance for the family. They chose to regard it as an achievement of sorts, evidence of his taste and knowledge, but his behaviour put a strain on them all. Then, when Emma's grandmother died, it was discovered that she had been spending her capital to keep them. There was very little money left, and the family was forced to move to Cornwall, where life was cheaper. They settled down to a restricted existence outside Bodmin, a quieter, duller place than Plymouth.

The three sons were educated for the professions, but there was

no money for anything else. Helen and Emma each worked for
six months as a governess and found that quite enough. Then
Helen became a companion to an old lady living in Tintagel, and
she, meeting Emma and observing her limp, generously gave her
a mare to get about on. The mare was named Fanny. Her father
taught her to ride Fanny with a side saddle and showed her how
to manage a long riding habit with the proper elegance. Riding
became her passion, and she was off, cantering about Cornwall on
her own, happily and fearlessly. Apart from the limp she was a
strong, well-built young woman: in old age she told a friend that,
as a girl, she was supposed to be getting consumption, 'but the
doctor said with *my width* and *shape* of chest it was quite impossible.'[5] When Helen was thirty she received a proposal of marriage
from a clergyman, the Revd Cadell Holder. He was sixty-five and
had been a widower for many years – he had a grown-up son and
grandchildren living in Cornwall – and he was now gamely taking
up a new living at St Juliot, where he felt he would need support.
It was not a romantic match but served the purposes of both well.
He got a young wife, and she got a cheerful, gentlemanly old
husband and became mistress of a comfortable and attractive, if
isolated, rectory. It had been built only a few years earlier, in 1847,
as part of the Church's crusade against the spread of Nonconform-
ity, and they had made a good job of it. Holder, born in Barbados
in 1803, came of a family with sugar plantations there; he had been
sent to England to study at Oxford and, as he was thought to be
delicate, went into the Church. The West Indian connection was
useful, the patron of St Juliot, who appointed him to the living,
being Richard Rawle, who had taught for many years in Barbados
and was soon to be consecrated Bishop of Trinidad. Rawle was a
Cornishman by birth and owned land around St Juliot. He was
childless, and it was he who had raised the income of the benefice
and was partly funding the restoration of the church, turning up
in person when it was reopened.[6]

Holder and Helen were married in 1867, and Emma was invited
to live with them in the rectory. Emma's biographer suggests that
he must have appeared to be marrying both sisters, but it was a
usual enough arrangement in days of large families, and perhaps he

did like the idea of a brace of young wives. Emma was only twenty-six, and she said Helen was always disposed to be jealous of her, but they kept one another company, and there was plenty of room at the rectory, and enough to do in the parish. They had a man in charge of the stables to look after Fanny, the other horses and the basket carriage. A romantic garden dropped away from the flagged terrace along the back of the house, part of it enclosed to make a greenhouse, and fruit and vegetables were grown in a large walled enclosure. By the time Hardy came to St Juliot they were well settled in; but there were few visitors to such a remote spot, and those who came were very welcome.

Hardy was there to work, of course, and he spent the whole of his first day at the church. It was a short walk from the rectory, standing quite by itself above the meadows falling steeply away to the Valency River below. In the churchyard were ancient Celtic crosses and modest gravestones marking the mostly short lives of the local people, and the first event in the morning of the day he worked there was a funeral, a single bell being tolled on the ground. All the five bells had been brought down from the tower, already condemned as unsafe. The church building, small and dilapidated as it was, contained a decrepit but fine carved wooden screen and pew ends with poppies, which Hardy drew. He went back to the rectory for lunch, returned to the church, and finished his survey and notes that evening. The next day he was driven by Emma, with Mrs Holder for company, along the narrow lanes through Boscastle and Tintagel village to the Penpethy slate quarry to look at the materials to be used in the restoration work on the church. The slates were greenish, and in 1925 Hardy published a poem called 'Green Slates', with the note 'Penpethy', recalling Emma standing in the quarry.[7]

On his third day he and Emma went out with no chaperone to the cliffs, she on horseback. And now he first became aware of another Emma, and his imagination was stirred by the discovery of this different creature as she rode along the cliffs with the Atlantic breakers crashing in below, the March wind blowing processions of clouds across the sky, black-faced Beeny Cliff jutting out to sea before them and the sea stretching away to the limitless west. She rode so well that she and Fanny were like one animal, and she sometimes told people pertly, 'I prefer my mare to any husband.'[8] She was wonderfully bold, careless of heights or weather, and even claimed to enjoy the feeling of rain running down her back and her hair floating in the wind. Sometimes, she told him, she dismounted to clamber down the rocks and explore the seal caves below. Hardy knew the Dorset cliffs well, but this was a fiercer, wilder coast. The landscape spoke to something in her, and she believed that 'no summer visitors can have a true idea of its power to awaken heart and soul.' Her response to her surroundings, her high spirits as she cantered along the cliff tops, and her freedom to wander about alone as she pleased, and unchaperoned, made her unlike the established pattern of well-behaved, timid, clinging Victorian girlhood. Hardy had read enough of the Romantic poets to see her as a spirit of the chasms and wild places, with her floating hair and her look of *la belle dame*. She could take on all the roles – a spirit yet a woman too – and she became for him the spirit of delight itself.[9]

In his pocketbook the brief notes he made that day trail away, helped along by Tennyson: 'On the cliff . . . "The tender grace of a day", etc. The run down to the edge. The coming home . . .' They talked about the poetry they liked, and she learnt that the blue paper sticking out of his breast pocket was not an architectural note but a poem of his own. At some point he told her that he had the manuscript of a novel in the hands of a publisher, and she confessed that she too jotted down ideas and hoped to write a novel, and to publish it. In the afternoon they walked down the valley with Helen to Boscastle, 'E. provokingly reading as she walked.' Then 'evening in the garden; music later in the evening.' Hardy noted the names of some of the ballads they sang, 'The Elfin Call' and 'Let Us Dance on the Sands'. When he left before dawn on 11 March – he had to be driven the sixteen miles to the nearest railway station at Launceston again – it was Emma who made sure the servants were up in time, sat with him as he took his candlelit breakfast and went out into the damp garden with him to say goodbye. Both knew that something had happened in those few days which might lead to more. They agreed to write to one another. Hardy's poem 'At the Word "Farewell"' tells us how he parted from her with a kiss:

> Even then the scale might have been turned
> Against love by a feather,
> – But crimson one cheek of hers burned
> When we came in together.[10]

It is easy to see what she liked about him. He was a stranger from a larger world. He was a man in charge of architectural work he understood thoroughly and dealt with authoritatively – a change from her idle, blustering father and valetudinarian brother-in-law, the two men she knew best. He had a neat figure and a sensitive face that could be eager and intent, or close up entirely when he chose to withdraw into himself. When he was with her, the eagerness was drawn out, and she bloomed like a flower in response: this is the mechanism of falling in love. On that they had much to build, laughing together and exchanging views on their common passion, literature, and their common wish to become writers. Whether she was likely to achieve that or not, he could see her as someone who could help and advise him with his writing.

The long slog back to Dorset gave him plenty of time to think about Emma on the one hand, and on the other to return to fretting over Macmillan and their response to *Desperate Remedies*. Back in Weymouth he worked on his plans for St Juliot Church. The bad news arrived in the post soon enough, on 5 April: Macmillan was rejecting the unfinished *Desperate Remedies* as too sensational. Another failure, another humiliation to be made light of or hidden from his family, and now also to tell his Cornish correspondent. He could not endure the idea of a second rejection from Chapman & Hall also, so, although it was their reader, Meredith, who had advised him to write a well-plotted novel, he

sent it immediately to Tinsley Brothers, a firm known to have
lower standards. Another wait. The daily detail of these transactions
shows just how agonizing they must have been. On 2 May, Hardy's
other life surfaced, as his plans for St Juliot Church were approved
by Crickmay; and on 3 May, William Tinsley wrote saying he
would *consider* publishing *Desperate Remedies* but thought there
should be alterations to the manuscript. On 5 May he laid out his
terms. They were steep. Hardy was to contribute the large amount
of £75 towards the cost of publication, to cover losses. He might
recoup some or all of it – or lose it all. Hardy agreed to this, and,
on 9 May, Tinsley proposed an edition of 500 copies, subject to
the book being revised and completed to his satisfaction.

Hardy now moved to London to get on with rewriting, taking
lodgings in Kensington, at 23 Montpelier Street, off the Brompton
Road, a better address than he had yet settled in. He kept afloat
by taking on odd architectural jobs, for Blomfield, and for an
architect called Raphael Brandon, whom he admired and whose
picturesque chambers in Clement's Inn, off the Strand, he observed
carefully, storing up the details for future use.[11] With Brandon he
discussed the outbreak of war between France and Germany in
July, and with Horace Moule too, who was in London again,
coaching for the Indian Civil Service examinations. They saw a
good deal of one another. Moule made no secret of his low opinion
of the Tinsleys as publishers, but Hardy was set on his arrangement
with them. He also told Moule about his Cornish trip and Miss
Gifford. He had never confided in him about a friendship with a
woman before. What made it possible was that for the first time
she was a mentionable person from Moule's world, the daughter
of a solicitor, living in a country rectory, well read and able to
discuss his work with him. He was not only corresponding regularly with her but sending her books to read, and he could imagine
that she and Moule might find something in common, and look
forward to their meeting.

In June he had his thirtieth birthday in London. It meant little
to him, his heart being in Cornwall. He could have visited his
cousin Martha, who had just given birth to twins, and Tryphena
was at her training college in Stockwell, but if he saw either he

made no record of the meetings. In July news of other cousins came to his mother in the shape of a tiny letter, just four inches wide, bearing a Canadian stamp. It was from Louisa Sharpe, the eldest daughter of his Aunt Martha, last seen in Hitchin in 1849, when they were children. Louisa reminded the Hardys that Thomas had written to them for his mother in 1858, not long 'before my dear mother's death' who had been 'sleeping so long in the grave'. Louisa knew that sending her letter was a sort of 'castle in the air', but she still hoped to hear from them. She expected it to be two months before she could. She added, 'I think I can remember you and Thomas but it is almost like a dream.' Her neat, wistful letter, posted in Medina, East Nissouri, Ontario, seems to have gone unanswered.[12] Perhaps Jemima put it aside for Tom to deal with later, but he was not much at home. London held him, and his mind was still further away, in Cornwall, and on his exchanges of letters with Emma, and the plans they were making for him to return to St Juliot. There he would have more time to work on his book. Emma offered to help with the fair copy. None of this could be explained at Bockhampton, where Emma's name had not yet been mentioned.

The Holders had invited Hardy to return to St Juliot for a summer holiday, and on 8 August he was there. Emma's brown winter dress, the only one he had seen, had been put away, and she appeared in blue: 'the original air-blue gown' was a sight he never forgot. They were very happy. 'August. Cornwall. The smoke from a chimney droops over the roof like a feather in a girl's hat. Clouds, dazzling white, retain their shapes by the half hour, motionless, and so far below the blue that one can almost see round them,' wrote Hardy in his notebook. The weather was hot, the sun shone and they explored the coast and the countryside together: the lush Valency Valley, with its river bubbling down to the port at Boscastle; the tidal sands at Trebarwith, where women gathered seaweed and collected sand, loading it on to their donkeys in panniers; and the ruins of Tintagel on its bare island, where they narrowly avoided being locked in. At the same time they were exploring each other, finding out each other's tastes, enjoying the long hours in each other's company, often unaccompanied. She was so *living*, he thought.[13] He was physically enthralled by her; after he left he wrote her initials against 'The Song of Solomon' in his Bible: 'Behold, thou art fair, my love; behold, thou art fair; thou hast doves' eyes. Behold, thou art fair, my beloved, yea, pleasant: also our bed is green.' They picnicked by the Valency, and Emma lost the glass they had drunk from; Hardy sketched her on her knees trying to find it in the river, in vain. It had disappeared for ever, like a magic cup lost in an old story.

There was something else. Emma remembered a particular word he had used when she wrote her memoir later: 'We grew much interested in each other and I found him a perfectly new subject of study and delight and he found a "mine" in me, he said.'[14] What he meant by calling her a mine was that she gave him material for his writing. He learnt from her exactly what it was like to be a young woman in her situation, and he could feed it into his fiction. He had already tried using the voices of women he was involved with in poems such as the 'She, to Him' sonnets, and now he had something more valuable: direct access to her life and feelings. He could ask her questions, study her, watch her movements and her manners, listen to her laughing, scolding and boasting, hear her confessions, her dreams and her stories, observe what made her smile and what upset her. He was in love with her, there was no doubt of that, but she was also a precious commodity – a 'mine', as he so frankly told her, a seam of gold for a writer who knew he had to study the market.

As the month went by they heard of the French defeat by the Germans at Sedan and the capitulation of Napoleon III. It was the biggest military encounter in Western Europe since 1815. Hardy wrote his poem 'In Time of "The Breaking of Nations"' during a later war, in 1915, but he explained then that it was inspired by his memory of walking in Cornwall after getting the news of the defeat of the French in 1870.

I

Only a man harrowing clods
   In a slow silent walk
With an old horse that stumbles and nods
   Half asleep as they stalk.

II

Only thin smoke without flame
   From the heaps of couch-grass;
Yet this will go onward the same
   Though Dynasties pass.

III

Yonder a maid and her wight
   Come whispering by:
War's annals will cloud into night
   Ere their story die.

His explanation suggests that the 'maid and her wight' may not be an anonymous rustic couple but Emma and Hardy themselves, distant figures viewed through the long telescope of time, and caught for ever moving across a patch of rough working Cornish land. You can believe that he remembered the old horse, the man with the harrow and the couch-grass giving off smoke just as he had seen them, and that he saw himself at the edge of the scene, walking closely with Emma – close enough for them to exchange loving whispers. The old word 'wight' nudges his past self and puts him in his place, and suggests that two lovers, whether lady and gentleman or maid and wight, have the same value in the end. He thought it was among his best poems, and it has the solidity of something truly remembered and realized.[15]

Other memorials from that summer are the drawings they did
of one another, Emma's showing Hardy sitting on a stile with a
tender, bemused expression and holding a flag (presumably a
French one), sketched on 18 August. The next day he drew Emma
on all fours searching for the cup lost in the river. She is deliciously
dressed, hatted and curled, with her bottom sticking up, her sleeves
rolled and her breasts clearly outlined. On the 22nd, the day
rain ended the heat wave, he sketched Beeny Cliff, showing an
indeterminate figure that must be Emma, wrapped up against the
rain.[16] She made tiny drawings of 'our stone' under the trees by
the Valency River, and of the pretty summer house with its table
in the rectory garden where they must have sat for shelter from
sun or rain, looking out over the fields. During these three August
weeks they fully acknowledged their love for one another, and
when Hardy left he considered himself engaged. It had to be a
private engagement. Of Emma's family he knew only the Holders,
and of his family she knew nothing unless perhaps he mentioned
his sister Mary as being a schoolteacher, and Kate, still a schoolgirl.
She had no money of her own – she must have managed on pocket
money from her father or Holder – and Hardy had savings of only
£125, of which £75 were going to be handed over to Tinsley.
Whether he knew it or not, she would be thirty on her next
birthday, in November. Their youth was passing, they had no
prospects, and two years went by before he felt able to speak to
her father about the possibility of marriage. When he left Cornwall
at the end of the month, he did not know even when he would
be able to see her next.

Letters kept their love going. Hardy, in a glow of remembered
emotion, later compared their correspondence with the exchanges
of Robert Browning and Elizabeth Barrett. One would give a
great deal to hear Hardy open his heart and Emma at full voice,
and there must have been many letters, given that the lovers were
separated for about eleven months of each year during the four
years of their wooing. Easy to imagine the bundles tied with ribbon
and neatly boxed, but every one of them was destroyed; not because they could not bear the thought of profaning their love by
letting them be seen, but through rage and bitterness – by Emma.

Nobody knows whether Emma ever read the jubilant lines inspired by Hardy's first journey to Cornwall, 'When I Set Out for Lyonnesse'. Lyonnesse was the old name he used for Cornwall; he put the date 1870 beside it but did not publish it until after her death, perhaps because it seemed too painfully ironical when he began to publish his poems in 1898.[17] She is not named, although she is part of the poem. It is an incantation about magic and falling in love, coming out of freezing darkness and loneliness into a life of limitless, shining possibilities.

> When I set out for Lyonnesse
>   A hundred miles away,
>   The rime was on the spray,
> And starlight lit my lonesomeness
> When I set out for Lyonnesse
>   A hundred miles away.
>
> What would bechance at Lyonnesse
>   While I should sojourn there
>   No prophet durst declare,
> Nor did the wisest wizard guess
> What would bechance at Lyonnesse
>   While I should sojourn there.
>
> When I came back from Lyonnesse
>   With magic in my eyes,
>   All marked with mute surmise
> My radiance rare and fathomless,
> When I came back from Lyonnesse
>   With magic in my eyes!

8. The True Vocation

For the next two years – 1871 and 1872 – he shuttled between Weymouth, Bockhampton, London and Cornwall. Ideas for new novels came tumbling into his head, but, although he had a few periods of concentrated writing, mostly he had to fit it into whatever spare time was left while he earned his living doing architectural jobs. He was short of money. Getting to Cornwall was difficult, and there was no question of Emma coming to him. She had no money at all, the idea of her staying with his parents was unimaginable, and unmarried ladies did not visit men. Some time in 1871 he wrote a sad sonnet, 'The Minute before Meeting', in which he spoke of the 'grey gaunt days' and 'slow blank months' of separation from Emma, and said he could hardly enjoy even the imminent prospect of seeing her because it was spoilt by knowing how soon they would have to part again.

His gloom was not lifted by his mother, who must have heard of Emma's existence after his return from Cornwall in September 1870 and noticed the regular arrival of her letters. Jemima's remark, entered in his notebook in October as the grim suggestion 'That a figure stands in our van with an arm uplifted, to knock us back from any pleasant prospect we indulge in as probable', may have been offered as a warning to him not to be too hopeful in his wooing, or in any other plans. Temperamentally he shared her bleak view of fate. Still, she was a good practical mother and looked after him while he was at Bockhampton that autumn, preparing *Desperate Remedies* for Tinsley. As a keen reader she must have been curious about his writing, but he says nothing about showing it to her. He may have worried about her response to his descriptions of country life, and it was said by a neighbour who knew her well that she did object to his use of local material. 'She rather bitterly complained of his not having kept his word to her that he would confine his productions to London. "And he don't say things right neither . . . He tells as how I did always come out of the front door to feed the chickens – and I never did! – I did always come out at back!" "[1]

She would have noticed the sheaves of pages going off to Emma for her to copy in her neat handwriting, and perhaps minded that, and felt a sense of rivalry. Emma did the work gladly. She wrote to him of 'This dream of my life – no, not dream, for what is actually going on around me seems a dream rather . . .'[2] Their collaborative effort was in the publisher's hands on 9 December, but they had no prospect of meeting for many months yet. Divided from her, unable to share his love for her with his family, or even to introduce her into it, and uncertain whether his writing would ever succeed, he read *Hamlet* while he waited for Tinsley's response and marked the Prince's words: 'Thou wouldst not think how ill all's here about my heart: but it is no matter!'[3]

There was a final tussle about terms with Tinsley, then he went to London in January 1871 and paid over the £75. This left him with a total fortune of £50. He would have to get work again once he had corrected the proofs. This at least went smoothly, and on 25 March his first published book was at last in his hands, a moment of rejoicing, surely, rapidly followed by intense anxiety, since it was also in the hands of the reviewers. His view was that *The Poor Man and the Lady* was a much better book, while this one was written to a formula, but it did not prevent him from hoping for a good response. It was in the usual three volumes, and there was no author's name on the title page, only a sentence from Scott explaining that 'the province of the romance-writer being artificial, there is more required from him than a mere compliance with the simplicity of reality.' It was not calculated to attract readers, and it was slightly misquoted: a bad start. Hardy corrected it on the copy he sent to Emma.[4]

He was already working on another book, cannibalizing some of the rustic scenes already written for *The Poor Man and the Lady* and building a simple narrative around a piece of his own family history: the conflict between the 'string choir' of viols and voices his grandfather had run in Stinsford Church, and a new vicar determined to replace the choir with an up-to-date organ. It was to be called 'The Mellstock Quire'. Wanting to get on with it, he still needed to earn and took himself to Weymouth once more, where Crickmay, busily building new villas and schools, was glad to employ him. Writing was again relegated to spare time. In April the first two reviews of *Desperate Remedies* lifted his spirits, praising the power of the plot, the characterization, the use of dialect and the presentation of rural life (this was 'almost worthy of George Eliot'). After this the *Spectator* put in the knife, suggesting that the whole book was itself a desperate remedy for 'ennui or an emaciated purse' and that the unknown author had 'prostituted' his powers 'to the purposes of idle prying into the way of wickedness'. 'Here are no fine characters, no original ones to extend one's knowledge of human nature, no display of passion except of the brute kind.' Miss Aldclyffe was described as 'a miserable creation – uninteresting, unnatural, and nasty'. It was the sort of attack an author never forgets, and Hardy never did forget it, any more than he developed a thick skin, as Moule urged him to in a kindly letter. Few writers do, although some brazen it out better than others. The *Spectator* review was long, and when he was able to look at it calmly he saw that it also contained a good deal of praise for 'talent of a remarkable kind', vivid powers of description and an especial skill in the presentation of country people. This was balm, and he copied out the encouraging parts.

Joy came in May, when he persuaded Crickmay to send him back to St Juliot, and he and Emma were able to exult together over the three volumes of 'their' book – she had after all copied most of it – and to talk about the new manuscript. In the course of the summer Hardy carried out radical changes, writing forty pages of extra material and shifting the main interest away from the tribulations of the choir to the love story.[5] Emma claimed in later years that she helped and advised Hardy with his writing, while he insisted that her help was pretty well confined to making fair copies, but the alterations to 'The Mellstock Quire', which became *Under the Greenwood Tree* during the summer of 1871, suggest that in this one instance she may have influenced him, or at least that he made adjustments to suit her taste and interests. What he did was to promote the village schoolmistress, Fancy Day, from minor figure to heroine, putting her at the centre of the plot and making it a much more conventional one. The main theme of the village musicians fighting to keep their church band became humorous background material to a pastoral love story in which three rivals pursue Fancy.[6] Hardy had started with his native village and his own people in mind, but he may have decided that this was not the way to introduce them to Emma, and by reducing the importance of their role he distanced them. The Shakespearean allusion in the new title, together with a subtitle, 'A Rural Painting of the Dutch School', distanced them further, inviting the reader to stand back and enjoy a scene framed and shaped for pleasurable contemplation.

Under the Greenwood Tree has charmed generations of readers who share Emma's view that there is an unbridgeable gulf between the gentry and the poor. You are charmed on condition that you accept Hardy's condescension towards his characters. His villagers are drawn sympathetically but as simpletons. He is tender towards them and gives them beautifully turned rustic dialogue, but he invites us to smile with him at their simplicity. They are comical without knowing they are. They have no hope of dealing with the new vicar effectively, because they cannot be other than deferential to his position, whatever they think of him as a man. They accept their own inferiority, and, even though he is not much brighter than any of them, his class and social status ensure that he will always win in any dispute. Hardy's tone is judicious, avuncular, staid. Fancy Day has had more education than most of the villagers, having been to a teacher training college. The villagers see she is pretty; the reader sees that she is vain and sly, bringing a chill breath of air into the idyll. But she is sensible enough to understand that rising socially by marrying the clergyman would not make her happy, and that she would do better by sticking to her own class. Both Hardy and Emma might have found ironies here, but if they did they kept silent, as Fancy did.

There is no sense of strain in the finished narrative, and there is a joyful account of the Christmas dance in the village, where Dick woos Fancy almost without words but instead with his concentrated physical energy during a long evening of festivities, up and down the country dance sets, urging the band to keep playing and holding her tighter and tighter in his arms until – as he remembers it afterwards – she was 'so close to me that not a sheet of paper could have been slipped between us'. They have reached a point where they understand one another's hopes and intentions – 'Fancy was now held so closely, that Dick and she were practically one person' – and after this he is not likely to lose her.[7]

Hardy modelled Mellstock on Stinsford and Bockhampton: the Dewys live in his family home, and Mrs Dewy grills bacon at the fireplace as Mrs Hardy did; but Dick Dewy is not his father and still less is he Hardy himself. He may, however, be what one part of Hardy would have liked to have been, because he loved dancing and listed it among the great things of life:

> The dance it is a great thing,
>   A great thing to me,
> With candles lit and partners fit
>   For night-long revelry . . .[8]

He and Emma do not seem to have danced together. The circumstances of their courtship did not give them the occasion. Neither had a supporting community which would welcome the other into it, and, even if Helen had offered to play for them to dance in the hall at St Juliot, Emma's lameness may have made it impossible for her.[9] A different sort of gently erotic scene between Dick and Fancy, when they wash their hands in the same bowl, could have been drawn from Cornwall experience, perhaps in the conservatory, where Emma was in charge. Hardy describes Dick's pleasure and Fancy's awareness that the mixing of fingers was vaguely improper: 'It being the first time in his life that he had touched female fingers under water, Dick duly registered the sensation as rather a nice one. "Really, I hardly know which are my own hands and which are yours, they have got so mixed up together," she said, withdrawing her own very suddenly. "It doesn't matter at all," said Dick, "at least as far as I am concerned." '[10]

The most entertaining character in the book is Fancy's step-mother, Jane Day, a woman who is 'terrible deep', as we are told by her husband. Hardy was writing just after the death of Dickens, whom he admired, and Mrs Day is his tribute to him, drawn with Dickensian exuberance. She celebrates Fancy's wedding day by ' "Claning out all the upstairs drawers and cupboards, and dusting the second-best chainey – a thing that's only done once a year. 'If there's work to be done I must do it,' says she, 'wedding or no.' " '[11] She appears suddenly from upstairs halfway through a meal her husband and daughter have laid out in the kitchen to lament that people would be saying 'that Jane Day's tablecloths be as poor and ragged as any union beggar's' and fetches a damask tablecloth which she unfolds and spreads by instalments, moving aside the plates and dishes as the meal goes on. After this she brings down her good cutlery, polishes it up and puts it on the table; then she takes away the teapot, cups and saucers, and brings a silver teapot and china cups. ' "Very strange woman, isn't she?" said Geoffrey, quietly going on with his dinner . . . "Ay, she's very quare: you'd be amazed to see what valuable goods we've got stowed away upstairs." ' Mr Day's straight-faced acceptance of her behaviour is as nicely done as Mrs Day's advanced eccentricity. There is no one quite like her in the rest of Hardy, perhaps because she has strayed in from another writer's imagination.

The beauty and precision of the descriptive writing is admirable, from the starlit beginning among the winter trees, each endowed with its distinct sighing voice, to the finale, when 'the landscape appears embarrassed with the sudden weight and brilliancy of its leaves . . . when the apple-trees have bloomed, and the roads and orchard-grass become spotted with fallen petals.'[12] And from its publication on there have always been readers who go to Hardy primarily for this: a plunge into the Dorset woodlands, streams and rivers, fields and meadows, cottages and churches, soft skies and birdsong. As the *British Quarterly* pronounced in 1881, 'the book is delightful because the sweet and liberal air of Dorset blows through it, because a county little known to the world beyond it, but loved well by those who are Dorset born, or have made it their home, is lovingly presented in all its pleasant aspects, its rough frank life, its genuine English language, the fair scenery of its woods and wolds.'[13]

An idea for another novel was already in his mind, this time a love story with a tragic theme. He thought of calling it 'A winning tongue had he', a line taken from the ballad 'By the Banks of Allan Water', in which a soldier with an eloquent tongue seduces and abandons the miller's daughter, who dies of grief. Its setting would be north Cornwall, which would mean many happy consultations with Emma. To be involved with his work gave her a sense that she was important to him during their long separations, and he needed her encouragement. Travelling back to Dorset in early June, he had the unpleasant experience of seeing copies of *Desperate Remedies* being sold at a reduced price on the bookstall in Exeter Station. Any chance of getting back his £75 now seemed small. He wrote to Tinsley urging him to advertise, the first salvo in a lifelong campaign of pushing his publishers into promoting his books effectively. In Weymouth, still in Crickmay's office, he went on working frenetically and writing whenever he could fit it in. In July he marked lines from *Macbeth* in his Shakespeare: 'Things at their worst will cease, or else climb upward / To what they were before.' By August he had a finished manuscript of *Under the Greenwood Tree* and posted it straight off to Macmillan.

The same old game began again. Morley liked the book, commenting on the careful, natural, delicate writing and harmony of construction and treatment, but now thought Hardy should study George Sand. The firm was hesitant, keeping the manuscript but doing nothing about it. Hardy had to write to them again in October, when he was at St Juliot once more, and this time Alexander Macmillan answered with a lukewarm letter, saying they could not do it for Christmas, but 'if you should not arrange otherwise before the spring I should like to have the opportunity of deciding as to whether we could do it for an early summer or spring book. I return the MS.'[14] This was the third book he had offered Macmillan, only to be half encouraged and then effectively rejected.

His disappointment turned to anger, and he says he threw the manuscript into a box and declared he might as well give up the struggle to become a writer. It was Emma who urged him to stick to writing, believing it to be his true vocation. Her attitude touched him deeply. He saw that she was prepared to 'set herself aside altogether – architecture obviously being the quick way to an income for marrying on' and decided he must think of *her* interests, which meant earning enough for them to marry and ignoring her selfless advice.[15] That winter he gave the best of his energies to architecture.

So things continued for another six months, Hardy and Emma exchanging letters, Hardy working through Christmas and until Easter for Crickmay, when he decided to go to London again and was given a job assisting an examiner for the Royal Institute of British Architects. News of his cousin Tryphena was that, having finished her treacher training at Christmas, she had applied for and got a position as headmistress of a primary school in Plymouth, with a salary of £100 a year. She was twenty, Hardy nearly thirty-two. If Hardy knew, or reflected on, their relative situations, he may have laughed.

But now things began to change. In April he asked Tinsley for an account of his earnings. Tinsley invited him round, gave him various small payments and wanted to know if he had anything else to show him. He remembered that Hardy had indicated in the autumn that he had another book planned. Hardy wrote home for the manuscript of *Under the Greenwood Tree*. Tinsley read it in a week and made an offer of £30 for the copyright. It was an outrageously low offer, but Hardy accepted. The copyright remained with Tinsley and his successors until after Hardy's death.

He corrected the proofs of *Under the Greenwood Tree* late at night, after his day's work. It was published on 15 June 1872 in two volumes, anonymously again, and immediately well reviewed, with especial praise for its freshness and originality. Tinsley now needed a serial for the magazine he put out monthly, and asked Hardy if he had anything else; Hardy agreed to let him have 'A winning tongue had he', although he had only five chapters completed. The first instalment had to appear in September, which meant he had to give up all his other work and turn out copy as fast as he could, but he was being paid £200.

In this way Hardy began his long career as a writer for serialization, which paid so much better than book publication at first. He renamed his current project *A Pair of Blue Eyes* and took the manuscript with him when he set off for Cornwall in early August, this time making the journey by sea, aboard a mail packet boat leaving from London Bridge; the voyage gave him useful copy for the serial. This time he was going to meet Emma at her father's home, Kirland House, near Bodmin, and he asked to have the next set of proofs sent there. Professionally, his star was rising at last, and he felt he could go confidently to Mr Gifford and speak of his wish to marry his daughter. He already had an idea for another novel which was to be *Far from the Madding Crowd*.

Nobody who was at Kirland House when Hardy and John Gifford met ever described or discussed what happened, but the upshot was that Hardy left the house and never communicated with either of Emma's parents again. Plainly Mr Gifford, on meeting him and learning of his family background, refused to countenance his marriage to Emma. He seems also to have made some accusations against him, because Hardy later used the word 'slander' without explaining further.[16] This absolute rejection by Emma's parents, attributable entirely to class snobbery and kept up for the rest of their lives, was another wounding humiliation that had long-lasting effects. For Emma it was a blow, painful no doubt, but nothing was going to deflect her now. She showed her spirit, ignored her father's outburst and appears to have left the house with Hardy. They went to stay with old friends of hers, the Sergeants – Captain Charles, his wife, Jane, and their children – at St Benet's Abbey in Lanivet, and from there they went on to St Juliot. The Holders, who took a different view of Emma's romance from John Gifford, made them welcome, and Hardy was given Mr Holder's seal of approval by being invited to read the lessons in St Juliot Church, morning and evening, on Sunday, 8 September. This may have given him some private amusement, but it was important to have someone in her family ready to countenance their engagement.

Hardy said later that when Emma was living in Cornwall 'and playing the harmonium in the church she had no religious opinions whatever – was, in fact, an Agnostic'.[17] It is his only mention of her indifference to religion in the days when he first knew her, and, if it was so, it would have been an important secret bond between them. She may have been influenced against religious belief earlier by her father's 'secular quotations and remarks' and encouraged further in this direction when Hardy talked to her about his freethinking ideas, or she may have simply wanted to please him by agreeing with them.[18] Living in a rectory, she naturally conformed to religious observance, and not only by playing the harmonium. In one of the few fragments he quoted from a letter of hers later in 1872, she speaks of believing what she can't understand in the Bible 'in a lump of simple faith', which does not exactly suggest agnosticism.[19] It looks as though she fluctuated between belief and disbelief, now influenced by Hardy in one direction, now reverting to the conventional norm and the prayers she learnt as a child. Later in life she returned to her mother's Low Church Protestantism and decided to be shocked by Hardy's atheism, which may be why he felt it worth recalling her earlier lack of faith.[20]

Hardy stayed on at St Juliot until mid September, absorbing the details he needed for the setting of his novel and consulting Emma on points of womanly behaviour and etiquette. The first instalment had already appeared in *Tinsleys' Magazine*, anonymously but 'By the Author of *Under the Greenwood Tree* and *Desperate Remedies* etc.', and he had to keep going fast. But he was writing well and confidently, with the comfortable thought that he had another good novel gestating in his head. When a letter came from Professor T. Roger Smith at the Institute of British Architects offering him more work in his office, he decided he could afford to refuse it.

This was the turning point in his professional life. He had made the leap into being a full-time writer. He was thirty-two, and he knew it might not last, but it was a great moment. He went home to Bockhampton and was able to give himself up entirely to writing. *Under the Greenwood Tree* got a good short review in the *Spectator* in November, and there was a stirring of interest in the

literary world. Later in the month the editor of the *Cornhill* magazine, Leslie Stephen, asked Moule for Hardy's address and wrote
to him saying 'it was long since he had received more pleasure
from a new writer' as he had from *Under the Greenwood Tree*, and
asking him if he would like to do a serial for the *Cornhill*. Hardy
wrote back explaining that he was busy at present but outlining
his idea for a novel about a young woman farmer, a shepherd and
a cavalry sergeant. Stephen approved and suggested a meeting, but
for the moment Hardy held back. He had been invited by Holder
to Cornwall for Christmas and the New Year, and naturally
accepted.

After Christmas with his beloved he was home in Bockhampton,
writing steadily. In March he sent off the last instalment of *A Pair
of Blue Eyes*, and in May it was published in three-volume form
by Tinsley Brothers, for the first time under his own name. It is a
book that charms the reader from the start, with its setting – the
wild northern coast of Cornwall – and its heroine, Elfride, the
daughter of the parsonage who writes her widowed father's sermons for him and lives as free as air, riding when and wherever
she likes on her horse, and busily composing a romantic novel
when she is not enjoying Tennyson. She is wooed by a young
visiting architect, Stephen Smith, who at first impresses her father
as a gentleman and is then rudely turned out of the house when it
appears he is merely the son of a builder. The resemblance to
Hardy's own Cornish experiences is obvious, but *A Pair of Blue
Eyes* is only passingly autobiographical, because Stephen leaves for
India and faithless Elfride meets and prefers his older friend and
mentor, Henry Knight. The scenes between Elfride and her two
successive lovers are wittily done, and Elfride is well drawn, a
clever, impetuous and independent young woman who yet allows
herself to be subjugated by the older, highly educated and pompous
Knight. He gives as his opinion of women that the best thing to
hear about one is 'not that she is writing but that she has married,
after which you hear no more about her' – a view shared by
many Victorian men. To Hardy's contemporaries, Knight, with
his insistence that a young woman may not be intellectually aspiring
and must be chaste, seemed like a sensible fellow, but Hardy's own

view was certainly closer to the modern one. In fact, Elfride can be seen as a predecessor of Tess, a woman cast off for no good reason by a lover who does not deserve her.

The book also contains one of the most surprising scenes in Victorian fiction. Knight slips on a cliff edge, along which he and Elfride have been walking in the rain, and finds himself clinging by his fingers and likely to fall to his death while she thinks how to rescue him. She is clever and bold enough to take off all her underwear, tear it into strips and make it into a rope to drag him back to safety. When he is safe, they embrace, full of relief and joy, but she is so embarrassed by her nakedness under a damp dress that she runs off home without him. He is left observing how very small she looks minus the usual layers of underclothing – 'small as an infant', he thinks. Hardy was raising a question which must have puzzled many young men at that time: what was the real shape and size of a fashionably dressed young lady? It was one no other writer of the period felt able to consider, and Hardy's readiness to do so shows what an original approach he had. The book bogs down into too much plot, as serialized novels tended to, but it is fresh enough to let you see why two poets, Tennyson and Coventry Patmore, said it was their favourite among Hardy's novels.

The reviews were generally good, some excellent. This did not prevent Horace Moule's brother Charles writing to Hardy – who had perhaps asked his advice – with the classic suggestion that he would be wiser to keep up some sort of steady professional work. The postscript to his letter is a fine example of social anxiety and snobbery rolled into one: 'I trust I address you rightly on the envelope. I conjectured that you wd prefer the absence of the "Esqre" at Upper Bockhampton.' What did this mean? That Hardy could not be a gentleman at his parents' house, whatever he might achieve in the world? Essentially, Charles Moule was backing John Gifford's view of things. It helps us to understand what Hardy had to take on in battling his way towards acceptance in middle-class society. The Moules were friendlier than the Giffords, but the note of patronage was always there. Horace Moule also sent an ineffably condescending letter, however well meant his correction of the

cast list Hardy had placed at the start of *A Pair of Blue Eyes*: 'Why
would you put Spenser Hugo Luxellian a Lord and not Spenser
Hugo, Lord Luxellian . . . Mind – I've read next to nothing as yet.
P.S. You understand the *woman* infinitely better than the *lady* –
and how gloriously you have idealized here and there, as far as I
have got. Yr slips of taste, every now and then, I ought to say
point-blank at once, are *Tinsleyan*.'[21] Hardy made the correction
to Lord Luxellian, but the Moule superiority was losing its power
to crush now that he was beginning to be successful in England
and about to be published in the United States for the first time.
In June, *Under the Greenwood Tree* appeared from the New York
firm of Holt & Williams. It was serialized there the following year,
and Hardy rose swiftly to popularity with the American reading
public.

The year continued well. He and Emma made plans to meet in
June in Bath, where she would be staying with an elderly lady
friend, Miss d'Arville, who could chaperone them. Before that he
delivered a few finished chapters and an outline of more of *Far
from the Madding Crowd* to Leslie Stephen. Hardy was in London
for a few days and dined with Moule, who was going to work as
a Poor Law inspector in Ipswich. They agreed to meet in Cambridge in five days' time. Hardy's brother Henry joined him in
town for a few days of sightseeing. Then Hardy made his first visit
to Cambridge, where he had once thought of applying as a student.
It was an intense experience. Cambridge is so perfect architec-
turally, the colleges placed along the river with their green courts
and gardens, that it can seem more like a dream than a real place.
Term was over, and Moule was in rooms in his old college,
Queens', in the heart of the town, between the river and the main
street, King's Parade. Hardy was given a guest room, dined in hall
and had a glimpse of the privileged academic life. It was 20 June,
midsummer, flawless weather:

By evening train to Cambridge. Stayed in College – Queen's [*sic*] –
Went out with H.M.M. after dinner. A magnificent evening: sun over
'the Backs'. / Next morning went with H.M.M. to King's Chapel early.
M. opened the great West doors to show the interior vista: we got upon

the roof where we could see Ely Cathedral gleaming in the distant sunlight. A never-to-be-forgotten morning. H.M.M. saw me off for London. His last smile.[22]

Hardy went happily on to Bath, where Emma awaited him, and they explored the city and its surroundings, going to Tintern Abbey and the Wye Valley, Chepstow and Clifton, during their ten days. Miss d'Arville did not feel obliged to accompany them, but Emma had to be returned to her house every evening. One night Hardy sat up on Beechen Cliff, overlooking Bath, through the short hours of darkness – 'Last eveglow loitering in the sky.' He thought of her in the sleeping city below, and how he would like to 'walk the world' with her, and how she matched 'the maddest dream's desire' – and wrote a poem saying so.[23]

9. Easy to Die

From Bath he went home to Bockhampton and settled down to write *Far from the Madding Crowd*. It is the warmest and sunniest of his novels. He tells us that some of it was written out of doors, on scraps of slate or stone, pieces of wood and even dead leaves, which is hard to imagine – how much can you write on a dead leaf? – but also absurdly appropriate to the rural setting of the book, and the storm scene was actually written during a night of thunder and lightning.[1]

It is a near-perfect mid-Victorian romance – Hardy intended it to be a contemporary story – with a heroine who challenges Victorian assumptions about young women through her natural energy. Bathsheba Everdene is autonomous, active, prepared to choose her own men and possessed of a strong erotic will of her own, characteristics usually allocated to bad women in nineteenth-century fiction. Several contemporary critics took against her: Henry James thought Hardy's depiction of her 'vague and coarse', and Andrew Lang found himself unmoved by her 'character and mischances' and thought she was not a 'firmly designed character'.[2] Perhaps they missed the originality of some of the ideas Hardy makes her express, among them 'it is difficult for a woman to define her feelings in language which is chiefly made by men to express theirs' – an idea hardly heard about again until the late twentieth century – and disapproved of her 'I *hate* to be thought men's property.'[3]

Although everyone in the parish where Bathsheba settles thinks she speaks like a lady, she is not a lady but the daughter of a country tailor, several times bankrupted and now dead. She has had some education but was considered 'too wild to be a governess'.[4] She is quite capable of running the farm she inherits from an uncle, and she is brave and bold, in contrast with her meek, passive, crushed rival in love, Fanny Robin. Bathsheba rides a horse with pleasure, not wearing a riding habit or using a side saddle like Elfride but astride 'in the manner . . . hardly expected of the woman', and is able to perform the acrobatic feat of dropping 'backwards flat upon the pony's back, her head over its tail, her feet against its shoulders and her eyes to the sky' as she rides beneath some low branches.[5] She also has the courage to open the coffin in which the dead Fanny has been laid, prising it open herself, because she wants to know whether there is a baby inside beside her rival.

Bathsheba is intelligent, playful and vain. At the start of the book both Hardy and his hero, Gabriel Oak, adopt a gently patronizing masculine stance towards her, but it is soon blown away. She feels herself entitled by her beauty, her position and her character to assert her own will in most matters. ' 'Tis the toss of the head, the sweep of the shoulder, and the dare of the woman in general' is how one of her labourers sums her up, adding, 'she said a man's Damn to Liddy when the pantry shelf fell down with all the jam-pots upon it.'[6] When she finds her bailiff stealing, 'She flewed at him like a cat – never such a tom-boy as she is.'[7] At the corn market, she argues, holds to her own prices and persistently beats down the prices of other farmers, winning their respect.[8] Love makes her lose her command and good sense, and she is chastened by her own mistakes but not defeated. Hardy does not condescend to her, as he does to Fancy and to Elfride, but instead seems to feel with her, giving her an irresistible intensity. Bathsheba starts as a girl and becomes a woman; she suffers and blooms at the same time. Some of the glow of his love for Emma is there in the writing, and you may wonder if he is offering her a picture of what he most admired in a woman: strength, high spirits, passion, and the power to recover from setbacks and mistakes. Bathsheba, with her dark eyes and hair, and her red jacket, careless of convention and in charge of her own life, is plainly not Emma, but at the same time she shares some of her enthusiasms, notably horse riding – something Hardy himself had never mastered.

If the setting was meant to be contemporary, the criticism it provoked was justified: that it painted much too pleasant a picture of farming conditions in Dorset in the 1870s. Hardy presents rural events and tragedies – the sheep driven over the edge, the ricks on

fire, the dishonest bailiff – and shows a hiring fair where Oak
fails to find work; but, as Andrew Lang remarked in his review,
'The country folk in the story have not heard of strikes, or of Mr
Arch; they have, to all appearance, plenty to eat, and warm clothes
to wear.'[9] When Joseph Arch, who travelled round England
organizing agricultural workers into unions, visited Dorset in
1873, he found 'the condition of the labourers in that county as
bad as it very well could be'.[10] The early 1870s were a low point
for agricultural workers all over England. Arch attended the
Dorchester Candlemas Fair in February 1873, and Hardy heard
him speak, either then or on a similar occasion. Arch spoke again
to an assembly of nearly 1,000 men and women on Fordington
Green, against the system of hiring labourers by the year.[11] In his
own account of his experiences, Arch wrote that

labourers were no better than toads under a harrow . . . We labourers
had no lack of lords and master. There were the parson and his wife at
the rectory. There was the squire, with his hand of iron overshadowing
us all. There was no velvet glove on that hard hand, as many a poor man
found to his hurt. He brought it down on my father because he would
not sign for a small loaf and a dear one . . . At the sight of the squire the
people trembled.[12]

Arch was recalling his own family's experiences in Warwickshire,
but the power of squire and parson over the poor was much the
same in all rural areas.

   This is not the world as described in *Far from the Madding Crowd*.
How much does it matter? Not much more than Shakespeare's
Arden representing no real part of France. Although Hardy has
been read as a realist, he was not producing documentaries but
writing fiction, and in this instance romantic fiction. He himself
wrote, in his preface to the edition of 1912, that it was 'partly real,
partly dream-country'. His characters and scenes are conjured out
of his imagination. There is poverty, cold, hunger, the workhouse
and early death in its pages, but not for the labourers, only for
Fanny, who has dropped out of the community. There are setbacks,
notably for Gabriel Oak, who thinks seriously of emigrating, as so

many were doing, Hardy's cousins among them; but he is able to overcome his problems through patience, diligence and love. There is no harsh squire, and what is heard of the vicar from his parishioner Jan Coggan is more favourable than you might expect from Hardy. Coggan is explaining why he will not desert church for chapel: 'when every one of my potatoes were frosted our Parson Thirdly were the man who gave me a sack for seed, though he hardly had one for his own use, and no money to buy 'em. If it hadn't been for him I shouldn't have had a tatie to put in my garden. D'ye think I'd turn after that?'[13]

In his determination to succeed, Hardy set out to write a novel of rural life that would please Leslie Stephen and the readers of the *Cornhill*. A grim picture of destitution and rage against oppression would not have done so. *The Poor Man and the Lady* had failed to find a publisher, so a novel devoted to the plight of the Dorset labourers and to the landowners and parsons who oppressed them was not likely to fare any better. Hardy made his chorus of villagers content with their lot, and their lot on the whole easy. He also made them comical, but at the same time he was anxious that they should not be seen entirely as figures of fun and asked his publishers to make sure the illustrator understood that the 'rustics, although *quaint*, may be made to appear *intelligent*, & *not boorish* at all'.[14] He knew he was treading a fine line, risking disloyalty to his own people by presenting a version of them intended to amuse educated readers. His uncles and cousins might remain blissfully ignorant, but his mother was another matter. The question of loyalty would be taken up in his next novel, *The Hand of Ethelberta*.

Some of the most striking passages in *Far from the Madding Crowd* are again the meticulous observations of the natural world. One describes standing on a hillside in midwinter, with a clear sky above, when the different colours of the stars are perceptible and the 'kingly brilliance of Sirius pierced the eye with a steely glitter, the star called Capella was yellow, Aldebaran and Betelgueux shone with a fiery red. To persons standing alone on a hill during a clear midnight such as this – the roll of the world eastward is almost a palpable movement . . . whatever its origin, the impression of riding along is vivid and abiding.'[15] This can be written only from personal experience, and allows us to think of Hardy taking a wintry night walk from Bockhampton, riding the world and sensing its roll eastward.

In another passage he writes of the splendour of buildings like the ancient barn used for sheep shearing:

The dusky, filmed, chestnut roof, braced and tied in by huge collars, curves and diagonals, was far nobler in design because more wealthy in material than nine-tenths of those in our modern churches ... One could say about this barn, what could hardly be said of either the church or the castle, its kindred in age and style, that the purpose which had dictated its original erection was the same with that to which it was still applied. Unlike and superior to either of those two typical remnants of mediaevalism, the old barn embodied practices which had suffered no mutilation at the hands of time ... the mind dwelt upon its past history, with a satisfied sense of functional continuity throughout, a feeling almost of gratitude, and quite of pride, at the permanence of the idea which had heaped it up ... So the barn was natural to the shearers, and the shearers were in harmony with the barn.[16]

Hardy takes the barn as his text to give us his credo concerning functionalism, architecture and the value of continuity. His words were true and powerful when he wrote them, but sadly they have become historical and melancholy for us, now that barn and labourers have both lost their function.

Only occasionally are there weak pages where Hardy falls into a plod, for example giving Sergeant Troy a flat introductory chapter headed 'The New Acquaintance Described'. An editor might have protested, but Leslie Stephen accepted the three pages of prosing, and their dullness is quickly redeemed by the next chapters showing Troy in action, first in conversation and then with his sword. Once read, the scene in the hollow among the ferns where he woos Bathsheba by outlining and enclosing her body with his dazzling sword play is never forgotten. Here Hardy the poet is at work, conjuring up a perfect metaphor for seduction, his imagination allowing him to *be* Troy as he slices off a curl and spits a caterpillar on Bathsheba's bosom, and also to be Bathsheba, shedding a helpless stream of tears when Troy kisses her and leaves her. As J. M. Barrie wrote, making up for earlier critics' dismissal, fifteen years after the book's publication,

He does not draw a male flirt to show that the species are contemptible, but because there are male flirts; nor are the two terrible scenes, Fanny's death and Bathsheba opening the coffin, introduced to warn womankind against the Troys ... Never until Troy was shown at work had we learned from fiction how such a being may mesmerize a bewitching and clever woman into his arms. Many writers say their Troys do it, but Mr Hardy shows it being done.[17]

Hardy worked steadily through the summer. In September he planned to walk over the heath to the annual sheep fair at Wood-bury Hill to pick up some local colour for his book. The fair was an ancient one, held over a week every autumn above the small town of Bere Regis, and Hardy thought nothing of taking on the twenty-six miles there and back on foot in the heat on the Sunday. Three days later, on 24 September, he heard from the Moule family that Horace was dead. His body was to be brought back from Cambridge to Fordington for the funeral.

He had cut his own throat, unable to face the cycle of depression and drinking in which he was caught. Anyone who has witnessed severe depression at close quarters knows how the sufferer is driven to prefer death to life on the terms on which he has to live it. No further explanation seems necessary for Horace Moule's final action. Feeling himself to be in crisis, he had summoned his brother Charles to Cambridge. It was still the long vacation, when the town was relatively empty. Charles came at once, and they sat talking in Horace's rooms in Queens' for three hours that evening. Then Horace, saying he felt ill, took himself to bed in the adjoining bedroom, while Charles remained in the outer sitting room, writing. He became aware of a noise, went into the bedroom and found his brother covered in blood. His first thought was that he must have burst a blood vessel. He ran to the porter's lodge and asked them to send for a doctor. When he got back to his brother, Horace said, 'Easy to die,' and 'Love to my mother.' They were his last words, and they have a touch of sublimity. The doctor found that he had cut his own throat, and when a nurse came she discovered the open razor he had used. Charles was able to arrange an inquest the next day, and presumably through his evidence a verdict of 'suicide whilst in a state of temporary insanity' was returned. It meant Horace could be buried in a churchyard.

It is a terrible story. How much of it was made plain to Hardy at first is not known, but the bare fact of the death was bad enough. The funeral was fixed for 26 September, and the day before he went out and sat on a weir on the River Frome, looking up at Fordington churchyard, where the newly dug grave had been prepared, not in the central part but in a side area a good way from the church. The spot is a beautiful one, high above the green open countryside and the river below, where Hardy sat that day. Years later he wrote a poem, 'Before My Friend Arrived', describing how he had looked up at the 'towered church on the rise' and made a drawing of the mound of white chalk taken from the ground to make the grave. Today the grave is covered in primroses in spring, and the Moule parents lie alongside their brilliant and unhappy son. Mrs Moule lost her sight in the year he died and followed him to the grave four years later.

Never again would Hardy have a friend who held his heart so wholly, and his last lesson was that death might be irresistible. Another wound was made that would never quite heal. But Hardy did not allow grief to distract him from his work. On 30 September he was able to send Leslie Stephen several further chapters of *Far from the Madding Crowd* and an outline of more. Stephen was so pleased with what he read that he offered Hardy £400 for the serial rights, twice what Tinsley had paid for *A Pair of Blue Eyes*. In October he asked if he might start running it in the *Cornhill* earlier than planned, in January 1874. Hardy agreed to this, although he knew it meant the early chapters would be appearing months before he could possibly finish the book, and he would be writing to close deadlines again. He also knew now that he could do it. Tinsley was pressing for another serial. Meanwhile *A Pair of*

Blue Eyes had been published in book form in America in July and
began to run serially in New York from September. All this brought
money, and money brought the prospect of marriage closer.
Although Emma's parents were now out of the picture since she
had broken with them, there was still his mother to be reconciled
to the idea. That autumn he helped his father with the cider-apple
gathering from the huge old trees in the garden: 'it was the last
time he ever took part in a work whose sweet smells and oozings
in the crisp autumn air can never be forgotten by those who have
had a hand in it.'[18] The two men were on good terms, and his
father on his own would no doubt have accepted Hardy's bride
whoever she was, but Jemima was a strong-minded woman, and
in this matter she had made up her mind. Miss Gifford was not the
right wife for her son. She was not a Dorset girl, she was well born
but penniless – poor gentry was the worst of all worlds – and she
was too old. For the moment Miss Gifford was still tucked away
in St Juliot.

In December, Hardy went to London to meet Leslie Stephen
for the first time. Having misunderstood an invitation to lunch, he
called at his house in South Kensington – 8 Southwell Gardens –
at a different time of day.

He welcomed me with one hand, holding back the barking 'Troy' [a
collie] with the other. The dog's name I, of course, had never heard till
then, and I said, 'That is the name of my wicked soldier-hero.' He
answered caustically: 'I don't think my Troy will feel hurt at the coincidence, if yours doesn't.' I rejoined, 'There is also another coincidence.
Another Leslie Stephen lives near here, I find.' 'Yes,' he said, 'he's the
spurious one.'[19]

Hardy decided to like him when he explained that he had played
as a child with his nurse in the fields near his present house, all
now being built over. 'I felt then that I liked him, which at first I
had doubted. The feeling never changed.'[20] Stephen was the same
age as Horace Moule, with a similar if more achieved educational
background, and in one way he stepped easily into Moule's role
as mentor and critic, and with real power of literary patronage;

but, although he returned Hardy's liking, he did not have Moule's charm.

Leslie Stephen's fame today rests largely on being the editor of the original *Dictionary of National Biography* and the father of Virginia Woolf, but in 1873 he had not yet embarked on the first project or attached himself to the mother of his renowned daughter. In fact, he was married to Thackeray's daughter Minny, and her sister Anny shared their house. Hardy remembers meeting both sisters at lunch the day after his first call on Stephen, and how they sat over the fire, the ladies wrapped in shawls against the cold, and talked about Thackeray, Carlyle, Browning, the Bible and Voltaire. The Stephens gave a dinner for Hardy later, described in a letter by Minny Stephen to her sister, who was away on the Isle of Wight. Minny said, 'the evening was a wild chaos. I tried to drown my cares in drink but it only affected my *feet* and not my head. Mr Hardy is a very damp young man and dampness I abominate.'[21] No doubt Hardy was nervous and trying too hard, faced with a daughter of the great Thackeray. Her remark was snobbish: a gentleman is not damp.

Stephen was as dry as a gentleman should be. He was very tall, his mouth and chin were concealed within a fuzz of whiskery hair, and above this was a long, prominent nose and shrewd, small eyes. His world was as different from Hardy's as it could be. Everything Hardy had to struggle for, mostly in vain, had been given to him: education, leisure, congenial friends and colleagues, the confidence that comes from knowing your family belongs among the intellectual elite of England. It was natural for them to send their sons to Eton and Cambridge, and at Cambridge Stephen had become a Fellow of his college, charged with the intellectual and moral guidance of the young gentlemen coming up from their public schools. He was an enthusiastic rowing coach, famous for his thirty-mile walks, and he relished the bachelor rituals of college life. He had taken holy orders, as was expected, and it had needed courage for him to acknowledge that he could no longer believe in the Christian doctrine he was supposed to uphold, and to leave his comfortable college and launch himself at the age of thirty into the choppy waters of literary journalism. Still, he knew almost everybody who mattered in London, had a small private income, was able to live in Kensington with his mother and continued to enjoy regular visits to his college, even drawing his stipend until his marriage in 1867. His chief passion was mountaineering in the Alps, and he was able to indulge it pretty often.

He had been settled in London for ten years when Hardy met him and editing the *Cornhill* for the last two, at a salary of £500 a year. The proprietor, George Smith, was a friend. It was a magazine intended for middle-class, middle-brow families, and it avoided politics, religion and anything that might offend. 'Thou shalt not shock a young lady' was the first commandment the editor had to enforce.[22] Stephen commissioned good writers and wrote articles himself, but he did not make a success of it, and the circulation fell steadily under his editorship. Hardy knew nothing of this, of course, only that Thackeray had edited the *Cornhill* and that it had a great reputation. He found that Stephen was a conscientious editor, but that he took his obligation to forestall any possibility of giving offence to lady readers to heart. In March he wrote anxiously to Hardy, 'Troy's seduction of the young woman will require to be treated in a gingerly fashion, when, as I suppose must be the case, he comes to be exposed to his wife? I mean that the thing must be stated but that the words must be careful – excuse this wretched shred of concession to popular stupidity; but I am a slave.'[23] In April he followed this up with 'I have some doubts whether the baby is necessary at all . . . perhaps if the omission were made it might be restored on republication . . . should somehow be glad to omit the baby.'[24] Fanny's baby, and the climactic scene in which Bathsheba discovers it in the coffin, was duly cropped for the *Cornhill*. Different views have been taken of how much Stephen minded making a change which damaged the book as badly as this one, but he was under pressure from Grundian complaints, and he can be given the benefit of the doubt. It remained exasperating for Hardy, who restored the passage for book publication and pointed out to Stephen that *The Times* singled out for praise the passage that had been cut. Stephen replied impatiently, 'I spoke as an editor, not as a man. You have no more consciousness of these things than a child.'[25] Hardy may have reflected privately that

Stephen had written in 1873, 'The one duty which at the present moment seems to be of paramount importance, is the duty of perfect intellectual sincerity' and 'Let us think freely and speak plainly, and we shall have the highest satisfaction that man can enjoy.'[26] On the other hand, Hardy understood that he was still an apprentice writer and wrote to Stephen in the course of discussing cuts, 'for the present circumstances lead me to wish merely to be considered a good hand at a serial.'[27]

After Hardy's meetings with Stephen and his family in December 1873 he went to Cornwall for a Christmas visit. He had kept the title of *Far from the Madding Crowd* secret from Emma, in order to surprise her, he explained, and it was only as he was leaving in January that she saw the first instalment in the *Cornhill*. It was presented anonymously, as all its serials were, but it was evidence of his literary success, and the auguries for their being able to marry were now good. At the same time he had retreated from discussing or sharing his work with her. She may have enjoyed the surprise of the title, but she must also have noticed that this time she had been excluded from the process of choosing it. Hardy's view of how helpful she could be with his work was not quite the same as hers. Later in the year she wrote to him with a touch of sadness, 'My work, unlike your work of writing, does not occupy my true mind much . . . Your novel seems sometimes like a child, all your own and none of me.'[28]

He had been working supremely hard in order to succeed so that he and Emma could be married. Now, as a result of this intense dedication to his work, the world was opening out for him, and he began to have the chance to meet people he found interesting. Emma, who had so dazzled him, may have begun to seem less extraordinary. On his return to Bockhampton, he was invited to dine with a neighbouring family, that of the Revd Reginald Smith, rector of West Stafford, and his wife, Geneviève. At their house he had once been offered a glass of milk as a schoolboy. Now they were aware of his literary success. Their son Bosworth was teaching at Harrow, and their two daughters,

Evangeline and Blanche, were both bookish. This was a notable social occasion for Hardy, the first formal invitation he had received from any member of the Dorset gentry. He went on his own, and the butler who served at table that evening was the father of Cassie Pole, with whom he had flirted in London. If it was a disconcerting situation for butler and guest – the butler is said to have resented it – it passed without anyone else being aware of it, and the next day Hardy sent a copy of *A Pair of Blue Eyes* to Mrs Smith, with a note of thanks for her hospitality, saying it had a 'peculiar charm' for him as a writer, the more so since he had been 'denied by circumstances until very lately the society of educated womankind, which teaches men what cannot be acquired from books, and is indeed the only antidote to that bearishness which one gets into who lives much alone'.[29]

He had London invitations too. In April the Stephens introduced him to George Smith, publisher and proprietor of the *Cornhill*, and in May to Helen Paterson, the young artist who was illustrating *Far from the Madding Crowd*; also to Mrs Procter, a lively and remarkable old woman who had known everybody, her stepfather having been a friend of Wordsworth and Coleridge, Mary Wollstonecraft and William Godwin.[30] Hardy greatly enjoyed her company. He also developed a *tendresse* for Helen Paterson on the one hand and Anny Thackeray on the other. Meanwhile he was preparing to be married to Emma.

And where was Emma? A mystery hangs over her whereabouts during 1874, which neither Hardy nor Emma ever chose to explain. The inscription he wrote for her memorial stone in St Juliot Church stated that she had lived at St Juliot until 1873. His last visit to Cornwall was made for Christmas 1873, and they were not married until September 1874. She wrote in her recollections that 'I went as a country cousin to my brother in London', but she gave no dates. Did she live with Walter for nine months? Did she go to friends? There was no reconciliation with her parents. Hardy was at Bockhampton for much of the early part of the year, with visits to London in April and in May. In late May he arranged a passport for himself and his wife 'travelling on Continent'. This was four months before it was needed.

A poem called 'The Change', written in early 1913 among the other poems recalling the time of his courtship of Emma, describes her arrival unaccompanied at what appears to be a London railway station. It sounds like a winter scene, with its 'murks of night' and 'lamps wanning her face':

Mid murks of night I stood to await her,
And the twanging of iron wheels gave out the signal that she was
      come.

. . . She said with a travel-tired smile,
   Half scared by scene so strange;
She said, outworn by mile on mile,
   The blurred lamps wanning her face the while,
'O Love, I am here; I am with you!' . . . Ah, that there should have
      come a change!

This suggests that Hardy met Emma in a place strange to her after a long railway journey made alone, very likely from Cornwall to London. Her sister and brother-in-law were unlikely to have agreed to her making such a journey alone to meet Hardy in London, which suggests further that there had been a falling out between Emma and the Holders. Had they been on good terms, it would have been natural for Emma to be married from their house. In fact, contact between the sisters seems to have been broken off for a time. Her journey must have been made between January and May 1874, but under what circumstances we can only guess. Hardy was absorbed in writing. He was much at home, where his mother's influence was felt, but sometimes in London, where he was experiencing the charms of the world into which Leslie Stephen had introduced him and meeting women he found attractive. Hardy wobbled, as happens during a long engagement, and thought he might have liked to woo Miss Paterson. She was quite uninterested in him and about to be married herself, to another writer, William Allingham, but Emma would have noticed a change of tone in his letters. If her journey to London was impulsive and meant to remind him of their engagement, it succeeded when in May he took out the passport for himself and wife. He says nothing about any of this in his memoirs, and Emma's own *Recollections* make her stay in London into a joke: 'I went as a country cousin to my brother in London, and was duly astonished, which gave him even more pleasure than it did me. I was rather bewildered with the size and lengths and distances, and very much embarrassed at going in an omnibus, which seemed a very undig-nified method of getting about.' Nothing about when, or how long her visit was, or how she occupied herself.

After Emma's and Hardy's deaths, his second wife put out various stories about Emma. One was that Emma's family put pressure on him to marry Emma. Another had Emma visit Bock-hampton alone to confront Hardy's parents.[31] Neither seems likely. A more probable scenario is that Emma began to worry that Hardy's affections might be wandering and told her sister she would like to go to London. Helen said, on no account, it is not done. Emma answered, I am going whatever you think, and let Hardy know she was coming. Hardy met her at the station. Now what? He could not take her to his lodgings. She had to go to her brother Walter, fortunately established in London, and stay there. The drama of the arrival fixed itself in Hardy's imagination and appeared in the poem.

Hardy applied for the passport for himself and wife to demon-strate his commitment, but he still had to go on writing *Far from the Madding Crowd*. He went back to Bockhampton to do so, remaining until July, when he returned to London. In August he brought the book to its conclusion with 'the most private, secret, plainest wedding that it's possible to have',[32] and at the beginning of September he wrote to Emma's uncle, the Revd Edwin Hamilton Gifford, a man in his fifties, Cambridge educated and at this time a Canon of Worcester, asking if he would officiate at his and Emma's wedding on 17 September. He also offered the Canon a bed at his own lodgings in Celbridge Place. Gifford declined the offer – he preferred Onslow Square, where he often stayed – but kindly declared, 'I shall be very happy to tie the knot for you', adding that he had left a little present of salt cellars and spoons for Emma, to be engraved at his expense.[33] It may have been their only wedding present. Hardy meanwhile was finishing a short story commissioned by the *New York Times*, 'Destiny and a Blue Cloak', which he posted off on 12 September. On the same day Canon Gifford wrote again, confirming that he would be at Chippenham Road, where Emma's brother lived, at 10.45 on the 17th and advising Hardy, who had evidently told him about his honeymoon plans, that Rouen was an expensive place.[34]

10. A Short Visit to the Continent

Hardy never wrote or spoke about his wedding to Emma. There is a short, serene account of the day by Emma in her *Recollections*, written some thirty-five years afterwards. 'The day we were married was a perfect September day – the 17th, 1874 – not brilliant sunshine, but wearing a soft, sunny luminousness; just as it should be.' Nothing more. At the time she wrote even less in her diary:

Married   *September 17th. 1874*
St Peter's Paddington from 54 Chippenham Rd. Westbourne Pk[1]

St Peter's Church was newly built and ugly, and must have been picked purely for its convenience, Elgin Avenue being within easy walking distance of Walter Gifford's house in Chippenham Road.[2] Canon Gifford's letter suggests that the ceremony took place in the morning. Emma was given away by her brother. The marriage certificate shows that Hardy's witness was the daughter of his landlady. Either he could find no friend or family, or he preferred not to ask any, out of shyness, or wanting to protect Emma. He put down his own and his father's occupations plainly as 'Author' and 'Builder'.

A line in Emma's diary has been scored over but seems to read 'Palace Hotel, Queen's Road', which could be where the small party had lunch, and almost certainly where she and Hardy spent their first night together before going on to Brighton.[3] The next entry is 'Brighton. Rough sea on Friday'. At Morton's Hotel in Brighton, Hardy wrote to his brother:

Dear Henry, I write a line to tell you all at home that the wedding took place yesterday, and that we are got as far as this on our way to Normandy and Paris. There were only Emma and I, her uncle who married us, and her brother, my landlady's daughter signed the book as one witness.

I am going to Paris for materials for my next story. Shall return the beginning of October . . . We sent an advertisement of the marriage to the Dorset Chronicle – Try to see it. Yours in haste / Tom.

Thanks for your good wishes.[4]

Hardy was never a florid letter writer, and this sticks to the barest facts, suggesting that Henry was at this point the only member of the family he felt inclined to write to.

If there was a celebratory lunch, if Emma looked beautiful with the soft, sunny light on her wedding dress, if she even wore a special dress, these things went unrecorded. Their happiness at being together at last after four and a half years of being in love and apart must be assumed. No need for a party, dancing, music, food and drink, neighbours, jokes, flowers, families. Yet weddings are not easy to negotiate without festivities of some kind, and Hardy, given a little encouragement, took pleasure in parties. The fact that when he came to write about his early love for Emma, calling up so many detailed memories in so many poems, he had nothing to say of either the wedding or the honeymoon makes you wonder whether the wedding seemed to him more like a necessary adjustment made to their circumstances than like the fulfilment of a dream, and whether the wedding trip was less full of tenderness and pleasure than he had hoped. Temperamentally, he was given to self-doubt after achieving long-cherished ambitions. It happened when he finished building his house, Max Gate, and was plunged into anxiety that he had done the wrong thing, and his wedding may have produced the same sort of reaction. Weddings demand buoyant spirits. Hardy was an anxious man and easily cast down. Away from Cornwall and buttressed by her clergyman uncle, Emma seemed less of a free spirit. His London acquaintance with the Stephens and their clever circle had by his own confession given a slight shake to his attachment to her, and she must have felt it. Whether both of them, having defied their parents, had regretful thoughts for them on the day, and whether lovemaking, at last licensed, was awkward for them, as for most newly married innocents, we shall never know, but there were many possible reasons for them to feel unsure of themselves. Yet they were doing what they had both dreamt of for four years and what he had worked for with unremitting dedication. Some sense of triumph and relief must have been in the air during their simple ceremony.

Emma's diary is a record of their travels, not of her feelings, and 'Tom' makes few appearances in it. They spent the weekend in Brighton, where, she notes, they visited the Aquarium and the Pavilion, and went out on to the old pier. On Sunday they went twice to church, rather surprisingly, and back to the Aquarium for more observation of turtles and seals. A cheerful note comes in with Paris in prospect: 'Brighton's Sunday is like a Parisian Sunday. All enjoyment gaiety and bands of music and excursionists.' On Monday 'Tom bathed' in spite of the rough sea; and in the evening they left for their Channel steamer and a choppy crossing to Dieppe. Once in Rouen she is in her element, describing the hotel, many details of the French dinner, among them 'Little pigeons delicate to a degree and salad eaten with it'; and the bedroom, 'night dresses laid out on bed . . . 2 *large* square pillows. Spring mattresses', and, as they sat writing, the chambermaid coming into their room in her white cotton jacket and short petticoats, smiling and chattering, and bearing a pail to go under the washstand.

Her delight in the trip grew as they reached Paris: 'Place de la Concorde first seen by moonlight! . . . Stars quite put out by Parisian lamps.' It was only three years since the Franco-Prussian War and the violence of the Commune, and they saw the half-destroyed Tuileries ('tells what a French mob can effect'). Otherwise tourist Paris was in good order, and they took trains to Versailles and Saint-Cloud, saw the Louvre and Notre-Dame, the Hôtel de Cluny, Napoleon's tomb and the morgue, so popular with Victorian visitors: 'Three bodies – middle one pink – Their clothes hanging above them. Not offensive but repulsive.' She was quick to notice children, cats also, the clothes and the flower shops, and she thought the working-class people of Paris very small, 'pigmies in fact', and the old women 'very *ugly* and dark – very fierce in the poorest streets'.

She also noticed that

Wherever I go, whoever I pass . . . the people gaze at me as much or more than I at them and their beautiful city . . . Query – Am I a *strange-looking* person – or merely picturesque in this hat – Women sometimes laugh a short laugh as they pass. Men stare – some stand – some look back or turn, look over their shoulders – look curiously, inquisitively – some . . . tenderly without my being mistaken – they do *in* a French manner.

As it is remarkable I note it –

Children gape too –

She does not say whether Hardy noticed people staring at her, or whether she asked him what he thought; there is nothing to suggest he teased her and they laughed about it together. He has simply disappeared from her narrative. But she loved the time spent in Paris, and on leaving on the last day of September she wrote, 'Adieu to Paris – Charmante ville / Adieu to the Boulevards. To the gay shops – To the "*gens*" sitting in the streets To the vivants enfants To the white caps of the femmes To the river and its boats To the clear atmosphere and brilliant colourings.'

Emma was a naive diarist, responsive to what she saw and fluent in a scatter-brained way. She makes you smile, sympathetically; and she shows her enjoyment of travel, but from our point of view she fails to seize her great opportunity – she might have been honeymooning with anyone, Hardy's presence being barely mentioned. No doubt there was an element of decorousness in this, and intimacy is hard to describe. His only surviving account of the trip is no better, written in old age and consisting of half a sentence mentioning 'a short visit to the Continent – their first Continental days having been spent at Rouen'.[5] On the train returning them to Rouen she continued to put down her impressions of Paris, remembering the white coats of the waiters on the boulevards, 'Blossom white – wonderfully pure and clean and smoothly starched and ironed'. Then, 'Thursday Oct – 1 – 1874 / Arrived at London – Dirty London. Very wet –'

They now had to begin their serious life together and establish themselves somewhere in England. Since neither possessed so much as a table, a chair or any household goods, they needed a furnished place. They looked in the south-west outer suburbs, Wimbledon and Denmark Hill, for cheapness, and after a few days took half a house in Surbiton, still mostly open country and farmland but with an efficient railway connection to central London. St David's Villa was a new double-fronted house with two staircases, a cellar, a carriage drive and a garden, and they would be sharing it with a retired brewer called Hughes, a friend of someone Hardy had known in Weymouth. Hughes had a wife, a small daughter and a dog.[6] There must also have been at least one servant to help out.

Emma had not been brought up to clean and cook, while Hardy had always been able to take for granted that he would be looked after by his mother or by landladies. Since during the years of their courtship they had spent only a few weeks together each year, almost always in holiday circumstances, they had a great deal to learn about each other and had to establish a domestic routine. There must have been shocks on both sides. Although Emma knew she was breaking away from her family and its traditions, her model of marriage came from her mother and her sister, both installed in their own well-appointed homes and always supported by servants. Hardy, on the other hand, had seen his grandmother and mother in charge of all the domestic activities at home, and when his mother was ill his aunt came to take over, and his sisters grew up learning household skills. Was Emma going to wash Hardy's linen? Out of the question. She could probably put together a light meal, but cooking and serving dinner would be outside her range.

The pattern of his days had to be that he wrote, and thought about his work, in a room set aside as his study. He may have read aloud to her some of what he had written during the day and given her pages to copy. Unfortunately the theme of the book he was now embarked on, planned before the wedding, did not appeal to her: it was the story of the social rise of the intelligent child of two servants. He would have appreciated the irony of the situation in theory but perhaps not in practice. How did she fill her days while he was working? She no longer had a horse to ride. Neither ever said what happened to Fanny, but Emma must have missed riding sadly. She had no piano either, no garden of her own, and no family or friends close by or inclined to visit. She read. A note in her diary listing knitting wool and crewel thread suggests she embroidered and knitted. They went for walks, and to church, and sometimes into London on the train together to go to a gallery or shop. She gave her orders to the servant. She thought about her own writing projects.

Their good fortune was that his books were selling well. Hardy began to be aware of the scale of his success only when he noticed ladies on the London train carrying copies of the just published two-volume edition of *Far from the Madding Crowd* with Mudie's Library labels on the covers. It became clear that his four years of bruising hard work had succeeded, and he was well able to keep Emma in comfort. In fact, there was no need for them to be living in Surbiton, a very modest setting for a popular writer. The winter of 1874 was cold, with snow, travelling was difficult, and there were no visits to or from families at Christmas. In the new year they decided to return to central London, and in March they moved to rooms in Newton Road, just north of Westbourne Grove and close to Emma's brother Walter. Hardy noted that all their worldly goods at this time fitted into four small packing cases, two full of books, one of books and linen, sundries in the fourth. It was not the way respectable middle-class couples were expected to start married life in the 1870s.

Before the move George Smith had advised Hardy to ask Tinsley to sell him back the copyright of *Under the Greenwood Tree*. Tinsley cannily put a price of £300, ten times what he had paid ('preposterous' said Smith) and threw in some criticism for good measure. 'I think your genius truer than Dickenses [*sic*] ever was, but you

want a monitor more than the great Novelist ever did. Apologising
for being so plain spoken.'[7] Hardy told Tinsley he was asking twice
what he was prepared to pay, and the matter lapsed. Meanwhile
the first edition of *Far from the Madding Crowd* sold out in January
and a second was printed.[8] In America *Publishers Weekly* talked of
'Mr Hardy's great novel' and predicted it would be 'one of the
hits of the season'.[9] And it was, in spite of Henry James's savagely
superior attack in the *Nation:* 'imitative talent . . . second rate . . .
fatal lack of magic . . . verbose and redundant style . . . little sense
of proportion and almost none of composition . . . Everything
human in the book strikes us as factious and insubstantial; the only
things we believe in are the sheep and the dogs.' Clever, and
funny, but, for all James's fine intelligence, wrong.

He was wrong because Hardy had found a true voice, sometimes awkward but tuned into experiences and feelings outside the
range of Henry James. It is a voice that speaks to readers in many
countries and to which successive generations have responded.
With this voice Hardy established the territory in which he worked
best in fiction, in which rural landscape is drawn with a naturalist's
eye and country people are shown playing out their lives 'between
custom and education, between work and ideas, between love of
place and experience of change'.[10] From now on all his best novels
– *The Return of the Native, The Mayor of Casterbridge, The Woodlanders, Tess of the D'Urbervilles* and *Jude the Obscure* – were built on this
foundation. But something wilful, or whimsical, or stubbornly
resistant to producing merely what people wanted made him turn
away repeatedly from what he did best. Few novelists maintain
their highest standards in book after book; Thackeray, George
Eliot, Henry James, even Dickens all had their failures. But Hardy's
output is exceptionally uneven. Over the next decade, the first
ten years of his married life, it went like this: failure (*Ethelberta*),
masterpiece (*The Return of the Native*), slight historical novel (*The
Trumpet-Major*), failure (*A Laodicean*), interesting oddity (*Two on a
Tower*), masterpiece (*The Mayor of Casterbridge*). To produce two
masterpieces in a decade is enough for any writer. Even the two
failures have their points of interest, and the second was written
during a painful and prolonged illness. But the first is a very curious

case, because it was written on the back of the great success of *Far from the Madding Crowd* and managed to dissipate almost all the goodwill, commercial and critical, it had earned.

While they were still at Surbiton, Stephen asked for a new serial for the *Cornhill*, and Smith wanted to sign him up for publication in volume form. They offered him £700 for the combined rights, and from America there was a further £550, the increased advances being the direct result of the success of *Far from the Madding Crowd*. Hardy had been planning a comedy of manners, perhaps encouraged by Anny Thackeray telling him that 'a novelist must necessarily like society.'[11] It was to be set largely in London and partly in France and called *The Hand of Ethelberta*. He was annoyed by the reviewers' insistence that his gift was for rural stories, and, although he had another idea for one with a woodland setting, he put that aside and started on *Ethelberta*. Stephen and Smith were both disconcerted by what he told them about it, but they were committed to it, and Stephen wrote politely of his pleasure in reading the early chapters.[12] But the public were disappointed in due course – it sold badly – and *Ethelberta* remains one of the least read of Hardy's novels.[13] You can see why. It is too long and too busily plotted, and the characters remain notional figures, there to make points. At the same time it is full of odd and arresting touches – as are all Hardy's novels – and Ethelberta herself, quick-witted and ambitious, and with an awkward path to negotiate, is a brave attempt to show a modern woman who finds herself outside the conventional structures of society and sets out defiantly to make the most of her situation. Some critics praised its originality and element of fantasy, and one saw it as 'a humorous fable' and an attack on the rich, which it partly is. But it is more than that.

Hardy had imagined a young woman whose parents are servants, father a butler, mother once a children's nurse in a county family, her aunt a maid who married a valet. Her many siblings are also all employed in lowly occupations, as cook, dressmaker, carpenter, housepainter, pupil teacher, page-boy, etc. She alone, educated well enough to become a governess in a wealthy family, has escaped from her class, first marrying the son of the house where she worked, then widowed almost as soon as married and taken abroad by her mother-in-law to have her education finished and a little polish put on. She now passes as a lady and has also become a published poet. She is beautiful, with what Hardy calls squirrel-coloured hair, and performs so effectively as an extemporizer that she can fill a London theatre. Society is at her feet, and suitors are queuing up. But, although she is ambitious for herself, she is unwilling to jettison her family and tries to lead a double life, sharing her London house with them – they pretend to be unrelated to her and merely her servants – while she makes up her mind how to proceed with her life. It was the emphasis on servants that upset Emma. Hardy called it a comedy, and some of it is farcical. It is also of course a commentary on his own position, which parallels Ethelberta's in obvious ways, and on the English preoccupation with class. What makes a lady or a gentleman? How central this question was: Leslie Stephen, on declaring himself an unbeliever, announced, 'I now believe in nothing . . . but I do not the less believe in morality . . . I mean to live and die like a gentleman if possible.'[14]

Hardy shows how uncomfortable Ethelberta sometimes finds her position. Attempting to communicate with one of her sisters, she thinks:

The wretched homeliness of Gwendoline's mind seemed . . . to be absolutely intolerable, and Ethelberta was suddenly convinced that to involve Gwendoline in any . . . discussion would simply be increasing her own burden, and adding worse confusion to her sister's already confused existence . . . As she ascended the stairs, Ethelberta ached with an added pain . . . *It was that old sense of disloyalty to her class and kin by feeling as she felt now which caused the pain, and there was no escaping it.* [my italics] Gwendoline would have gone to the ends of the earth for her: she could not confide a thought to Gwendoline![15]

As you read this passage, you think at once of Hardy's relations with his own family, parents, brother, sisters and cousins. While he was writing *Ethelberta* his sister Kate was working as a pupil teacher in Piddlehinton's mixed National School and his brother

Henry as a builder with their father; his cousin Martha and her husband, ex-lady's maid and butler, were preparing to emigrate to Queensland, Australia, despairing of making a good life in England.[16] So the book was among other things a farewell to Martha, and one of its most striking scenes may have come from something she told him about her working years. It describes an evening when the family are at dinner downstairs and the staff decide to come up from the basement and play games in the first-floor drawing rooms.

'Now let's have a game of cat-and-mice,' said the maidservant cheerily ... Away then ran the housemaid and Menlove [the lady's maid] and the young footman started at their heels. Round the room, over the furniture, under the furniture, through the furniture, out of one window, along the balcony, in at another window, again round the room – so they glided with the swiftness of swallows and the noiselessness of ghosts. Then the housemaid drew a jew's-harp from her pocket, and struck up a lively waltz *sotto voce.* The footman seized Menlove ... and began spinning gently round the room with her ... 'They'll hear you underneath, they'll hear you, and we shall all be ruined!' 'Not at all,' came from the cautious dancers. 'These are some of the best built houses in London – double floors, filled in with material that will deaden any row you like to make ...'[17]

The scene must have caused a stir in some London households.

The whole book is built around class encounters. Ethelberta moves through the social layers, while her older sisters end up emigrating to Australia. Her brothers remain working men, rough in their speech and appearance, and so radical in their views that one does his best to prevent Ethelberta marrying into the peerage. A London society lady gives her views on not spoiling servants by lending them books 'of the wrong kind for their station' and making them dissatisfied – 'and dreadfully ambitious!' suggests Ethelberta slyly.[18] A smooth, well-connected gentleman who courts her prides himself on his nonchalance and 'never disturbed the flesh upon his face except when he was obliged to do so'. Ethelberta rather likes him but goes off him when she finds he owes his fortune to buying up old horses for slaughter and selling horsemeat for hounds.[19]

A sensation is caused at a dinner when an apparently disembodied voice is heard to exclaim 'Good God'. It turns out to be the butler, Ethelberta's father, reacting to hearing the diners he is serving gossip about her impending marriage. His employers are shocked, first by his speaking at all, and then by the discovery that they have unknowingly entertained their butler's daughter at this same dinner table. The mistress of the house wants to sack him at once, and his job is saved only because the master values him too highly to let him go and is prepared to excuse his lapse into human behaviour.[20] When Ethelberta takes her builder brothers on an educational visit to the Royal Academy, they arrive in their best clothes, 'chests covered with broad triangular areas of padded blue silk', and walk through the gallery 'with the contrite bearing of meek people in church', admiring the construction of the skylights overhead. Dan observes, superfluously, 'I feel that I baint upon my own ground today.'[21]

Ethelberta is worldly enough to opt in the end for marriage to the disreputable – but very rich – old peer who pursues her. In making her choice, she consults a treatise on Utilitarianism, and in pondering whether to tell the old man about her background she picks up another on Casuistry. This is Hardy determined to show her serious intellectual qualifications. She chooses to tell her aristocratic lover the truth, and he of course doesn't give a damn – he knew already, and relishes it. She neither loves him nor even likes him much, but sees him as the solution to her problems and is confident she can keep him in order. Her brother Sol scolds her for 'creeping up among the useless lumber of our nation that'll be the first to burn if there comes a flare. I never see such a deserter of your own lot as you be . . . When you were a girl, you wouldn't drop a curtsey to 'em . . . But, instead of sticking to such principles, you must needs push up, so as to get girls such as you were once to curtsey to you.'[22] Sol need not have worried. By the end of the book the old viscount has been tamed, and his lady is running the estate and, in her spare time, working on an epic poem, inspired by her admiration for the republican poet Milton (her epic ambitions curiously predict Hardy's composition of *The Dynasts* three decades later). She is also helping her family. Her parents are installed in a villa on the south coast. She gives her younger sister a dowry and enables her youngest brother – the page-boy – to go into the Church, a nice Hardy joke. Even her builder brothers Sol and Dan have acquired their own business with a loan from her and signed a contract to build a hospital for £20,000.[23] Hardy passes few overt judgements, letting the story do its own work. It is a pity he packs it with too much material and too many thin sketches of people, because he has a good theme that deserves better treatment. Its failure is tantalizing, but it is a failure. Leslie Stephen should have made him work it over, cutting, sharpening and rewriting.

But Stephen had other things on his mind, and he made few suggestions beyond bowdlerizations. He asked Hardy not to describe Ethelberta's poems as 'amorous' and fussed, 'I may be over particular, but I don't quite like the suggestion of the very close embrace in the London churchyard,' where she is kissed by one of her admirers on a visit to Milton's tomb.[24] The two men met and talked in March 1875 but not about Hardy's intentions for his new book. Stephen wrote to him inviting him to call alone, as late as he liked in the evening, without giving a reason.

I went, and found him alone, wandering up and down his library in slippers; his tall thin figure wrapt in a heath-coloured dressing-gown. After a few remarks on our magazine arrangements, he said he wanted me to witness his signature to what, for a moment, I thought was his will; but it turned out to be a deed renunciatory of holy orders, under the Act of 1870. He said grimly that he was really a reverend gentleman still, little as he might look it, and that he thought it as well to cut himself adrift of a calling for which, to say the least, he had always been utterly unfit. The deed was executed with due formality. Our conversation then turned upon theologies decayed and defunct, the origin of things, the constitution of matter, the unreality of time and kindred subjects.[25]

Hardy could only be flattered that Stephen should make a request so personal, trusting and friendly.

The Hardys stayed in London until July, and the two men

exchanged further letters. There was, however, no invitation to them as a couple. Minny, as we have seen, did not like Hardy, and that was a good enough reason. She was also experiencing a difficult pregnancy, and Stephen took her to Switzerland in the summer. So there is no knowing what Minny would have made of Emma, whose inconsequentiality and chatter was faintly in the style of her sister Anny. In November, almost without warning, Minny died of convulsions brought on by her pregnancy. Stephen was broken with grief. Her death came on his birthday, and he never celebrated the day again. It was a ceremonious gesture of a kind Hardy understood and observed himself in the same spirit later in his own life, feeling the need to give love and death and sorrow their due.

☞

In London, Hardy took a first cautious step as a professional author speaking up for his profession when he joined the Copyright Association and was one of a delegation to the Prime Minister, Disraeli, encouraging him to set up a Select Committee to look into the law of copyright. This was in May. In June he went house hunting in Dorset without Emma, visiting Shaftesbury, Blandford and Wimborne, all at a discreet distance from Bockhampton, although he must have taken the opportunity of dropping in on his parents. None of the houses he saw appealed, but he and Emma agreed to leave London in July in any case and make for Swanage on the Dorset coast, where he said he intended to set some scenes in *Ethelberta*.

On the way they stopped in Bournemouth and on St Swithin's Day spent a rainy afternoon at a hotel. The day is sadly commemorated in his poem 'We Sat at the Window', published after her death with the inscription '(Bournemouth, 1875)' below the title.[26] They had been married for ten months, and this is his first known utterance about the state of things between them – a case of true Hardyesque irony. Far from describing the enjoyment of a trip out of town together, it is about their discontent as the rain falls and neither can find anything to like in the other. 'We were irked by the scene, by our own selves; yes' – and this is toned down from the manuscript's sharper 'We were irked by the scene, by *each other*, yes.' It is a stiff, remorseful poem about a bad moment. It is also entirely theoretical, giving no impression of either as individuals. The only physical detail is the rain. He says he failed to 'see' her then, but he also fails to let us see her in the poem. For a poem that takes on an intensely personal moment to be so impersonal is disconcerting.

What had happened to the living, high-spirited girl in Cornwall? Hardy had killed off Elfride at the end of *A Pair of Blue Eyes*, and he may have begun to think that the Emma he had fallen in love with was as insubstantial as Elfride. A friend who met her a few years further into their marriage said of her, 'Mrs Hardy belonged essentially to the class of woman gifted with spirit and the power of deciding for herself, which had attracted Hardy in his early manhood. She had the makings of a Bathsheba, with restricted opportunities.'[27] Perhaps she was finding that her opportunities were as restricted within marriage as they had been before. He knew he ought to value her, just as she doubtless knew she ought to praise the chapters of *Ethelberta* he showed her, and failed to. When things were not going well between them, his response was to withdraw into himself. He preferred silence to quarrels, which might have cleared the air and sent them into each other's arms.

With Hardy it is usually easier to find evidence of things going badly than accounts of happiness, but it was not all gloom. The steamer carried them on to Swanage, 'a seaside village lying snug within two headlands as between a finger and a thumb', with beach, boats and spectacular cliff walks with views over outlying rocks and sea, a spot likely to please Emma as much as himself. It was not yet a popular resort, and they had no difficulty finding lodgings with a retired sea captain and his wife at West End Cottage, a modest house on the hill leading out of town. Captain Masters told them sea stories and took them out in his boat; Mrs Masters looked after them. Asked about her later, Emma said she was fairly pleasant, adding that she stole from them.[28] Since the Hardys possessed almost nothing, it must have been money she took. It can't have been much, and they liked the place enough to stay there for nearly a year, until May 1876.

Swanage was near enough to Bockhampton for Hardy to make a gesture to his family. Mary and Kate were invited over for a holiday, and to meet Emma, at the beginning of September. It was the first encounter between his sisters and his wife, an anxious moment for all of them. Again the only account comes from Emma's diary, and again it is studiously impersonal, not mentioning their presence at all on one trip, the only evidence of which comes from Mary's sketch book. Mary was never talkative, but her brother's love was precious to her. Years later Emma accused her of trying to make division between her and Tom from the start, but things appear to have gone well enough in Swanage, and some sort of friendship was established. Mary was well read and well spoken, and could discuss books and poetry with Emma, and Kate was cheerful and prepared to make friends. Her letters to Emma after this are affectionate, and she was eager to be invited for further visits. Hardy took them all on a day trip to the Isle of Wight aboard a steamer, past the Needles, Ventnor and Ryde and back through the Solent, stopping at Bournemouth and reaching Swanage again by moonlight. On the last day of the visit they had what Emma described as a 'Breakfast Picnic' at Corfe Castle, a few miles inland. It was too far to walk, and they got into 'Sommer's Van, leaving Swanage at 7. with 15 people'. On the road they picked up more passengers 'until we were 21. and were packed as close as sardines', wrote Emma in her diary, adding 'Sun shining carelessly and lazily.' They took a kettle and brewed their tea on the green slopes below the ruined castle, and in the afternoon Mary and Kate said goodbye and walked off along the Wareham road with their bits of luggage. Hardy and Emma returned to Swanage on the top of the horse bus, three horses abreast, with views over the lush late-summer landscape: 'Hedges flowing over into the wide-sided roads, growing freely into the fields behind.'[29] She sounds content.

They kept up a habit of walking daily on the shore or the cliffs, even when Hardy was working. The first instalment of *Ethelberta*, with dully conventional illustrations by George Du Maurier, had appeared in the *Cornhill* in July, and he kept going steadily, the last sent off in January. Whatever people thought of it, his reputation was growing. To his delight, a dialect narrative poem he had written ten years before, 'The Bride-Night Fire', was published in November both in the *Gentleman's Magazine* and in *Appleton's Journal* in America; offending words were removed ('her cold little buzzoms' becoming 'her cold little figure') and some dialect words changed, but it was still entertaining.[30] Emma made a copy of the original version, which Hardy then corrected again, giving them a chance to talk about it and share it, which meant much to her. Also in November came a favourable critical article in the French fortnightly *Revue des deux mondes*, one of the most influential journals in Europe.

In the same month Hardy told an editor seeking a story from him that he intended 'to suspend my writing – for domestic reasons chiefly – for a longer time than usual after finishing *Ethelberta*, which I am sorry to say is not nearly done yet'.[31] Domestic reasons could have meant house hunting or a hope that Emma was pregnant. She had her thirty-fifth birthday at the end of November, and each month must have brought its private drama of expectation and disappointment, and anxiety about her age. Whatever his reasons, he had made up his mind to take a break from writing. In March they moved again, settling briefly in lodgings in Yeovil.[32] *Ethelberta* appeared in volume form, and the Leipzig publisher Tauchnitz, who sold English-language novels all over Europe, approached Hardy for the first time with an offer for it, going on to publish editions of nearly all his books. Hardy started a new notebook in which he planned to collect source material. Like many nineteenth-century novelists, he saw newspapers as a useful repository of human-interest stories, and Emma was given another task of copying out likely stuff.

Money was not short, there was nothing· to keep them in England, and Emma loved travelling abroad. They decided to take another foreign trip in May, this time to Brussels and the Rhineland. Before setting off for the Continent, Hardy wrote to Leslie Stephen for advice on his reading, particularly critical books. Stephen, still stunned with sorrow, sent an admirable reply: 'if you mean seriously to ask me what critical books I recommend, I can only say that I recommend none. I think as a critic that the less authors read of criticism the better. You, e.g., have a perfectly fresh and original vein, and I think that the less you bother yourself about critical canons the less chance there is of your becoming self-conscious and cramped. I should therefore, advise the great writers – Shakespeare, Goethe, Scott, &c &c, who give ideas and don't prescribe rules.'[33]

In Swanage Emma had been doing some writing of her own, a short novel which she called *The Maid on the Shore*.[34] It is in nineteen chapters, set in north Cornwall, and the best parts of it are the descriptions, of the seashore where the country women come at low tide with panniered donkeys, collecting sand for the farmers, of the bleak moorland and 'dreary interminable roads', of the miserable mud cottages with dirty children and of the poor farms, each with a few fields, barn, poultry, pig, horse, cart and plough. Against this she tells an unhappy love story of two cousins, Claude and Rosabelle, who are engaged, until Claude deserts her and runs off to London with an uneducated but exotically beautiful Cornish girl he has met on the beach. After complications Rosabelle finds happiness with Claude's quiet and steady best friend. Claude is disappointed in his love and grows ill living a hectic life in London, returns to Cornwall, falls off a cliff and dies. Emma had no gift for characterization and little idea of how to write fiction, and it would be hard for even the most determined editor to make anything of her story, but she did get it written to the end, it is reasonably coherent, and it uses what she knew of Cornish life. It is not absolutely unreadable, even if you keep hoping it will improve, and end by feeling sorry for Emma having worked so determinedly to so little effect. If she showed it to Hardy and he commented, it may have made a difficult moment for both of them.

Hardy managed to maintain a quite spectacular anonymity well into middle age. There is not a single written description of him – or of Emma – throughout the first six years of the marriage, although his name as an author was becoming known. It is true that for a whole decade he and Emma were on the move between London, the Continent and various parts of Dorset, going from place to place, living in lodgings with landlords and ladies who would not have noticed or cared who they were, travelling, renting houses in out-of-the-way places and making few friends – none of them the sort of people who would think of writing down their impressions of the Hardys. Marriage across class boundaries was also isolating. Some of their relatives complained, not entirely without reason, that they appeared to be wandering about like tramps.[35] Part of Hardy always wanted to guard his privacy. Like Ethelberta, he was unsure where he belonged and could not solve his problem by marrying into the peerage. Emma was also shy.[36] Even the friendship with Leslie Stephen became inactive with Hardy's marriage and the death of Minny, and, although the two men corresponded, they met only occasionally.[37]

Hardy's own recollections were written down fifty years afterwards. Then he approached those years with as much caution as Leslie Stephen would have recommended in his most stringent editorial mood. His second wife, acting as adviser and editor, had no interest in expanding his account of his best years with Emma, since she was hostile to her memory. A few of his notebook entries are copied into the *Life*, almost all worth reading. But really we know little more than where they settled and where they travelled, what Emma wrote in her diary and he in a handful of letters, almost all professional, and how his career progressed. We have to accept that he intended his personal life to be kept private except for the very occasional confession, and that the story he wanted told was what he put into his books.

They left England on 29 May, taking the train from Liverpool Street and crossing from Harwich to Rotterdam. Emma started a new and rather disorganized diary in the back of her honeymoon one. She observed German ladies with many babies on the steamer, and that the sea is higher than the land at Scheveningen in Holland. They took a Rhine steamer, saw Cologne (where 'T. was angry about the brandy flask'), Coblenz and Heidelberg, Baden-Baden and the Black Forest. In Strasbourg she was ill with an ulcerated throat that was treated with the brandy and a patent medicine fetched by Hardy. From Brussels they visited the battlefield of Waterloo, where a woman brought out two baskets, one of bread, the other of skulls, with perfect teeth, before giving them cake to eat and some flowers to take away. That day they walked a long way in the heat, and the next day she noted, 'I am still greatly fatigued and Tom is cross about it.' At the end of the trip she wrote, 'Going back to England where we have no home and no chosen county.' This was on 18 June, and on the next page she was able to write 'July 3. 1876. Riverside Villa. Sturminster Newton'. Here Hardy started work on a book that surpassed any he had yet written.

PART THREE
1875–1905

11. Dreaming the Heath

Within days of their return to England the Hardys found and agreed to rent an unfurnished house in the ancient market town of Sturminster Newton on the River Stour, spanned by a grey stone bridge built in 1500. Sturminster is in north Dorset, above the Vale of Blackmore, and a good twenty miles from Dorchester – and Bockhampton – with no direct rail connection. If Hardy was making a cautious approach to the area of his childhood home, he was not yet ready to ask Emma to settle any closer to his mother. The house they took stands at the edge of Sturminster, or rather just out of town, separated from the paved streets by an expanse of grass on which sheep are often put to graze and placed high above the river, flowing past at the bottom of a steep bank. The spot is undeniably romantic, and the site of an old mansion, but the house taken by Hardy was one of a pair of standard mid-Victorian semi-detacheds, bow-windowed and two-storeyed, built further along the bank.[1] They shared a garden at the back, with a pump. There is unlikely to have been either a bathroom or indoor plumbing when they lived there. The fronts of the houses were their glory, facing west over the riverside walk, the river below and the miles of water meadows beyond. The sunsets were spectacular: 'the west is like some vast foundry where new worlds are being cast,' wrote Hardy one autumn evening.[2] Not surprisingly he set up his study in the west-facing bedroom upstairs. The houses were known as Riverside or Rivercliff Villas – he uses both names in his letters – and were newly built, and the Hardys were the first tenants. Here the marriage got into its stride. They found a way to be happy, Hardy wrote well, and they stayed for nearly two years.

Before they could move in they had to acquire some furniture. Bristol, they decided, was the place to do this, and off they dashed to buy '£100 worth of mid-Victorian furniture in two hours'.[3]

What he meant by 'mid-Victorian' was simply modern, as opposed to the ancient furniture he had grown up with. The sum he laid out was substantial, and he must have felt some pride at being able to spend so freely to make this first real home for Emma. Why they chose Bristol for furniture is a mystery. Prices may have been lower, and the transport to Dorset cheaper. One of his carpenter cousins was living there, Nathaniel Sparks, who had become a restorer of violins since their London days and was about to be married to Mary Hardy's college friend Annie, but, since Hardy was not eager to introduce Emma to his cousins and Annie was pregnant, it seems unlikely that Nat was the draw, or that he looked them up.[4]

They next had to find their first servant girl, Georgiana, who lasted only a few months, Emma giving 'Notice to Geo' on 13 November.[5] She was replaced by Jane, the daughter of a labouring family from a nearby village, 'said to be an old county family' come down in the world, much liked by both Hardy and Emma.[6] So they settled into the house where, as he recalled, they spent their happiest time together. Looking back later, he wrote a lucid and expressive poem about their time there. He called it 'A Two-Years' Idyll':

> Yes, such it was;
> Just those two seasons unsought,
> Sweeping like summertide wind on our ways;
> Moving, as straws,
> Hearts quick as ours in those days;
> Going like wind, too, and rated as nought
> Save as the prelude to plays
> Soon to come – larger, life-fraught:
> Yes, such it was.

The poem goes on to say how little they valued their happiness then, and how they failed to realize that what they thought of as a prelude to better things – 'larger, life-fraught' – was really, as it turned out, the high point of their life together. So it becomes a sorrowful poem about how easy it is to live through the best parts of life without realizing it, always looking forward, and how you regret it afterwards. It may be one of the standard poetic subjects, but Hardy writes about it in strong, unstandard phrases:

> 'Nought' it was called,
> Even by ourselves . . .

he says bluntly, and

> What seems it now?
> Lost: such beginning was all . . .[7]

A charm of the poem is that after you have finished it and are reduced to sadness, you can go back to the opening lines and call up the remembered delight again, of their hearts quick to be moved, of the wind characterized by Hardy's rare and lovely use of 'summertide' that makes you pause to enjoy it, and of time passing speedily for happy people for whom the speed itself becomes part of the happiness.

☞

Another part of the happiness was that Hardy was working on a new novel, and that its theme was drawn from the deep places of his imagination. The greatness of *The Return of the Native* is that it is as much the work of Hardy the poet as Hardy the novelist. All his novels have elements of poetry, but this is the first in which, although he has made his concepts into fiction, essentially he is setting down a poetic dream. Leslie Stephen had urged him back to Shakespeare, and you can read *The Return of the Native* almost as a complement to *A Midsummer Night's Dream*. It is the dream of a winter's night, with witches instead of fairies, fateful journeys through difficult terrain, marriage plans which falter, and lovers who exchange their partners for no sensible reason. There is a moonlit love scene, there are fierce quarrels, and there are rustics who put on a dramatic entertainment. In good Shakespearean tradition there is also a young woman who disguises herself as a boy. Hardy shows us mats of 'perfumed shepherds' thyme' to match Titania's bank, and snakes that shed their skins; lizards, grasshoppers and glow-worms make their entrances. Venn the reddleman acts as a sort of Puck, moving rapidly about the heath to intervene in the plot, sometimes speaking in riddles as when he tells Thomasin, who believes her husband has been out to buy a horse, that he has seen him leading one, 'A beauty, with a white face and a mane as black as night'.[8] In the opening chapter Hardy suggests the element of dream when he writes that in winter the heath becomes 'the hitherto unrecognized original of those wild regions of obscurity which are vaguely felt to be compassing us about in midnight dreams of flight and disaster'.[9] Dreams, or nightmares. His tale ends in tragedy for most, with three of the principal figures caught up in flight and disaster ending in death, but he leaves a future for Thomasin and her baby daughter, and for Venn.

All this is drawn out of an imagination inspired and nourished by memories of his native heath, where he took his first steps with his once all-powerful mother, and by other dreams and fantasies of his boyhood. The proud, intelligent mother Mrs Yeobright is made into a widow, but, like Jemima, she is fiercely ambitious for her son, Clym. He is an only child, although his cousin Thomasin is virtually a sister, and just such a quiet, steady girl as Hardy's sister Mary. Clym is a distant version of himself, a man who has been away and returns with high-flown philosophical ideas, and who enrages his mother by falling in love with a woman she dislikes. Clym's beloved, Eustacia, is presented as a queen of the night, mysterious, alluring and changeable, the beauty of a boy's dreams. The scene in which she allows young Charley to hold her hand for fifteen minutes in payment for his help has more of an erotic charge than her scenes with Clym, surely because Charley is standing in for young Tommy in the days when he yearned after inaccessible women. Charley makes her take off her glove – what good is a gloved hand to a lover? – and later he brings her presents from the heath, 'white trumpet-shaped mosses, red-headed lichens, stone arrowheads used by the old tribes on Egdon', trying to please her, rather as Hardy made drawings of animals to please Mrs Martin.[10] And when Eustacia dies, her husband acknowledges

Charley's position as one who loved her and takes him to see her lying dead and restored to beauty.

The quarrel between Mrs Yeobright and Eustacia – where she accuses the older woman of having set herself against her from the start, and claims to be better born, and Mrs Yeobright acknowledges that she had tried to stop her son marrying her, and rages against her audacity – is painfully realistic in its fury and bitterness. The two women are virtually tearing him limb from limb between them, each intent on taking him from her rival.[11] How clearly Hardy could imagine such a quarrel between his mother and Emma, and he may even have seen it as a way of pre-empting it and warding it off. There is a good deal of magic in the book. Eustacia is held to be a witch by some of the heath dwellers, and she is partly brought down by an act of witchcraft in turn. Hardy is ambivalent about witchcraft, 'rationally sceptical but emotionally sympathetic . . . both qualities exist within him,' as Simon Gatrell has observed.[12] In his first draft of the book Wildeve was called Toogood, and he was not an engineer turned publican but a herbalist, a white witch, known as Conjuror Toogood. The first draft was different in several other ways. Venn was a less solid figure; Eustacia had no foreign father, naval grandfather or girlhood in Budmouth, but had always lived on the heath. Mrs Yeobright was not socially superior to her neighbours, and Clym had been no further away than Budmouth to work. To quote Gatrell's excellent account of the changes again, a 'wave of gentrification . . . struck the text'.[13] Thomasin, coming into money, is seen with no fewer than three servants at the end, which seems a little superfluous for a heath dweller, but was perhaps what Hardy had learnt a genteel household required. Many of the names were changed too, the Yeobrights starting as the Brittans and Eustacia as Avice. Interesting as these adjustments are, they are no more than incidental. They do not affect the essential nature of the book, its fervent linking of place and feeling, its quality of a poet's dream.

Years later Hardy said *The Return of the Native* was the novel for which he had most affection: 'it had a suggestive atmosphere and he thought Clym an interesting and loveable figure, though he had no personal connection with himself.'[14] You might say the book is all atmosphere, but there are many other things to be admired. One is its virtuoso structure. Hardy has given it the unity of a Racine tragedy, not only by confining all the action to the heath but by assembling his group of men and women so tightly clenched together in love, hate and mutual dependence that they are like fingers in a fist. They are so tightly held that they destroy one another.

There is also his usual loving attention to details of natural history woven into the narrative. Either he was blessed with an unusually good memory for the minutiae of his native heath as he sat writing above the River Stour or – more likely – he had kept notes almost as meticulous as Gilbert White's. He writes confidently, for instance, of the 'strange amber-coloured butterflies which Egdon produced, and which were never seen elsewhere' that 'alighted on Clym's bowed back, and sported with the glittering point of his hook as he flourished it up and down'. Reference to a modern butterfly book confirms what he says and names them as Lulworth Skippers.[15] He describes the precise effect of the wind on different forms of vegetation, giving each a different voice, 'the linguistic peculiarity of the heath'. Here is the dead heather, its bells 'now washed colourless by the Michaelmas rains, and dried to dead skins by October suns . . . each of the tiny trumpets was seized on, entered, scoured and emerged from by the wind as thoroughly as if it were as vast as a crater'.[16] And here the reeds growing behind Wildeve's inn announce their presence 'by sounds as of a congregation praying humbly, produced by their rubbing against each other in the slow wind'.[17] In Mrs Yeobright's garden a hot August day makes the large-leaved plants flag by the clock, the rhubarb bending downward by eleven, 'and even stiff cabbages were limp by noon.' It sounds like a memory of his father's vegetable garden at Bockhampton.[18] And this is Mrs Yeobright's exquisite observation of a heron flying towards the late-afternoon sun: 'He had come dripping wet from some pool in the valleys, and as he flew the edges and lining of his wings, his thighs, and his breast were so caught by the bright sunbeams that he appeared as if formed of burnished silver.'[19] The heron is one of the last things she sees in her life, and he makes her wish for a moment that she could arise and fly as he flew, to what seemed a 'free and happy place' in the sky. She dies soon after, from exhaustion and unhappiness and the bite of an adder. A Christian writer would have seen this as her release into just such a free and happy place. Hardy did not, but at least he gave her, and us, the wonderful image of the bird lit up by the sun.

Writing the book was one thing; placing it as a serial and finding a publisher another. If Hardy started with justified confidence on his first chapter, it was soon under attack. While he was still in an early stage of writing, in February 1877, he sent a few chapters to Leslie Stephen to consider for the *Cornhill*; he also wrote to George Smith, asking him 'if you think it a kind of story likely to create a demand in the market'.[20] Neither committed himself, so Hardy turned to John Blackwood – George Eliot's publisher and editor of *Blackwood's Magazine* – to see if he were interested.[21] Blackwood politely declared himself unable to place it in the near future and offered some criticism. He complained that 'There is hardly anything like what is called Novel interest' in the first chapter – it describes the heath – although he found Eustacia 'a remarkable character and might have been educated in Paris' (ambivalent praise from a British editor).[22] Hardy went back to Stephen, who now said he would not consider it without seeing the finished novel: 'he feared that the relations between Eustacia, Wildeve and Thomasin might develop into something "dangerous" for a family magazine.'[23] Hardy decided to give up on the *Cornhill* and wrote to two more magazines, finally setting up the serialization with the poorly regarded *Belgravia* and getting only £20 for each instalment. At least they were prepared to take it sight unseen, as was *Harper's* in New York. By November 1877 the first five instalments were sent off, and it ran monthly through the whole of 1878. Arthur Hopkins, brother of the poet Gerard Manley Hopkins, did the illustrations, but, although Hardy discussed them with him, and he was a competent artist, they do not begin to suggest the wild expanses of the heath or the originality of the conception. Instead they weaken its power by making the characters into nicely dressed people you might expect to meet on a croquet lawn.

Hardy may have realized this, because the book was published in volume form without illustrations, except for a map of the heath drawn by Hardy himself.[24] It was not a success, only 900 of the 1,000 copies printed being sold, and British reviewers were grudging about it. Hardy was found guilty of imitating Victor Hugo, and Eustacia was described as belonging to 'the class of which Madame Bovary is the type', which was not meant as praise. Any supposed French influence was regarded as objectionable by British critics. So was what they saw as pretentiousness and low moral tone exhibited through the portrayal of selfish and sensual characters, because novels were required to be straightforwardly morally uplifting. The anonymous writer doing a batch of novels for the *Athenaeum* said it was Hardy's worst book yet and was puzzled by the 'low social position of the characters' and the way they were made 'to talk as no people ever talked before'. Perhaps he missed the comforting condescension to the lower orders shown in *Under the Greenwood Tree*.

W. E. Henley, a young poet and a protégé of Leslie Stephen, found it less good than *A Pair of Blue Eyes*, 'very French' and 'disagreeable' but also 'acute, prescient, imaginative, insatiably observant and . . . rigidly and finely artistic'. Only the *Spectator*'s reviewer saw that it was the book of a poet, and one of brilliant talent, 'even of high genius', although he also had unfavourable comments about the rustics and Hardy's failure to present 'grief of the deepest and noblest type'. Hardy felt the pain of the onslaughts and hardly noticed the praise. He wrote in his notebook for 28 November 1878, 'Woke before it was light. Felt that I had not enough staying power to hold my own in the world.'[25] He was always exceptionally anxious and sensitive about reviews, and he sent a letter to the *Athenaeum* defending his presentation of 'intelligent peasant speech'.[26] He might have spared himself the trouble: the divide between those who disliked his language, his lower-class characters, his troubling women and his gloom, and those who appreciated the beauty and imaginative power of his work, was already there and remained firmly fixed throughout his career as a novelist.

☞

This is to run ahead of the Sturminster years. Emma had the pleasure of organizing and ordering her new home above the river, and two of her brothers came for a three-day visit in October 1876. The Hardys were for the first time accepted as solid, respectable citizens, and they made friends, particularly with the Dashwoods, the local solicitor and his wife, to whom Emma confided her literary ambitions.[27] At Christmas, Hardy took her to stay with his parents, her first visit. His father was always genial, Kate was enjoying her last bit of freedom before starting teacher training at Salisbury, Mary was home for the school holidays and Henry was solid and unexcitable. Six adult Hardys and Emma in the cottage meant it was crowded, and you can imagine the men going out to look at the garden together to get away from the women's tongues. There was the walk to church on Christmas Day, and the familiar service, still taken by Mr Shirley. Did Hardy introduce Emma to the man who had preached against the over-ambitious poor? We don't know, because nobody has left any account of the visit. What is certain is that everyone understood that the danger point was between Jemima and Emma. They did not make friends, but there was at least a truce – although there is no record of any later visit.

Winter, spring, summer were spent writing. Hardy sometimes took Emma boating on the Stour, and they still read poetry together. He often also took long walks by himself – her lameness did not encourage her to join him – and he kept an image of her standing in the porch, wearing a white muslin dress, eager for his return, the notes from her musical box coming faintly from indoors.[28] Looking back, he was in no doubt that he loved her then: 'And beneath the roof is she who in the dark world shows / As a lattice-gleam when midnight moans.'[29] But he also remembered how often he failed to notice her, withdrawn into his own world as he needed to be.

Both of them expected and hoped to have children. During 1877 Emma's brother Walter had a boy, Gordon, Hardy's cousin Nat also had a son, and Nat's sister Tryphena, Hardy's one-time flirt, gave up her teaching career to marry a publican and soon had a family. Early in the next year Leslie Stephen remarried, choosing a widow with three children, and they were to have four more together.[30] During the summer the Hardys' maid Jane also became pregnant. They caught her as she crept out of the back door in her nightdress, after midnight, to meet a lover hiding in an outhouse in the garden, believing she intended to bring him into the house, because the bolts on the kitchen door had been oiled. They led her back inside and the man fled, but she got out of the dining-room window early in the morning, taking her best clothes with her, and was not seen again. Hardy went to her family – they were haymaking – but she was not with them. In August they had news of her. Hardy wrote: 'Aug. 13. We hear that Jane, our late servant is soon to have a baby. Yet never a sign of one is there for us.'[31] If he reflected that he himself had been conceived in similar circumstances, while his mother was in service and his father without any thought of getting married, he could hardly talk about it with Emma. When Jane gave birth at the end of November, she was still unmarried, named no father and called her infant son Tom. The child died two days later, and no more was heard of her.[32]

Hardy and Emma's failure to have children is the saddest thing about their life together. He would have made a gentle and humorous father, and a child would have given Emma a focus for her attention and love, and filled up the long hours when he was absorbed in his writing. It would have relieved the tensions and resentments that built up between them, and might even have helped to soften relations with Bockhampton. As it was, Jemima could claim that Emma brought Hardy neither youth nor wealth, small intelligence and no children.

The episode prompts the question, when did Hardy find out the circumstances of his parents' marriage and his own birth? It is not something children think about or parents talked about. The most likely source of information was his Sparks cousins, whose parents had been instrumental in getting his father to marry his mother. Maria Sparks was the closest of Jemima's sisters, and their children knew each other well enough to discuss family history as they grew up. It could help to explain the distinct cooling in his relations with the Sparks cousins who remained in England, who remembered and talked about the story of Jemima's forced wedding. If Hardy did not already know, the approach of his own wedding may have aroused his curiosity about that of his parents, and so led him to find out. However and whenever he did, he kept it to himself.

☞

In October 1877 Hardy performed the duty of a son towards his father, whose rheumatism was getting worse. A cure in Bath was recommended; Hardy met his father there and helped him find lodgings in Church Street, took him to the theatre and departed the next morning. Two weeks later Mr Hardy wrote a lively letter to his daughter Kate, interesting in itself and because it shows the width of the cultural gap between father and son:

Bath is a very Grand Place and I like it very much. I have taken 6 Baths and am to take one to Day and I am to Drink two Glasses of the Water a Day But Have not gaind much Benefit by it as yet the Dr Says its a good Sign when it make any one Worse at first as it tis likely to do good.

I have very Comfortable lodgings . . . there is a man and His Wife and 3 more Respectable Gents and one Young lady Lodge in the Same House all of us in Separate rooms and 3 of us have the rheumatism and take the Same Baths.

there is so very many Cripples about Bath and most of them Seems to be respectable people and thousands and thousands of Bath Chairs you can scarcely move for them as they all go on the Pavement – the Drapery Shops are very grand and numerous.

I Have been Hear a month . . . Mrs Gill of Stafford Has fell Down and broken Her Leg She is gone in the Hospatle to Have it off and Henry tell me she is not expected to come out again a live. Yours afftly Thos Hardy.[33]

☞

For some time Hardy had been thinking of writing a historical novel set during the Napoleonic Wars. This was partly what made him so determined to walk over the field of Waterloo. He had also, when in London with Emma, twice taken her with him to visit the Chelsea Pensioners, among whom there were still survivors from the battle with stories to tell. And, although they were happy at Sturminster, he was restless. With *The Return of the Native* nearly finished at the end of 1877, he began to think of returning to London, where he could more easily do the necessary background reading for his new book at the British Museum. Emma was agreeable, but both felt disinclined to live in the centre of town. The 1870s was a time when the middle classes made a mass move to the leafier suburbs, and they decided to look to the south of London again. In February they decided on a house in Tooting, close to Wandsworth Common, with a regular train service to Victoria. 1 Arundel Terrace, Trinity Road, was an end-of-terrace house, larger than the one in Sturminster. There was nothing picturesque about it or its situation, but it was undoubtedly genteel.[34] In March they packed up their things and left Dorset. The two-years' idyll was over.

12. Hardy Joins a Club

Hardy had decided that 'the practical side of his vocation of novelist demanded that he should have his head-quarters in or near London,' and three years based in Tooting followed.[1] Although he later, characteristically, doubted whether it was a wise move, it was, in fact, a highly successful strategy for meeting publishers and editors, writers, artists and distinguished men and women with an interest in literature, and he put a lot of energy into taking up the invitations he received. Within weeks he was being welcomed to social events as one of the younger writers people wanted to meet, and he must have become a familiar figure on the Wandsworth–Victoria train. Very early on he and Emma were invited by their near neighbour Alexander Macmillan, the grand old man of British publishing, who had started life in much the same way as Hardy, a penniless, half-schooled Scots boy who came south and worked his way to the top of his profession – and who had also turned down Hardy's first three novels. At his house Hardy met Morley, his earliest reader, again, and scientists of the calibre of T. H. Huxley, whose high intelligence and modest manner Hardy particularly admired, and whom he knew to be the friend and ally of Darwin. Another influential figure, Charles Kegan Paul, a Dorset clergyman who had left the Church and become a writer and publisher, admired Hardy's work, asked him to dine and supported his election to the Savile Club. He was elected to the club only three months after his arrival in Tooting, and in early August he spent an uncharacteristically riotous evening there and at the Lyceum, where Henry Irving, a fellow member, dispensed champagne to a party from the club, whose members were for the most part writers.

The Savile had been going for only a decade, one of a growing number of such establishments where gentlemen enjoyed something between the comforts of hotel and home in central London

without being troubled by their families. You could have any meal
served and spend any hour of the day or night there, knowing you
would meet no one but your carefully chosen fellow members,
and no women at all – female servants being effectively invisible.
Did Hardy ever think of his mother's ambition to become a cook
in a gentlemen's club? It is likely it was from her that he first knew
a gentleman should have a club. Almost at once he was using the
Savile as his address in his correspondence – 15 Savile Row, W –
and inviting visiting American literary men to lunch there. But,
although the Savile was undoubtedly a convenience for him, it did
not make him into a clubbable man. The evening with Irving was
not repeated, and Hardy did not become a fixture either at the
lunch table or in the card room. 'Considering his eminence, Hardy
seems to have made ... small impact at the Savile,' writes the
historian of the club.'[2]

He did all the same make an effort to take part in some of the
rather forced jollities of the literary world. When a fellow member
of the Savile, Walter Besant, pressed him to join the Rabelais Club,
set up to celebrate virility in literature, Hardy was flattered enough
to agree, confessing at the same time that he had barely read
Rabelais. His account of the inaugural dinner makes you glad not
to have been there. It was held at the Tavistock Hotel, on a dismal
winter night, the fog in the Bloomsbury streets creeping into the
'large, empty, dimly-lit, cheerless apartment' in which they met.[3]

He told Kegan Paul, 'I have only settled temporarily in this
suburb, to have a foothold from which to choose some permanent
spot. We might have ventured on Kensington, but for such utter
rustics as ourselves Tooting seemed town enough to begin with.'[4]
This was not literally true, since he had taken the lease for three
years, but it probably expressed a true wish or intention. Something
similar was at work when, having been asked by an American
paper to provide autobiographical notes about himself, he left
out any mention of his early struggles and presented himself as
effortlessly cultivated, having received his 'higher education' from
a Cambridge scholar and visited 'several of the great collections of
paintings in Continental Capitals from time to time'.[5] He was
striking what he thought was the right note.

The friendship with Leslie Stephen remained low key, partly no doubt because Stephen's faith in Hardy as a novelist was fading. In 1880 he wrote to a friend, 'there is no one now who is to the rising generation what Mill and Carlyle were to us; nor have we a really good novelist . . . to replace the old idols.'[6] Fortunately Mrs Anne Procter, the ancient literary lady to whom Stephen had introduced Hardy before his marriage, stepped into the breach. She already took a great interest in his work, and she invited him to bring Emma to meet her as soon as she heard they were in London, and took a liking to her.[7] Mrs Procter was now nearly eighty, widowed, and had seen one daughter, a gifted poet, die young, and another fall into a decline, but she faced such blows gallantly, kept her salon in regal style and even managed to be coquettish. Hardy thought she moved through rooms of celebrities 'like a swan', and he noticed a 'momentary archness' in her glance now and then. Another of her admirers, Henry James, carried a flirtation with her to the point of making a formal, if light-hearted, proposal of marriage.[8] James saw in her 'a kind of window into the past', and like Hardy loved the fact that she had known everyone in the literary world from childhood on. She received on Sunday afternoons in her flat in Queen Anne's Mansions, and here Hardy often saw Browning, then at the height of his fame. Hardy was pleased to meet the great man, but Browning liked lions, and Hardy was shy, and they failed to make much of an impression on one another. Mrs Procter also tried Hardy with Tennyson, taking him to dine with the laureate when he was in London for his annual visit. Mrs Tennyson received lying down 'as if in a coffin', wrote Hardy, but got up to greet him, and her husband was genial and forthcoming, strikingly dressed in a shirt with a large loose collar and wearing old steel spectacles. He explained that they hated London but needed to come up once a year, because they got rusty living on the Isle of Wight. Hardy thought him quite unlike his portraits and was especially taken with the humorous twitch to his mouth as he talked. He said *A Pair of Blue Eyes* was his favourite among Hardy's novels and told him stories about misprints in his own work, 'airy' changed to 'hairy' pleasing him particularly. Hardy was charmed, and the Tennysons warmly invited him to visit them in Freshwater. Yet he never went, even though he and Emma had read Tennyson's poetry from their earliest days together, and she would have adored to go. Perhaps that was part of the difficulty, feeling that he could not go without Emma, and that she might dominate the conversation or say awkward things, her style far from that of the self-effacing Emily Tennyson. Yet it would have been an easy trip from either London or Dorset, and it was a missed opportunity.

One clue to the state of things between Hardy and Emma at this time comes from the account written by Richard Bowker, the young London representative of Hardy's American publishers Harper, who had just serialized *The Return of the Native*. Bowker, newly arrived in London in the summer of 1880, called on the Hardys in Tooting in July and wrote about it in his journal. It is the earliest description of them as a couple, Hardy just forty, Emma thirty-nine:

I was received in a pretty parlor by Mrs Thomas Hardy, with her Kensington-stitch work, and her pet cat; she is an agreeable youngish English lady, immensely interested in her husband's work, and we were at once good friends. Hardy presently came down, a quiet-mannered, pleasant, modest, little man, with sandyish short beard, entirely unaffected and direct, not at all spoiled by the reputation which *Far from the Madding Crowd* and its successors have won for him. He was originally an architect, and had little thought of writing novels. Told me he had the greatest difficulty in remembering the people and incidents of his own stories so that Mrs Hardy had to keep on the look-out for him. We three fell to discussing a title for a new story which he is writing . . . Before I went, tea and cake were served. I came home, having made two pleasant friends I think.[9]

Hardy's remark about not being able to remember the people or incidents in his writing and having to rely on Emma to put him right is a joke, even if Bowker did not notice it. But it is a joke that makes you wonder whether Emma, so 'immensely interested in her husband's work', could be rather too ready to intervene with comments and suggestions. Hardy's humorous words sound like a very gentle, affectionate mockery of her behaviour and mark the early stages of what was to become a problem. Both were victims of the limitations placed on genteel women. Emma still had nothing to do except embroidery, keeping a cat, ordering about a servant or two and shopping. Hardy did his best to entertain her, escorting her to see the Lord Mayor's show and to her fashionable dressmaking establishments in Regent Street.[10] He also took her for another French holiday in the summer of 1880. But these diversions could not fill the emptiness in her life. In his memoirs he says that it was in the Tooting house 'that their troubles began' and that 'they seemed to begin to feel that "there had passed away a glory from the earth".'[11] She made no progress with her own writing and became one of those wives who regards her husband's work as 'our work' and refers to it in that way in public.

In London the introductions continued. The son of his publisher George Smith invited him to dinner with Matthew Arnold, who modestly explained he was only a hard-worked school inspector; however, on being asked his views on style, he unhesitatingly recommended Swift as a model for narrative writing. Two other writers also present, both at the beginning of their careers, were Henry James and Richard Jefferies, neither of them likely to adopt Swift as a model. Hardy had no reason to like James personally after his review of *Far from the Madding Crowd*. He was also conscious that they were too far apart in their approach to writing fiction to find common ground, since the sort of people Hardy wrote about did not register on James at all, and James, in Hardy's view, was without poetry, humour or spontaneity in his writing. He nevertheless admired him as a novelist, and he and Emma both read his novels. Of Jefferies, Hardy had nothing to say, surprisingly, since his essays and stories of Wiltshire life and landscape, ecstatic in their response to nature and detailed in their account of the men and women who worked the land, had something in common with his own work. He may have been simply too high-flown for

Hardy; but when Jefferies published his striking study of rural labourers, *Hodge and His Masters*, in 1880, Hardy responded by attacking the use of the word 'Hodge' as a general and demeaning term.[12] Jefferies never had Hardy's success. He had to grind at journalism to make money, and he died relatively young of an untreatable and agonizing spinal disease.

Lord Houghton, better known as Monckton Milnes, Liberal politician, friend of Swinburne and champion of Keats, whose *Life and Letters* he had brought out when Hardy was still a child, expressed a wish to see more of Hardy. The painter W. P. Frith, best known for his panoramic studies of crowds, *Derby Day*, *Ramsgate Sands* and *The Railway Station*, became a friend, and at his studio Hardy met Sir Percy Shelley, only surviving son of the poet he idolized and about as different from Percy Bysshe as could be imagined. Another figure from the past was a well-wrapped-up old lady who, Frith assured him, had been the dedicatee of Byron's *Childe Harold*. Hardy was greedy for such remnants of the past. He went to talk to the Chelsea Pensioners yet again. He also took himself to Chislehurst to watch the funeral of the young Prince Imperial, killed in Africa, carefully observing the Prince's uncle Joseph as he passed in order to get the Bonaparte features fixed in his mind.

Lowell, the American minister in London, was another he met; the cheerful Du Maurier, illustrator and novelist, and the Pre-Raphaelite Thomas Woolner, who sculpted Hardy's old hero, John Stuart Mill. Not everyone was so agreeable. 'Also met a Mrs H., who pretended to be an admirer of my books, and apparently had never read one,' he noted after a party. He attended an International Literary Congress, where he met Monsieur de Lesseps, followed by a Soirée Musicale at the Hanover Square Club, to meet members of the Literary Congress again, plus members of the Comédie-Française, and wondered why he was there. In short, he lived the literary life much as it still goes on.[13]

He acquired a reader's ticket at the British Museum and went to the great reading room to study the background for his historical novel. The plan for *The Trumpet-Major* included an account of George III and his family staying in Weymouth during the Napoleonic Wars, as well as references to the Captain Hardy who served with Nelson at the Battle of Trafalgar. The setting was mostly Weymouth and the steep-sided downs behind it, where the English regiments were encamped and where a few villages were placed, and the wild isle of Portland, across which the heroine walks to see her lover's ship, the *Victory*, passing at sea in full sail until she disappears over the horizon. It is neatly told and slight, a harmless pot-boiler written as though Hardy had made up his mind to avoid conflicts with editors about propriety or any possible comparisons with modern French novelists, and it reads almost like a book for children. There is some vivid description, an exciting scene with the press gang, military drill and a lot of rustic foolery. Also a bland heroine Anne with a row of tight curls across her forehead, who dithers between two brothers, the faithful soldier John – the Trumpet-Major – and his sailor brother Bob, fickle as every sailor is known to be. Leslie Stephen saw it and declined it as a serial. Hardy tried to sell it to Blackwood ('it is above all things a cheerful story, without views or opinions') with no better luck, then to *Macmillan's Magazine*. It was finally taken by *Good Words*, whose editor obliged him to remove swear words and references to Sunday travel.[14] They paid him £400 and it ran throughout 1880, and simultaneously in America, bringing in another $500.[15] Smith, Elder published a three-volume edition of 1,000 copies in October 1880 for which they paid £200, so it kept the pot boiling well enough.[16] £1,000 a year was an income that put you in the highest levels of middle-class earnings, and, although Hardy was not regularly earning that much, he must have been setting aside substantial sums. His determination to promote his reputation then led him to a striking further step: he wrote to Queen Victoria's private secretary, offering her a copy of *The Trumpet-Major* and pointing out that it featured her grandfather George III. When the offer was accepted, he explained that the details of the King's appearance had been given to him by 'an aged villager' who had actually seen him. Whether the Queen would be as struck by this as Hardy hoped, he did himself no harm. A few months later he dispatched a second copy to the Prince of Wales.

He remained uncertain about the pleasures of London life. On the last day of 1878 his father wrote to him to say his mother was ill, that they had 'drunk both their healths in gin and rhubarb wine' and hoped to have a visit soon. Hardy responded quickly, going down in chill weather, and alone.

Feb. 1 To Dorchester. Cold. Rain on snow. Henry seen advancing through it, with wagonette and Bob [the horse], to the station entrance. Drove me to Bockhampton through the sleet and rain from the East, which shaved us like a razor. Wind on Fordington Moor cut up my sleeves and round my wrists – even up to my elbows. The light of the lamp at the bottom of the town shone on the reins in Henry's hand, and showed them glistening with ice. Bob's behind-part was a mere grey arch; his foreparts invisible.[17]

Not even the sleet shaving like a razor stopped him noting the details, and Hardy was always as interested in describing bad weather as good. He found his parents in tolerable health, though they must have felt the absence of both of their daughters. He talked a great deal with his father, who told him stories of old times; also to local people, always making notes: 'A villager says of the parson, who has been asked to pray for a sick person: "His prayers wouldn't save a mouse."' And during his two weeks' visit he walked with his usual energy, one day as far as Portland, where the wind blows so fiercely you can be blue with cold in half an hour.

   Thinking about his parents, he reflected that both were getting on for seventy, then regarded as the normal life span. Kate was away, and, although Mary was returning to Dorchester, it was as headmistress of the National School, which would keep her busy. He began to consider building a house for himself in the area. He could afford it, but what Emma would think of the idea was another matter. They had married as two people isolated by their defiance of their families. She remained isolated, and if Hardy meant to return to the fold, where she had no wish to be and felt unwelcome to his mother, their life together would be changed for the worse as she saw it. It would no longer be a great adventure, more like a sort of captivity. But there was not much she could do if he made up his mind. She deserves some sympathy. But the shifting feelings in a marriage, and in a family, are as complex and unpredictable as cloud formations. In August, Hardy spent another week at Bockhampton, and this time he persuaded Emma to come down to Weymouth to join him for a second week. His sisters were at home, Jemima consented to make some expeditions with them, and everything went well. By the next spring he was writing to his brother Henry about the possible purchase of a 'plot of ground we want to get in Dorchester'.[18]

So there were two processes running counter to each other in this period. Hardy was achieving the sort of success he wanted, he and his work were in demand, he was making enough money to live comfortably in a middle-class suburb, to belong to a club in town and to take Emma to fashionable hotels in France when they spent a holiday touring in Normandy in the summer of 1880. He could just about hold his own at dinners and in a salon, and he had the confidence to offer the Queen his book. Emma still compelled him physically: a paragraph in his poetry notebook describes how he watched her reading by candlelight behind a screen in his firelit study, a shadow of her head thrown on to the ceiling and wall, light 'shining through the loose hair about her temples' and reaching her skin 'as sunlight through a brake'.[19] It reads like a foretelling of Tess. At the same time he was feeling the pull of his old home, turning back to the places and people of his past. He worried about the condition of his parents: their generation was dying off. Mr Moule followed his wife and son to the grave early in 1880; his mother's brother William Hand also died in 1880 and her sister Mary's husband John Antell soon after. Who was to say how much longer before they too went, taking not only themselves but their precious stores of memory and knowledge?

And he was sometimes oppressed by the problems between Emma and himself, knowing that she disliked the idea of settling permanently in Dorset, that she grieved over having no children, and being unlikely now to have any, and that she would like to be more involved in his work and more fully acknowledged for her involvement.

In the autumn of 1880 he was well into his new novel. It had a title that meant more to his generation than later ones, *A Laodicean*, taken from the Book of Revelation and meaning a person who blows neither hot nor cold but remains cool and indecisive. This was the heroine, daughter of a millionaire railway engineer who has left her a fortune and an ancient castle in Dorset which she loves for its antiquity but also wants to modernize. The early chapters were already written and being printed for serialization when, as though fate had decided to change the plot of his life, he was struck down by an illness so severe that it kept him out of action for many months. He does not describe or name the illness, but years later he called it an attack of bladder inflammation and says it recurred throughout his life, although never so badly as on this first occasion.[20] He blamed a chill brought on by too much swimming off the Normandy coast in July, whose symptoms he must have ignored. He began to feel really ill in October, when he had to call in a neighbouring surgeon. Internal bleeding was diagnosed. Bladder infections are agonizingly painful and debilitating. It does not seem to have been caused by a stone but was rather a severe form of cystitis. Nowadays antibiotics work their wonders, but then suffering was likely to be prolonged, and patients had to rely on careful nursing care. Hardy endured a great deal of pain. Emma, aghast, asked the Macmillans' advice, and they sent their own doctor. There was talk of an operation. Then they were told that if Hardy was prepared to rest in bed for several months, he might avoid the operation. This was the least dangerous course and fortunately what he chose to do.

His decision was not made only on medical grounds. He realized that an operation and a stay in hospital would have made it impossible for him to go on writing, whereas from his bed at home he believed he might manage to keep up his commitment to deliver his monthly instalments to *Harper's*. There was a good reason for

this. He was being paid £100 for each of the twelve instalments
of the new book, which was to be the first serial in the new *Harper's*
European monthly magazine, with Du Maurier's illustrations, and
there were ten more to be written and delivered: he stood to lose
£1,200 if he failed, and he made up his mind he would not. He
had to rely on Emma as he had never done before. She became
his chief nurse and also his amanuensis, and as soon as he was able
to they set up a programme of work which they kept to doggedly,
day after day, as he dictated the novel to her from his bed. She was
also responsible for keeping his publishers reassured, making light
of his indisposition and insisting that there was nothing seriously
amiss.

Worried as Emma was, it was also a high point for her. It gave
her an occupation and responsibility. She was in charge of his
health and his correspondence, and indispensable to his writing.
The bitterly cold winter made extra problems in running the
Tooting house and nursing, and in January snow was blowing in
through window cracks and doors. 'Our passage (downstairs) is
sole-deep, Em says, and feet leave tracks on it.'[21] She proved herself
stalwart and good at what she had taken on. It was not easy,
because his condition did not improve steadily but fluctuated in
an alarming way. A Savile acquaintance, Edmund Gosse, came to
see him and afterwards remembered getting the impression he had
jaundice; he may well have had more than one affliction. In January
one of his Puddletown cousins, Mary Hand, offered to come to
help out, and, although it is not known whether she did come,
Emma was ready to accept help or service from his family in a
crisis. She kept in touch with Mary, one of whose letters survives
from January; it suggests that Hardy had been suffering a relapse
of some sort: 'My dear Emma, I was very glad to hear from you
but the iron has again entered my soul respecting Tom's illness. I
am glad you told me just how he was and I hope he is again
recovering.' And she goes on to describe conditions in Dorchester,
where the schools are closed by the weather:

I don't think there has been such a winter since Granny went to Church
walking on the hedges . . . I have heard nothing from home during the

sharp weather except the Dorchester news which has been that the Bockhampton folk had to live wholly on potatoes. No bakers could get there I know: but don't be alarmed. Henry is young and strong and they killed a pig quite recently, but I suppose they don't wish to risk Bob's legs if they can avoid it . . . I should very much like to come and see you again. All this dull weather Katie has been quite lonely and so have I. I wish we could have been with you – if you would have liked us. Yours affectionately, M. Hardy.[22]

The wistful last words suggest a degree of uncertainty about her welcome, but Emma was at her best when most was asked of her.

In February, Kegan Paul advised Hardy to consult Sir Henry Thompson, specialist in bladder disease, who came, examined Hardy and said he did not think an operation necessary, though he told him he must continue to rest. By now he had only five more instalments to write and was recovering his strength. His sickbed notes are charming.

Jan. 31. Incidents of lying in bed for months. Skin gets fair: corns take their leave: feet and toes grow shapely as those of a Greek statue. Keys get rusty; watch dim, boots mildewed; hat and clothes old-fashioned; umbrella eaten out with rust; children seen through the window are grown taller.

Feb. 7. Carlyle died last Saturday. Both he and George Eliot have vanished into nescience while I have been lying here.

'Nescience', as Hardy lovers know, was a favourite word and means having no knowledge, particularly appropriate for George Eliot who, alive, had so much.

Feb. 21. A. G. called. Explained to Em about Aerostation, and how long her wings would have to be if she flew, – how light her weight, etc., and the process generally of turning her into a flying person.[23]

A. G. was Alfred Greenhill, an engineer friend of Hardy, interested in aeronautics, and aerostation was aerial navigation. They perhaps shared a joke about Emma being a ministering angel to Hardy, and how differently she would have to be constructed before she could take to the skies. It sounds like a cheerful scene, the two men complimenting and teasing her, as though the hard work she had put in through the winter had earned her some lightness of being.

13. The Tower

In April 1881 Hardy was able to get up again and spend his days by the fire, feet on the mantelpiece and pen in hand – so he described himself in a letter to a friend.[1] He said he was not writing much, but in fact he was working on the twelfth and last instalment of *A Laodicean*, and he finished it by the end of the month. The result was poor and scrambled together, but it was a triumph to have got it done at all, and to have kept the severity of his illness from *Harper's*. Now Emma was able to go into town again when she liked, and he made his first outing in a carriage, and then resumed a daily walk. Together they went for another consultation with Sir Henry Thompson and were reassured. After this they made up their minds to leave London for Dorset yet again. Hardy blamed the bad metropolitan air for undermining his health and believed he would work better in the country. The search for a building plot had been set aside during his illness, but it was not forgotten. Meanwhile they must rent a house.

In June they were in Dorchester, staying at the King's Arms while they looked about.[2] They found what they wanted in Wimborne, near the Hampshire border and ten miles north of Bournemouth and the sea. Wasting no time, they went back to Tooting to pack up their things and moved in before the end of the month.[3] It was Emma's third Dorset home. Memories of their good days living at Sturminster above the Stour may have played a part in their decision, since Wimborne also stood on the Stour. It has water meadows to the south and west, a cluster of streets with handsome old houses and a minster church dating back to the twelfth century. Hardy had thought of moving there in the year after their marriage, when his house-hunting led him past the minster at dusk and he had gone in to hear an organist playing, lit by a single candle, and was pleased by the music and the brilliance of the candlelight in the dark arcaded building. But what they rented was once again a solid modern brick villa, as close to the railway station with its good service to London as to the river or the minster. Lanherne, The Avenue, had been built for a gentleman, with stables and a carriage house at the end of the garden. Not needing the stables, Hardy allowed a neighbour to use them and chose to charge him nothing. He found immediate pleasure in the well-planted garden, the conservatory and the vine on the stable wall, and he made a careful note of what was growing, from Canterbury bells and Sweet Williams to 'strawberries and cherries that are ripe, currants and gooseberries that are nearly ripe, peaches that are green, and apples that are decidedly immature'.[4] On the night of 25 June they were in the garden to enjoy a new sight in the sky, a large comet named after the Australian astronomer who had predicted it, Tebbut's Comet.

Hardy began to think of a story with an astronomical theme. In 1881 astronomers were preparing to travel round the world to observe the rarely occurring Transit of Venus in front of the sun, due to take place in December 1882, which would allow a more exact measurement of the distance between the sun and the earth to be calculated.[5] Hardy incorporated the Transit of Venus into his tale, making his young hero an astronomer eager to get to the Pacific to gain a good observation point. He also applied for permission to visit the Royal Observatory at Greenwich. Visitors were not normally allowed, and he was sent a form to fill in, inquiring whether he had an observatory of his own or planned to build one. He replied disingenuously that he was 'sketching the plans for one' and wished to ascertain 'if a hollow memorial pillar, with a staircase inside, can be adapted for the purpose of a small observatory – and how it can be roofed so as not to interfere with observations – etc. etc.'. He was also asked to produce 'the name of any gentleman of either of the Scientific Societies of London, or who has repute in Science to whom you are known'. Hardy offered three names eminent enough to unlock most doors, although only one, Thomas Huxley, was a scientist. He added Tennyson and Lord Houghton for good measure and was admitted to the Observatory in December 1881, where he presumably found answers to his questions.

He wanted to know whether a tower could be converted into an observatory, because he had decided his hero would install one in an existing tower, lent to him by the lady on whose land it stood. Hardy had three Dorset towers in mind, but his principal model was in the park of Charborough House, an eighteenth-century mansion five miles from Wimborne.[6] This tower, a magnificent construction, with stairs and rooms, was put up in the 1790s and improved fifty years later. There was no question of asking to visit it, because Dorset landowners did not open their properties to the public, but, in July, Hardy took Emma and his sister Kate for a jaunt to see an Iron Age camp, Badbury Rings, in a hired wagonette, and, as they passed Charborough and glimpsed the tower over the wall of the estate, their driver told them this was 'heiress land', meaning that it had passed down through the female line. The present owner, Miss Drax, lived there alone and unmarried, a quiet little lady, he said. She had inherited from her mother, Jane Erle-Drax, the previous heiress, while her father was a mere young officer, with nothing but good looks and a smooth manner to recommend him. Jane Erle-Drax had been thirty-nine when they married in 1827; he was twelve years younger and he took her name. Their only child, Maria Caroline Sawbridge-Erle-Drax, inherited it in 1853 and was now the quiet little lady, living in entire seclusion.[7]

Hardy snapped up gossip and snippets of information like this and used what he wanted. He set his tower on a private estate, made its mistress an older woman and her lover a clever boy. His tower stands far from the house, on a small tree-covered hill in the middle of a great ploughed field of ninety acres, which, as Hardy points out, provides a better barrier than a lake. He has it built over what might have been a Roman camp, and it emerges from trees into the open sky 'a bright and cheerful thing, unimpeded, clean, and flushed with the sunlight'.[8] He claimed that *Two on a Tower* centred on the contrast between the hero's astronomical studies, voyaging through the vastness of space, and the intimacies of love between him and the older woman, and that he had intended to 'set the emotional history of two infinitesimal lives against the stupendous background of the stellar universe'.[9] In practice the lives of characters in a novel cannot seem 'infinitesimal', because they have to claim the foreground of the writer's imagination and our attention, and, whatever Hardy intended, it is not the starry spaces but Viviette and Swithin who fill the foreground of this novel, with the questions raised by their love – whether they can or will marry, whether she will wreck his life, or he hers, and how they can manage to keep any secrets in a country village where the farm labourers and the domestic servants know just about everything that is going on – all pressed urgently and effectively. Viviette, Lady Constantine, is the 28-year-old wife of a baronet, Swithin a poor, clever boy of nineteen, and their love leads to many complications. Once again, Hardy was raising the question of the poor man and the lady.

Swithin is given some impressive astronomical talk. 'The actual sky is a horror,' he says and 'horrid monsters lie up there waiting to be discovered . . . Impersonal monsters, namely Immensities . . . the voids and waste places of the sky.' He talks of 'a quality of decay' in the sky that adds 'a new weirdness to what sky possesses in its size and formlessness', possibly an allusion to the Second Law of Thermodynamics, formulated at the mid century.[10] 'If you are cheerful, and wish to remain so, leave the study of astronomy alone. Of all the sciences, it alone deserves the character of the terrible.'[11] This is what he tells Viviette, who is eager to hear and learn. There are times when he is so excited and absorbed by his intellectual pursuits that he forgets about her, and times when she asks herself if she is right to distract him from his ambitions and makes up her mind to leave him alone.

The tower itself is the centre of the book, and Hardy makes it, as well as a solid structure, a poetic dream place where things are possible that are not allowed in the real world. It also sets the events of the story going and sees their conclusion. It is at various times observatory and work place, love nest, refuge, object of curiosity and suspicion, tourist attraction and place of death. He describes it with loving attention in all seasons and at all hours of the day and night. At the top of the tower, Viviette, wife of the landowner on whose estate it stands, first lays eyes on Swithin, a trespasser from the village, whose interest in astronomy has led him to use the tower as an observatory without asking permission. He is the orphaned son of a curate and a farmer's daughter, brought up by his simple grandmother in the village but educated at the local grammar school. He is gifted, and ambitious to become nothing less than the Astronomer Royal, as he announces to Viviette. He is also a strikingly beautiful young man. She grants him permission to continue working in the tower – her husband is away indefinitely in Africa – and offers to assist him with his astronomical ambitions in every way. To begin with she purchases the equipment he badly needs. It is not long before she realizes she might 'soon be plunging across the ragged boundary which divides the permissible from the forbidden'.[12]

The book has a strong sexual charge and is especially insistent on Viviette's wooing of the boy. She is Venus to his Adonis, only a successful Venus.[13] One day she finds him sleeping in the tower and cannot resist cutting off one of his curls to keep. Hardy writes of her 'superiority of experience and ripeness of emotion exercising the same peculiar fascination over him as over other young men in their first ventures in this kind'.[14] When she has lunch served to him in her library, it is highly symbolic: first pheasant – the land-owner's food, traditionally denied to the lower classes – and then an apple, 'in whose flavour he recognized the familiar taste of old friends robbed from her husband's orchards'.[15] She sits down to talk to him with 'warm soft eyes which met his own with a luxurious contemplative interest . . . [and a] voice not far removed from coaxing'.[16] Later in their romance Swithin's voice becomes husky with desire when he says, 'I won't go away from you,' and she yields to 'all the passion of her first union with him': as straightforward an account of a sexual embrace as could then be made.[17] Ten years on, Hardy told a friend that 'ever since I wrote "Two on a Tower" in 1881 – I have felt that the doll of English fiction must be demolished.'[18] This suggests he knew exactly what he was doing, and why.

Marriages between older women and young men were also very much in the news. Hardy's friend Anny Thackeray had recently married, at the age of forty, a cousin seventeen years younger, to the intense disapproval of Leslie Stephen. In 1880 George Eliot, a few months before her death, married a man twenty years her junior. In the same year the 67-year-old Baroness Burdett-Coutts caused general consternation by announcing she was going to marry her secretary, a young American half her age, and against all advice the marriage went through in February 1881. Hardy's Viviette was not yet thirty, but she was still an older woman, and Hardy knew that for a baronet's wife or widow – there is doubt over her status for some time – to be attracted to a village youth was a shocking theme for the 1880s. But his tone is easy and his sympathy strongly with Viviette, as she and Swithin flout the conventions of class, age and morality.

Swithin's clergyman father had married a farmer's daughter and been dropped by the gentry as a result; like Hardy, he is between two worlds, brought up in the village by his Gammer Martin, who bears some resemblance to Hardy's grandmother, as we have already seen.[19] Later in the book Viviette behaves still more disgracefully, when, finding herself pregnant by Swithin after sending him to the other side of the world on his astronomical expedition, she has not the courage to brazen things out and instead deceives a bishop into marrying her and passes off the child as his.

Viviette and her story developed in Hardy's mind through the summer and autumn of 1881, but he did not write anything down yet. He negotiated the sale of a short story through a 'Newspaper Fiction Bureau' and delivered it for Christmas publication, read the proofs for the serialization of *A Laodicean*, which continued until December, and in September the proofs for its publication in volume form.[20] He enjoyed the proofreading because he was able to sit in the sunshine under his vine: 'The sun tries to shine through the great leaves, making a green light on the paper, the tendrils twisting in every direction, in gymnastic endeavours to find something to lay hold of.'[21] The green light on the paper is from Hardy the poet making notes, like the candlelight reaching Emma's skin through her loose hair 'as sunlight through a brake', when he was ill in the winter. He believed, and said, that he was a poet and not a novelist, and that he wrote novels to make money; and his businesslike attitude to getting well paid for them, and relative indifference to making them as good as they could be, relate to this belief. His method was as far as possible from the perfectionism of a Flaubert, and he had very little to say about his approach to writing fiction. When a novel turned out badly for one reason or another, he dealt with it briskly, but he does not appear to have tormented himself; he never even considered withdrawing *A Laodicean* from publication. It was work done and paid for, and that was it.[22]

The Hardys were now accepted as solid people and invited to dull provincial dinners, Shakespeare readings and even to the annual ball given by Lady Wimborne, where Hardy exchanged mild jocularities with his host. The eldest of the Moule brothers, Henry, who had first made friends with him and introduced him into his family, called on them in Wimborne; he was about to become curator of the Dorset County Museum, currently being built in Dorchester to the design of Hardy's old boss, Crickmay. Emma suggested that Moule and Hardy might collaborate on a book about Dorset, Moule doing the pictures and Hardy the text, but Hardy thought it unlikely to make money and did not pursue the matter. In August he took Emma for a northern trip: visiting Edinburgh, Glasgow and Loch Lomond, and returning by way of Windermere and Chester. In September the *Atlantic Monthly* asked him for a new serial to appear simultaneously in America and England. He offered them *Two on a Tower*, and the deal was made in January 1882, the story to run from May to December. Now he began to put on paper the ideas he had already developed in his head. 'Thus ended 1881,' he wrote, 'with a much brighter atmosphere for the author and his wife than the opening had shown.' The cheerfulness is rare enough to suggest that Hardy and Emma enjoyed their Christmas season in Wimborne.

He had no difficulty in keeping up with the instalments of *Two on a Tower* and managed to cram in a great deal of other activity during 1882. In February a dramatized version of *Far from the Madding Crowd* opened in Liverpool, and he took Emma north to see it in March.[23] On the way back they stopped in London to see Henry Irving in *Romeo and Juliet*, tickets provided by Irving as a fellow Savilian. In April he was in London to attend the funeral of Darwin at Westminster Abbey and to see 'his' play again, which

had transferred from Liverpool to the Globe Theatre; it did not
please him. In September he finished writing *Two on a Tower*
and made a tour around the West Country with Emma, visiting
Salisbury and the coast, Lyme Regis, Charmouth and Bridport.
They travelled in horse-drawn coaches, and Hardy was proud of
his wife when she complained about the ill-treatment of a horse:
'E., with her admirable courage, would have interfered, at the cost
of walking the rest of the distance: then we felt helpless against the
anger of the other passengers who wanted to get on.'[24] On their
way home they called on William Barnes in his thatched vicarage
near Dorchester, at Winterborne Came. He was now in his
eighties, still sprightly, cared for by his unmarried daughter with
the help of several servants in neat uniforms, still a good pastor to
his parishioners and still a revered figure to other poets, Tennyson
foremost among them.

Two on a Tower came out in volume form in October. It was
found shocking, even repulsive, and called his 'worst yet' by one
critic. Hardy must have expected, or even intended, to produce
some sort of shock and indeed had suggested an advertisement, to
go in the *Athenaeum*, that singled out the age gap between hero
and heroine and her 'desperate *coup d'audace*' involving a bishop;
but he was still worried by the attacks.[25] There was some reassur-
ance from the young Henry Havelock Ellis, who took the occasion
to write a long essay in the *Westminster Review* in which he discussed
all Hardy's work, praised him for his presentation of women who
are 'not too good' and very real, and hailed him as 'a writer who
has a finer sense of his art than any living English novelist'.[26] Ellis
was not upset by sexual passion, young lovers of older women or
by the presentation of a bishop as a self-satisfied fool; he was only
ahead of his time, and Hardy wrote him a grateful letter. But many
readers were horrified, and Hardy was reduced to making lame
excuses, saying the plot had required a bishop, that he meant no
disrespect to the Church, that another character was an entirely
honourable clergyman, that the heroine was deeply religious and
so forth. Since Emma's uncle Canon Gifford, who had conducted
their wedding, had just married a daughter of the Bishop of Peter-
borough, she also may have felt the book to be embarrassing. In

the preface to the 1895 edition Hardy again lamely pointed out that 'the Bishop is every inch a gentleman.'

Pompous bishops have been known to exist, women to fall in love with younger men and to pass off babies on the wrong man. The love affair is perfectly believable, the best of the book being its exploration of the situation that arises when a clever youth is wooed by a lady: delicate, ecstatic, sometimes absurd and sometimes painful. The real problem with *Two on a Tower* is a quite different one, and it is that, after the arresting start that seems to promise a brave, original story, the heavy paraphernalia of the Victorian thriller is wheeled out creaking: coincidences pile up one after another, letters appear at the wrong moment and are read by the wrong people, distant uncles leave wills with upsetting clauses, a marriage turns out to be invalid, Viviette's meddling brother appears suddenly from abroad for no good reason, and her husband Sir Blount is first reported dead, then alive, then again dead. Some of this can be put down to the usual problem that Hardy was writing for serialization, which drove him to pack in far too much plot, and that he wrote too fast, without time to think or reconsider. This time he did not even trouble to revise the serialized text for book publication. So the narrative veers between comedy, some light, some black, and pathos, confusing our responses.

The one thing no reader can miss is that Hardy had a good time imagining Viviette. He was captivated by her, still more than he had been by the beautiful pagan Eustacia. He gives her the allure of a woman who can be thought of as part sister, part mother, part lover, describing her look 'that was neither maternal, sisterly, nor amorous; but partook in an indescribable manner of all three kinds'.[27] She is 'fervid, cordial, and spontaneous'.[28] Even the virtuous vicar of the parish is made aware of her 'soft dark eyes . . . the natural indices of a warm and affectionate, perhaps slightly voluptuous temperament, languishing for want of something to do, cherish, or suffer for'.[29] She is driven to behave badly only when circumstances have trapped her and she is desperate, and, although she is punished by her author with a severity that should have reassured conventional readers, she appears throughout as a charming woman who has the author's sympathy, admiration and tenderness. She was one of the well-loved dream women who kept him company away from the real world. Some years later Emma complained that he cared more for the women he imagined than for any real woman, a remark that suggests she understood him better than she is usually given credit for.[30]

On the other hand, he failed to revise or improve *Two on a Tower* precisely because he set off with his own real woman, Emma herself, for a prolonged holiday in Paris in the autumn, 'playing truant', as he put it cheerfully to Gosse, just when he should have been working on revisions.[31] They took a flat in the rue des Beaux-Arts on the Left Bank for more than a month, bought their own groceries and vegetables 'in the Parisian bourgeois manner', dined out in restaurants every night, walked about Paris together visiting the Louvre and other galleries, where he jotted down his ideas about the paintings, and appreciated the beauty of the city. They also revisited Versailles, where they had been on their honeymoon. Hardy notes that they both caught colds, and Emma kept no diary this time, but it was the sort of jaunt she loved.[32] There were no distractions, and it's a fair guess that they enjoyed themselves, and even each other's company. George Douglas, who first met them in Wimborne in 1881, said of Hardy that he was 'at his best and happiest about the year '81. Besides his work – ever with him the first consideration – there were, of course, other things to minister to his happiness – most notably his wedded life, and unmistakable, though all too slow recognition by the public of his work . . . the Hardy of 1881 was a robuster figure than any I ever saw again, robuster and less over-weighted by care. His talk, too, was light and cheerful – mainly about literature.'[33]

If he was happy with Emma in Paris, he was still set on moving back into the orbit of Bockhampton. Like a migrating bird or a salmon driven to return to the place of its origin, he seems to have been drawn by an irresistible force. Early in 1882 he wrote to Lord Ilchester's estate office asking the price of a freehold site on which to build, at Stinsford Hill, between Bockhampton and Dorchester.

He had no luck with this request, but he had made up his mind to build himself a house in the district. The builders were there, in the shape of his father and brother, and he was to be his own architect.

Emma's family, apart from her brother Walter, was as distant as ever. A letter from Helen at this time shows what Emma had to put up with in the way of condescension, ignorance and insult from her sister. Helen does not mention Hardy. 'I am glad that you have at last settled in the country I am certain it is best, and you can always go to town,' she wrote. 'Have you ever read Zenobia, Queen of Palmyra – We have had it lent us, a most delicious book.' A postscript reads, 'One of our servants tells me that one of the books on the drawing room table "Far from the medelling [sic] crowd" is *so nice*.'[34]

In November 1882 Helen wrote to Emma again, this time with the news of the death of her husband. Cadell Holder had been nearly eighty when he died peacefully: 'I asked him if he was happy and he looked earnestly and said "Yes darling" his last words . . . Pa is coming on Thursday,' she wrote to Emma, still without mentioning *her* husband.[35] Hardy regretted the death of Holder and kept a friendly memory of the man who had encouraged his wooing of Emma.

At the end of the year he decided to take a house in Dorchester, where he would be best placed to look for the building site he wanted. They moved in the summer of 1883. In the eight years of their marriage they had lived in seven different places and made three trips to the Continent. Hardy had worked steadily, producing five novels, but nothing he had written during this time had matched the success of *Far from the Madding Crowd*. Still, like Dickens and George Eliot, he had established himself by his pen as a solid member of the middle class within a decade of his first book appearing. He had understood the business side of writing, the importance of serialization, and how to deal with the American market, and the Australian, as well as British publishers and magazine editors. Even when one of his books was badly reviewed and sold poorly, the demand for the next remained strong enough for him to turn from one magazine to another, and from one pub-

1. This is the view of Dorchester – Fordington Church on the left and the water meadows in the foreground, with Grey's Bridge over the Frome – that Hardy knew from his earliest years.

2. Hardy's drawing of his birthplace at Higher Bockhampton, built in 1800 by his great-grandfather for his newly married grandparents, shows it as it was in the 1890s, extended from the original two-up, two-down cottage. His earliest-known poem describes it as his grandmother remembered it:

> Our house stood quite alone, and those tall firs
> And beeches were not planted. Snakes and efts
> Swarmed in the summer days, and nightly bats
> Would fly about our bedrooms. Heathcroppers
> Lived on the hills, and were our only friends;
> So wild it was when first we settled here.

3. and 4. Hardy's parents are old in these earliest picture but they suggest his father's easy-going nature and the powerful character of his mother, Jemima.

5. Melbury House, the seat of the Earls of Ilchester, one of the great land-owning families of Dorset, on whose favour the rural poor depended. Jemima worked as a maid for members of the family from the age of thirteen.

6. Stinsford House, near Bockhampton, belonged to the Ilchesters. Here Jemima was a servant and the Hardy men did building work.

7. Hardy's first school at Lower Bockhampton. At ten he went on to school in Dorchester, and at sixteen he was articled to a Dorchester architect.

8. The most interesting family in Dorchester was that of the Revd Moule, here on the lawn in front of his Fordington vicarage. He worked tirelessly for his poor parishioners and ran a school for boys in the vicarage, educating his seven sons, all of whom went on to universities, two becoming bishops.

9. Horace Moule was the most brilliant of the sons and became Hardy's friend and mentor, giving him books and encouraging him to question orthodox religion. But Horace was depressive: he drank, failed to take his exams, caused scandals and finally killed himself. He made an indelible mark on Hardy's life, and Hardy never forgot how cruelly Horace was destroyed by forces outside his own control.

10. Hardy aged nineteen, when he was an architectural pupil in Dorchester, studying Latin and Greek in his spare time and enjoying Moule's friendship. Two years later he took himself to London, found architectural work, wrote poetry and took a great interest in politics and science. John Stuart Mill was his hero; he read Darwin and gave up Christianity. After five years he went home to write a radical novel, but failed to find a publisher.

11. In 1870 Hardy was sent to north Cornwall to work on a dilapidated church at St Juliot near Boscastle. He stayed at the rectory. The garden terrace is shown here, with the rector, his wife seated, and her sister, Emma Gifford, standing. Hardy and Emma fell in love on this first visit.

12. and 13. The Giffords were gentry but Emma was free-spirited and unconventional, and believed in Hardy as a writer from the first.

14. Hardy's sketch of Emma on her knees searching in the river for the glass they shared on a picnic, bottom in the air, breast clearly outlined and hair tumbling. He marked in his Bible, 'Behold, thou art fair, my beloved, yea pleasant: also our bed is green.' She had dropped the glass while rinsing it, and both bared their arms to search for it in vain. 'No lip has touched it since his and mine / In turns therefrom sipped lovers' wine,' he makes her say in 'Under the Waterfall'.

15. Emma's sketch of Hardy holding a flag, probably showing support for the French during the Franco-Prussian War in 1873. He was not able to visit Cornwall often, and their courtship was mostly by letter. She copied his manuscripts for him and encouraged him to persist with his writing, as he struggled to establish himself as a novelist while earning his living by architecture.

16. and 17. Emma later destroyed their letters, but these little drawings made during their courtship were preserved, showing the summerhouse in the garden of the rectory where they sat together, 'Boscastle Valley' and 'The Watercourse' of the Valency River.

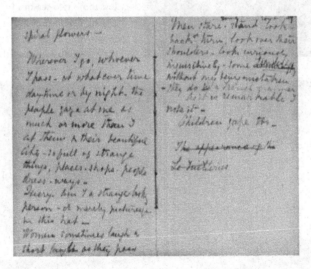

18. A page of Emma's honeymoon diary. Hardy left no account of his wedding, to which neither his parents nor Emma's came, but she described the day, 17 September 1874, as 'not brilliant, but wearing a soft, sunny luminousness; just as it should be'. And in her diary she showed her delight in France, Rouen and better still Paris, 'charmante ville' of 'gay shops . . . gens sitting in the streets . . . vivants enfants . . . white caps of the femmes . . . the river and its boats . . . the clear atmosphere and brilliant colourings'.

19. and 20. The house above the River Stour where Hardy and Emma enjoyed two happy years from 1876. Riverside Villas stand outside the market town of Sturminster Newton, and Hardy's upstairs study window gave him a fine view over the Blackmore Vale (*below*). Here he wrote *The Return of the Native*, the novel he held in greatest affection. Years later he also wrote tender reminiscent poems about his life with Emma: how they went boating together and how she would wait for him in the porch in her white muslin dress, eager for his return. 'A Two-Years' Idyll' speaks of this time:

> Yes, such it was;
> Just those two seasons unsought,
> Sweeping like summertide wind on our way,
> Moving, as straws,
> Hearts quick as ours in those days . . .

21. Hardy has made himself look the part of the successful Victorian literary man, bearded and bewhiskered in the pattern of Dickens, Trollope, Meredith, Henry James and Wilkie Collins. The photograph is from the time of his marriage in 1874. He had published four novels during the four years of his courtship, *Desperate Remedies*, *Under the Greenwood Tree*, *A Pair of Blue Eyes* and *Far from the Madding Crowd*, serialized in the *Cornhill* magazine and immediately popular, as it has remained ever since. His books were welcomed in America too, and he was making serious money.

22. Leslie Stephen with his dog Troy. Stephen was the editor of the *Cornhill* and had commissioned *Far from the Madding Crowd*. His background – he had been to Eton and Cambridge, had a private income, knew everybody and was married to Thackeray's daughter – was as different as possible from Hardy's, but the two men took to one another. In the last year of Hardy's life Stephen's daughter Virginia Woolf made a visit to her father's old friend and wrote an admirable description of him in her diary.

23. The Hardys took this house in Tooting in 1878 in order to enter into London life. Hardy joined a gentlemen's club and was invited to meet the literary lions of the day – Tennyson, Browning, Matthew Arnold. But he became seriously ill in the winter of 1880, and after his recovery they moved back to Dorset, first Wimborne and then Dorchester.

24. Hardy bought a piece of land outside Dorchester, designed his house and had it built by his brother. In June 1885 he and Emma moved in. At once he doubted whether it had been a wise move, and she never liked Dorset, but they lived out their lives there – only going to London every summer for the Season.

25. The hall at Max Gate, with its grandfather clock, and the sun coming in through the drawing room. On the left is the dining room, at the back the kitchen and the bicycle room: Emma started to bicycle in 1885, taught Hardy, and they both became enthusiasts. Upstairs he wrote *The Woodlanders*, *Tess of the D'Urbervilles* and *Jude the Obscure*, the last two regarded as scandalous – and read all over the world.

26. Hardy dressed for the road, with his bicycle – 'the loveliest "Byke" . . . "The Rover Cob"'.

27. Hardy met and fell in love with Mrs Florence Henniker in 1893, as he was embarking on *Jude*. She was the daughter of Richard Monckton Milnes, the first Lord Houghton, an aristocrat with literary tastes, and she translated poetry and wrote and published stories. Hardy misread her charm as encouragement, hoped for a love affair and sank into gloom when she turned him down, but they remained friends, and some of his best letters were written to her.

28. Emma Hardy in her later years, dressed up for one of her garden parties, with one of her impressive hats. 'How she would have loved / A party today! – / Bright-hatted and gloved, / With table and tray / And chairs on the lawn . . .' wrote Hardy later, but there were years of estrangement and mutual hostility as he withdrew from her. She came to dislike his writing; he preferred the company of other women; she retaliated by moving up to the attic. Her situation as a wife whose husband no longer needed her was pathetic, and, although she was mocked by many and disliked by some, there is something touching about her childlike face.

29. and 30. Florence Dugdale, a young schoolteacher with literary tastes, wrote to Hardy asking if she might visit him in 1905. She was twenty-six to his sixty-five. He was now one of England's leading writers and had much to offer her. He was also starved for affection and soon in love with her. It was the beginning of a semi-clandestine relationship: here they are on the beach at Aldeburgh. The situation turned to farce when Emma met and innocently befriended Florence in 1910, inviting her to Max Gate.

31. When Emma died suddenly in 1912, Hardy was stricken with sorrow and remorse and began on a sequence of poems recalling his love for her. Florence was bitterly offended, but agreed to marry him in 1914. She liked living at Max Gate no better than Emma had done. Here she is in front of the house with Hardy and their dog Wessex, a biter, feared by everyone else but cosseted and spoilt by both of them.

32. In 1923 it was arranged that the Prince of Wales, who was visiting his Duchy of Cornwall estates, should be given lunch at Max Gate to meet the great writer. Hardy was pleased, Florence was flustered, the Prince had not read a line of Hardy's work, but the occasion went well, not least because Hardy liked old institutions and royalty was one. He may have reflected that his mother had watched from the roadside Princess Victoria driving by in 1833, and felt understandably proud that royalty now came to him.

33. Hardy's tragic novels and his picture of man's powerlessness against the malign workings of fate gave him his reputation for pessimism, a charge he rejected, seeing himself as a realist with an eye for the ironic element in life. If he sometimes harassed his fictional characters, in life, as he aged, he laughed with friends, enjoyed the company of younger poets and other admirers, and gave his time generously to visitors, who found him spruce, lively, cheerful and vigorous, and took away an impression of charm and simplicity. He saw the funny side of old age and remained 'a human being, not "the great man"'.

34. Augustus John's portrait of Hardy was painted in 1923, showing a face
carved, seamed and furrowed by a long, reflective life, 'refined into an
essence', as T. E. Lawrence described him. 'I don't know whether that is
how I look or not – but that is how I feel,' said Hardy of the portrait.
He had four more years to live and continued to work in his study
every day, writing poems, interesting himself in every aspect of their
publication, and also in theatre productions of his novels. He read widely
as well. When Einstein's theories caught his attention, he jotted in his
notebook: 'Relativity. That things and events always were, are, and will be
(e.g. E.M.F. etc. are living still in the past).' 'E.M.F.' stood for Emma, Mary
his dead sister and Florence Henniker, who had died earlier in the year.

He approached his own death serenely, clear in his mind to the end,
unwavering in his atheism, and died at home in January 1928.

lishing house to another. All this was negotiated by Hardy himself. No one had yet thought of becoming a literary agent, and it is unlikely he would have employed one if they had. He was not yet ready to start on another novel, but he kept going with short stories: 'The Three Strangers', a dramatic and sinister tale with a Dorset setting, greatly admired by Robert Louis Stevenson, a sentimental pot-boiler called 'The Romantic Adventures of a Milkmaid', specifically for the American market, and a fresh and lively adventure story for children, 'Our Exploits at West Poley'.[36]

He was also persuaded to provide an article, 'The Dorsetshire Farm Labourer', for *Longman's Magazine*, in which he praised Joseph Arch, whom he had heard speak and greatly admired. Arch had been setting up trades unions among agricultural workers and was shortly to go into Parliament as a Liberal. There was widespread anxiety about conditions on the land and the future of farming, and against this background Hardy gave his personal view that things had improved for Dorset farm workers during his lifetime in terms of education and freedom, and that they were less exploited by their employers than they had been. At the same time he warned that rural communities were breaking down, as villagers left to live in towns, many moved from job to job, and the loss of 'long local participancy' left them without any comforting sense of belonging to a particular place and group. He was then asked to write another article about labourers and the vote but declined on the grounds that it was 'a purely political subject'. Liberal by family tradition and personal conviction, he now decided not to take a public stance on politics, saying that a writer was more effective if he appeared open-minded on strictly political questions.[37] In his letter to the commissioning editor, however, he commented privately that the insecurity of labourers' lives caused them painful anxiety, and he believed that 'some system by which he could have a personal interest in a particular piece of land' would be desirable.[38] Some of the ideas that helped to shape his later novels, *The Woodlanders*, *Tess of the D'Urbervilles* and *Jude the Obscure*, in which he shows the insecurity of the lives of the rural poor, were slowly building in his mind.

14. The Conformers

In 1883 he and Emma moved into a rented house in Dorchester, and he bought a lease on a building site just outside the town, making it clear that he planned to settle permanently. He was even ready to take up his responsibilities as a prosperous citizen and soon accepted a nomination to sit on the bench as a Justice of the Peace. The place had not grown or changed very much in the twenty years since he left it, although there was a new museum, a new brewery and a few more churches. Strolling players still came to perform in the market field, and the proprietor and leading actor playing Othello, whose voice could be heard as far as the town pump, had to reproach people for laughing in the murder scene. 'Is this the nineteenth century?' he asked his ignorant audience, reducing them to silence, although they clapped the placing of the pillow over Desdemona's face.[1] Circuses came to Fordington Field, itinerant girl musicians played in the high street, and old men rang in the new year in the belfry of St Peter's as they had always done. Hardy began to meditate a novel in which Dorchester itself would figure as prominently as the characters. Within a year he would start searching the files of the *Dorset County Chronicle* for stories from the 1820s that he might make use of. He became absorbed in the history and fabric of the town, its pattern of streets based on the camp set up by the Romans and now 'shut in by a square wall of trees, like a plot of garden ground by a box-edging'. Viewed from the hills above, it was still small enough to appear 'clean-cut and distinct, like a chess-board on a green table-cloth'. He noticed that most of its citizens left their front doors open so that you could look right through their houses to the flower gardens at the back. The shops were full of agricultural implements, and the people remained rough, humorous and down to earth.

In August he had the gloomy task of attending on an old friend, Hooper Tolbort, one-time pupil of Horace Moule and William

Barnes, who had done so brilliantly in the Indian Civil Service examinations in the 1850s. He was now ill with tuberculosis and back in England, bringing with him a half-written study of 'The Portuguese in India' which he asked Hardy to have published, should he prove unable to see it through himself. It was a sad business. Hardy said he would, Tolbort died in August, and on examining the manuscript Hardy found it was unpublishable. He wrote an obituary for the *Dorset County Chronicle*, and brooded on the waste of hope and promise: 'Tolbort lived and studied as if everything in the world were so very much worth while. But what a bright mind has gone out at one-and-forty!'[2] Praising his friend's commitment, intelligence and enthusiasm, he saw that 'everything in the world', far from being worth while for him, had been rendered useless by his early death.

His own planned progress continued smoothly. In June he had signed a lease with the Duchy of Cornwall for a plot of land of an acre and a half on which to build, committing himself to spending at least £1,000 on the house (and in 1886 he paid £450 for the freehold).[3] A visit to the house and walled garden today, with encircling main roads, traffic, suburban housing and thickets of trees, gives almost no impression at all of how it was then, a bare plot with open land and wide views all around, a mile outside Dorchester in a still unenclosed part of Fordington Field, 'with rolling, massive downs, crowned with little tree coronets before and behind'.[4] He had made time to draw up his own plans, and his father and brother were to be the builders, although old Mr Hardy's participation cannot have been great, given his age and poor health; but Bockhampton was near enough for him to drive over to give his advice. Work started on the site almost at once, and at the end of the year Hardy himself planted an infant forest around the site, mostly beech trees and Austrian pines, to provide shelter from the wind as they grew. He had never planted trees before, as far as we know, but either he knew instinctively how to set about it or he sought expert advice. Two years later, when he described Giles Winterborne and Marty South at work in *The Woodlanders*, he was able to draw on his own experience:

Winterborne's fingers were endowed with a gentle conjuror's touch in spreading the roots of each little tree, resulting in a sort of caress, under which the delicate fibres all laid themselves out in their proper directions for growth . . .

'How they sigh directly we put 'em upright, though while they are lying down they don't sigh at all,' said Marty.

'Do they?' said Giles. 'I've never noticed it.'

She erected one of the young pines into its hole, and held up her finger; the soft musical breathing instantly set in, which was not to cease night or day till the grown tree should be felled – probably long after the two planters should be felled themselves.

'It seems to me,' the girl continued, 'as if they sigh because they are very sorry to begin life in earnest – just as we be.'

Giles plants skilfully, but it is only Marty who notices the sighing of the newly set trees. Hardy must have heard it when he planted his. He became their protector and would never have them lopped back or cut down, even when they grew into dense thickets. He spoke of 'wounding' them, and refused to curtail the 'soft musical breathing' he had initiated and given to Marty to appreciate.[5] His trees were silenced only after his death, when his widow had most of them cut down.

During the preliminary work of digging a well, three feet below the surface, three skeletons were found in separate graves, cut into the solid chalk, each an oval about four feet long and two and a half feet wide. The bodies had been laid on their right sides, with their knees drawn up to their chests and their arms extended so that their hands rested on their ankles. 'Each body was fitted with . . . perfect accuracy into the oval hole, the crown of the head touching the maiden chalk at one end and the toes at the other,' wrote Hardy, as tightly fitted as chicks inside the egg shell.[6] Two had metal circlets with clasps fixed around their heads, and one was a woman, from whom Hardy himself removed 'a little bronze-gilt fibula that had fastened the fillet across her brow' with his own hands.[7] All were buried with urns of a design that suggested Roman work of the third or fourth century. Near them was a deeper hole with the horn, teeth and bones of a bull. Hardy assumed that this was an out-of-town, single-household resting place. Later the workmen making the drive to the house found they had decapitated five more skeletons. The link with the ancient past interested him, but he did not tell Emma about the skeletons at the time, thinking she might be frightened, and it occurred to him that they might be an evil omen.[8]

The site was on the Wareham road, near a disused toll gate whose last keeper had been Henry Mack, and the place was known as 'Mack's Gate'. Hardy changed it to Max Gate, a name that has always seemed unsuitable, with a suggestion of sophistication and urbanity. Even he had doubts about it and once jokingly made it 'Porta Maxima' in a letter to Gosse. Bockhampton has the ring of an ancient English place name; 'Max Gate' has nothing of what Hardy described as 'the quaintnesses of a primitive rustic life'.[9] But so he named it. Within months of moving into the finished house he was doubtful that it had been right to build it at all: 'Whether building this house at Max Gate was a wise expenditure of energy is one doubt, which, if resolved in the negative, is depressing enough. And there are others,' he wrote in his notebook.[10]

In September 1883 Oscar Wilde, who was raising money by lecturing before he got married, spoke in the Town Hall in Dorchester on one of his standard subjects, 'The House Beautiful'. He led his audiences round an imaginary house, telling them what was good and what to avoid, for example no wallpaper in the entrance hall but wainscoting, and tiles rather than carpet. Only secondary colours on walls and ceilings. Windows must be small to avoid glare. No gas chandeliers but sidelights instead. Furniture should be Queen Anne, and stoves should be Dutch porcelain. He then turned his attention to the people in the house and advised the women to give up corsets and wear simple Grecian drapery, and the men to return to knee breeches.[11] As long as you could afford Queen Anne furniture and had the figure for simple Grecian drapery, there was nothing outrageous about his advice. He had given the talk with great success all over America, and he went on from Dorchester to Bournemouth and Exeter with it. Hardy was invited to meet the lecturer after the talk, but no local reporter was taking notes, and it may be these two remarkable men failed to exchange any words. Later Hardy gave his opinion that Wilde's wit relied on a formula by which he took a well-known saying and distorted it to make it shocking, 'Never put off till tomorrow what you can do today' becoming '*Always* put off till tomorrow what you can do today'. This was clever of Hardy but not quite fair – Wilde is funnier than that.[12] And, as far as the House Beautiful went, he does not appear to have considered any Wildean adjustments to his arrangements for Max Gate, where the hall floor was of polished wood, some windows were made small and others large, and where there were never any gas chandeliers for the good reason that there was no gas supply. 'I never have cared for possessions,' he once said. 'What is in this house has come together by chance. The things I have bought, I bought as I needed them, and for the use I needed them for.'[13]

Was Hardy a good architect? The question is unfair, since he built so little and got out of the profession. He had won a prize for the design of a country mansion when he was at Blomfield's, and he drew efficient-seeming plans for cottages and villas in his notebook, but Max Gate was his first house, designed and built in a proud and thrifty gesture after he had abandoned architecture. Few have admired it, and no one could call it beautiful. It was not a country mansion but a small house of two reception rooms, two bedrooms and a study. The outside is starkly proportioned and weighty for such a modest place; the inside is uninspired but comfortable, with a kitchen and service rooms at the back and bedrooms for servants in the attics. Hardy specified a flush lavatory, for which the water had to be pumped up daily, but there was no bathroom and no running water: maids carried jugs to the bedrooms, as was normal in the 1880s, when half the female population must have spent hours carrying water up and down stairs. Seeing Max Gate today, you have to subtract the additions made since. In the 1890s Hardy built for his brother and sisters another house at West Stafford, about two miles away, recognizable by a similarly ungainly exterior.

No one else ever commissioned Hardy to design a country house, but he kept up his interest in architecture, mostly through William Morris's Society for the Protection of Ancient Buildings, which he joined in 1881 and which tried to prevent architects from spoiling churches with the sort of work he had been employed in as a young man. He regretted what he had done and worked with the Society energetically, trying and failing to keep Puddletown Church (among others) from being 'improved', and speaking eloquently of how buildings hold together 'memories, history, fellowship, fraternities'.[14]

In the spring of 1884, after his three-year pause, he started on his new novel. *The Mayor of Casterbridge* is an extraordinary book and another new departure for him, not a love story but a tragedy built around a single man. As in *The Return of the Native* he created an almost closed setting, giving a dramatic intensity to the action. The scene was the town of Dorchester – renamed but recognizable – and the action was set back to the 1840s. The Mayor himself, Michael Henchard, was supposed to be about as old as the century, older than Hardy's parents and no kin of the people of Mellstock but a stranger to the district. It is the first of his books to be named for one person, the subtitle variously 'The Story of a Man of Character' or 'The Life and Death of a Man of Character', both good.

The book is squarely centred on this one man, strong, ignorant, energetic, driven by a sense of what he might achieve, which he fulfils once he sets his mind on doing so. Never for a moment do we doubt that becoming mayor of a small country town is a huge achievement, so well does Hardy establish the world he has chosen to write about. Henchard is undermined by guilt for his actions as a young man, and he craves affection, but has a temper that drives it away. So the basis for a classic tragedy is set up, the hero not a king or even an educated man but an unschooled, roughly spoken working man: 'bad at science' and 'bad at figures – rule o'thumb sort of man', is how he describes himself.[15] Henchard comes from nowhere, first seen as an itinerant hay-trusser walking through the countryside looking for work, owning nothing but what he can carry. He was married at eighteen and regrets it at twenty-one, and the only family he ever mentions is a brother, long since dead.

By moving him into the small community of Casterbridge, Hardy allows him to appear as a great figure within it, powerful, respected and also resented. He is again alluding to Shakespeare: Henchard's behaviour in ridding himself of his family and ill-treating his mild daughter, and his strength that turns into self-destructiveness, partly mirror the behaviour of Lear. He has the ambition and the strength to be a hero, and the failings to become a tragic one. He is without subtlety, but he is built on a large scale, morally and physically – Hardy tells us he is 6' 1½" in his shoes – and he has an intuitive sense of what life should be. When he knows he has gone wrong, he seeks to put things right, clumsily but honourably; and when he knows he has gone irretrievably wrong, he decides that the right course is to end his life, asking that his memory should be blotted out with his life. When his daughter Elizabeth-Jane reads his instructions that he should not be commemorated, she accepts them 'from her independent knowledge that the man who wrote them meant what he said. She knew the directions to be a piece of the same stuff that his whole life was made of, and hence were not to be tampered with to give herself a mournful pleasure.'[16]

Deeply imagined and meditated work, dramatic and poetic, the narrative is shaped on a grand scale and paced with extraordinary moments. Henchard at the weir hole, intending to drown himself and seeing himself in the water, remains a terrifying incident even when you know the explanation. The words spoken over the departed Susan Henchard by Mother Cuxsom, momentarily setting aside her class belligerence in acknowledgement of the power of death, contrive to be one of the most perfect elegiac statements ever made: 'Well, poor soul; she's helpless to hinder . . . anything now . . . And all her shining keys will be took from her, and her cupboards opened; and things a'didn't wish seen, anybody will see; and her little wishes and ways will all be as nothing!'

The descriptions of Casterbridge/Dorchester combine what Auden called Hardy's 'hawk's vision' and a countryman's wit:

Bees and butterflies in the corn-fields at the top of the town, who desired to get to the meads at the bottom, took no circuitous course, but flew straight down the High Street without any apparent consciousness that they were traversing strange latitudes. And in autumn airy spheres of thistledown floated into the same street, lodged upon the shop fronts, blew into drains; and innumerable tawny and yellow leaves skimmed along the pavement, and stole through people's doorways into their passages, with a hesitating scratch on the floor, like the skirts of timid visitors.

Or

The farmer's boy could sit under his barley-mow and pitch a stone into the office-window of the town-clerk; reapers at work among the sheaves nodded to acquaintances standing on the pavement-corner; the red-robed judge, when he condemned the sheep-stealer, pronounced sentence to the tune of Baa, that floated in at the window from the remainder of the flock browsing hard by; and at executions the waiting crowd stood in a meadow immediately before the drop, out of which the cows had been temporarily driven to give the spectators room.[17]

The Mayor of Casterbridge is a great book in detail and conception, flawed by having too much plot, too many incidents packed in too fast, so that you long for a pause in the action. At two thirds of the length it could have been still better than it is. Hardy himself complained that he had been driven by the demands of serialization to over-elaborate, and, although his inventiveness is impressive, he was right about there being too many twists and turns.[18] Sometimes the chapters gallop through revelation and counter-revelation at a pace hard to keep up with or believe in. The central device – of a man who has made good out of a bad start and, just when it seems he can redeem himself, is drawn down into another spiral of mistrust, jealousy and misunderstanding – is quite enough, and the central trio, Henchard, his supposed daughter and his assistant Farfrae, strongly and subtly balanced, are always living presences. Around them the other characters gesture and play their parts picturesquely and impressively but without their depths. Henchard and Elizabeth-Jane turn through hope, conflict, hatred, forgiveness, love and despair, never quite predictably, as we watch his strength draining and hers developing. When she looks at Farfrae, she notices 'how nicely his hair was cut, and the sort of velvet-pile or down that was on the skin at the back of his neck, and how his cheek was so truly curved as to be part of a globe, and how clearly drawn were the lids and lashes which hid his bent eyes'.[19] Hardy is showing her appraising a man, finding him desirable and imagining how it would feel to touch his skin and hair – not what a nineteenth-century girl was supposed to imagine, but he was not going to deny her sexual feeling.

When Henchard torments her halfway through the book, she is described as a 'dumb, deep-feeling, great-eyed creature', reduced by unkindness almost to a suffering animal; Hardy also knew the ways in which men are cruel to women, and women submit.[20] Towards the end Henchard reflects that out of his wronging of the social law had come 'that flower of Nature, Elizabeth. Part of his wish to wash his hands of life arose from his perceptions of its contrarious inconsistencies – of Nature's jaunty readiness to support bad social principles.'[21] He is thinking of her illegitimacy, although you might expect him to take some comfort from 'Nature's jaunty readiness', this man who moves like a great tree in the wind, who gazes 'stormfully' (a word Hardy coined for him) and emits 'a blaze of satisfaction' when he carries a point; who is described as leonine and with tigerish affections. But Henchard has been defeated, and Nature has become his enemy.

Hardy's portrait of Henchard – depressive, black-tempered, self-destructive and also lovable, as a child is lovable – is one of his strongest achievements. He told a friend that the only tragedy that made him weep while writing it was *The Mayor of Casterbridge*.[22] Henchard's will forbidding mourning or memorials is a sort of soliloquy addressed to everyone who might read it, a way of cheering himself before he dies, negating the bad things he has done, choosing his own end, dramatizing himself against his environment; and 'it is the moment at which we identify with him most completely.'[23] Although Horace Moule was an entirely different case, it is still possible there were thoughts of him – drinker, charmer and suicide – coming into play in Hardy's mind. In everyone there is some guilt, some fear that events from the past may turn out to have unforeseen consequences, and it may be that the gossip Hardy had heard of Moule's bad behaviour to a poor Dorchester girl who went to Australia, pregnant with his child, was in his mind.

Another tenuous link with local life is in the naming of Abel Whittle. The manuscript shows him fiddling with Henchard's name, trying out Giles and James before he settled on Michael, and with Farfrae's, but he had most trouble with the name of the foolish workman humiliated by Henchard for being late, who appears variously as Smallbone, Small, Wringbone and John Wringbone in the manuscript before he is finally named Abel Whittle. When Whittle first appears he is shown as a near-pauper and a near-idiot, but at the end he becomes a saintly fool who goes to help the dying Henchard. The fact is there was a real Abel Whittle who had been a prosperous farmer at Maiden Newton where Jemima Hardy worked at the vicarage as a girl. His name appears in the census for 1851 and for 1861, when he was sixty-four, a farmer with 1,000 acres, living in Church Street close to the vicarage, with wife, three adult children and several servants; before that he was at nearby Up Cerne. Jemima would have known about him from her friends and could well have known him herself. She may have given Hardy the name, and she may have had reasons of her own for suggesting it to Hardy, or he may simply have found it himself and liked the sound of it. Even the faintest hint that he talked about his work with his mother is intriguing, since he is silent on the subject.[24]

If Hardy himself experienced rage like Henchard's, he turned it inwards. He said he suffered from depression, telling a friend in a letter of 1887, 'As to despondency I have known the very depths of it – you would be quite shocked if I were to tell you how many weeks and months in byegone years I have gone to bed wishing never to see daylight again.'[25] He went on to say that 'this blackest state of mind' was something he suffered from rarely now, but that there were times when it returned. In November 1885, between finishing *The Mayor of Casterbridge* and seeing it published, he noted that he was 'in a fit of depression, as if enveloped in a leaden cloud'. Then he wrote, 'a tragedy exhibits a state of things in the life of an individual which unavoidably causes some natural aim or desire of his to end in catastrophe when carried out.' This was putting prosily what his book had demonstrated dramatically. Was he now thinking of Henchard or of himself? A few weeks later, 'This evening, the end of the old year 1885 finds me sadder than many previous New Year's Eves have done.'[26] This was just before the book began to be serialized in January 1886, and four months before it was published. A reader at Smith, Elder complained that the 'lack of gentry among the characters made it uninteresting'. They printed only 750 copies and remaindered the book in under a year.

He must have planned the book in his head before he put pen to paper, writing it at a gallop in not much more than a year, and that a year full of interruptions as he supervised the building and furnishing of Max Gate and took up his position as a JP in the spring, sitting on the bench for the first time in the autumn. He was also away in London for part of June and July. In 1883 he and Emma made their first venture into taking part in the London Season, and from this point on it became an annual habit. It is one of the unforeseen and even shocking oddities of Hardy's life that for the next twenty-five years, almost without a break, as the weather grew warm each spring, he chose to make the long train journey to Waterloo – still nearly four hours – and to exchange the beauty of the countryside, the birdsong and sweet air he celebrated in his writing, for a sooty atmosphere and unpredictable quarters in town in order to join in the upper-class rituals of the Season.

In the early years they stayed in modest hotels or lodgings in Bloomsbury, partly to be close to the British Museum, where Hardy used the reading room. As time went by they tried a great many lodgings, rented flats and occasionally houses, rarely returning to the previous year's perch but experimenting boldly, sampling life in various parts of town: Bayswater, South Kensington, Holland Park, St John's Wood, Marylebone, Manchester Square, Maida Vale and Victoria. As Hardy prospered, there were summers when they took their own servants with them, just as

Hardy's mother's employers had taken her with them to London for the Season. Jemima herself may well, directly or indirectly, have put the idea that one should go up for the Season into her son's head. It was what you did when you were rich, as she knew, and she must have been impressed and pleased to see her Tom marked out as one of the rich. It was not something Emma's family had ever been in a position to contemplate doing, but she was pleased too, happy to sample the pleasures and amusements of the great world with him. The bonus for her was that she got him away from his mother's influence at the same time. It was still a surprising way to choose to spend the best months of the year. They made occasional visits to town in winter and spring also, but the Season dominated their year. He considered himself 'half a Londoner'.[27]

Hardy did some reading, and even a little writing, during his London Seasons. He went to the Savile, which moved to new premises on Piccadilly in 1882. He saw the summer show at the Royal Academy, and took in theatres and concerts. He attended 'At Homes', 'crushes', luncheons and dinners, even balls. In London he met the Dorset landowners who had not noticed his existence in Dorchester and found that in London he was a well-known figure. He kept an eye on politics. In 1886 he took himself into the House of Commons, admired the benevolence on Gladstone's face and saw 'the dandy party enter in evening-dress, eye-glasses, diamond rings etc. They were a great contrast to Joseph Arch and the Irish members in their plain, simple, ill-fitting clothes. The House is a motley assembly nowadays.'[28] As his own fame grew, the society hostesses who took him up as a celebrity introduced him to politicians, Liberal and Conservative – Lord Salisbury, Balfour, Joseph Chamberlain, Asquith among them. When tea on the terrace of the House of Commons became fashionable, he was there taking his tea.

It was understandable that he should be pleased to lunch with a man of letters such as Lord Houghton, friend of Swinburne and editor of Keats, but he also ate and drank with men and women he could not have found congenial. Sometimes he wrote sardonic notes about them, how men just going into the Cabinet talked with no greater insight than you would expect from a group of Oxford Street shopkeepers, or how the political conversation at another dinner was 'when the next election would be – of the probable Prime Minister – of ins and outs – of Lord This and the Duke of That – everything except the people for whose existence alone these politicians exist'.[29] Looking at the expensively dressed ladies at an evening party, he famously asked himself, 'If put into rough wrappers in a turnip-field, where would their beauty be?'[30] He also found himself face to face with many landowners who spent the winter doing what he most detested, shooting game birds for pleasure.[31]

Yet Hardy was delighted to receive invitations from the aristocracy. These were the people who ran the country. They had the power and the money, and if they offered a glimpse into their privileged world, it was hard to resist. He saw too that entry into high society impressed Emma and made her happy. To her it was the proof of his success, the answer to her family's disapproval and condescension. When Lady Portsmouth invited the Hardys to stay in the country, Emma wrote to her uncle, now Archdeacon Gifford, to boast about this social conquest.[32] And Hardy was every bit as gratified as Emma. The snobbery of titles is still strong in the twenty-first century, and in the nineteenth it reigned supreme. Hardy might mock 'Lord This and the Duke of That', but he enjoyed being taken notice of by them, and he liked other people to know that he was taken notice of by them. He was also susceptible to the charm and flattery of their ladies, and they liked him, not only because he was a well-known author, but because he did not challenge or make demands; small, gentle and respectful, he was no danger to their daughters.

One society hostess became a real friend. In 1886 he met Mrs Jeune, five years younger than him, nice-looking, very rich in her own right and given to good works as well as to hospitality. She came from the Highland aristocracy and was related to the Duke of Wellington, and royalty had been present at her wedding to her first husband, a son of Lord Stanley of Alderley, who died young, leaving her with two infant daughters. Her second husband was Francis Jeune, son of a bishop, himself a lawyer and Conservative

MP who became a judge, was knighted and finally accorded a peerage. They lived at the very heart of the Establishment.[33] During the Season she ran almost non-stop lunches, dinners and crushes in her Wimpole Street house, moving in 1891 to Harley Street. Edith Wharton described her as 'a born "entertainer" according to the traditional London idea, which regarded ... the act of fighting one's way through a struggling crowd of celebrities as the finest expression of social intercourse ... She took a frank and indefatigable interest in celebrities, and was determined to have them all at her house.'[34] Wharton nevertheless found her charming, became her close friend and loved staying with her. So did Hardy, who called her 'the irrepressible Mrs Jeune', but found that for him she would make time to sit quietly. She encouraged him to talk about his writing, which she admired, as she admired his modesty, and they came to know one another very well. He was there so often that Lord Rowton, who built lodging houses for the homeless, jocularly described him as Mrs Jeune's dosser.[35] He was captivated by her warmth and also by her small daughters. They filled a need for him, as he did for them, since they had no memory of their father, and by now he must have given up any hope of having children of his own. He stayed often enough in Wimpole Street to become 'Uncle Tom' to Madeleine and Dorothy, romping up and down the stairs with them and, as they grew older, taking them to the theatre. Long after she was grown up, married to a Conservative politician and a mother herself, he went on writing to 'My dear little Dorothy', and she went on calling him 'Uncle' for the rest of her life. They not only gave him their affection, they showed him what family happiness could be. There was always a bedroom for him at the Jeunes' if he was in town on his own. Emma was also invited, although she rarely stayed with them. A surprising family connection was made when her uncle Archdeacon Gifford married Francis Jeune's sister. It was a pity that Madeleine and Dorothy disliked Aunt Emma as much as they liked Uncle Tom, but they were too well brought up not to do their best to hide what they felt.[36]

Another who nudged Hardy slowly into friendship was his fellow Savilian, Edmund Gosse. Gosse was the man who had appointed himself the fixer of the London literary world. He was nine years younger than Hardy and had grown up in a modest household in Devon with a scholarly father whose interest in science existed alongside a rigid religious faith which rejected Darwin's account of evolution. The younger Gosse was as clever as his father and soon they were in intellectual conflict. There was no money for university, and at seventeen he was given a probationary job at the British Museum, where he found the work 'tedious slavery' but stuck at it. His ambition was to become a poet, and he had an easy way of making friends with the younger lights of the world he aspired to enter; soon he was close to Ford Madox Brown, Rossetti and Swinburne. He began to review books. He was a fine linguist, took a holiday in Norway, discovered Ibsen's work and introduced it to the English, to great effect. He married in the same year as Hardy, and his new brother-in-law, the artist Lawrence Alma-Tadema, lent him a house close to Regent's Park in which to begin his married life, which was a cheerful one and blessed with children. At the same time he was offered a well-paid sinecure as permanent translator to the Board of Trade. He had earned his luck, but it was astoundingly good luck, and from now on Gosse published his own indifferent poetry and a great many quickly forgotten studies of writers. He entertained energetically at home and in clubs, flattered his friends and proposed them for honours, became librarian to the House of Lords and dedicated himself to living the literary life more seriously than anyone else has ever done. There was something absurd about him, but he was not all absurd, because in his fifties he produced a masterpiece, one of the most powerful autobiographical books ever written, an account of his childhood, *Father and Son*.

Gosse's eagerness to be Hardy's friend came out of a sincere admiration for his work, and he persevered so successfully that in June 1883, having known him for several years and visited him during his illness in Tooting, he persuaded him to stay with his family for a weekend. Inevitably it culminated in a literary party at the Savile in honour of Howells, the American novelist, editor and friend of Henry James. Hardy found Howells amusing and noted down his stories. Howells found Hardy shy.[37] But the friendship was now well launched, and Gosse was rewarded with a reciprocal invitation for a weekend visit to Dorchester in July, as well as a promise that Hardy would take him to meet William Barnes.

Gosse came when the Hardys had just made their move from Wimborne and were installed in Shire Hall Place, the rambling old house in the highest part of the town, where they were to live while the purchase of a building site was negotiated and their own house built. Hardy must have felt satisfaction in returning to Dorchester after so many years away, visibly successful, with a reputation as a writer, a wife and enough money to run a comfortable household and take himself to London or abroad whenever he chose, and the invitation to Gosse shows he felt at ease with his situation. Henry Moule was asked over to meet Gosse, and the three men went out for a stroll round the town together. Gosse was struck by the 'colour and animation' of Dorchester on a Saturday evening: 'it looked in the dusk like a bright foreign town,' he wrote to his wife, who had stayed at home with their children.[38] The liveliness of the streets came from farmers and labourers in town to do their shopping at the Saturday fair, and the brilliantly uniformed infantry and cavalry soldiers from the barracks.[39] On Sunday, Hardy escorted Gosse to hear the 82-year-old Barnes preach with undiminished energy to his flock at Winterborne Came, and accepted his invitation to take high tea with him afterwards.

Gosse's letter to his wife Nellie included a careful comment on Emma: 'she means to be very kind,' he wrote. Hardy was too observant not to notice that his friend was sometimes rather at a loss in his attempts at conversation with his wife. To find that Emma's zest for life, so much prized by him during their wooing, was not so attractive to others, and that her charm fell flat, was upsetting. Of course she was middle aged now. She no longer wore her glorious hair over her shoulders in curls, her strong features were settling into heaviness, and her talk sometimes strayed from the point and followed its own track in a way that had once seemed delightful but now sometimes disconcerting. Feeling unappreciated brings out the worst in everyone, and when people failed to warm to Emma she became more difficult. She had lost her hope of children, hardly saw her own family and was suspicious of his. A letter this year from her friend in Sturminster, Mrs Dashwood, also reminded her of her failed literary ambitions: 'I hope your stories will emerge one after the other and pleasantly astonish the literary world, they have been concocting in your brain long enough and should now see the light . . . When will you and Mr Hardy spend a day with us? You have not visited this gay city for a long time, and ought to renew your acquaintance once with it.'[40] Emma could say nothing of any publication prospects, alas, and there was no visit to the gay city of Sturminster. Gosse's friendship with Hardy was strong enough to include Emma, but he never warmed to her in her own right.

The following summer, in August 1884, Hardy made a trip to the Channel Islands with his brother Henry, and without Emma. In October he was in London to dine with the Lord Mayor, and early in 1885 he went to stay with Lord and Lady Portsmouth in their 'very handsome' house in Devon, where he was fussed over by the ladies of the family. As well as this he worked at copying stories from local newspaper files of the 1820s and 1830s, using some of his findings in the current book: for instance, three stories about wife-selling and an account of wrestling. Emma took on a good deal of the copying for him.[41] Their tenth wedding anniversary had been reached in September. In the previous year Hardy had written a poem called 'He Abjures Love', which he is unlikely to have shown her.[42] No wife would be overjoyed to read:

> At last I put off love,
>   For twice ten years
> The daysman of my thought,
>   And hope, and doing . . .
>
> No more will now rate I
>   The common rare,
> The midnight drizzle dew,
>   The gray hour golden,
> The wind a yearning cry,

> The faulty fair,
> Things dreamt, of comelier hue
> Than things beholden! . . .

Even if the last lines set it in perspective:

> – I speak as one who plumbs
> Life's dim profound,
> One who at length can sound
> Clear views and certain.
> But – after love what comes?
> A scene that lours,
> A few sad vacant hours,
> And then, the Curtain.

Hardy's poems are as likely to be dramatic statements of mood as expressions of fixed feeling, and moods are changeable. This terse farewell to love was by no means his last word on the subject, and there was a good deal more of it to come in his life. Another poem printed in the same group is 'The Conformers', which is also about the end of romance, this time for a couple, now settling down in 'a villa chastely gray'. In it they will 'house, and sleep, and dine . . . / friends will ask me of your health, / and you about my own'; and, their 'dreaming done', they will be remembered as 'A worthy pair, who helped advance / Sound parish views'.[43] For all the scorn in the poem, Hardy had become a JP, Emma was a regular churchgoer – often joined by him – and they were giving up their peripatetic life and building their own villa – plum-red rather than grey but solid enough to qualify as the home of a worthy pair of conformers, as Hardy saw, and was protesting about to himself.

15. The Blighted Star

Hardy was now for the first time in his life a householder and a man with civic responsibilities. His imagination responded by leading him into dark places. The three novels he published during his first decade at Max Gate, from 1885 to 1895, were marked by a fierce questioning of accepted ideas about society and by a gloom that grew deeper from book to book. He sometimes denied that he was a pessimist, and it is true that he kept up his cheerful social life in London, was an assiduous party-goer, took many holidays, indulged in flirtations and wrote several light-hearted stories at the same time as he was working on these novels. More than most writers he knew how to keep an absolute division, a closed and barred door between the polite and quietly spoken person who enjoyed London society and dispensed justice in Dorchester, and the raging, wounded inner self who chastised the values of the world he inhabited. The books are powerful, bleak and sometimes savage in their representation of human experience: the Hardy who moved between his London club, visits to distinguished friends and a home well staffed with servants is not easy to connect with them.

The reception of these books, especially *Tess of the D'Urbervilles* and *Jude the Obscure*, was such that Hardy became a rich man with a world reputation. They also caused scandal, and even the critics who saw they were master works were disturbed by them. What especially worried them was that he seemed to suggest that human beings might be brought down by malignant forces at work in the world, using their power to turn things to evil. Already in *The Mayor of Casterbridge* he had asserted that Henchard gave up his struggle partly because the odds were fixed against him by 'that ingenious machinery contrived by the gods for reducing human possibilities of amelioration to a minimum'.[1] And when Elizabeth-Jane finds love, marriage and wealth, she still believes that happiness can be only 'the occasional episode in a general drama of pain'.

This thought of hers closes the book. Hardy wanted the reader to remember it.[2]

He had written enough about Arcadian country life to show that at one time he believed in the possibility of happiness being more than an occasional episode, even something quite substantial. In *Far from the Madding Crowd*, Fanny Robin dies with her baby, Troy is killed and Boldwood destroyed, but there is light as well as shade, and Bathsheba is allowed to recover and given a second chance with Gabriel Oak. The signs are that they will live a decorous and happy life together. *The Woodlanders*, which he embarked on in 1885 and wrote entirely at Max Gate, is like a black version of *Far from the Madding Crowd*. This time the good man dies needlessly, and the bad man wins his woman and keeps her in spite of his blatant infidelities. All the women are humiliated, suffer and end in sorrow. Grace, educated out of her class by her ambitious father, fits nowhere, makes a bad marriage and fails to get the divorce she wants. She brings about the death of one of the men she loves. The rich Felice Charmond is murdered. The village wench, Sukie Damson, is carried off to New Zealand by an angry, cheated husband. Giles Winterborne, a fine, upright, skilled, hard-working man, first loses the girl who had been promised to him and whom he loves, then his family home and much of his livelihood, and finally his life. Of the two women who love him, one is left trapped in a bad marriage, the other in poverty and mourning, stoically endured. Richard Hutton, an editor of the *Spectator* and usually an admirer of Hardy's work, reviewed *The Woodlanders* as a 'powerful book, and as disagreeable as it is powerful . . . written with an indifference to the moral effect it conveys . . . [that] lowers the art of his works quite as much as it lowers the moral tone'.[3] Hutton, although he claimed not to be asking for poetic justice, in fact disapproved of Hardy making things too easy for the badly behaved Fitzpiers and unleashing punishment on the blameless Winterborne. He saw Hardy as setting out to shock and depress, and skewing the plot accordingly, and this worried him quite as much as the sexual misbehaviour of the characters.

The criticism has been repeated in a different form by one of

Hardy's most intelligent twentieth-century critics, Irving Howe, who writes:

> Because Hardy remained enough of a Christian to believe that purpose courses through the universe but not enough of a Christian to believe that purpose is benevolent or the attribute of a particular Being, he had to make his plots convey the oppressiveness of fatality without positing an agency determining the course of fate . . . The result was that he often seems to be coercing his plots . . . and sometimes . . . he seems to be plotting against his own characters.[4]

The Woodlanders has been read in many different ways: as a lament for the changes affecting rural life, or as a pastoral elegy, partly comic, and pathetic rather than tragic. This is David Lodge's reading. He diagnoses its pessimism as evolutionary and suggests that Fitzpiers survives because he is fitter to do so in the modern age than Winterborne, who represents the old order. He supports this view by pointing out that Hardy's description of the natural world stresses the brutal evolutionary struggle among trees and other plants. Lodge thinks that Hardy, well read in Darwin, accepted the inevitability of the process that destroyed the old-fashioned rural worker, and that it is simple and sentimental to read his novel as tragedy. Hardy himself partly endorsed this when he wrote, in October 1888, 'If you look beneath the surface of any farce you see a tragedy; and, on the contrary, if you blind yourself to the deeper issues of a tragedy you see a farce.'[5] He sounds like a modernist, well aware that his work is open to alternative interpretations. But when he later described it as his favourite among his own books, he took a much simpler stance: 'I think I like it, *as a story*, the best of all. Perhaps that is owing to the locality and scenery of the action.'[6] And for many readers his descriptions of the woodlands, apple orchards and north Dorset landscape have more substance than most of the characters.

There is pastoral magic in the book: Grace thinks of Giles as a fruit god or a tree god, 'cider-stained and starred with apple pips', and he blends into the woodlands, carrying an emblematic apple tree in his arms, taller than himself. Marty's father believes he will die when the great tree by his house falls, and he is proved right. 'English trees! How that book rustles with them,' wrote E. M. Forster.[7] There is comedy, both light-hearted and dark: Grace finding a slug on her plate at Giles's party, Fitzpiers caught out when his three women realize they have been sharing him, a man-trap set off by the wrong person. But there is nothing to smile at in the fate of Giles or Marty. Solid and steady, they are the two characters who carry the book on their shoulders and are remembered when the rest of the story fades. To deny that their fate is tragic is to deny them their dignity and truth, and to miss Hardy's gloomy point about the vulnerability of the poor.[8]

The next book goes a stage further. *Tess of the D'Urbervilles* sets out to show the crushing of its innocent heroine by the society in which she lives, its Christian hypocrisy, its double standard, its exploitation of cheap labour, all combining to reduce her to desperation, so that she ends her life as a ritual sacrifice to society's values. Early in the book Tess tells her brother that they are living on a 'blighted star'. She is giving her own opinion only, but her subsequent history goes to confirm her view. In the final paragraph Hardy famously invoked the idea of the President of the Immortals sporting with her, taking the phrase from Aeschylus. When he was attacked for it, he explained that 'the forces opposed to the heroine were allegorized as a personality', and that this was 'not unusual in imaginative prose or poetry'.[9] To suggest that readers should see that 'the President of the Immortals' is meant only to symbolize the forces of society that brought Tess down will not do as a defence. There is something more there, something that makes sport with her sufferings, and making sport with suffering is cruelty.

Hardy's defence is made weaker because there are other examples in his fiction of people suffering from exceptionally bad luck – luck so bad that it looks as though it has been willed, by the gods, or fate, or possibly by the author. For example, when the young Jude falls into despair at the difficulty of learning Latin and Greek, 'he wished he had never seen a book, that he might never see another, that he had never been born.' This is a reasonable account of a sensitive boy's reaction to severe disappointment, but

Hardy continues, 'Somebody might have come along that way who would have asked him his trouble, and might have cheered him . . . But nobody did come, *because nobody does*.'[10] I have put the last words in italics because this is not a true account of life. Hardy is not only coercing his plot, he is generalizing falsely. There are times when nobody comes, but there are also times when somebody does come. For example, Hardy himself had been helped to learn, not only by schoolmasters but also by Horace Moule and William Barnes, and encouraged by his architectural masters, and he had made other friends who read the classics with him for pleasure. A good many people had come along for him. Jude is not Hardy, of course, but, in so far as he represents Hardy's own unfulfilled wish to go to a university, he is put through a very much worse experience than anything Hardy went through. This is part of what made even Hardy's friend Gosse ask in his review, 'What has Providence done to Mr Hardy that he should rise up in the arable land of Wessex and shake his fist at his Creator?'[11] Part of the answer might be that he was writing at a time when Britain seemed to be permanently and bitterly divided into a nation of the rich and a nation of the poor.[12]

Hardy made a case for his insistence on 'the tragical conditions of life' in a letter to John Addington Symonds, written while he was working on *Tess*. 'I often begin a story with the intention of making it brighter and gayer than usual; but the question of conscience soon comes in; and it does not seem right, even in novels, to wilfully belie one's own views. All comedy, is tragedy, if you only look deep enough into it.'[13] It is hard to believe that any of Hardy's late, gloomy novels could have started off with comic intentions. Henchard restored to prosperity and dandling Elizabeth-Jane's grandchildren, Tess happily married to Angel, Jude getting his BA at Oxford – such ideas are an insult to the characters as he drew them. And can he really have believed that the study of tragedy in fiction might be 'the means of showing how to escape the worst forms of it . . . in real life'?[14] He was too much of an artist to think girls might be warned off bounders by reading *Tess*, or married women deterred from quarrelling with their mothers-in-law and leaving their husbands by reading *The*

Return of the Native. His novels spoke for themselves, and he was not at his best producing theoretical justifications for them.

Neither Hardy nor anyone else has explained where his black view of life came from. I have suggested that something in his constitution made him extraordinarily sensitive to humiliations, griefs and disappointments, and that the wounds they inflicted never healed but went on hurting him throughout his life. In a sense too he never got over his own loss of Christian belief, which removed hope. He was always defensive about it, so much so that when his friend Frederic Harrison attacked him for his pessimism in 1919, saying that the gloom in his poetry was 'not human, not social, not true', and that it sorted ill with Hardy's long, happy and well-rewarded life, Hardy reacted by ending his friendship with Harrison.[15] Like most people, he gave different accounts of what he believed at different times. While he was working on *The Woodlanders* he was reading Hegel and noted, 'philosophers seem to start wrong; they cannot get away from a prepossession that the world must somehow have been made to be a comfortable place for man.'[16] Years later, when he came to write *The Dynasts*, he wrote of the Immanent Will, a morally indifferent force that controls events without awareness of what it is doing (like a machine):

> The Will has woven with an absent heed
> Since life first was; and ever will so weave.

This at least works better than the idea of a malign President of the Immortals. Later still he said he saw the Cause of Things as 'neither moral nor immoral, but *un*moral'.[17] At the same time, atheist or agnostic as he was – he was not sure which – he could never quite get away from the Christian God. In his poem 'God's Education' he suggests that 'God' has something to learn from man and accuses him of cruelty; God thinks about this and says it is a new idea for him.[18] Hardy took some of his pessimism from Schopenhauer, who saw the world as malignant, God and immortality as illusions, and the extinction of the human race through chastity as an end to be sought: best of all not to be born. Yet he was always too imaginative to follow any one philosopher consistently. 'This planet does not supply the materials for happiness to higher existences [meaning human beings],' he noted in 1889. 'Other planets may, though one can hardly see how.'[19] In his own life, however, he did not entirely give up on locating happiness, however grim the messages he put out.

In 1891, when he was working on the proofs of *Tess*, he wrote to a friend, Henry Rider Haggard, whose ten-year-old son had just died, expressing 'sympathy with you both in your bereavement. Though, to be candid, I think the death of a child is never really to be regretted, when one reflects on what he has escaped.'[20] Did Hardy really believe this? And even if he did, could he not see that it was not the thing to say to the parents of a newly dead ten-year-old, for whom they must have planned and desired a long and happy future? What was in Hardy's mind as he wrote this letter? Was he trying out an idea or just being awkward? Was Schopenhauer's recommended preference for non-existence being offered as a tonic? And did he look at Mrs Jeune's daughters and privately hope they too might die before they grew up? Surely not. He had enough imagination to write feelingly about a mother grieving over her dead daughter in 'A Sunday Morning Tragedy'.[21] Haggard was tough enough to take the letter in silence. He may have understood that Hardy's ability to believe several conflicting things at once meant he sometimes expressed himself strangely.

And behaved strangely. His idea that death was preferable to life led him into playing a game in which he imagined he was already dead. He describes it in a note made in 1888 after a conversation with Leslie Stephen's sister-in-law Anny Ritchie (*née* Thackeray):

if there is any way of getting a melancholy satisfaction out of life it lies in dying, so to speak, before one is out of the flesh; by which I mean putting on the manners of ghosts, wandering in their haunts, and taking their views of surrounding things. To think of life as passing away is a sadness; to think of it as past is at least tolerable. Hence even when I enter into a room to pay a simple morning call I have unconsciously the habit of regarding the scene as if I were a spectre not solid enough to influence my environment.[22]

The idea that you could get past death and still want to pay morning calls is more fanciful than morbid, and you wonder what he supposed the views of a ghost might be. He took things a stage further in a poem written in 1896, 'The Dead Man Walking', in which, with a passionate gloom, he described himself as having become 'a corpse-thing' that only seemed to be walking, talking and smiling – really, he was dead.[23] This is a poem in which he brings up the losses and disillusionments of the past. Death came on in stages, he says, first from seeing how men lived and losing his youthful enthusiasm, then from the loss of his friend – Moule – and members of his family. It culminates in a bitter reference to finding 'my Love's heart kindled / In hate of me', which sounds like a reference to a quarrel with Emma. What is interesting is that he sees himself being killed progressively by these bad experiences, but, although the idea of a living corpse is horrible, it reads like an ingenious exercise, too ingenious to be painful. Hardy was of course abundantly alive in 1896, but, as at almost any time in his life, he could plunge suddenly into misery and blackness, and follow up a grim fancy of death to see just how far he could take it.

He could also use his sense of the world's random cruelty to make a masterpiece. To read *Tess* is an emotional experience; to write it must have been an overwhelming one. Hardy said later that 'he had put too much feeling into it to recall it with pleasure.' To another friend he wrote at the time of its publication, 'I am glad you like Tess – though I have not been able to put on paper all that she is, or was, to me.'[24] To a third he confessed that he had lost his heart to Tess as he wrote about her.[25] There is no missing this in his descriptions of her physical presence: her 'diapason-stopt voice' which, mysteriously, 'will never be forgotten by those who knew her' (a stopt diapason is an organ note); her warmth of 'a sunned cat' after she has been lying down; her arms fresh from crumbling curds at the dairy, as cold and damp as a new-gathered mushroom; her eloquent dark eyes whose colour defies naming; or 'the brim-fulness of her nature' breathing from her. Whether formed from memory or dream, she was palpable to him. He saw her, and felt the movements of her inner being. Here she is reviving after disaster: 'some spirit within her rose automatically as the sap in the twigs. It was unexpended youth, surging up anew after its temporary check, and bringing with it hope, and the invincible instinct towards self-delight.'[26] The 'invincible instinct towards self-delight', a perfect phrase to describe something we instantly recognize in certain people, and especially the young, was something Hardy himself possessed in very small measure, which may be why he saw and valued it so highly in Tess.

He was exact when he said a novel is not an argument but an impression, and this novel lives through its impressions of Tess and the landscapes through which she moves.[27] He watches her, and sometimes he *is* her, giving her thoughts which are recognizably cast in his own mode: for instance, when she thinks of the past and how, 'whatever its consequences, time would close over them; they would all in a few years be as if they had never been, and she herself grassed down and forgotten.' The 'grassed down' is a pure Hardy image. Again, reflecting on anniversaries and birthdays, she suddenly thinks that one day must be the day of her death, 'a day which lay sly and unseen among all the other days of the year, giving no sign or sound when she annually passed over it; but not the less surely there. When was it? Why did she not feel the chill of each yearly encounter with such a cold relation?'[28] The idea, quaint and slightly sinister, bears the marks of being one of Hardy's own, taken out of his store to be given to Tess.

Hardy places her in a sequence of settings, so that she appears at times an emblematic figure as she moves through the seasons of the year with their appropriate countryside activities, like a figure in a series of paintings. She is seen dancing on the green in her white dress in spring, then reaping in the fields with the villagers and sitting down to feed her baby among them; she is at the dairy in summer, where everything in nature is lush and the milkmaids abandon themselves to the open air of the meadows 'as a swimmer to the wave'; then she is at winter work in colourless fields, with other labouring girls crawling over the surface like flies as they pick swedes under a white sky. She stumbles into the pheasant shoot and shelters among wounded birds whose plight mirrors hers. She is threshing when a new machine sets a diabolical pace of work. And finally she is at the secret house when she and Angel share their few days of bliss.

Tess's name is embedded in the consciousness even of people who have never read the book, but it did not start as 'Tess'. Hardy's particular care in naming his characters often led him to change them in the course of writing, and the evolution of her name can be tracked in the manuscript. In the early stages he tried out three names, Love, Cis and Sue. She was Love Woodrow, Cis Woodrow or Sue Woodrow; occasionally Sue Troublewell or Sue Troublefield. In July 1889 he suggested 'The Body and Soul of Sue' as a title for the work in progress. Then she transmutes to Rose-Mary or Tess: Tess Woodrow or Rose-Mary Troublefield. Turberville makes a first appearance, and 'Too Late, Beloved!' is a possible title in August 1889. At this point he thinks of making the villain, till then named Hawnferne, take the ancient name of Turberville: Alec is being woven into a wider pattern. Tess Troublefield appears next and transmutes into Tess Durbeyfield. When Hardy saw that Durbeyfield could be traced back to the noble D'Urbervilles, giving him a central theme for the book, he wrote a new first chapter, the dazzling scene beginning '"Goodnight, Sir John"', in which Tess's drunken and shiftless father is told of his Norman blood by the local clergyman with an interest in genealogy. It must have been the moment when he knew he was on exactly the right track with the book. This was in November 1889.

Throughout much of this time Hardy was in negotiations with editors. He used the book not only to tell a story close to his heart but to fight a battle, and the long-drawn-out business of how it was written, revised, cut, restored and revised again shows how important the battle was to him. In September 1889 he cancelled his original agreement with Tillotson's syndicated fiction firm, rather than make the changes they asked for, thereby losing the 1,000 guineas he was to have been paid. He then offered it to two magazines, fully expecting them to reject it, and used their letters objecting to its frankness when writing his essay 'Candour in English Fiction', published in January 1890. In this he accused magazine editors and circulating-library managers of standing in the way of good novel-writing by their prudery. 'If the true artist ever weeps it probably is . . . when he first discovers the fearful price he has to pay for the privilege of writing in the English language – no less a price than the extinction, in the mind of every mature and penetrating reader, of sympathetic belief in his personages.' He had suffered from bowdlerizing editors throughout his writing career, and he was determined to have *Tess* published as he wanted it and to 'demolish the doll of English fiction' at last.[29]

To do this he adopted a complicated strategy which involved producing a heavily cut and changed text for serialization. He accepted that in the version published by the *Graphic* Tess should go through a mock marriage instead of being raped, and that she should have no baby; and that Angel, instead of carrying the milkmaids through the flooded stream, should wheel them in a barrow. In *Harper's Bazaar* the changes were less severe, although anything likely to offend Christian readers was removed. And in order to have time to negotiate his way through all the work this would involve, he set *Tess* aside in the autumn of 1889 and switched his attention to writing something entirely different. This was a collection of linked historical stories about titled women – *A Group of Noble Dames* – intended to make another major serial for the *Graphic* and *Harper's*. These, and his essay 'Candour in English Fiction', kept him fully occupied through the winter and spring. Meanwhile the manuscript of *Tess* lay on the shelf. Nothing shows so clearly how much he regarded himself as a craftsman, able to turn out six light pieces of fiction to order while he was in the middle of a quite different and much more serious sort of book. The *Noble Dames* stories, not much more than light reading, were delivered in May 1890, just before his fiftieth birthday. At the end of June he was told that they too would need to be bowdlerized: although the editor was not worried by the references to illegitimate births in noble families, the directors of the *Graphic* objected to them strongly. 'Here's a pretty job! Must smooth down these Directors somehow I suppose,' wrote Hardy in his notebook, and promptly did so.[30]

While he attended to this, he was in London for the Season as usual. That year he entertained himself by going to music halls and also to police courts, low-life entertainments to vary the high life. Emma had to leave London in July when her father died, and she went to Portsmouth for the funeral. Hardy stayed away. He could hardly have gone with her, since the family had never accepted him as Emma's husband. He was restless, and in August he took his brother Henry to Paris to show him the sights. They included a visit to the Moulin Rouge to see the can-can performed. What either of them made of the dancing girls he does not say, but they were two men on the loose, free to do as they pleased. He and Henry got on well as holiday companions, and you wonder whether they sometimes spoke dialect together and laughed more freely than they could when the women – mother, sisters and wife – were there. It was the first time he had been to France without Emma.

Back at Max Gate, *Tess* was waiting as well as Emma. He settled to work again and was able to deliver the 'finished' *Tess* – i.e., the copy expurgated for serialization – in December; he was correcting the proofs in the new year of 1891. This version appeared in the *Graphic* from July. Meanwhile he arranged for the separate publication in other magazines of two of the sections that had been cut, one of them being Tess's christening of her baby. While he restored the rest of the cuts for book publication, he did more revision, including the last-minute addition of a subtitle, 'A Pure Woman', on the title page. This was undoubtedly intended to be a red rag to the delicate-minded, and they complained bitterly.

The first edition, in three volumes, finally appeared in November 1891, with new publishers, Osgood, McIlvaine, Americans who had set up in London. The 1,000 copies sold out quickly. Another 16,000 were sold during 1892. As further editions

followed, Hardy, always reluctant to allow that any of his work
was finished, did more revising. The complicated history of the
text accounts for some of the unevenness in the writing, but at the
same time it allowed him to reconsider and enrich the book. In
America three different versions of *Tess* came out in three years.
As late as 1912 he was still making changes, cutting down Tess's
use of dialect in favour of more standard English. Not surprisingly,
textual studies of Hardy have kept scholars busy. So have arguments
about his intentions. Did he withhold information about Tess's
rape, or seduction, because he was not a realist but a modernist,
deliberately introducing ambiguity to represent the ambiguities in
Alec's intention and Tess's response? To challenge the standard
Victorian response to a fallen woman? Or to nudge the reader
into seeing how relative all values and judgements are in such
matters?[31] *Tess* has provoked many such questions and stood up
bravely under the massive weight of critical discourse that has been
piled on it.

In the first reviews several critics pointed out that Hardy had
won his battle against the editors and circulating libraries triumphantly. *Tess* marked 'a distinct epoch in English fiction', wrote one,
and 'Mrs Grundy and her numerous votaries must, for a time at
least, hide their heads in shame.'[32] It was greeted as a tragic masterpiece, 'brave and clear-sighted', 'one of those books which burn
themselves in upon the soul', full of 'subtlety and a warm and
live breathing naturalness', a book that 'permanently enlarged the
boundaries of one's intellectual and emotional experience'.[33] Tess
herself was seen as a Shakespearean creation and the greatest character in recent fiction: 'She seizes one at once and never looses her
hold.'[34]

It was sneered at too, by critics of both sexes, for its 'terrible
dreariness', its inauthentic picture of country life, its failure of good
taste and lack of intellectual cultivation, its jarring defects of style,
its 'succulence', i.e., insistence on Tess's physical beauty, and
its stagey characters and general unpleasantness. Robert Louis
Stevenson and Henry James exchanged private letters in which
they shared their dislike of the book. Stevenson wrote,

Tess is one of the worst, weakest, least sane, most *voulu* books I have yet read . . . no earthly connexion with human life or human nature; and to be merely the unconscious portrait of a weakish man under a vow to appear clever, or a rickety schoolchild setting up to be naughty and not knowing how . . . *Not alive, not true* was my continual comment as I read; and at last – *not even honest!* was the verdict with which I spewed it from my mouth.

To which James, who had previously given some faint praise to the book, excused himself for it and replied, 'I grant you Hardy with all my heart, and even with a certain quantity of my boot-toe . . . oh yes, dear Louis, she is vile. The pretence of "sexuality" is only equalled by the absence of it, and the abomination of the language by the author's reputation for style.'[35] No one has ever claimed that the book is perfectly written or constructed, or without clumsiness, but it glows with the intensity of his imagination; and Tess's capacity to arouse visceral distaste in some and profound affection and admiration in others is a measure of the sexual power he built into his heroine. To Irving Howe, one of Hardy's best and fairest critics, she is his 'greatest tribute to the possibilities of human existence, for Tess is one of the greatest triumphs of civilization: a natural girl'.[36]

It was said that *Tess* divided families and broke up friendships. Dinner parties had to be rearranged to take account of the warring opinions. And it sold and sold. This, and the effects of the passing of the US Copyright Act in 1890, made Hardy seriously rich. He was able to buy two houses in Dorchester, one for his sisters, both now teaching there, and one as an investment. It also meant that in 1893 he and Emma could for the first time take a whole house for the London Season, moving all their staff to St John's Wood with them. His social ascent continued. He was elected to the Athenaeum Club, from whose balcony he and Emma watched the German Emperor William II progress through London. He moved in the highest circles, and his fame brought him some amusements. Regarded now as an expert on social problems, he was invited by Millicent Fawcett, a leader of the women's movement, to write a story for working boys and girls, warning them of the dangers of treating love lightly. He excused himself, saying that to do it properly demanded clear, direct talk, which he knew the public would not tolerate. He went on, 'The other day I read a story entitled "The Wages of Sin" . . . expecting to find something of the sort therein. But the wages are that the young man falls over a cliff, and the young woman dies of consumption – not very consequent, as I told the authoress.'[37] He smiled again when Arthur Balfour, speaking at a fund-raising dinner of the Royal Literary Fund, gave it as his opinion that literature was in decline and there were now no writers of great merit alive. Hardy was among the guests, who were mostly writers; and noted that not much money was subscribed.[38]

Even as *Tess* was published, Hardy was already at work on another serial promised to Tillotson the year before, a light-hearted story called *The Pursuit of the Well-Beloved*, in which he imagines one man falling in love, at the ages of twenty, forty and sixty, with a woman, her daughter and her granddaughter. He intended it only as a serial, but later rewrote and published it as *The Well-Beloved*.[39] In 1892 he also produced the most haunting of his short stories, 'The Fiddler of the Reels', in which a demonic travelling musician steals the love of a girl away from her country sweetheart, abandons her and returns years later to steal their child.[40] It is a small masterpiece, crackling with energy. And he had another book planned. This one would crown his thirty-year career as a novelist, and also cut it off for good.

16. Tom and Em

As he worked up to his most powerful fictional attack on conventional views of religion and marriage, in his private life he remained conventional and conservative. At Max Gate they took *The Times*, gave employment to two maids, a cook and a gardener, and kept to regular habits. Hardy did not smoke and drank very moderately. Although he venerated Shelley and said the poet was the person he would most like to meet from the past, there was never any question of him behaving as Shelley had towards his wife Harriet, who was simply abandoned when he decided she was uncongenial. For all the disappointments of their marriage, the Hardys conducted it with great decorum for many years. They took frequent holidays together, in England, in Scotland and on the Continent. They entertained and made visits together, giving ambitious luncheon parties in London and garden parties in the late summer at Max Gate. They read together, and went to concerts and the theatre together. They even went to church together, both in London and in the country. Hardy agreed to have two of the children of Emma's brother Walter Gifford, Gordon and Lilian, for occasional holidays at Max Gate within a year of settling there.[1] The arrangement may have been set up to please Emma, but he grew fond of them too and became a notably kind uncle. Their own childlessness remained a sorrow to both of them.

An equal devotion went to their many cats, and they mourned the death of their dog Moss together: some of the tenderness they failed to give one another went to the pets, providing an alternative form of bonding. Up to the mid 1890s he was still writing to her as 'My dearest Em' or 'My dearest Emmie', and in 1895 he sent her a letter from London urging her to come and join him and saying he was 'lonely and dismal' without her. They shared a bedroom and a bed for twenty-five years, which may have been a comfort to them both; it is, however, possible to withdraw into celibacy in the marital bed. Once Emma gave up hoping for a child, she may have become a reluctant participator, but it was not until 1899 that she moved herself upstairs to a bedroom in the attic. Hardy always had an eye for women, on the bus ('in their fluffy blouses' he wrote), in the street, at the music hall, at dinners and crushes.[2] He made notes about their appearance, found many attractive, and at the end of the 1880s he began to fall noticeably in love.

Yet he always admired the Bathsheba side of Emma, wonderfully displayed when, at the age of fifty-five, she learnt to ride a bicycle. She showed great spirit and energy, and persuaded Hardy to learn to bicycle too. They both became enthusiasts, and her initiative opened up their lives significantly. To Emma, with her lameness, the bicycle was a substitute horse, and she even talked about going for a canter. It makes you wonder why he had never bought her a horse at Max Gate. She had a special green velvet bicycling suit made to match her first bicycle, which was green and known as 'The Grasshopper'. Later she acquired a blue one, with matching blue costume. People laughed at her in Dorchester, but Hardy saw the point. The English roads were rough and dusty, but they were also empty, the stagecoach having long disappeared and the motor-car not yet arrived, and so they had the best bicycling ever enjoyed, and after they had mastered their machines were able to cover many miles together. In August 1899 they rode for seventeen miles by moonlight after a harvest festival at Turnworth, arriving home at midnight – and this was only the return journey. By then they were both fifty-nine, and Hardy said he could do forty to fifty miles a day, and Emma almost as much.[3] It suggests camaraderie and shared enjoyment, because it is difficult to keep up a quarrel or a sulk as you pedal along country roads.

Meanwhile, in March 1887, after finishing *The Woodlanders* and accepting the 1,000 guinea advance for *Tess* which he later paid back, he carried Emma off to Italy for six weeks. Once again she kept a holiday diary, a vivid, disorganized, enthusiastic and entertaining record that began on 14 March, when they set off from Max Gate in an east wind that turned into a snowstorm. Thick fog and driving snow greeted them at the coast. 'It seemed the height of madness to start. Tom went below, I stayed on deck.'

Intrepid Emma. In France their train took them to Paris, then to Dijon, where they had an excellent five-course dinner. 'Paid six francs each. Tom very vexed. Dyspeptic before and worse now.' On into the mountains of Savoy, deep snow and tunnels, then Turin and Genoa, where 'Our Hotel Smith quite full, turned out to be Germans and Americans.' Where Hardy noticed the marble palaces and the washing lines strung between the houses, Emma was overwhelmed by the colours of Genoa.

Bright colours everywhere, house[s] yellow, salmon colour very often, sometimes pink. A jammed sensation, on account of the narrowness of the street & great height of houses, palaces[,] continually views of narrow streets, going uphill or downhill, looking like gullies, figures passing in brilliant colours . . . We drove up hill, catching peeps of the sea between the high houses and winding slowly up to the crest of the hill where we got out and a sight burst upon our view which I shall never forget – the whole city lay before us, and the sea – the Mediterranean beyond the houses. I never saw such a superb city.

She has less to say about Florence, where William Barnes's daughter Lucy Baxter had arranged for them to stay in the old Trollope villa, now run as a pension, and they did the usual round of sightseeing. Her first impression of Rome was that the 'large fashionable shops and people and carriages give it the appearance of an ordinary city. disappointing.' But this soon changed: 'stupendous ruins of the Palatine hill and the Forum overpowering – quite easy to realize the life in rooms where the decorations were still distinct.' She picked up a piece of marble on the steps of the Temple of Jupiter. They drove about and took the omnibus but mostly walked, determined to get to know Rome properly. Hardy regretted that the ancient ruins had recently been tidied up, the thickly growing shrubs, flowers and foliage Shelley had liked so much removed. They visited the English Cemetery to see his grave and Keats's, Emma noting the sad inscription, the violets on the graves and the crimson camellias in flower. Hardy picked some violets and sent them to Gosse; Emma welcomed '2 nice letters for Tom about Woodlanders', one from Gosse.

One day, as they walked down opposite sides of a narrow street near the Capitol, three thieves closed in on Hardy, Emma shouted a warning and rushed at the thieves 'with her usual courage', he wrote, driving them away. In the Capitol Museum she studied the Venus and described her with charming precision: 'her hand touches her right thigh, fingers being spread out naturally *both* little toes crumpled under as if she had worn boots.' They succumbed to weariness, fever and colds from time to time, and had to move from a hotel with bugs to the Hotel Allemagne in the Piazza di Spagna, where she admired the 'scarlet carpet, white fore-post [*sic*] iron bedstead covered with muslin curtains', and he could look out at the house where Keats died. She wrote, 'Looked at Ruins over again today. Feel we know the Forum and Colosseum. Shops in narrow streets are always square holes in wall with no wood work . . . no doors, always open for vegetable & provisions.'

Then back to Florence, which now seemed like home: 'the Arno, today a lovely blue – with a dash of opal in it, below sparkling and foaming over rocks like a Devonshire river.' On the other hand, 'old frescoes are horrid entre-nous (note-book and I).' Tom went off on his own to see Siena, then both of them to Venice on 12 April, his thoughts on the poetry of Browning, Shelley and Byron. They had no idea that Henry James was travelling in the opposite direction on the same day, leaving Venice for Florence, where he wrote his great story *The Aspern Papers*, inspired by what he had heard of Claire Clairmont, mother of Byron's daughter Allegra and closer to Shelley than anyone in his circle. She had died only eight years before. So these two writers, each acutely sensitive to the literary associations of the places they were visiting, passed each other unawares. James had been staying with a rich American friend, Mrs Bronson, who lived in the Casa Alvisi on the Grand Canal, opposite the Salute Church, and returned a few weeks later to stay with the super-rich Daniel Curtis of Boston and his English wife in their still more princely Palazzo Barbaro. These were the same people to whom Hardy carried letters of introduction, no doubt from Robert Browning.

Emma wrote, 'T.H. cross at finding we are not on Grand Canal.' 'T.H. has taken letters of Int: to the ladies – Very disappointing for me – (*For the best always*).' The last phrase seems to indicate forgiveness and understanding. In any case she soon met the ladies, Mrs Bronson and Mrs Curtis, the daughter of an English admiral, and was entertained by both families. Emma had nothing to say about them personally, malapropped the names of their palazzi into Barbarossi and Casa Vecchia, and boldly summed up the decor at Mrs Bronson's as 'Well furnished Maple style – and with Liberty combined and Venetian ornaments thrown in.' She could have been right, of course, and intended to be rude, since Maple's furniture was generally known to be for 'monied nobodies', only Liberty's for the discerning.

Otherwise she rose to Venice with enthusiasm. 'The whole city makes one feel fantastic, or beyond. Romantic. You are in a planet, where things are managed differently, or you are gone to the bottom of the sea, and this is a phantom city, or you are simply dreaming.' She noticed that 'None of the Campaniles quite perpendicular. Numerous buildings out of it – walls are all or nearly all in the narrow alleys in a bulging state, & crumbling, many timbers rotting.' And she gives a graphic impression of a night trip along the canals:

Resting[,] the gondola is quite motionless. Stars innumerable and very bright. Then gliding into the narrow canals, though lighted here and there – seems dark and dangerous and very dark places continually beyond, and to pass, shoot under narrow bridges, the gondolier shouting a warning note before he turns sharply round each corner – prime or stati, according as he goes in opposite direction – if he goes stati he calls 'left' to the other who may be coming. Nobody comes generally – but he shouts each time.

In Milan, they went up to the roof of the cathedral, where Emma admired the 'marvellous profusion of marble statues and decorations, flying buttresses, crocketted pinnacles and marble steps' and then felt frightened and descended rapidly while Hardy remained, thinking about Napoleon. She went shopping alone and bought a necktie for Henry Hardy – the only present she mentions – then confidently summoned an open carriage, told the driver to

take her to the principal churches and managed to get round five
or six. She and Hardy were on the evening train for Lucerne, via
Como and St Gothard ('Cascades and mountains'), and so to Paris
and home.

It had been their most ambitious holiday, fulfilling his wish to
follow in the steps of Shelley and Keats, and he was pleased to
have done so; but, although he was inspired to a handful of poems,
his responses to the cities they visited and the landscapes through
which they travelled were muted. Emma's diaries, naive and scatty
as they are, breathe an intense enjoyment and are worth the short
time it takes to read them. She was curious, observant and ready
to explore. They allow you a glimpse of what had first caught
Hardy's fancy. Her social ineptitude may have exasperated him,
and by her own account they were not always the best of friends,
but they came back in good spirits. They proceeded at once to
enjoy the London Season, and on 21 June he took her to view
the Queen's Golden Jubilee procession from the windows of the
Savile Club.

☞

Holidays, and London, distracted them from the discontents of
their marriage. In Dorset they loomed larger. She had seen herself
from the start as his literary companion and helpmeet, and she did
a great deal of dogged work for him, copying manuscripts and
looking through old papers for stories that might be useful to him.
But she had always wanted to become a writer herself, and as the
years passed she infuriated him by dropping remarks that suggested
she had played a part in his creative process. She talked of 'our
books' and of 'emendations' she had made to his work.[4] His
resentment was understandable, although he might have done
better to make a joke of it. Alfred Pretor, a Cambridge scholar
who became their friend and Emma's correspondent and consoler,
went so far as to assure her that 'there is a general and most
widespread belief . . . that you help, and can compose passages, in
the writing of the books.'[5] Since there is no textual evidence that
she composed any passages, it looks as though Pretor was chiefly
concerned to soothe her. Hardy did on one occasion give her

credit for suggesting a scene, when he was speaking to an interviewer about Tess putting on the jewels from Angel's godmother, and said, 'I think I must tell you that was an idea of Mrs Hardy's.'[6] Still, she resented his failure to make any formal acknowledgement of the hard work she put in for him. The manuscript of *The Woodlanders* showed so many pages fair-copied in her hand that Hardy felt obliged to apologize to its purchaser.[7] A dedication would have cost Hardy nothing and meant a great deal to her. He did not choose to put dedications to his books.

He wrote fast, worked hard and for much of the time he needed to be absorbed in his private mental world. He was in his study early at Max Gate and often late too, so that there were days when he hardly noticed her existence or anyone else's. And even when he did notice her, he refused to give her encouragement or to help with her attempts to write, something that became more wounding when he began to show interest in other women's writing, offered to help them and even collaborated with them. A woman friend who knew the Hardys from their Tooting days and stayed at Max Gate with them described Emma as 'very countryfied and scatter-brained . . . [she] wanted to be a poet or novelist . . . and found it hard that no one took her literary accomplishments seriously . . . She had not the intellectual value nor the tact it would have needed to hold the heart of her husband against all the world, but she had loved him dearly and was a nice loveable inconsequential little lady of whom one grew very fond.'[8] There were unkinder comments. When Robert Louis Stevenson called at Max Gate with his wife, Fanny, in 1885, she described Hardy as 'a quite pathetic figure', a 'pale, gentle, frightened little man, that one felt an instinctive tenderness for, with a wife – ugly is no word for it'.[9] George Gissing found her foolish, discontented and paltry when he stayed with them ten years later, but then he did not think too well of Hardy either: 'I admire Hardy's best work very highly, but in the man himself I feel disappointed.' He thought he retained 'much of the peasant's view of life', cared too much for lords and ladies, and did not read many books, and he was shocked that he did not know the names of the wild flowers in his own fields.[10] An American writer, Gertrude Atherton, who saw them in London in the 1890s, described Emma as 'an excessively plain, dowdy, high-stomached woman with her hair drawn back in a tight little knot, and a severe cast of countenance', and told a joke about the journalist T. P. O'Connor attributing the pessimistic nature of Hardy's work to her presence in his life: it suggests the sort of gossip that went about.[11]

Emma described herself once, for an American magazine in 1892: 'In appearance Mrs Hardy is striking: her hair is dark and slightly tinged with grey; her eyes are also dark. She is dignified and very graceful, and looks as though she might be the wife of some ecclesiastical dignitary.'[12] There is something pathetic as well as absurd in her dream of being attached to a clergyman rather than to Hardy, the writer and freethinker, but increasingly the Church became the symbol of her social superiority over him, recalling her gentlemanly brother-in-law at St Juliot and her uncle the Archdeacon. Although Hardy often went with her to church services, she knew very well that his beliefs were unorthodox, while hers became more and more fixed in what she called '*Low Church* Protestantism', learnt, she said, from 'my saintly mother'.[13] Sometimes, when there were guests for lunch at Max Gate and Hardy said something that indicated he did not believe in God, she would murmur that he did not really mean what he said. In the last years of her life she wrote her own account of the 'High Delights of Heaven', full of exuberant imaginings that included the abolition of evil, a glance at hell and the 'obliteration' of those who reject salvation; 'lost pets and martyred ones' were to have their place in heaven as well as angels. There would be flying for all and a new body at Judgement Day, which would give the blessed 'the joy of a healthy child'.[14] Perhaps she was thinking of being free of her lameness at last.

In the summer of 1889 Hardy was sent a book of poetry by a woman poet, Rosamund Tomson. He wrote to thank her and presently they met at the Jeunes'. A striking beauty with large, luminous eyes, she was twenty years younger than him, with a career as a journalist and editor in the literary world. She was also a markedly emancipated woman, had already divorced one husband and married another, Arthur Tomson, a landscape painter, whom she would leave for a third in another five years. Hardy asked for her photograph, flirted with her and pursued her for 'a season / Of love and unreason' that 'took me by storm,' as he wrote later.[15] She was flattered by his interest in her and found it professionally useful, and she seems to have encouraged him enough to keep him dancing attendance. But by 1892 he decided she was merely 'exhibiting him as an admirer' for her own purposes and broke off the friendship 'with considerable disgust'.[16] Emma met the Tomsons, and Hardy's infatuation can hardly have escaped her notice. It was the first time in the fifteen years of their marriage that he had plainly shown he was attracted to another woman.

In the 1890s there were deaths in both Hardy's and Emma's familes. First, in the spring of 1890 he heard of the death of his cousin Tryphena, not yet forty. They had lost touch altogether, she married to a publican in Exeter, with several children. He says he began to think about her for no reason on a London train and started a poem which became the tender 'Thoughts of Phena' when he heard of her death a few days later. 'Not a line of her writing have I,' it begins, 'Not a thread of her hair,' and it goes on to recall her as 'my lost prize'.[17] He was remembering how fond he had been of his pretty cousin, the youngest of the Sparks girls, now all dead or else in Australia, and expressing a sense of loss and regret. His sister Mary kept in touch with Tryphena's brother Nathaniel Sparks in Bristol, but Hardy had offended him by failing to attend his father's funeral in Puddletown in December 1874, when Hardy was newly married and living in Surbiton. He did not go to Tryphena's funeral either.[18]

Over the next few years there were more deaths in both the Hardy and the Gifford families. Emma's mother died a year after her father, in 1891. Losing her parents made her think again about their opinions and prejudices, and especially perhaps what they had said to her about her husband. A grandfather clock and some other Gifford furniture came to Max Gate, a source of pride to Emma. There is a story that she once pointed it out to Lady Newbolt with the words, 'These were mine, Mr Hardy's family didn't have any furniture like this.'[19] Whether the story is true or not, her father's remembered warnings and dislike of her husband may well have helped to fuel any anger he now provoked, and it was about this time she began to keep diaries in which she gave expression to her disappointment with the marriage and resentment at his behaviour.[20] About this time too Hardy changed his appearance, shaving off the beard he had worn throughout their marriage. Instead of continuing as a respectably bewhiskered Victorian, he gave himself a smooth chin and cheeks and kept only a moustache, which he waxed with dashing effect and which proclaimed him a man of the world.[21]

In November 1891 Hardy's aunt Mary Antell died. She was the last of his mother's sisters and the widow of John Antell, the shoemaker with radical ideas who had taught himself Latin, Greek and Hebrew and, frustrated by his inability to make anything of his learning, took to drink; their daughter Polly, friendly with Kate Hardy, was often at Bockhampton and sometimes kept an eye on Max Gate when Tom and Emma were away. Antell was followed in 1892 by Hardy's father, who died in July at the age of eighty-one. He had been confined to the house and unable to see anyone outside his immediate family for several years, and his wife and daughters between them nursed him to the end. It was eighteen years since Hardy had last helped him with the cider-making, and fifteen since he had travelled from Sturminster to Bath to visit him when Mr Hardy went to have his rheumatism treated there. On the day of his death Hardy was in London, but he at once began to arrange a memorial service to be held at Stinsford Church. He also produced a leaflet, pointing out that his father had been born and died in the same house, played his violin in the church for as long as he was allowed to and possessed the virtues of Horatio, 'A man that fortune's buffets and rewards / Has ta'en with equal thanks'. His father's cheerful and equable spirit meant much to him, his own being so different. He left an estate of £850 – some of it perhaps given to him by his successful son – with money to his daughters and the various small bits of property he had acquired in his working life to his widow, and after her death to his son Henry. On one of his father's plots of land, Talbots, at West

Stafford, Hardy and Henry agreed to collaborate in designing and building a house, with the idea that Jemima and her unmarried children could live more comfortably there than at Bockhampton. The house went up, but Jemima was unwilling to move, and the house, Talbothays, was let out. Thomas's inheritance from his father was £5 and any piece of furniture he wanted. We don't know what he chose, but it may have been another grandfather clock, because there were three at Max Gate.

Two months later, Stinsford House was partly destroyed in a fire. It was where Jemima Hardy had been in service; and where before that Lady Susan O'Brien had lived for many years and employed Hardy's grandfather to build the vault in the church for her husband and herself; and where Hardy's father 'when a boy chorister in the gallery of the church used to see her, an old and lonely widow, walking in the garden in a red cloak'. 'A bruising of tender memories for me,' wrote Hardy. 'Met Mary in the churchyard, who had been laying flowers on Father's grave, on which the firelight now flickered.'[22] Although Jemima lived indomitably on, it was symbolic of the end of the era of the older Hardys.

It was also the time of the height of the success of *Tess*, about to appear in a one-volume edition owing to the very great demand. Hardy went to London in September to see his happy publisher at the Café Royal. Then he travelled on to Berkshire, to the village where his father's mother, Mary Head, had been an unhappy orphan. The village was Great Fawley, and Jude Fawley became the name he gave to the hero of his next book. It had been in his mind for several years. There is a note dated April 1888 for a short story about a young man 'who could not go to Oxford'.[23] He had started to jot down a scheme for it in 1890, and the death of Tryphena, stirring memories of his cousins as young women, gave the germ of another element in the story.[24] The book had a long gestation. In Berkshire, Hardy noted, 'Entered a ploughed vale which might be called the Valley of Brown Melancholy. The silence is remarkable . . .'[25]

Then he was back in London to attend another funeral, that of Tennyson in Westminster Abbey, which he reported to 'My dearest Em'. He told her he had looked into the grave as he walked past among the other literary grandees. Since he and Em had shared their pleasure in Tennyson's poems as they fell in love in Cornwall, he knew that 'the tender grace of a day that is dead' would come into her mind as well as his, and he signed off 'Yours always, Tom' – the only time he used this form.[26] There was still a residue of the old feeling.

17. The Terra-cotta Dress

The next emotional lurch in Hardy's life occurred in 1893. As often happens, it came with success. This was the year he and Emma first took a whole house for the Season, and they chose a big, handsome one at 70 Hamilton Terrace in St John's Wood. They were there with their servants from mid April, and in May they travelled to Dublin at the invitation of the Lord-Lieutenant. He was the second Lord Houghton, and Hardy had known his father, Richard Monckton Milnes, the first Lord Houghton, who died in 1882. The Hardys stayed at the Viceregal Lodge and were welcomed by Houghton's married sister, the Hon. Florence Henniker. Mrs Henniker had the exquisite manners of her class and a *joie de vivre* inherited from her father. She had grown up in a cultivated, privileged and cosmopolitan atmosphere, in Upper Brook Street in Mayfair, on the family's Yorkshire estate and with visits to her maternal uncle, Lord Crewe. Her godmother was Florence Nightingale, whom her father had hoped to marry, and he always made much of this youngest child, encouraging her to write poetry, which she did even before she could form her letters, dictating verses to her elder sister. At her seventh birthday party Swinburne playfully proposed marriage to her. When he told Lady Trevelyan of the 'engagement', she expressed herself 'only too thankful to hear that I have a chance of being saved by a virtuous attachment'.[1] Her father took her to Paris when she was sixteen and allowed her to be seated next to President Thiers at dinner at Versailles, and she was well able to hold her own, in French as well as English. At seventeen she was composing cheeky limericks about Harrow boys and young army officers: 'There once was a youth in the Blues / Who thought he knew how to amuse / He was somewhat loquacious / And very flirtatious / That airified youth in the Blues.'[2]

Monckton Milnes was active in politics, a patron of writers, a

traveller, often abroad, President of the London Library, Foreign
Correspondence Secretary to the Royal Academy, a Trustee of
the British Museum, equally at ease addressing a Social Science
congress and exchanging risqué letters about flagellation with
Swinburne. Florence's mother died when she was nineteen, and
she acquired a reputation for being clever and rather fast. She did
not marry until she was twenty-seven, in 1882. Arthur Henniker
was a younger son of a Suffolk peer, an adjutant in the Coldstream
Guards, with no interest in literature, although he acquired a
volume of Byron as ammunition in his wooing of Florence, casting
it aside after the wedding. He had to work for his living, and
almost as soon as they were married he left with his regiment for
Egypt, where political disturbances were threatening the safety of
the Suez Canal. Florence's father had wanted a rich husband for
his daughter and was disappointed by the marriage. Three years
later he died at Vichy, leaving a characteristic joke to amuse his
friends: 'My exit is due to too many entrées.'

Florence had no children, and Henniker was more often over-
seas than in England, leaving her free to entertain for her brother,
and to write. When she and Hardy met, she had already published
two novels, *Sir George* in 1891 and *Bid Me Goodbye* in 1892. They
were competently written and politely received, and a third, *Foiled*,
came out in 1893. Hardy knew many aristocratic women, but he
had never met one so congenial, so delightful, so intelligently
responsive and intuitive. As soon as he and Emma were back in
London after their Irish trip, he made sure he saw a great deal of
Mrs Henniker. She did not put him off. They went with her sister
to see Ibsen's *The Master Builder*, newly translated and scandalizing
the critics in much the same way as Hardy, by presenting ordinary
people struggling with large emotions and tragic events. He offered
to give her lessons in architectural history as a way of securing
frequent meetings tête-à-tête, she accepted his offer, and they
began with Westminster Abbey. He took her adventurously
'through the pestilential vapours of the Underground'. She let him
see her translations of love poems by Théophile Gautier and the
melancholy Spaniard Gustavo Bécquer. He misread the charm and
informality of her manner. A well-known and evidently admiring

author was an intriguing figure, to be flattered and flirted with, and he allowed himself to imagine she meant more than she did. He gave her an inscribed copy of *Tess*, with notes allowing her to follow Tess's wanderings in Dorset should she so wish; and of *A Laodicean*, with an allusion to the fact that he had just missed meeting her when writing it, by 'an adverse stroke of fate', when her father had invited him to Yorkshire and he had been prevented by illness. But for that, he told her, 'you would be – a friend of 13 years standing.'[3] Soon he was invoking Shelley's *Epipsychidion*, talking of plunging into wild dissipation and hoping they would become lovers. She was interested in his friendship, and she liked him, but not enough for that. Like any lovelorn youth, he told her, 'I sleep hardly at all, and seem not to require any.'[4] Later she discreetly destroyed some of his early letters, but those that survive are alive, sprightly, confiding, flirtatious, frank: name-dropping apart, which he could not resist, here suddenly is a different Hardy. There is fresh energy in his poems too. 'A Thunderstorm in Town' (later subtitled 'A Reminiscence: 1893') gives a graphic glimpse of the two meeting in London, of his pleasure in her fashionable dress – a new one, which he may have thought, reasonably enough, she had put on especially for him – and of his intense desire and frustration:

> She wore a new 'terra-cotta' dress,
> And we stayed, because of the pelting storm,
> Within the hansom's dry recess,
> Though the horse had stopped; yea, motionless
>   We sat on, snug and warm.
>
> Then the downpour ceased, to my sharp sad pain,
> And the glass that had screened our forms before
> Flew up, and out she sprang to her door:
> I should have kissed her if the rain
>   Had lasted a minute more.[5]

He keeps the tone light in the poem, but he was unabashed in scheming to be with her. When she went to Southsea in August, he persuaded her to travel from there to Winchester to visit the cathedral with him. Both arrived by train and met at the George, and he was delighted to notice that the inn people assumed this was an assignation. They were observed with 'veiled smiles', and supposed to be 'more than friends' who had 'all resigned / For love's dear ends'. But the poem describing the day, 'At an Inn', moves sharply into sorrow after its humorous start. Things were not as they seemed, and there was no kiss and no consummation of love. Florence Henniker was prepared to play, but she would go no further. She explained that her Christian beliefs would not allow her to break her marriage vows.

To find that she, like Emma, was a conventional Christian and ready to invoke religion in defence of her marriage vows, instead of the emancipated person he had supposed her, was especially galling. This is how in his next novel she became a model for Sue Bridehead, to whom he gave the second name Florence, who liked to be loved and pursued while refusing to give any return of sexual love, and who gave up being a free spirit and turned to Christ in a hideous scene of penitence. Hardy told a friend later that he and Mrs Henniker had clasped hands beside the high altar in the cathedral, but a clasped hand is a scant offering to a man desperate for an embrace.[6]

Nine or ten poems of Hardy's allude to his love for Florence Henniker. Most are wistful, a few desolate. It is wonderful to see him being shaken by a new subject into new adventurousness in his writing of verse. 'A Broken Appointment' is set at the British Museum:[7]

> You did not come,
> And marching Time drew on, and wore me numb. –
> Yet less for loss of your dear presence there
> Than that I thus found lacking in your make
> That high compassion which can overbear
> Reluctance for pure lovingkindess' sake
> Grieved I, when, as the hope-hour stroked its sum,
> You did not come.

You love not me,
And love alone can lend you loyalty;
– I know and knew it. But, unto the store
Of human deeds divine in all but name,
Was it not worth a little hour or more
To add yet this: Once you, a woman, came
To soothe a time-torn man; even though it be
You love not me?

It must have caused a pang of remorse to Mrs Henniker when she read it, if not in 1893 when it was written, then in 1902 when it was published. She was not a heartless woman by any means. Her stories, which tend towards the pathetic, show great sympathy for the unhappy and the unfortunate. The first story in her collection *Outlines*, published in 1894 and dedicated to 'To my friend Thomas Hardy', is a sad, sentimental piece called 'A Statesman's Lapse'. The central figures are a distinguished politician with an invalid wife and three children, and his wife's young cousin, Aileen. The climactic scene takes place in the country, beside the Thames: he has gone to see his son's future housemaster at Eton, taking Aileen with him.

As by a lightning flash was revealed to this man and this woman an enchanted country untrodden as yet by the feet of either. Side by side they had unknowingly passed through the fateful gate. When they should retrace their steps the summer would be over in the land whence they came, the skies a chill expanse, the world a colourless plain. Yielding to an overmastering impulse, Gaspard Fludyer drew his companion towards him and kissed her, once only, on her cheek. She turned pale. Then he took her hand in his; and pressed first the fingers, then the little pink palm to his lips. She turned her head away, and he saw that she was crying. 'Aileen – forgive me – I had no right to kiss you. But it is for once only – one little miserable caress for a whole lifetime! Think of that, my child, and don't be angry with me. It will never be again.'

She trembled from head to foot. He passed her hand within his arm, and they walked silently back, out of their solitude, away from their dying dream, into the discord of life once more.

Mr Fludyer and Aileen part for ever. The passage gives an idea of her tone as a writer, which found admirers in her day. It is just possible that the story relates to a scene between the author and Hardy. He may have thought it did and enjoyed the idea of a secret literary link. He praised it, urging her to make it the title story and call the whole collection 'A Statesman's Lapse' – advice she did not take.[8]

In September she was away in Ireland and then at her uncle Lord Crewe's. Hardy was 'a trifle chilled' to hear that she was reading passages from his letters aloud to the house party, and he 'much regretted having sent the effusive ones'. 'I lost confidence in you somewhat,' he told her.[9] Nothing could have made plainer the difference between his feeling for her and hers for him. She seemed to be showing him off as a conquest, just as Mrs Tomson had done. This time Hardy could not bring himself to break off the friendship and, having stated his objection, by the end of the letter had written himself back into being her friend again.

In October they were collaborating on a story, 'The Spectre of the Real'. It was Hardy's idea, and the plot, involving a woman who believes herself to be a widow and is about to marry again when her husband reappears, was his, as was most of the narrative. He consulted her – as he had once consulted Emma – about womanly details: 'please insert in pencil any details that I have omitted, and that would only be known to a woman.'[10] He was now using a hired typist, Miss Tigan, rather than Emma, to make copies of his work, something that was likely to upset her, given everything else she could observe of his behaviour, movements and fluctuating moods. To cheer herself, perhaps, Emma borrowed or hired a horse and took to riding again.[11] She need not have felt too much literary jealousy at least. 'The Spectre of the Real' is a poor story, with a large element of Grand Guignol. It took a year to be published in a magazine and was reprinted by Mrs Henniker in a collection of her own work in 1896, when it got a drubbing from the critics. The *Spectator* called it gruesome and repulsive, and proof that Hardy was not a 'judicious literary counsellor'.[12]

Accepting that he could hope for nothing more than friendship, Hardy worked assiduously at being a useful friend. He recommended her work to a magazine editor, who took one of her stories. He badgered the same editor to get a review of *Outlines*, ending his letter cynically, 'This is log-rolling, is it not?' Then he wrote an anonymous puff of her work in another magazine.[13] While this was going on, Emma began to interest herself in the suffrage cause and complained that Hardy's interest in women's suffrage was 'nil' and that he cared only about the women he invented.[14] At the same time Hardy, with protean energy, was engaged in writing *Jude*, and some of Emma's bitterness was provoked by the fact that, whereas throughout their marriage he had consulted her, asked her to copy pages and showed her or read to her from each novel in progress, now for the first time he did none of this.[15] Instead he was discussing it with Mrs Henniker. He had started writing it about the time of their Winchester assignation, and when it was published he wrote to her. 'My hesitating to send "Jude" was not because I thought you narrow – but because I had rather bored you with him during the writing of some of the story, or thought I had.'[16] He had also asked her opinion at an early stage about the naming of the heroine, and she can't have failed to notice that he added her name to Sue's.

Things settled down. A steady friendship was established on both sides; they continued to take an interest in each other's work and to exchange letters, his more freely expressed and entertaining than any others he wrote.[17] She went to Emma's parties in London, and in 1896 she introduced Hardy to her husband. Hardy decided to like him. Three years later, when Major Arthur Henniker was setting off for Africa to fight the Boers, Hardy wrote him a letter with the rather curious declaration that he regarded him as 'the most perfect type of the practical soldier that I know'. He had received many glamorous photographs of Mrs Henniker. Now he asked her to let him have a photograph of the Major, in uniform, and told her, 'he is to be framed with our other celebrities.'[18]

In September 1895 Hardy fell half in love with another younger married woman, Agnes Grove. It was a less consuming experience than his love for Mrs Henniker and helped to distract him from it.

Mrs Grove was born into an interesting family, her father General Pitt-Rivers, her grandfather Lord Stanley of Alderley, and her husband a good-natured country baronet who called her 'my little pepper pot' for her advanced views and determined character. Her brilliant aunt Kate died young, leaving a baby son, Bertrand Russell. Mrs Grove was in her thirties, with a brood of children, and was also set on becoming a writer on social questions, among them women's suffrage. The Hardys were invited to the Pitt-Rivers' for the week in September when they gave their annual open-air dance in Wiltshire. A warm night, soft grass and a full moon, with extra light provided by hundreds of lanterns strung in the trees, offered a magical setting, and Hardy and Agnes led a country dance together. He was as entranced as a child by the experience, and perhaps it was something boyish about him that made her allow him to hold her hand when they sat out together, listening to the music while others danced on.[19] Since Lady Jeune's daughters were her cousins, he was quite at ease with her, and she had the confidence of a beautiful aristocratic woman of the world. She was also astute enough to see that her literary ambitions might be advanced by a friendship with Hardy.

For him it was not so much a matter of replacing Mrs Henniker as adding another name to his pantheon. He needed a muse, the position Emma had once filled but did so no longer. Ideally his muse should also be his mistress – as Mary Godwin became Shelley's – and there is no doubt he longed to take hold of a woman and make her his own in defiance of the rules of the Church and conventional society. But Mrs Henniker had taught him a lesson by her cool, definite withdrawal from anything more than flirtation, and he had to settle for admiring beautiful women, taking his inspiration from them, accepting their flattery when offered without considering its motives too closely, helping them where he could, and taking pleasure in being with them, talking with them and, if he was lucky, getting a hand to hold. He was now fifty-five years old. When he looked at himself he was dismayed by what he saw: his hair receding and thinning, and his skin showing the creases of age. Yet his eyes remained bright, and he still aspired to a youthful look: the moustache with long twirled points carefully maintained, extended across each side of his face, announcing, I can be dashing and dangerous when I choose to be.

His muses did not inspire him to flights of love, but there is one near-perfect short poem in which he talks about appearing old and feeling young:

> I look into my glass
> And view my wasting skin,
> And say, 'Would God it came to pass
> My heart had shrunk as thin!'
>
> For then, I, undistrest
> By hearts grown cold to me,
> Could lonely wait my endless rest
> With equanimity.
>
> But Time, to make me grieve,
> Part steals, lets part abide;
> And shakes this fragile frame at eve
> With throbbings of noontide.[20]

Although God appears in the first stanza, death in the second and Time in the last, there is nothing portentous here. There is not a spare word either. His skin is wasting (and by suggestion also wasted, with no lover to caress it). He feels distress at other hearts not responding to his. If only his own were cooler, he could remain as calm as his coming death will one day make him – but it is not cool. Time has stolen his youth – like Milton's 'Time, the subtle thief of youth' – but only a part of it, and the last two lines expand into a burst of feeling. The fragile frame shaken suggests a flight of birds alighting on a tree, full of life, energy and song. And the 'throbbings' are not only the beating of his heart, they are also the sensations of the flesh. It is not cool evening for him at all but sultry midday. When you finish reading the poem, you see that it is about sexual desire, and that it declares he is not old, but a man who aches to express his love through his body.

During this period he was also in the middle of writing *Jude the Obscure*. Reading *Jude* is like being hit in the face over and over again. I think Hardy intended this, although he expressed surprise at the response of his earliest critics. The 1890s were the decade of Decadence; 1894 saw the scandalous trials and conviction of Oscar Wilde, with all the hysteria they engendered. *Jude* was seen by many as another attack on sound English moral values, and it was found intensely shocking when it appeared in November 1895: the serial version had preceded book publication and was, as usual, bowdlerized to an idiotic degree. But *Jude* is still distressing to read. If the Book of Job was partly its model, it was Job retold for a godless world that offers no final consolation or redress. And, although it told a different story from Hardy's first, rejected, novel, *The Poor Man and the Lady*, it returned to the theme of a penniless young man with ambitions and radical ideas, and showed that Hardy's anger had never been extinguished. Jude Fawley is orphaned, village bred, intelligent and aspiring, and he is repeatedly knocked off course as he tries to go forward in life. First there is his poverty, and the fact that he has no home or supporting community. There is no one to help him or advise him when he needs help and advice. Then there is the distraction of sexual desire, and the trap of marriage to an uncongenial wife. There is the indifference of the educational establishment to people of his class. Then the torment of meeting and loving a clever, congenial young woman, his cousin Sue, who would be a good life companion for him but that she is a tease, wanting to be loved while sexually unarousable, and emotionally a masochist, so that, although she does love him in her comradely way, she is prepared to leave him for a man she finds physically loathsome. The only sexual release available to Jude is with the wife of his youth, with whom he has nothing in common. Towards the end of the book, he says, 'There is something external to us which says, "You shan't!" First it said, "You shan't learn!" Then it said, "You shan't labour!" Now it says, "You shan't love!" '[21] It is his own summary of his experience of life.

Jude's great-aunt has warned him from the first against marriage, saying the family history showed the Fawleys were not meant for it. He learns that his own mother committed suicide after separating from his father, and he makes an early unsuccessful attempt at suicide himself. On top of this Hardy piles bad luck, malign coincidence and then horror, when Jude's son hangs his little half-brother and sister and then himself. That he intended the horror to hit his readers hard is plain from the manuscript, where there was originally only one younger child to be killed; a second child was added at a later stage. This is a clear instance of Hardy 'coercing his plots' and piling on the agony. Seeing it in the manuscript gives the reader who finds it pause, because it suggests a degree of relish. Hardy is saying, 'Look! Look how bad things can be! Even as horrible as this!'

But most readers have not consulted the manuscript, and *Jude* does not impress only by shocking. It speaks sense about the painful difficulties of life for the poor and intellectually aspiring who have lost their roots in any place and their faith in any god. When Ruskin College was founded in Oxford for working men some years later, people wrote to Hardy saying it should be called after Jude, something he was rightly proud of.[22] The book also offers an interesting corrective to any idea that the countryside is inherently cheering or consoling, by giving an unrelieved view of the dark side of rural life. There are no lush meadows and rivers, no great medieval barns as in *Far from the Madding Crowd*. Jude is seen first in a bleak and dreary upland Berkshire village in which many of the old cottages have been pulled down; even the ancient church has been replaced by an ugly modern one. In the process, the graves of the village forebears have also been destroyed, leaving the villagers without any record of the past. As a small boy Jude works for a farmer scaring birds in a vast upland field: 'How ugly it is here!' he thinks; and he is sorry for the birds, and troubled by the law of nature that makes cruelty to one creature kindness to another. There are no Wordsworthian lessons or inspirations here. His dream of becoming a student at Oxford is unattainable. He is trapped into marriage, too young and without love, and the marriage fails. Later he is broken by Sue, the woman he loves who is all nervous intelligence without sexual warmth. He becomes an itinerant stonemason, walking or taking trains from place to place, carrying a few possessions, never able to settle or make a secure life for himself, never finding true friends, turning to drink to forget his misery. In many ways his experience forecasts the brutality of life a century later, when economic migrants wander the earth, having lost their natural support systems of family and home, and encountering incomprehension, hardship, hostility and often early death. When Jude has lost everything he cares for, and the last dregs of his self-respect, he deliberately seeks his own death by exposing himself to cold and soaking rain.

Hardy told Florence Henniker the book was 'addressed to those into whose souls the iron of adversity has deeply entered at some time of their lives'.[23] He added that it was not a novel with a purpose and not a manifesto against marriage, as many critics took it to be, and he insisted that it was simply a story of 'two persons who, by a hereditary curse of temperament, peculiar to their family, are rendered unfit for marriage, or think they are'. This point is made several times in the book. Warning words are spoken by Jude and Sue's great-aunt Drusilla, who tells Jude, 'The Fawleys were not made for wedlock: it never seemed to sit well upon us. There's summat in our blood.'[24] Later she tells Sue, 'Ah – you'll rue this marrying as well as he! . . . All our family do.'[25] After her funeral, the two cousins talk about her idea again. ' "She was opposed to marriage, from first to last, you say?" murmured Sue. "Yes. Particularly for members of our family . . . She said we made bad husbands and wives. Certainly we make unhappy ones." '[26] And Aunt Drusilla turns out to be horribly right, whatever the reason. Whether Hardy wanted us to believe in hereditary curses of temperament, or was describing a piece of witchlike rural super- stition, is not clear. The most likely explanation is that, as with the witchcraft in *The Return of the Native*, his position was somewhere between belief and unbelief. In his own life, the person who warned her children against marriage was his mother, who advised all her children against it and told them to look after each other instead – advice disobeyed only by Thomas.[27] Neither the spirit in which she gave such advice nor her reason for giving it was ever disclosed, but by the time he came to write *Jude* part of him at any rate may have been ready to think his mother had been right.

He told Mrs Henniker in the same letter that he believed he
had written 'a novel which "makes" for humanity more than any
other I have written'.[28] It is true that Jude, boy and man, is drawn
with a sympathy that makes readers like him, and feel the unfairness
and anguish of his repeated disappointments. All the same, there *is*
something of the manifesto about the book. Its determined grim-
ness suggests that Hardy set out to shock and horrify people to
force them to take notice of the things he found detestable in
society. In *Tess* it had been the double standard and the general
view that a woman once 'fallen' could not redeem herself. In *Jude*
it was the class system's denial of education and opportunity to the
intelligent poor, and the resulting wastage, as well as the problems
and pain of dealing with failed marriages.

On the same day he wrote to Mrs Henniker he sent another letter
to Gosse, thanking him for a review, regretting that *Jude* was not
as good as it had been in his mind, and also suggesting that he had
allowed it to take its own course: 'It required an artist to see that
the plot is almost geometrically constructed – I ought not to say
constructed, for, beyond a certain point, the characters necessitated
it, and I simply let it come.'[29] 'I simply let it come' suggests that it
was dreamt as much as it was planned, and that he allowed Jude
and Sue to take over the book and make their own fates. If, as this
implies, he either wrote with no advance plan, or jettisoned his
plan when he felt his characters taking charge, it would also help
to explain some of the horrors. Many writers have said their
characters take charge or take over the narrative. It may be objected
that they are his inventions, the children of his brain, carrying out
his wishes. But what if they are carrying out wishes he has not
consciously formulated? A writer deeply engaged and absorbed in
his work may surprise himself, and this may be what happened as
Hardy wrote *Jude*, and may help to explain its unrelenting power
and gloom. If the poetic dramas of the Elizabethan and Jacobean
writers come to mind, where horror is part of the fabric, we should
remember that Hardy said he aimed to keep his narratives 'as near
to poetry in their subject as the conditions would allow', and that

he sometimes spoke of his poems coming to him: 'the verses came,' he told Arthur Benson.[30] So perhaps we can believe that the worst parts of Jude and Sue's story also came partly unbidden, out of the place inside him where the wounds made by grief and loss and humiliation and failure had never ceased to ache.

Hardy made the standard novelists' denial that there was anything autobiographical in the book. True, he makes Jude an orphan, taken in by a great-aunt who calls him a useless boy and says it would have been better if he had died with his parents, and this is quite different from Hardy's experience of nurturing parents. Yet, in a memorable scene in the novel, he shows Jude looking through his straw hat as the sun shines through it and thinking, 'If only he could prevent himself growing up! He did not want to be a man.' This is exactly what Hardy described as his own experience, looking through his straw hat as a child and thinking 'that he did not wish to grow up'.[31] The power of the scene in the novel comes from Hardy's memory of himself. The oddity is that he transposes the thought of a boy who had no conscious reason to be unhappy or to fear growing up into the mind of one who was already unhappy and had good reason to approach adult life with small enthusiasm. Hardy appears to be reinventing his childhood and making it worse. This prompts the question as to whether he had only lately learnt the facts of his own conception and birth, and become aware that he had been an unwanted child whose existence forced his parents into a marriage neither desired; or only lately brooded on the implications of this knowledge.[32] A retrospective blight cast across his life is a very Hardyesque possibility.

He also makes Jude embark on learning Latin and Greek with the idea of getting to a university and becoming an educated man, exactly as he did. Hardy's circumstances were again more propitious, but, although he asserted that he might have attended a university in his twenties, there was always an underlying bitterness at his failure to do so. No success ever sweetened it and the force of that bitterness appears in *Jude*. Sue's experiences at her teacher training college were drawn from his sisters' grim accounts of Salisbury. More tenuously, but still clearly enough, his fluctuating relation to Sue alludes to the frustrations of his love for Florence Henniker.

Hardy did not let Emma read *Jude* until it was published. The hurt and humiliation of this were such that she felt free to say how much she disliked it in his presence, and to a guest at their own lunch table. She hated its attacks on the Church, to which she was so firmly attached, and on marriage, which were hard for a wife of twenty years to read.[33] But Emma's objections were as nothing before the first onslaught of the critics, described by Hardy as 'booing'. He knew, because he was subscribing to Durrant's press-cutting agency. Some ridiculed; more were shocked. 'A titanically bad book', 'Mr Hardy running mad in right royal fashion', 'dangerously near to farce', 'Jude the Obscene', 'a shameful nightmare', 'too deplorable a falling-off from Mr Hardy's former achievements to be reckoned with at all'. In spite of this, many of the bad reviews conceded that *Jude* was also 'manifestly a work of genius' and, although 'coarsely indecent', delivered 'from the hands of a Master'.

And very soon the praise came: 'the most powerful and moving picture of human life which Mr Hardy has given us', 'the greatest novel written in England for many years'. W. D. Howells in *Harper's Weekly* gave a long, carefully considered appreciation: 'All the characters . . . have the appealing quality of human creatures really doing what they must while seeming to do what they will. It is not a question of blaming them or praising them; they are in the necessity of what they do and what they suffer.' Of the most upsetting incidents in the book, Howell wrote, 'They make us shiver with horror and grovel with shame, but we know that they are deeply founded in the condition, if not in the nature of humanity.'[34] The *Saturday Review* for February 1896 ended its account by quoting from Jude's last words and describing them: 'That is the voice of the educated proletarian, speaking more distinctly than it has ever spoken before in English literature . . . There is no other novelist alive with the breadth of sympathy, the knowledge, or the power for the creation of Jude. Had Mr Hardy never written another book, this would still place him at the head of English novelists.'³⁵

A letter from Swinburne, to whom he had sent a copy of *Jude*, gave Hardy deep pleasure: 'The beauty, the terror, and the truth are all yours, and yours alone . . . The man who can do such work can hardly care about criticism or praise.'³⁶ But Hardy did care, and minded very much when he heard that the Bishop of Wakefield had burnt his copy and written to the *Yorkshire Post* to announce the fact, as well as persuading W. H. Smith to withdraw it from their circulating library. The public took less notice of the Bishop than Hardy did, and three months after publication 20,000 copies had been sold. Scandal had brought success. All the same, he noticed that some of his acquaintances turned away rather than speak to him, and he was upset and furious when Gosse, having reviewed *Jude* well, told Hardy it was 'indecent' at the Savile Club lunch table.³⁷

Paradoxically, he was now assured of an income large enough to allow him to give up writing fiction. It was said that he was driven to do so by the attacks on *Jude*, but his own account is subtler. He maintained that he had always tried to keep close to natural life in his novels, 'and as near to poetry in their subject as the conditions would allow', and that he had long wanted to return to poetry proper, while being forced to earn his living through fiction. Once financially free to give up a form which he found increasingly problematical, he abandoned it.³⁸ It was a dramatic gesture from a novelist at the pinnacle of success, controversial but hugely admired, translated, discussed all over the Western world and rich from his royalties. In 1894 and 1896 he took an expensive house in Pelham Crescent for the Season.

There were times when Hardy could laugh at the ludicrousness of reactions like the Bishop's, but others when he sank into gloom at the disapproval piled on him.³⁹ During the winter he wrote three black poems, the first with an epigraph from Psalm 102, 'My heart is smitten, and withered like grass.'⁴⁰ The speaker in each is suffering: in the first from a winter of the spirit – he speaks of bereavement, friends turned cold, heart and strength destroyed; in the second he decides it would be better for him not to exist, since he disturbs the breezy, optimistic world; and in the third he looks back on moments in his life when he might have died, apparently regretting that he had survived to feel the bitterness of life. All the sorrows and grievances of his life were revived in his mind and went into the poems – plus, no doubt, the miseries of Jude, of Henchard and of his grandfather Hand too. The three poems were first called 'De Profundis', Hardy changing the title to 'In Tenebris' after Oscar Wilde's *De Profundis* appeared. It makes a curious link between the two men who upset England so badly in their different ways in 1895; luckily for Hardy, his offence was not a felony.

A year later, in December 1896, he wrote an autobiographical poem, 'Wessex Heights', in which he imagines himself standing on one of the high points in Dorset he loved to climb, where you can see for miles over the countryside. He says it is a place good for 'thinking, dreaming, dying on' and thinks his essential self may have been up there before his birth, and will return after his death. It offers him what he loves: solitude, silence and a wide view. Here he worries about how he has become 'false to myself, my simple self that was, / And is not now'. He deplores the sneering and disparagements of the critics who have attacked his work; the stress of the publication of *Jude* is still affecting him. His anguished mood leads him to remember past loves – like ghosts – and to regret his failures in love. He feels sorry for himself, as Shelley, whom he so much admired, allowed himself to feel when he wrote, 'I fall upon the thorns of life, I bleed' in his 'Ode to the West Wind'. Hardy's poem is also written in long, finely constructed, musical lines, and Mrs Henniker is given a particularly graceful stanza:

As for one rare fair woman, I am now but a thought of hers,
I enter her mind and another thought succeeds me that she prefers;
Yet my love for her in its fulness she herself even did not know;
Well, time cures hearts of tenderness, and now I can let her go.

Hardy's moods shifted from one hour to the next, and he habitually worked out an emotion by writing a poem about it. The most striking words in this one are his admonition to himself about being false to 'my simple self that was'. Yet he had never been innocent in the way that his father was (or Dick Dewy, or Gabriel Oak, or even Jude) – at least after the age of sixteen. He had been driven by ambition, determined to succeed in a society that had no connection with the heights of Wessex, to write books many people would read, to marry up, to have worldly friends, to make money – and he had done it all. Some of his gloom may have come precisely from the realization that there were not so many more heights to scale, or women to love.

Hardy worked on this poem on a December day. If he was in his study, he would be sitting in his socks, his boots or slippers always removed 'as a preliminary to writing'.[41] He completed it with another invocation of the pleasure of being on the heights, 'Where men have never cared to haunt, nor women have walked with me, / And ghosts then keep their distance; and I know some liberty'. He kept a neat desk, and a finished poem would be put carefully aside to be reconsidered. Then, slippers on again, he could go downstairs for a cup of tea and a slice of cake with Emma, before turning with renewed energy to pursue his life: a letter from a friend to be answered, a young woman writer needing his advice and encouragement, an arrangement to meet a portrait painter, plans for a trip to London. And in London, Mrs Henniker would doubtless invite him to lunch, and he would accept her invitation with pleasure.

18. A Witch and a Wife

Although Hardy joked about *Jude*'s reception to Mrs Henniker, saying that 'the only people who faint and blush over it are fast men at clubs', the furore reached into Dorset, and he noticed what he called 'extensive and peculiar' responses among their country neighbours, 'they having a pathetic reverence for press opinions'. Emma also said *Jude* had made a difference to them 'in the County'.[1] He did not say anything about what his family at Bockhampton made of it, merely telling Gosse that he had enjoyed a very quiet Christmas and New Year at Max Gate. It was immediately after this, in the first days of January 1896, that Emma persuaded him to try bicycling: 'I have almost forgotten that there is such a pursuit as literature in the arduous study of – bicycling! – which my wife is making me learn to keep her company, she doing it rather well.'[2] There was more fun when Mrs Patrick Campbell came to visit them, hoping to be allowed to play Tess in the theatre production Hardy was trying to set up; he had dramatized the book in five acts during 1894 and 1895.[3] He greeted her by getting out his fiddle and playing old English dance tunes, and she obligingly improvised her own dance steps to his music. 'It was a sight for London Town,' she wrote to a friend.[4] But London theatre managers were unexpectedly wary of *Tess*. Hardy believed they were put off by the response to *Jude*.[5]

He was in London in February, to allow a young woman painter to finish her portrait of him, to attend Lord Leighton's funeral – Hardy never willingly missed a funeral – and for a masked ball, a 'most amusing experience' he told Emma, where he and Henry James, the only unmasked men, were 'recklessly flirted with by the women'.[6] Emma was also invited, but stayed in Dorset suffering either from eczema or shingles – if shingles, excruciatingly painful. He too, he informed her, was suffering from 'the most fearful depression, slight headache etc.', but he did not allow it to interfere with his multifarious activities. Lady Jeune, even though she was preparing for her daughter Dorothy's wedding, insisted on putting him up, and he was in heavy demand. He was introduced to the brilliant American actress Elizabeth Robins, who had helped to promote Ibsen's plays in England, and they took a long walk together; also to Violet Hunt, novelist, feminist and friend of another rising writer, H. G. Wells. He called on 'Mrs Pat [Campbell]' twice. He visited his investment brokers to discuss shares and bonds held by him and by Emma. He wrote excitedly to her, 'I have seen the loveliest "Byke" for myself – it wd suit me admirably – "The Rover Cob". It is £20! I can't tell if I ought to have it.' He decided he would have it.[7] Emma, rather than staying alone at Max Gate, went by herself to Worthing, to nurse her health. From there she launched an attack on Hardy's sister Mary in the form of a letter of astonishing force and fury. The letter has survived because Mary coolly decided to hand it to the family lawyers.[8] 'Miss Hardy,' it began: 'I dare you, or any one to spread evil reports of me – such as that I have been unkind to your brother, (which you actually said to my face,) or that I have "errors" in my mind, (which you have also said to me,) and I hear that you repeat to others.' The truth was, she went on, that 'he has been outrageously unkind to me – which is *entirely your fault*: ever since I have been his wife you have done all you can to make division between us; also, you have set your family against me, though neither you nor they can truly say that I have ever been anything but, just, considerate, and kind towards you all, notwithstanding frequent low insults.'

One thing the letter proves is that Emma could use her pen to good effect when she was roused. She accused Mary of describing people she disliked as mad ('I have heard you say it of myself . . . And it is a wicked, spiteful and most malicious habit of yours'). She said she had been a 'causeless enemy' to her and pandered to Hardy's 'many weaknesses' in order to secure him 'on your side'. 'How would you like to have your life made difficult for you by anyone saying, for instance, that you are a very unsuitable person to have the instruction of young people?' – Mary being the headmistress of a girls' school. It is the letter of a distressed and furious woman, and it rises to a terrific climax in which she draws on Hardy's own depiction of the heath and its inhabitants: 'You are a witch-like creature and quite equal to any amount of evil-wishing and speaking – I can imagine you, and your mother and sister on your native heath raising a storm on a Walpurgis night.'

She went on to say that she proposed to tell Hardy what she had written and added, with considerable, if ungrammatical, dignity, 'I can understand your desire to be considered cleverer than I which you may be I allow.' These are not the words of a mad woman but of an angry one, as Mary must have seen, but – understandably perhaps – she did not respond and made no move to mend things with Emma. It was far too late for that, and the effect of the letter on her and her sister Kate was simply to encourage them in their view that Emma was mad. This seems to have been the end of any communication, written or spoken, between the Bockhampton women and the mistress of Max Gate.[9] No one from Bockhampton set foot inside Max Gate again in Emma's lifetime, and if any of them came face to face with her on the pavements of Dorchester, they presumably cut one another. Such situations are the dramas of provincial life. Mary's health was poor, and Emma's attack may well have shaken her. She was asthmatic, and, although she was only fifty-six, she retired from her position as headmistress the following spring.

Hardy was caught between the two embattled households. Whether he was shown Emma's letter or only heard about it, he understood what it meant. He had grown up with a mother who complained ferociously and a father who took evasive action; and, since there was no question of him reading the riot act either to his wife or to his sister, he likewise took evasive action. From the spring to the autumn of 1896 he simply removed himself from Dorset, taking Emma with him. He was pleasing her, letting her feel she had won the battle, allowing everyone to calm down and protecting himself; also, conveniently, getting out of the way while builders did some work at Max Gate. He took the Pelham Crescent house again, earlier than usual, in March, installing their servants again to run it. He escorted Emma to Brighton for two weeks in May, for the good of her health and his own, and after this they remained in London well into July. The Season went by with many convivial moments. He was under no pressure to work, and he appeared to be in high spirits. They were often on the terrace at Westminster at tea-time, and in the evening at concerts given by the Continental bands that came each year to entertain Londoners at the Imperial Institute. 'Here one evening they met, with other friends, the beautiful Mrs, afterwards, Lady, Grove; and the "Blue Danube" Waltz being started, Hardy and the latter lady danced two or three turns to it among the promenaders, who eyed them with mild surmise as to whether they had been drinking or not.'[10] The dancing skills acquired at Almack's and the Argyle thirty years before had come into their own. When Mrs Henniker accused him of preaching free love, he defended himself wittily, and disingenuously, claiming that 'I hold no theory whatever on the subject, except by way of experimental remarks at tea parties.'[11] No witnesses have come forward with accounts of his experimental remarks, but the impression he gives this summer is not of the self described in 'Wessex Heights' – crushed by sneering critics, disparaged by the women he meets and free only in solitude – but rather of a jolly, outgoing figure who has achieved the summit of social as well as intellectual success. The wedding of his old favourite, Lady Jeune's daughter Dorothy, to a young politician, celebrated with much splendour at St George's, Hanover Square, brought the Season to a cheerful close.

In August, after making a flying visit to his mother, and observing that her face looked smaller, he set off on another prolonged holiday with Emma. They were to be away for eight weeks, and she took her bicycle with her, although he had not yet had time to master fully his Rover Cob. They toured the Midlands, Malvern, Worcester, Warwick and Stratford-upon-Avon, and looked at Reading, in which town Hardy knew that his father's mother had lived almost a hundred years earlier. Their next destination was the Continent, but Emma was knocked off her bicycle by another cyclist at Dover. She had no serious injuries but needed to rest in bed, so they decided to stay put for a fortnight. During this time they read Matthew Arnold's 'Dover Beach' together, which he marked with their joint initials and the date, 'Sept.

1896 – T.H./E.L.H.'. September was the month of their wedding anniversary – the twenty-second – which would have prompted both of them to think of the past and make an effort to revive old feelings.

The next part of their tour was to be made in Belgium, where '*le véloze de Madame*' aroused interest among staff of the railways on which they travelled from town to town, Ostend, Bruges, Brussels, Namur, Dinant, Liège. In Brussels they went sentimentally to the hotel they had stayed in twenty years before, in 1876, 'for association's sake', but found it had 'altered for the worse since those bright days'.[12] Hardy wanted to make another visit to the field of Waterloo. Emma sensibly pleaded exhaustion – she could scarcely take her *vélo* across the battlefield – and he went on his own. On 2 October he walked from the English line, along the Charleroi Road, to the French, and was struck by how close the fighting lines were to one another. His mind was working on the idea of a drama about the Napoleonic Wars, in which the battlefield of Waterloo would figure. For the moment it was to be called 'Europe in Throes', and he imagined it on a large scale.

Then it was time to end their long break from Dorset and go home. He had shown that, for all his devotion to his mother and his sisters, he would not take their side against his wife. Similarly, while he admired – even adored – the elegance of Mrs Henniker and Agnes Grove, and delighted in their crisp worldly conversation, they did not make him despise Emma's muslins and ribbons and hats like collapsing birthday cakes. Nor did they prevent him from reading and discussing other writers' works with her. The sharing of 'Dover Beach' was only one example. She was reading Ibsen assiduously early in 1897, and they went to performances of his plays together that spring. In 1903 they both enjoyed Henry James's *The Wings of the Dove*, as he told Mrs Henniker, saying they had been arguing about what happened to James's characters, 'and find we have wholly conflicting opinions thereon'.[13] Emma also tackled some difficult books on her own. One was Jean-Jacques Rousseau's *La Nouvelle Héloïse*, read daily over a long period 'with my morning cup of tea' and finally abandoned with the comment 'queer morals': it is an account of high-minded illicit love and a nobly complaisant husband. Another was Tolstoy's *Resurrection*, which she read in a French translation and found 'powerful but unpleasant too'.[14] She also puzzled over Yeats's 'The Shadowy Land' [*The Shadowy Waters*].[15] Her responses were simple, but she was prepared to make an effort.

Hardy supported her in many ways during the 1890s. For example he was consistently kind to her nephew and niece. Gordon Gifford became a semi-permanent guest at Max Gate while he went to school in Dorchester. Lilian, red-cheeked, pretty and, although silly, liked by Hardy, was there for long periods too. They made a fuss of her, and in 1898 gave her 'the desire of her heart, a "bike"'.[16] Gordon showed enough aptitude to be sent to Paris as part of his education, and Hardy himself then gave him some training. In 1899 Hardy arranged for Gordon to be taken into the Blomfield architectural office, enabling him ultimately to work as an architect for the London County Council. This was a strikingly generous and helpful assumption of responsibility for the children of her brother, who had decided that Gordon had weak lungs and whose best idea for his son had been to find a gentleman living in Switzerland to whom he might become a companion.[17] Hardy also backed Emma strongly in her work for animal rights, and a few months after their return from abroad in 1896 she held an anti-vivisection meeting at Max Gate.

During 1895 and 1896 the house was enlarged: both front rooms were extended, a new kitchen was put in behind the old one – which became the bicycle room – and a warren of service rooms were added at the back. Extra rooms were also added in the attic. Emma began to use one of these as a daytime retreat, and Hardy moved to a new study. There was still no bathroom: neither thought it a necessary innovation, preferring to have the water for their basins and hip bath carried up and down stairs by the maids. The next improvement was to the garden, where a swing was installed and the lower lawn relaid, so that croquet and tennis could be played. This was in the winter of 1899.[18]

Here, then, was a hugely successful, worldly, enlightened Victorian husband behaving generously to his wife. But hurt and anger simmered inside Emma. She could not forgive him for no longer consulting her about his work, for refusing to encourage her in her efforts to write, for failing to help her find an agent or a publisher, as he did for his women friends, and for his barely concealed attachments to them. She made up her mind that it was his rejection of Christian doctrine that was at the bottom of all this bad behaviour. The diaries she kept in which she expressed her anger against him gave her a private outlet for her grievances, but she went further, making herself look foolish by inflating them and insisting that she was superior to him in birth, education, manners and even talents, and giving the impression that she did not value his achievements as a writer.[19] Visitors were embarrassed, and Hardy himself responded increasingly with silence and withdrawal when they were at Max Gate, making his study his refuge. He was often there in the evening as well as during the day.

Yet there was another jaunt abroad together in 1897, when they toured Switzerland energetically in June, having decided to miss the racket of the Queen's Diamond Jubilee celebrations in London. Emma kept a holiday diary again, not as lively as her Italian one, although she liked the Genevan musical boxes, the Alpine flowers and the glaciers, and noted with pleasure how she ate some snow to cool herself after a long upward trek. In Lausanne they stayed in the Hotel Gibbon, and Hardy, realizing that its terrace garden was the exact place and 27 June the very day on which Edward Gibbon had finished his *Decline and Fall of the Roman Empire* 110 years before, was inspired to a poem. He imagined the spirit of Gibbon, formal in pose, grave and grand, flecked with light from the lamps beyond the acacia trees on the terrace, asking, 'How fares the Truth now? – Ill?' – and proceeding to answer himself in the affirmative. Hardy makes Gibbon invoke Milton, deliberately ranging himself alongside the fearless truth-tellers of the seventeenth and eighteenth centuries.

Later that summer he and Emma went on a bicycle tour to Wells, Longleat, Frome and Salisbury, where they attended Evensong together several times, Hardy unable to resist the lure of the cathedral service.[20] His enthusiasm for bicycling was now fully as great as hers, and he was 'gradually getting to climb a fairly steep hill'.[21] He agreed to inspect the White Horse Inn at Maiden Newton, the village where his mother had worked when she was young, and told the Society for the Protection of Ancient Buildings, for whom he looked at it, that they owed him 'no expenses in travel worth mentioning, the visits having been made on a bicycle'.[22] He also took Kipling, whose company he enjoyed in spite of disapproving of his imperialist ideas, on a bicycling expedition to search for a house near Weymouth. When Kipling said he would like to build on the top of the Ridgeway, Hardy explained to him that any house there would be shaken by the guns firing off Portland, and Kipling replied that he would particularly like that. But no house was bought or built.[23] From time to time one or other of the Hardys fell off their machines and sprained or scraped themselves, but they both kept up their bicycling well into the next century.

                               ☞

March 1897 saw the publication of one further novel, a revised version of the serial he had written hastily in 1891 for *Harper's*, *The Pursuit of the Well-Beloved*.[24] It was now renamed *The Well-Beloved*. By Hardy's own account it is unlike his other novels in being 'frankly fantastic', built around a single idea. It centres on a sculptor, Jocelyn Pierston, who falls repeatedly in love with girls or women who seem to embody his ideal, only to find they soon lose whatever it was that had attracted him. He is always recognizing what he calls his well-beloved, but, 'Lucy, Jane, Flora, Evangeline, or what-not, had been merely a transient condition of [the well-beloved] . . . Essentially she was perhaps of no tangible substance; a spirit, a dream, a frenzy, a conception, an aroma, an epitomized sex, a light of the eye, a parting of the lips. God only knew what she really was; Pierston did not. She was indescribable.'[25] One of Pierston's friends advises him never to marry, another more cynically recommends marrying 'the first nice woman you meet. They are all alike.'

The book can be read as an account of the impossibility of

finding satisfaction in human love, each of us dreaming of a perfect love, pinning the dream on one person after another because (of course) no one can embody it. It is the creed of the romantic, not of the respectable family man, and neither subject nor tone was calculated to appeal to Emma, and her only known comment on it is that she did not like it. Although there is no trace of autobiography in *The Well-Beloved*, it is unmistakably an *apologia pro vita sua*. Hardy is not justifying the waywardness of the male who is helpless in giving and withdrawing romantic love, he is simply describing the condition as he has experienced it – with a bow to Shelley, who lived it before him.[26] Proust found it 'very beautiful', because he thought it approached what he himself was attempting, but, although there is a fascination in the book, it is in the idea, not in the telling. Pierston himself is so faintly sketched as to be a shadow rather than a man, and his women are fainter still. For the book to be interesting, they would have to have been made substantial, like Bathsheba or Sue. Hardy also excludes any suggestion that the love is sexual, making Pierston a still dimmer figure, and making his loss of interest in each of them almost entirely painless to both parties.

Whether you find the idea as compelling as Proust did and regard the book as a triumph of modernism, or take it as a mildly original exercise without much force, depends on what you look for in fiction. If you want Dorset scenery and customs, the descriptions of Portland and its inhabitants are well worth reading. Hardy's fiction is never dull, and there are some strong and surprising paragraphs about London life too. Here, for instance, is Pierston fighting his way through a society hostess's crush with Swiftian relish for the unpleasantness of the experience: 'After ten minutes given to a preoccupied regard of shoulder-blades, back hair, glittering headgear, neck-napes, moles, hairpins, pearl-powder, pimples, minerals cut into facets of many coloured rays, necklace clasps, fans, stays, the seven styles of elbow and arm, the thirteen varieties of ear; and by using the toes of his dress-boots as coulters with which he ploughed his way'.[27] Written straight from Mrs Jeune's drawing room, no doubt.

Pierston is looking for an ideal, or perhaps a goddess, and his response to the new moon in the sky suggests he worships as a pagan wherever he finds beauty: 'In a crowd secretly, or in solitude boldly, he had often bowed the knee three times to this sisterly divinity on her first appearance monthly, and directed a kiss towards her shining shape.'[28] Hardy may be imagined doing the same, offering his tribute to the goddess who is always changing, always beautiful and always inaccessible. The book turned out to be prophetic. Pierston, looking through old photographs, comes on one of an early love whom he now thinks dead. The effect on him is that 'He loved the woman dead and inaccessible as he had never loved her in life . . . the times of youthful friendship with her, in which he had learnt every note of her innocent nature, flamed up into a yearning and passionate attachment, embittered by regret beyond words.'[29] Hardy seems to be seeing ahead to 1912 when precisely this process would be enacted, following Emma's death, and he would find himself in thrall to her, dead and inaccessible, as he had not been for many years in life.

☞

For the living Emma, *The Well-Beloved* was another insult to be borne. In August 1899 she was asked for her advice on marriage by Elspeth Thomson, who, with her sister, a painter, had been on friendly terms with the Hardys for some time. Elspeth had just married Kenneth Grahame, the children's author. Their wooing had been conducted in baby-talk, and he turned out to be more set in his bachelor ways than she had expected. Hence her appeal to Emma. Elspeth may have suspected that Hardy was not an ideal husband either. In any case Emma seized on the opportunity to lay out her own disappointments in marriage, say what she thought of Hardy's behaviour and cast herself as an ideal wife, inexplicably undervalued. 'I can scarcely think that love proper, and enduring, is in the nature of men . . . and at fifty, a man's feelings too often take a new course altogether. Eastern ideas of matrimony secretly pervade his thoughts, and he wearies of the most perfect, and suitable wife chosen in his earlier life. Of course he gets over it usually, somehow, or hides it, or is lucky!'

She went on to lament interference from in-laws and suggested that 'keeping separate a good deal' was a way of dealing with crises. This was sensible enough, and it was advice she was putting into practice herself. She went on with a grim warning to expect 'little neither gratitude, nor attentions, love, nor justice, nor anything you may have set your heart on'. And more: 'If he belongs to the public in any way, years of devotion count for nothing.' At the end of her letter she acknowledged that happy marriages do exist, but usually when both partners are Christians.[30] Mrs Grahame accepted the advice about keeping separate, although she hardly needed it.[31]

Emma presented Hardy with a Bible that summer of 1899, intended to rekindle his Christian faith. Later in the year, pursuing her interest in women's suffrage, she wrote her name in a copy of Mary Wollstonecraft's *A Vindication of the Rights of Woman*, one of the great feminist texts, which included, although she probably failed to realize it, some strongly anti-clerical passages. The tragi-comedy pursued its course. During that year she moved out of the marital bedroom: 'I sleep in an *Attic* – or *two!* . . . My boudoir is my sweet refuge and solace – not a sound scarcely penetrates hither. I see the sun, and stars and moon rise.'[32] During the next year she made notes for a novel in which divorce looms, because the hero is so indifferent to his wife that he never looks at her. Meanwile Hardy, ever unpredictable, was inspired to write a poem called 'Wives in the Sere', distinguished by the acuteness and tenderness of its observation:

> Never a careworn wife but shows,
> If a joy suffuse her,
> Something beautiful to those
> Patient to peruse her,
> Some one charm the world unknows
> Precious to a muser,
> Haply what, ere years were foes,
> Moved her mate to choose her.

But, be it a hint of rose
    That an instant hues her,
Or some early light or pose
    Wherewith thought renews her –
Seen by him at full, ere woes
    Practised to abuse her –
Sparely comes it, swiftly goes,
    Time again subdues her.[33]

In October 1899 the rumbling dispute between the Dutch settlers
in southern Africa and the British, fired by imperial ambitions,
broke out into war. Hardy was no imperialist, but he had grown
up in a barracks town, watched soldiers in the streets, and observed
the arrivals and departures of regiments as part of everyday life
since his childhood, when he had also pored over his grandfather's
illustrated military magazines. He could not help being curious
about war. He went to watch the regiments leaving Dorchester,
and bicycled to Southampton – fifty miles there and back – to see
the troops embarking for southern Africa. He told Mrs Henniker
that he took pleasure in tactics and strategy, as in a game of chess,
but that the human side horrified him – horrified, and fascinated
too.[34] He struggled with the philosophical question as to how wars
began, and how men became willing to embark on mass slaughter.
Meeting Henry Moule, he suggested that Buddhism might be
more effective than Christianity in promoting peace. Moule, a
good Christian who thought the Boers were in the wrong, was
shocked.[35] Emma took the view that 'the Boers fight for homes
and liberties – we fight for the Transvaal Funds, diamonds and
gold . . . Why should not Africa be free, as is America? . . . Well,
we gabble all day long about this war.'[36]

In the first months of the war Hardy produced a series of poems,
meditations on the feelings of departing men and wives left behind,
the putting up of the lists of killed and wounded outside the War
Office in December 1899, and what the souls of the slain might
ask and conclude about the relative merits of military glory and

quiet domestic life. They are workmanlike and agreeably idiosyncratic. In one, he imagines himself meeting the souls of slain soldiers
flying home and hearing them ask how they are remembered; they
divide into two groups for ever, the loved, whose spirits return
home, and the unloved, who plunge into darkness. In another, a
Colonel reflects that 'the Girl I leave behind me' is now a grandmother and that she suffers much more than the young wives.
One short poem, 'The Dead Drummer', rises to sublimity. It
comes through Hardy's observation that a country boy, for whom
the stars he has grown up with and seen every night are an integral
part of his experience, would be disconcerted by the strangeness
of the southern sky; it was a response to Hardy's hearing that a
Dorset drummer boy had been killed in Africa. In the poem he
gives the boy the pejorative name of Hodge, as applied to the
lumpish and ignorant peasant: 'Drummer Hodge'. He goes on,
with exquisite courtesy, to offer him a perfectly shaped elegy.

I

They throw in Drummer Hodge, to rest
   Uncoffined – just as found:
His landmark is a kopje-crest
   That breaks the veldt around;
And foreign constellations west
   Each night above his mound.

II

Young Hodge the Drummer never knew –
   Fresh from his Wessex home –
The meaning of the broad Karoo,
   The Bush, the dusty loam,
And why uprose to nightly view
   Strange stars amid the gloom.

III

> Yet portion of that unknown plain
>   Will Hodge for ever be;
> His homely Northern breast and brain
>   Grow to some Southern tree,
> And strange-eyed constellations reign
>   His stars eternally.[37]

⁕

The particular significance of the year 1900 for Hardy and Emma was that it brought the thirtieth anniversary of their first meeting at St Juliot in March. A visitor to Max Gate at this time described how her mind ran on the past: 'It is pathetic to see how she is struggling against her woes. She asserts herself as much as possible and is a great bore, but at the same time is so kind and goodhearted, and one cannot help realising what she must have been to her husband. She showed us a photograph of herself as a young girl, and it was very attractive . . . She says it was she who encouraged him to give up the architect's profession.'[38] The anniversary also prompted him to make an effort to put things on a better footing between them. His account of the process is given in a poem called 'A Second Attempt'. It begins:

> Thirty years after
> I began again
> An old-time passion:
> And it seemed as fresh as when
> The first day ventured on:
> When mutely I would waft her
> In Love's past fashion
> Dreams much dwelt upon,
> Dreams I wished she knew.

He goes on to describe how he retraced his first sensations of love, its hopes and fears, then marriage and life together, and how he hoped to revive his past love. Only,

> . . . when I looked around
> As at the former times,
> There was Life – pale and hoar;
> And slow it said to me,
> 'Twice-over cannot be!'

The striking thing is that he describes a purely internal process, communing with himself and listening to 'Life'. He is not just telling us that Life forbids a return to earlier feelings, but that Emma has become inaccessible, and real communication is no longer possible between them.[39]

There was no London Season during the war, and they did not take a London house or flat; when Hardy went to town he stayed at a Bloomsbury hotel. Gordon was now working in the Blomfield office, and Lilian was at Max Gate for long periods. In October, Emma's sister Helen was taken ill, and she went to nurse her in Hampshire. Hardy worried about the strain on her, wrote affectionately ' "take it stiddy" as they say here' and advised her on investing her sister's money: 'Corporation stock . . . is as good as anything. It pays about 3 per cent; and if you are offered more anywhere you may be sure there is some risk.'[40] Meanwhile he had Lilian, and visits from a persistent American admirer, Rebekah Owen. He took Rebekah bicycling with Lilian, and for a night-time tour of the rougher streets of Dorchester – Mixen Lane, in *The Mayor of Casterbridge* – which may have seemed rather tame to a New Yorker. Emma dashed home in November, then went back to stay with Helen to the end; she died in December. Hardy lowered the blinds at Max Gate respectfully on the day of the funeral.

The last of the year was quiet, and he produced what became his most famous poem. It was printed in the *Graphic* on 29 December 1900 and was called 'The Century's End, 1900', but a deleted '1899' on the manuscript suggests he had written it a year before. Later he renamed it 'The Darkling Thrush'.[41] He manages a perfect balance between his unbelief and his nostalgia for the faith in which he had been reared, and this is what gives it such wide appeal: you can respond to it from either side of the divide. He places himself in the romantic tradition by invoking Keats's nightingale, to whom the poet listened 'darkling', while the bird sang with 'full-throated ease': Hardy's thrush delivers a 'full-hearted evensong / Of joy'.[42] The bleak scene is scrupulously set, the dying light of a cold country afternoon, shrivelled hedge plants and bare twigs from which comes the voice of the bird, so ecstatic

> That I could think there trembled through
>   His happy good-night air
> Some blessed Hope, whereof he knew
>   And I was unaware.

19. Cat, Bird, Eagle, Sphinx

When Queen Victoria died in January 1901, a short poem by Hardy saluted her as 'serene, sagacious, free'. She had won the heart of the world, he wrote, with 'deeds well done'. His poem appeared in *The Times*. With the Boer War and the new century a transformation was taking place, the shocking novelist and outrager of bishops emerging in a fresh light as a grand old man of English letters, confidently addressing the nation from its most respected newspaper, no longer as a novelist but as a poet.

He remained practical about the business of selling his work, and the twentieth century prompted him to put his publishing affairs in order. The failure of Harper's, his American-based publishers, allowed him a change of direction, and he decided to transfer all the British rights in his work to the house of Macmillan, the firm to which he had shyly and unsuccessfully submitted his first novel in 1868, and which was now headed by the shrewd Frederick Macmillan. Kipling and Wells were on their list, and they had already acquired, in 1894, the right to publish a 'Colonial Edition' of Hardy's novels. A new agreement was signed early in 1902, a year in which Hardy noted that his investments had depreciated in value. He negotiated for himself with Macmillan, bargaining hard for his royalties.[1] He got 25 per cent on any of his books sold at 6 *s.*, 20 per cent on those sold at 4 *s.* and 5 *s.*, and 16½ per cent on cheaper ones.[2] From now on a stately procession of Uniform Edition, Pocket Edition, Wessex Edition and Mellstock Edition kept all his prose, and his poetry as he produced it, available to the public in handsome volumes. Hardy himself had already suggested the marketing strategy of presenting his fiction as a unified series of 'Wessex Novels', and it worked still better when readers could collect complete sets and study a special map in each volume showing North Wessex, Mid Wessex, Lower, Upper and Outer Wessex. The many young women, mostly schoolteachers and musicians, he said, who wrote to him asking how they might return to country life could pick their location from it if they chose. Tourists came to see for themselves where Bathsheba and Tess had lived, and there was a steadily growing interest in attaching the fictional names of towns and villages to their originals.[3] This was a game Hardy enjoyed playing, sometimes insisting that the link was tenuous, at other times pointing out to favoured friends particular houses or places he had used. His friendship with Hermann Lea, farmer, builder and keen photographer, who settled in Dorset in the 1890s and became one of his bicycling companions, led to Lea's *Handbook to the Wessex Country of Thomas Hardy* in 1904, and a larger guide, *Thomas Hardy's Wessex*, was published by Macmillan in 1913 – and reprinted in the 1960s.

He also made the Wessex connection with his first published collection of poetry in 1898, *Wessex Poems and Other Verses*.[4] It contained fifty-one poems: a third were gathered from as far back as the 1860s and were mostly written in London; others were recent. Some, but not all, have dates assigned. They are written in a great variety of styles, from the expansive ballad narrative to the intensely concentrated utterance, and they are arranged with no regard for chronology. From the 1860s, 'Neutral Tones' is one of the best in the volume.[5] There are four sonnets in the voice of a woman, the first a free reworking of Ronsard's '*Lorsque vous serez vieille*'. There is a batch of run-of-the-mill historical verses, several set during the Napoleonic Wars, and a group of sprightly and entertaining Dorset ballads, 'The Dance at the Phœnix', 'The Bride-Night Fire', 'Her Death and After' and 'Friends Beyond'. Personal poems crop up randomly, several easily linked with known incidents and people such as Horace Moule ('A Confession'), Mary Hardy ('Middle-Age Enthusiasms') and cousin Tryphena ('Thoughts of Phena'), the young Emma ('Ditty') and Florence Henniker ('At an Inn').[6] Emma was upset by allusions and tributes to other women and took 'The Ivy-Wife' to be an attack aimed at her, although it seems no more than a *jeu d'esprit* about a woman who tries to climb to fame by attaching herself to a series of men, destroying one of them in the process. The volume ends triumphantly with 'I Look into My Glass', which suggests that Hardy knew how good it was.[7] Only 500 copies were printed, and the book had a poor reception, but it was a difficult collection to review. The inclusion of his own illustrations was a distraction. They are the work of a skilful draughtsman, but some are distinctly weird, especially the drawing of a dead woman lying under a sheet accompanying the poem addressed to his late cousin Tryphena, and the blank humanoid shapes manoeuvring a coffin on a staircase to illustrate a grim architectural joke in a poem dedicated to Blomfield. You have to admire Hardy's determination to extend his range by providing decorative drawings, but it is a relief that he did not repeat the experiment. All Hardy's eight collections, making up something like 1,000 poems, were presented in the same jumbled way, partly divided into sections but made up of poems taken from different decades, with few signposts and no notes for the reader, and it took time for the world to see that something remarkable was in the making.

His second collection, *Poems of the Past and the Present*, published at the turn of 1901 and 1902, is richer than the first. It contains 'Drummer Hodge', 'Wives in the Sere', 'The Darkling Thrush', 'The Ruined Maid', all discussed already. There are witty and elegantly constructed triolets and songs like 'I Need Not Go' and 'At a Hasty Wedding'. 'A Broken Appointment' is here, and the three 'De Profundis' poems. So is 'An August Midnight', written at Max Gate in 1899, which reveals Hardy sitting in his study, working late as he so often did. The clock beat he hears is likely to come from the grandfather clock in the hall downstairs, the lamp is an oil lamp, and the ink is liquid from the inkwell on his desk, given to him by Mrs Henniker. A dumbledore is a cock-chafer or maybug, a large insect with a hard shell that flies about on warm summer nights in the country. Hardy's courtesy to his animal visitors – 'my guests' – comes naturally to him, along with his appreciation that life is lived on different scales, and that their 'Earth-secrets' are as significant to them as his ink markings on the page are to him. It shows him at his most tender, at ease in what still sometimes seemed to him to be God's creation:

I

A shaded lamp and a waving blind,
And the beat of a clock from a distant floor:
On this scene enter – winged, horned, and spined –
A longlegs, a moth, and a dumbledore;
While 'mid my page there idly stands
A sleepy fly, that rubs its hands . . .

II

Thus meet we five, in this still place,
At this point of time, at this point in space.
– My guests parade my new-penned ink,
Or bang at the lamp-glass, whirl, and sink.
'God's humblest, they!' I muse. Yet why?
They know Earth-secrets that know not I.

Hardy's public persona was now secure. He remained hard to know. The poet in him was developing; the man avoided intimacy. None of his friends quite fathomed him. Gosse, one of the oldest, found him 'sphinx-like' and 'unrevealed', his genius a mystery.[8] Yet, although he resented intrusions into his privacy, he accepted a surprising number of visitors and allowed himself to be much painted, photographed and drawn. Most of those who came to see him spoke of his gentleness and sensitivity, although H. G. Wells was aghast to see that the brave author of *Tess* and *Jude* was nothing more than 'a little grey man'.[9]

In February 1901 William Archer, a friend since Hardy sent him a copy of *Tess* in 1892, stayed at Max Gate to conduct a formal interview, intended for publication. Hardy spent a sleepless night afterwards, worrying whether he had been guilty of 'self-conceit'. He had not: when Archer praised the depths of his knowledge of 'Wessex', he modestly replied, 'some of what you take for my knowledge may be "only my artfulness".' Much of their exchange was about local lore and legend, and Archer tactfully kept off family history. The one subject on which Hardy was categorical was war, still being waged in southern Africa, and on this subject he expressed a most surprising optimism about human behaviour: 'Oh yes, war is doomed. It is doomed by the gradual growth of the introspective faculty in mankind ... Not to-day, nor tomorrow, but in the fullness of time, war will come to an end, not for moral reasons, but because of its absurdity.'[10] A year after Archer's interview a literary journalist, Desmond MacCarthy, made the first of several visits. He found Hardy

very small, very quiet, self-possessed and extraordinarily unassuming. I seem to remember that his laughter made no sound ... a gentle eagerness which was very pleasing showed in his manner when he wanted sympathy about some point. He would instantly recoil on being disappointed. I observed in him once or twice a look, a movement, too slight to be called a wince but not unlike the almost imperceptible change one sees in a cat when a gesture has perturbed it.[11]

MacCarthy also picked up 'a glint in his eye which one might have associated with slyness in a mindless and insensitive man'. Where he saw a cat, the artist William Rothenstein made Hardy into a bird, with 'a small dark bilberry eye which he cocked at you unexpectedly'.[12] Another visitor found that 'the whole face gave the impression of a bird.'[13] And a young woman, taken by the Lord-Lieutenant of the county to one of Emma's garden parties, liked Mrs Hardy's 'homely welcome' and long table spread with jam, scones and 'large Mad-Hatter sandwiches', but thought the great writer himself resembled nothing so much as 'an ancient moulting eagle, with ... his bald peering head moving ceaselessly from side to side'.[14] Turning him into a bird, an animal or a sphinx was one way of dealing with his elusiveness.

Gosse had angered Hardy when, after his good review, he spoke rudely of *Jude* to Hardy's face at the Savile Club, but he was too buoyant to allow him to escape from his proprietorial friendship. Appointed librarian of the House of Lords in 1904, he was in a still better position to promote the careers and reputations of his literary

friends, and he enjoyed nothing more. That summer he invited
Hardy to tea at the House of Lords with the Conservative leaders
Lord Salisbury and Balfour. A few months later Gosse arranged a
meeting with Asquith, leader of the Liberal Party, already slightly
known to Hardy, and Asquith marked Hardy down as a Liberal
supporter.

An account of Hardy in conversation at a literary gathering in
1904 comes from Arthur Benson, who had recently left a teaching
post at Eton to settle in Cambridge. Benson was an expansive
diarist and a shameless snob, and both his virtue and his vice appear
here:

Entered Henry James, Thomas Hardy and another . . . Hardy came up
and sat down . . . looked at me, then looked away, suffused by a misty
smile and I presently gathered that this was a recognition – he seemed
hurt by my not speaking. I watched his seamed, pale, shy, kindly face;
which yet always to me has something inherently shabby and undistin-
guished about it: it is the face, not of a peasant, like old Carlyle, but of
a village tradesman. Then we had an odd triangular talk. Hardy could
not hear what Henry James said, nor Henry James what Hardy said; and
I had to try to keep the talk going. I felt like Alice between the two
Queens. Hardy talked rather interestingly of Newman; he has read the
Apologia, & I *thought* he said 'I joined the RC church for a time, but it
has left no impression whatever on me now.' Then he said very firmly
that Newman was no logician; that the *Apologia* was simply a poet's
work, with a kind of lattice-work of logic in places to screen the poetry
. . . Then Hardy went away wanly and kindly.[15]

In 1905 the University of Aberdeen proposed to confer an
honorary doctorate on him. This gave him intense pleasure. It was
his first degree – his and Jude's, you might say – and soothed his
pride after the long years of condescension. He travelled north in
April, to be cheered by the students, spoken of in the same breath
as George Eliot and Balzac, and praised for having done for Wessex
what Scott did for the Borders and Highlands. The granite city
was still under snow and crowded with eminent visitors assembled
for the opening of a new sculpture gallery; and he was splendidly

entertained by the senior members of the university with recep-
tions, eulogies, dinners, pipers and 'Auld Lang Syne'. While he
was there, he insisted on visiting the grave of a friend from the
1870s, William Minto, who had given him a good review for *Far
from the Madding Crowd*. Hardy did not forget these things. And he
gave a provocative interview to a journalist, declaring strong views
on the duties of the state towards children, and that 'illegitimacy –
so far from being the blackest blot in a community – may be
regarded in one aspect as a form of virtue'.[16] Among people interested in ideas, his spirits rose, and he was ready to speak out as he
rarely did in Dorset or London, and on this topic he was in the
forefront of a subject that was attracting attention in intellectual
circles. Within two years Dr David Eder published his pamphlet
The Endowment of Motherhood, arguing for state support for single
mothers, and there were debates at the Fabian Society on this
subject and on marriage reform. Hardy was never going to join a
political association, but his views had their influence.

As his fame brought him rewards, the life of the Hardys as a
couple lost its momentum, shrank and decayed. He did not take
Emma to Aberdeen, and there were no more holidays together,
either abroad or in England. She became less willing to spend
time in London and found the running of a second house or flat
burdensome. She began to worry about crossing the streets in
town, as her eyes and her limp gave trouble, and, when she did
venture there, she was sometimes 'very languid' and hardly went
out.[17] This was how it was in 1901. In 1902 they kept away from
London on account of the coronation and reduced investment
income. The next year Hardy took bachelor rooms in St John's
Wood for himself, and that autumn Emma, determined to follow
her own advice about separate lives, set off with her niece Lilian
for Dover, crossed the Channel and settled in Calais for three
weeks. It was a brave move, although it fell short of venturing as
far as Paris, which she had so much enjoyed before. Hardy reacted
uneasily and took himself to a London hotel, where he fell ill with
influenza, returning miserably to Max Gate. He disliked being
alone at home.

Emma went to Calais again in the autumn of 1908, on her own

this time, and stayed away for nearly two months, taking pleasure in French hotel life. She had a good practical reason for going then – her attic rooms were being redecorated and improved – but Hardy fussed in his letters, warning her against being friendly with strangers, 'as you don't know who's who in a town through which the worst (and no doubt best) of the earth pass on their way out of our country when it gets too hot for them'. He kept her up to date with the doings of the cats and the drowning of the latest batch of kittens at Max Gate, and then suggested a return date, saying, 'It is very dull staying here alone,' which was perhaps what she hoped to hear; and she did return a little sooner than she had planned. Only to be affronted. Mr Asquith, as Prime Minister, offered Hardy a knighthood, an honour Englishmen traditionally accept with the excuse that they are doing so to please their wives. Hardy sent a curious reply to Asquith, expressing his warm admiration for his policies, but saying he would like to think over the proposed knighthood for a year. Although this was politely agreed to, it does not seem to have been brought up again, and Emma remained plain Mrs Hardy. She felt this as a deliberately aimed slight, especially when two years later he accepted the Order of Merit, a much more distinguished award but one that carried no 'Sir' or 'Lady'. The nearest she got to her wish was that among her Dorset neighbours some of the children called her 'Lady Emma' behind her back, in mocking tribute to her sense of her own importance.[18]

One of the activities she kept up determinedly was party-giving, and the Max Gate garden parties were a feature of every summer. There are photographs showing large groups of assembled guests, all in the thickly layered clothing favoured by the middle classes of the period, even when the thermometer soared upwards, and the women under elaborate hats. In June 1901 a journalists' group, the Whitefriars' Club, insisted on travelling down from London en masse to pay their respects to Hardy. There were a hundred of them, and a tent was put up in the garden to receive them. The last part of their journey was made in open carriages, and the most interesting feature of the occasion was that Hardy's mother heard of their visit and insisted on being wheeled in her chair down

Bockhampton Lane to see the carriages go past. Her daughters reluctantly agreed to her plan, and the three women waited under the trees, Mrs Hardy with a hat to keep off the sun and a rug over her knees in view of her advanced age – she was nearly ninety. She told Mary and Kate she intended to wave her handkerchief at the carriages. They said it was not the thing to do, but, as the last carriage passed, she drew out her handkerchief all the same and waved it defiantly.[19] This was perhaps what she had done when she saw Princess Victoria driven past in the 1830s, and, while a group of journalists hardly equalled a princess, they were there to honour her famous son. She was not invited to Max Gate to meet them, because Emma refused to have his family there. And why did Hardy not for once override Emma's prohibition? Reluctance to do battle with her was probably the chief reason, but he may also have been ambivalent about bringing his admirers face to face with his old mother.

When Jemima Hardy entertained at Bockhampton, she served tea in the garden with dough cake, raspberries and blue vinney cheese, according to one of her brother William Hand's grand-daughters, who remembered such an occasion in 1900 and described her great-aunt wearing a tight-fitting bodice of blue satin with tiny buttons down the front. The four Hardy uncles and aunts were all there, and Thomas Hardy presented the child, Lillie May, with a two-shilling piece. She came from sophisticated Weymouth, and the local children asked, 'Towner, bain't'ee?' when they heard her speak.[20] Jemima's last years were spent, as her husband's had been, confined to the cottage at Bockhampton, served and nursed by Mary – in her sixties herself – and Kate. Early in 1904 she heard of the death of Henry Moule, whom she had known for most of his life, and decided to send a wreath to his funeral from her sickbed. Hardy described how she made one from their own meagre winter flowers with her daughters and, finding there was not enough greenery to finish it, sent one of them out in the dark with a lantern to cut more, so that it would be ready to be taken to the Moule house early in the morning. In less than a month she was dead herself. As a mother she had been powerful, rather than tender, with her dark streak of gloom and anger, but

Hardy wrote to a friend, 'I shall miss her in many ways – her powers in humorous remark, for instance, which were immediate. It took me hours to be able to express what she had at the tip of her tongue.' He also talked of her always thinking of him as 'her rather delicate "boy"' and said the gap she left was 'wide, and not to be filled. I suppose if one had a family of children one would be less sensible of it.'[21]

His poem 'Shut Out That Moon' was written this year. It speaks of the failure of love and writes a line under the past – as the death of a mother does.[22] It also draws on the imagery of the Romantic poets:

> Close up the casement, draw the blind,
>   Shut out that stealing moon,
> She wears too much the guise she wore
>   Before our lutes were strewn
> With years-deep dust, and names we read
>   On a white stone were hewn.

What is the moon stealing? Hearts, hopes, time, dreams, even wits: dangerous but also stealing like a lover, pleasurably. Lovers steal kisses, and the moon reminds us of the pleasures of youth, of music once made, of people known and loved who are now lying under gravestones. The poem goes on to warn against looking at the stars ('Immense Orion's glittering form') as well as the moon, and against 'midnight scents' in the summer garden and their power to arouse feeling; and, in doing so, it becomes more of a tribute to romanticism than a warning against it. The last stanza speaks of the unromantic world, the 'common lamp-lit room' that prisons 'eyes and thought', the 'mechanic speech' that replaces music and lyricism and laughter. These are the prosaic, limited options of adulthood, set against youthful romantic values, and Hardy seems to suggest they are a way of dealing with the disappointments of life. He ends the poem with bitter words:

> Too fragrant was Life's early bloom,
>   Too tart the fruit it brought!

Yet Hardy himself never allowed his eyes or thought to be imprisoned or his speech to become mechanic, and if, as he suggests, romantic values lead to disappointment, the poem chiefly invokes the exquisite pleasure they give. He might appear as a bald old eagle and be unreadable as a sphinx, but he kept his direct access to the world of nature and feeling as freshly as a young man.

Emma did not go to her mother-in-law's funeral, any more than Hardy attended her family funerals. Soon she had her own intimations of mortality. In May 1906, while Hardy was in London, she was at Max Gate on her own for a few days. Working in the garden, she had a fainting fit. 'My heart seemed to stop; I fell, and after a while a servant came to me.'[23] Whatever the cause of her collapse, which does not seem to have been investigated but sounds as though it could have been a small stroke, it may have contributed to her becoming more eccentric in conversation and style. Gosse wrote a merciless description of her in the last year of her life, 'absurdly dressed as a country lady without friends might dress herself on a vague recollection of some nymph in a picture by Botticelli'.[24] More kindly, the French portait painter Jacques Blanche caught the pathos of her appearance: 'Nothing remained to her of the full-blooded, rosy, jovial freshness attested by those who had seen her while still young. Instead, shrunken as if age had made her smaller, she adopted a defensive shield, retaining in stereotyped form the smile of former days as if fixed for all time by a photographer.'[25] Photographs of her in old age still show two curls emerging from the cap on her forehead, curls that had once pleased Hardy so much he gave them to Anne, the pretty heroine of *The Trumpet-Major*.

Emma was surely never mad, although Mary and Kate Hardy were not the only ones to suggest she was. She was eccentric, sometimes to the point of absurdity, her conversation could be dismayingly inconsequential, but she was always able to organize her own life and activities, to make travel arrangements, to write, to run the house and to communicate with her few friends and her maids. The most disconcerting and upsetting part of her behaviour was her open display of hostility towards Hardy, her snobbish claims for her own family and her dismissal of his family as 'peasants'. Married people are known to make covert attacks on one another in company, but Emma's attacks were not covert. In 1909 Hardy wrote to a friend explaining that 'my domestic circumstances . . . make it embarrassing for me to return hospitalities received, so that I hesitate nowadays to accept many.'[26] The friend was the rationalist banker Edward Clodd, who regularly invited Hardy to Aldeburgh for house parties where he gathered congenial intellectuals, occasions much enjoyed by Hardy, who went without Emma.

Her far from mad interest in the question of women's suffrage led her to support the suffragette movement. Hardy was in general agreement with the principle, although cautious as always about making any public commitment to it. But Emma joined marches in London in 1907, went to rallies, and wrote a long and well-argued letter on the importance of women's participation in government to the *Nation* in 1908.[27] The following year she resigned from the London Society for Women's Suffrage, but purely because she disapproved of militancy; she continued her allegiance to the cause itself. She kept abreast of current affairs in other ways: sending a donation to Israel Zangwill for the Zionist movement, with a letter of support; and writing various letters to the press about the conditions endured by the children of the poor – urging better care, better food, better schools, better housing – and about specific cruelties to animals, such as circus tigers and bulls in bullfights. Less sensibly, she also submitted poems to magazines, none of them even competently written; a few were printed because she was 'Mrs Thomas Hardy'. She lacked judgement to assess her own efforts, but this is a common fault, and she had the spirit to keep trying.

She made friends with one of her husband's most ardent American admirers, rich Rebekah Owen from New York, a repeated visitor to England who got herself and her sister an introduction to the Hardys in 1892 and thereafter put in frequent appearances at Max Gate. Emma was hospitable to them and kept up a correspondence with Rebekah that to a degree deflected her from bothering Hardy directly. Miss Owen was happy to accept Emma's kindness and her confidences and at the same time to gossip about her being 'half-cracked' and 'phenomenally plain' behind her back with other Dorset acquaintances.

When Hardy took holidays with other friends, Emma made her own arrangements. At sixty-eight she went bicycling alone round Dorset, sometimes stopping at roadside cottages for meals. She kept up her painting, her sewing and her music. She refused to become an invalid, making light of her physical problems and pains. At sixty-nine she sat down to produce *Some Recollections*, her best piece of writing, entirely on her own. What she could never do was to rediscover in her own mind what had made her proud of Hardy, or restore in her behaviour what had made her dear to him. And so they remained locked in mutual incomprehension.

With the twentieth century Hardy had put novel writing behind him, and there were to be no more shockers to upset Emma or the public. Instead he devoted much of the first decade of the century to a project to which no one could take exception, a work historical and patriotic in theme, composed largely in blank verse. *The Dynasts* could be seen as a fitting and respectable crown to the career of a man of letters. He had for many years been turning over in his mind the idea of writing about the Napoleonic Wars. As early as June 1875, when he had taken Emma with him to visit Waterloo veterans at the Chelsea Hospital on the anniversary of the great battle, and one old soldier had put his arm round her waist and called her 'my dear young woman', Hardy had thought of writing 'A Ballad of the Hundred Days. Then another of Moscow. Others of earlier campaigns – forming all together an Iliad of Europe from 1789 to 1815'.[28] In 1889 he was planning 'A Drama of Kings', and in 1896 it was to be 'Europe in Throes'. He did some research and writing in 1897 but did not settle to steady work until 1902. What emerged from his long labours became *The Dynasts: An Epic-Drama*, which absorbed him until 1908. It was history but also a vehicle in which he expressed his views about human motivation, how people are driven by the Immanent Will even when they think they are making their own choices. It was published in three parts, in 1904, 1906 and 1908. It was not intended for performance – Hardy took Shelley's *Prometheus Unbound* as his model here – and he hoped it would be read like a novel. As it turned out, this was a vain hope, and today it is among the least read of his works.

The scope of what he took on was ambitious: he started from the invasion scare in England in 1805, when Napoleon assembled an army on the French coast and Pitt and Sheridan clashed in the House of Commons, and covered all the main events in the European wars over the next ten years to the final defeat of Napoleon in 1815. The best effects are the cinematic stage directions in which we are given aerial views of Europe, looking down from a great height at advancing or retreating armies moving like caterpillars across the various landscapes, and at the great land and sea battles: Trafalgar, Ulm, Jena, Austerlitz, Corunna, Talavera, the retreat from Moscow and Waterloo. They are an extraordinary feat of imagination, original and dramatic. Moving the scale from the panoramic to the minute, there is an account of the effect of battle on animal, vegetable and insect life at Waterloo which no one but Hardy could have thought of and where his poetic voice is perfectly pitched:

> The mole's tunnelled chambers are crushed by wheels,
> The lark's eggs scattered, their owners fled;
> And the hedgehog's household the sapper unseals.
>
> The snail draws in at the terrible tread,
> But in vain; he is crushed by the felloe-rim;
> The worm asks what can be overhead . . .
>
> Trodden and bruised to a miry tomb
> Are ears that have greened but will never be gold,
> And flowers in the bud that will never bloom.[29]

These are the two best features of the vast enterprise in which Hardy asks his reader to take on nearly 300 characters, ranging from kings and emperors to common soldiers and Dorset rustics, as well as a group of presiding spirits, or 'phantom intelligences', who hover about commenting on the action, some sympathetically, some with irony or gleeful hostility. They are there to explicate the workings of the Immanent Will through humanity, but as celestial machinery they are feeble. Where Homer and Wagner made their gods into glorious and badly behaved beings with instantly recognizable feelings and behaviour, Hardy offers etiolated voices speaking without urgency or beauty. The demands of research and the scale of his enterprise seem to have absorbed his energy, so that when it came to writing there was little left to give life to the language. With a few exceptions like the passage above, it plods along, worthy and banal. Occasionally it becomes ludicrous. Blank verse needs a spring in it, and this has neither spring nor strength, but feebly apes Shakespearean historical writing:

> The hostile hatchings of Napoleon's brain
> Against our Empire, long have harassed us,
> And mangled all our mild amenities.
> So, since the hunger for embranglement
> That gnaws this man, has left us optionless,
> And haled us recklessly to horrid war,
> We have promptly mustered our well-hardened hosts,
> And, counting on our call to the Most High,
> Have forthwith set our puissance face to face
> Against Napoleon. – Ranksmen! officers!
> You fend your lives, your land, your liberty.
> I am with you. Heaven frowns on the aggressor.[30] –

It would be cruel to quote more. The first part was not received with much enthusiasm, although Max Beerbohm was fascinated by the thought that it was the 'first modern work of dramatic fiction in which free will is denied to the characters', set on their courses by the Immanent Will. He veered between finding it a 'quite fugitive and negligible little piece of work' and deciding he had been reading 'a really great book'. He mocked gently, talking

of the 'autumnal works of great writers' and suggesting it would
have required 'a syndicate of much greater poets than ever were
born into the world, working in an age of miracles' to carry out
Hardy's intentions. He asked himself why Hardy had written it
and wished it had been in prose, yet in the end he was won over.[31]

By the time Part III appeared the critics were generally respectful, and it was greeted as 'a great work of art' and 'the most
notable literary achievement of the last quarter-century' and proof
of 'undoubted genius'.[32] Hardy, now approaching seventy, had
earned the right to be taken seriously. It has never been popular,
however much respected, and it is quite hard to find anyone who
has read it for pleasure for many years. Still, there have always been
those whose love and commitment to his work have caused them
to embrace *The Dynasts*.[33] Granville-Barker put on a dramatized
version in the early years of the Great War, and there have been
more adaptations for stage performance since, and for radio. A
Major-General, Sir Harry Marriott Smith, who lived near Hardy
in the 1920s, had bought and read it between the retreat from
Mons and the landing in Gallipoli; he decided it was the greatest
book written in his lifetime, because of its uncanny knowledge of
how soldiers think and behave. When he asked Hardy how he
knew about such things, Hardy replied, 'Oh, well, I just knew it.
I didn't read that anywhere, I just knew it.' Marriott Smith saw
this as evidence of genius, and it is not for a civilian to argue with
his opinion.[34]

Macmillan brought out a complete edition of *The Dynasts* in
November 1910. It is in small type and runs to 525 pages, and it
has a portrait of Hardy, engraved from a painting made by his sister
Mary, as frontispiece. He is almost smiling, and his hair, eyebrows
and moustache are now quite white and look as soft as cotton
wool.

PART FOUR

1905–1928

20. Convergence

Letters from strangers came to Hardy from all over the world, and in August 1905 one with a Weymouth postmark caught his fancy. It was from a Florence Dugdale, who was holidaying on the coast; she declared herself a true admirer of his work and asked if she might call on him. He replied, 'Dear Madam, As you are not going to print anything about your visit I shall be at home to you some afternoon this month, if you will send a post card a day or two before you are coming.'[1] She seems to have made her visit, to have met Hardy but not Mrs Hardy and left such a good impression that she was invited to call again. Towards the end of the year she was back. As her home was in the London suburb of Enfield, she must have made a particular effort to travel to Dorset again. After this second visit, when she again failed to meet Emma, she sent Hardy flowers. He thanked her in a letter in January 1906, with an assurance that she had not stayed too long. She was twenty-six.

A few months later, in May, Hardy gave his publisher instructions to allow the publication of *The Pocket Thomas Hardy*, a selection of his prose and verse put together by an unknown journalist called Alfred Hyatt. Hyatt was Florence Dugdale's best friend in Enfield, so this was without doubt in response to a request from her, and it suggests she was not shy about asking favours. She and Hyatt both aspired to be writers, he as a poet – he went about in a cloak and broad-brimmed hat like Tennyson – and she through journalism and writing for children. It was a coup for her to get permission from the great Hardy for Hyatt's booklet. He ran his own tiny press and produced hand-printed books. But he was delicate – tubercular, in fact – and had not many years to live. After his early death Florence wrote that he was 'more to me than anything else in the world' and that she would '*gladly* have died' for him.[2] She makes it sound as though he was the true romance of her life.

Florence was a hero worshipper, kind and sensitive, and also determined, and she learnt to be devious. She gave various accounts of her first meeting with Hardy, none of which fits with the evidence of his first two letters to her. One was that she was taken to meet Mrs Hardy at Max Gate that August by Mrs Henniker, only to be told by a 'page' that Mrs Hardy was not at home, although she was clearly upstairs, and entertained to tea by a cheerful Hardy.[3] But Florence did not meet Mrs Henniker until 1910, when Hardy introduced the two women. She seems to have given two of her sisters different stories, telling one that she had been introduced to Hardy by W. T. Stead, the journalist, and another that she met Emma Hardy at a women's club in London, the Lyceum, before she met Hardy; yet her first meeting with Emma at the Lyceum was in 1910.[4] A further variant has her making friends with both Mr and Mrs Hardy when they met by chance on holiday in Dorset, and being invited by Mrs Hardy to stay at Max Gate as a result.[5] If Florence was trying to protect herself from any suspicion that she had pursued Hardy, and from any prying into the details of their early relationship, she did not set about it very efficiently. She emerges as someone whose word is not always to be believed.

Hardy found no fault with his new admirer. She was young enough to be his granddaughter, and she showed herself as sweet-natured and deferential. She was also very pleasant-looking, with dark hair and large grey eyes – 'large luminous living eyes', he wrote in his poem 'After the Visit'. Her manner was mild, her voice gentle and she moved lightly on her feet:

> Come again, with the feet
> That were light on the green as a thistledown ball,
> And those mute ministrations to one and to all
> Beyond a man's saying sweet.[6]

In all this she was unlike Emma. Where the two women were alike was in their love of reading; Florence shared Emma's enthusiasm for Tennyson and had even given a talk on *The Idylls of the King* to the Enfield Literary Society. Her background was modest, her father being the son of a Wareham blacksmith, something that was never mentioned, although Hardy was delighted when he found there was a Dorset connection. Mr Dugdale had risen to become headmaster of a Church of England school at Enfield in his twenties and gone on to be a pillar of the community and the local Conservative Party. Florence was one of five daughters, all brought up to understand that they must earn their own livings. At fifteen she became a pupil teacher, and in 1905 she was still teaching in her father's school. It was a rigidly controlled faith school, which she disliked, and keeping order in classes of forty boys took more strength and energy than she could easily muster. She was delicate and often ill, and the quietness of her voice was partly a result of persistent throat infections. She realized she must find some other occupation, and in 1906 she took up the old-fashioned position of lady's companion in the household of Sir Thornley Stoker, a rich Dublin surgeon with an invalid wife.

The snobbery of the age made her understandably reticent about her early working life. To admit to having worked as a pupil teacher would have been humiliating, and she chose to describe her job as a companion as 'staying with friends'. She seems to have divided her time between Dublin and London from 1906 to 1910, when Lady Stoker had to be moved to a nursing home. In both cities she made the hearts of old men beat faster. Sir Thornley grew warmly attached to her and, when he learnt of her ambition to write, gave her a typewriter; then, when his wife died, he presented her with an antique ring. Hardy's approach was different: his way of making sure they kept in touch was to ask her to do occasional research for him at the British Museum reading room. She insisted later that she worked unpaid for him.[7]

A letter from Hardy to Florence in April 1907, when he was living in a flat in Hyde Park Mansions, proposes a meeting at the South Kensington Museum: 'I will look for you in the architectural gallery at 4 – say by the Trajan column.' It is reminiscent of his early meetings with Florence Henniker, and in September of the same year he sent a story of the second Florence's to the editor of the *Cornhill* with a letter of recommendation. 'The Apotheosis of the Minx' is a sad little impression of a sensitive suburban school-master and a vulgar girl who jilts him for a grocer, regrets it and dies young: it is perfectly readable, if no more than that, and it was accepted. Hardy explained to the editor that 'Her family is an old Dorset one which I have known of all my life.'[8] This might just possibly have been true, and to others he sometimes described Florence as his cousin, which was not true by any stretch of the imagination.[9] A web of small deceits was being woven.

Armed with her typewriter from Sir Thornley, she taught herself to type, and one use she made of it was typing for Hardy. He was at pains to explain that 'my young friend and assistant . . . is not really what is called a "typist" . . . only doing my typewriting as a fancy.'[10] But it meant that when in 1909 she joined the Lyceum Club – established in 1904 at 128 Piccadilly as a meeting place for women with an interest in the arts – she could describe herself as Hardy's secretary.[11] That winter she talked again to the Enfield Literary Society, and this time her subject was Thomas Hardy. She was writing for children's annuals, and the Oxford University Press took her *The Story of Mr Prickleback* as one of their Story Readers.

In the summer of 1909 an operatic version of *Tess* was produced at Covent Garden, the work of an Italian librettist and German-American composer, Baron d'Erlanger. It had opened in 1906 at the San Carlo in Naples, coinciding with an eruption of Vesuvius that closed the opera house, then played in Milan. When Hardy understood that Emma wanted to be present at the first perform-ance, he asked Edward Clodd, who had not yet met Florence, to be the young woman's escort, and Clodd agreed. The first night was a social event, the soprano being the same who had premiered *Madame Butterfly*, and Queen Alexandra was in the royal box. Clodd was intrigued by the situation, took Florence out to dinner and saw her back to her club after the performance. He too found her charming, and when Hardy hinted that she would benefit from sea air, Clodd invited the two of them to Aldeburgh together. That August they stayed for ten days. Hardy's relations with Emma were by now such that he felt no need to account even for such long absences. The holiday was a success for him and for Florence: they went sailing, they spent a day at Cromer, and they were photographed together beside a breakwater on Aldeburgh Beach. Even getting stuck on a mud bank in the treacherous tidal estuary of the river and having to be rescued did not spoil their pleasure. 'Hardy and the Lady are enjoying themselves,' wrote Clodd to his friend Clement Shorter, who also knew them both. From now on Florence naively confided in Clodd, and Clodd passed on titbits to Clement Shorter, editor of the *Sphere* magazine, who knew all those involved, including Emma; and Hardy and the Lady were invited every spring and autumn to Aldeburgh.[12] Meanwhile the opera failed. D'Erlanger apologized to Hardy for not having proved worthy of him and sent him £34 in royalties.[13]

Hardy now began to arrange more elaborate trips in which Florence Dugdale accompanied him when he went to look at cathedrals and other places of interest. In October they travelled with his brother Henry to York, Durham and Edinburgh. The following March she and Hardy went together, unchaperoned, to the Isle of Wight to visit Swinburne's grave; then they spent Easter at Aldeburgh. That spring she borrowed a flat in Baker Street, where she introduced Hardy to her sister Ethel, who brought her small son along. Hardy took the child on his lap and spoke to him with grandfatherly kindness. Florence also encouraged him to take a place of his own in town and introduced him to a woman writer with a flat to let. Her impression was that Hardy was 'very much taken in hand and "run"' by Florence, an 'efficient, business-like young woman'.[14] He did not take the flat, but he helped Florence to find work as a journalist by recommending her to the *Evening Standard* and the *Standard* got its reward when he allowed them to print the profile she prepared for his seventieth birthday. Various other editors had letters from him recommending her work as a journalist and a short-story writer.

Florence was grateful for what he did for her, and fond of him, but she was never in love with him. He was not a figure of romance like poor Hyatt, now dying of tuberculosis, but a strictly literary hero. He gave her encouragement and got her paid work, and there was considerable cachet in being associated with him as his secretary and protégée. He took her on agreeable holidays. She was flattered that he was in love with her and wrote poems about her, but he was an old man. The balance of power was on her side. He was eager to grant her favours. He could not ask for more than her companionship.

He was also married. He seems never to have considered a formal separation, let alone divorce, from Emma, although he gave his opinion publicly early in 1912 that divorce should be granted at the wish of either party, if that party prove the marriage to be a cruelty to him or her (provided that children continued to be maintained by the bread-winner).[15] He could well afford to maintain Emma and set up somewhere else on his own, but a divorce would have taken time, and what grounds would he be able to give for one? And where would he have lived? He had put down his roots at Max Gate and had no wish to leave. More than that: something held him to Emma, not just fear of what she might do, or of scandal, but the years they had lived together. He did not like to be alone, so that even the company of a woman he hardly talked to, who kept out of his bedroom, whom he kept out of his study, and who was at enmity with him on fundamental points like religion and his family – even her company was preferable to being alone. He had to endure the situation even if he lost Florence as a result, by not being able to offer her marriage.

In May, Edward VII died. Hardy, invited to write a poem, explained that he did not feel 'any impulse, or faintest power, to write anything upon the sudden termination of the late reign. I will not attempt to explain why.'[16] To Agnes Grove he wrote, 'I fear the new court will not be much more intellectual than the old. I am inclined to go away on the day of the funeral, to avoid the frightful crush.'[17] Yet he could not resist watching the procession as the King's body was taken to Westminster, and the funeral cortège three days later, from the windows of the Athenaeum. In his absence, Emma invaded his study: she wrote to a friend about 'ensconcing myself in the Study in *his* big chair foraging – he keeps me *out* usually – as *never* formerly – ah well, I have my private opinion of men in general and of him in particular!'[18] After this she joined him in London, where he had taken a flat at 4 Blomfield Terrace in Maida Vale. And now things moved on in a surprising way.

Emma delivered a lecture at the Lyceum Club. Florence was present, and at the end she went up to Emma to congratulate her. She must have thought hard about whether to do this and consulted with Hardy, because it committed both of them to a more sustained and complicated deception. As it turned out, Emma was not difficult to deceive. Charmed at finding herself appreciated by someone, she at once invited her new friend to tea at Blomfield Terrace and then for a weekend at Max Gate. She had no idea that Florence knew the place, or its master, already. She eagerly took up Florence's offer to help her with her writing, and to approach publishers for her. The deference and flattery in Florence's letters to her are thickly laid on but they went down well with Emma, and Florence did some typing for her, including her short novel *The Maid on the Shore*, and even tried to place her work with publishers. Emma believed that Florence was her ally and friend, and when Hardy was given the Order of Merit in the Birthday Honours, she deputed her to keep an eye on him and check that he was properly got up to receive his award.

As in a black farce, Florence found that Mr and Mrs Hardy were competing for her company, assistance and affection. She added an extra strand to the plot with her own indiscreet letters to Clodd about her two admirers. For two and a half years, from the summer of 1910 until November 1912, the three played out a bizarre triangular game. In September 1910 Hardy and Florence spent five days at Aldeburgh. In September, Florence was at Max Gate helping Emma. William Strang came to draw Hardy, and Hardy persuaded him to draw Florence too, although he had never drawn Emma. In October, Hardy managed to take Florence to Bock-hampton and introduce her to his sisters, without letting Emma know. Florence wrote to Clodd, 'The "Max Gate menage" always does wear an aspect of comedy to me. Mrs Hardy is good to me, beyond words, and instead of cooling towards me she grows more and more affectionate. I am *intensely* sorry for her, sorry indeed for both.'[19]

In November, Hardy was awarded the freedom of the Borough

of Dorchester at a ceremony attended by Emma, Florence, Mary, Henry and Kate Hardy. He joked that he had already made free with the town in his writing and spoke of the disappearance of all the shopkeepers of his youth. Afterwards the Dorchester Debating and Dramatic Society put on a performance of *The Mellstock Quire*, adapted by a local chemist, A. H. Evans, from *Under the Greenwood Tree*, which delighted Hardy, although not Florence.[20] She was further exasperated by the poem he was writing on the death of his cat, described as his only friend. When she objected that the cat was not by any means his only friend, he explained that he was 'not exactly writing about himself but about some imaginary man in a similar situation'. On the same day Emma asked Florence if she had noticed 'how extremely like *Crippen* Mr TH is, in personal appearance. She added darkly that she would not be surprised to find herself in the cellar one morning . . . I thought it was time to depart or she would be asking me if I didn't think I resembled Miss Le Neve.' Emma then suggested that she and Florence might go to live abroad together for some months. It would have 'a good effect' on Hardy, she believed.[21] Florence made an excuse.

She did, however, agree to spend the Christmas of 1910 at Max Gate, and on the festive day a frightful row blew up. Hardy told Emma he was taking Florence to meet his family at Bockhampton, and Emma objected that they would poison Florence's mind against her. After a sharp exchange Emma retreated to her attic, while Hardy strode off to Bockhampton alone, not returning until half past eight in the evening. Florence vowed to herself that no power on earth would ever persuade her to spend Christmas at Max Gate again.[22]

☞

The year 1911 continued much the same, except that Florence now avoided Max Gate, and there are no surviving letters from her to Emma after January 1911. Perhaps Emma had been right in fearing that Florence would be turned against her. Emma was writing her *Recollections* in the attic, unknown to anyone. In them she returned to what she remembered as an idyllic childhood in Portsmouth, to her time in Cornwall and her gallops along the coastal paths there. The narrative ends with her wooing and marriage, described calmly and without a bitter word. Hardy introduced Florence to Mrs Henniker, for whom she began to do secretarial work. A second story attributed to Florence was fulsomely recommended to the *Cornhill* and appeared there. 'Blue Jimmy: The Horse Stealer' begins with an allusion to Hardy's ballad 'A Trampwoman's Tragedy' and consists largely of transcriptions from newspaper reports of the career, trial and hanging at Ilchester of a real horse thief, James Clace, in the 1820s, collected by Hardy in his notebooks.[23] In April he and Florence visited Hereford, Lichfield and Worcester cathedrals in a family party consisting of his brother Henry and her sister Constance, and then they went together to Aldeburgh as usual.

In May, Hardy escorted Emma to a party in London, telling Mrs Henniker, 'Emma wants me to take her to the reception at the Foreign Office ... so I suppose I must.'[24] He declined his invitation to the coronation of George V. He spent the day of his seventy-first birthday at Bockhampton with Florence and his family, and then took her to the Lake District with Henry and Kate and with the addition of Mr Dugdale, who seems to have accepted the absence of Mrs Hardy from the party without question. In July, Hardy went to Somerset with Florence and Kate. Then it was Emma's turn to be with Florence. The two women spent a fortnight in a hotel beside the sea at Worthing. This seems to have been the last time they were together: or at any rate there is no record of Florence being at Max Gate again, and Emma made no more visits to London.

Florence was typing Hardy's revised prefaces to the novels for the new Wessex Edition in preparation with Macmillan. She may also have helped Emma with advice on putting out two privately printed booklets with a Dorchester printer: one of her prose meditations, the other of her pathetically unskilled poems, although there is no written record of this. There was the usual Aldeburgh visit in October, and then Florence sometimes stayed in Weymouth, where Hardy could easily visit her, and did so. While she was there, Alfred Hyatt died suddenly of a haemorrhage of the lung. He was forty, and Florence was now thirty-two. This is when she told Clodd that he had been more to her than anything else in the world since she was twenty.[25]

In February 1912 Mrs Henniker's husband, the Major-General, who had survived the Boer War, was kicked by a horse and died of heart failure. Florence went to help her in London, and the two women produced a small memorial book, to which Hardy contributed some verses, written at Florence's request. From now on Mrs Henniker regarded Florence as a friend, and Florence became genuinely devoted to her. She suffered a second loss when Sir Thornley Stoker died. Generous to the last, he left her a bequest of £2,000, enough to give her a degree of independence.

☞

In Dorset, Hardy wrote his great poem 'The Convergence of the Twain' in response to the sinking of the *Titanic* – and he wrote it to order.[26] It stands apart from his other work in its superb simplicity, and marks an advance in power and extension of his range as a poet – with it he moves into the twentieth century. Donald Davie compared it to the ship that is half its subject: 'The poem itself is an engine, a sleek and powerful machine; its rhymes slide home like pistons inside cylinders.'[27] He might have added that the poem stays afloat to the end. It is grim and exuberant at the same time, as Hardy conjures up the simultaneous shaping of the ship and its 'sinister mate' the iceberg, seeing their conjunction as a working of the mysterious power behind the universe:

> And as the smart ship grew
> In stature, grace, and hue,
> In shadowy silent distance grew the Iceberg too . . .

> Till the Spinner of the Years
> Said 'Now!' And each one hears,
> And consummation comes, and jars two hemispheres.[28]

☞

Hardy and Florence enjoyed four days together in Aldeburgh in May. On Hardy's birthday, on 2 June, Yeats and Henry Newbolt travelled to Max Gate to present him with the gold medal of the Royal Society of Literature. Newbolt, just back from Italy, described what turned out to be an occasion 'beyond all others unusual and anxious'. Over lunch,

Hardy, an exquisitely remote figure . . . asked me a hundred questions about my impressions of the architecture of Rome and Venice . . . Through his conversation I could hear and see Mrs Hardy giving Yeats much curious information about the two very fine cats, who sat to right and left of her plate on the table itself . . . At last Hardy rose from his seat and looked towards his wife: she made no movement, and he walked to the door. She was still silent and unmoved: he invited her to leave us for a few minutes, for a ceremony which in accordance with his wishes was to be performed without witnesses. She at once remonstrated, and Yeats and I begged that she should not be asked to leave us. But Hardy insisted and she made no further appeal but gathered up her cats and her train with perfect simplicity and left the room.[29]

Emma must have exasperated Hardy beyond endurance for him to have treated her as he did on that occasion, in the presence of two eminent visitors. What was worse was that her presence made him so uneasy that all his considerable charm took flight, and he appeared nervous and uneasy with his guests as well as cold and unkind to his wife. He insisted on reading out his speech of acceptance to Yeats and Newbolt at the dining table. It began with a personal allusion, half jocular, half melancholy, as he said that he was 'rather an old boy to get a medal, and that, unfortunately, he had no boy of his own to whom to pass it on'.

There was another visit from literary dignitaries in early September, this time Gosse, bringing with him Arthur Benson, agog with curiosity. Benson was a poet himself and had sent Hardy a volume of his verse in 1892, getting a polite, if cautious, note of thanks: 'I am much struck with the poems so far, but I have not yet reached a critical estimate.'[30] Benson had also walked past Max Gate in 1905 as he toured Dorset and judged it a 'feeble, ugly

house'. 'It is walled in, and thickly planted with firs &c, so that it
looks like a house in a tray of vegetation.'³¹ He was the son of an
Archbishop of Canterbury, with all the advantages and disadvantages that brought. He had taught at Eton and was now a Fellow
of Magdalene in Cambridge. He was a gifted as well as a privileged
man, and a repressed, and depressed, homosexual. Like other
members of his family, he suffered periods of mental breakdown.
As well as being snobbish and quarrelsome, he kept a vast, detailed
diary. His entry for 5 September 1912 gives his impressions of Max
Gate, Hardy and Mrs Hardy, with much carefully observed detail
and feline condescension.

We made our way out among the neat villas and suburbs – at the very
end of the town where it melts into the country, there appeared a little
hedged and walled plantation – Max Gate – with a red house dimly
visible, bordered by turnip-fields. We descended at the gate and made
our way by a winding little drive to a small gravel sweep, all ill-kept, to
the door of the house. It is a structure at once mean and pretentious,
with no grace of design or detail, and with two hideous low flanking
turrets with pointed roofs of blue slate. In the vestibule a frightful
ornament of alabaster, three foliated basins tiara-wise with doves drinking
. . . There was a smell of cooking all about. A tiny maid took us into a
rather nice drawing room with a bow window, with many pictures and
ornaments and a large portrait of Hardy. Here was a small, pretty,
rather mincing elderly lady with hair curiously puffed and padded rather
fantastically dressed. Gosse took her by both hands and talked to her in
a strain of exaggerated gallantry which was deeply appreciated. A solid
plebeian overdressed niece was presented. Then Hardy came in – very
small and lean and faintly browned. His features are curiously worn and
blurred and ruinous. He has a big rather long head, bald, with thin
longish hair at the back, fine expressive brows and rather lustreless dark
eyes. One would take him for a retired half-pay officer, from a not very
smart regiment. He greeted Gosse very warmly and me cordially, and
enquired sedulously after our health, complimenting us on our books,
as if discharging a natural courtesy. Presently we went in to lunch. It was
hard to talk to Mrs H who rambled along in a very inconsequential way,

with a bird-like sort of wit, looking sideways and treating one's remarks as amiable interruptions.

Lunch was long and plentiful – rather coarse fare. We were served first with odd little cakes of mincemeat, one for each, a little high perhaps. The solid niece regarded hers stolidly with an air of knowing too much about its composition but didn't taste. Hardy offered claret, and rose on each occasion to pour it in my glass. Mrs H struggled with and chipped at a great chicken, stuffed, with an odd little dish of bits of cold bacon beside it. She stood to carve, and treated the chicken as if she were engaged in some curious handicraft – after which she devoted herself in a serious silence to her meal. Hardy filled my plate with odd thin slices of lamb, and sluiced his own plate of cold lamb with hot gravy. Then came a great apple tart. It was a meal such as one might have got at a big farmhouse – two tiny youthful maids waited, bursting with zeal and interest. The room was a dull one, rather slatternly. It was distempered in purple, much streaked and stained . . . Mrs H produced cigarettes, and Hardy said he never smoked; but Gosse playfully insisted that Mrs H should have one. She said she had never smoked, but lit a cigarette and coughed cruelly at intervals, every now and then laying it down and saying, 'There that will be enough' but always resuming it, till I feared disaster. Hardy looked at her so fiercely and scornfully that I made haste to say that I had persuaded my mother to smoke.

Benson goes on for many more pages, describing the garden with its lumpy grass and weedy trees planted too close together. He thought Hardy was 'not agreeable' to his wife, but saw that his patience was tried by one so odd who yet had to be treated as rational. He decided there was 'something secret and inscrutable' in him. He added that 'their kindness and courtesy were great'.[32]

We know that by now Emma was ill with an undiagnosed condition, and often in pain. Sometimes she felt that her usual bicycle ride to church at Fordington on Sunday was too much for her and had herself pushed in a bath chair by the gardener. Still, she summoned her energy to entertain, and she was friendly with the vicar there, Mr Bartelot, and with his wife. She gave a late-summer garden party and took a group of children from

Fordington for a beach picnic, bringing all of them back to Max
Gate afterwards for presents and tea. As Benson noted, she also had
her niece Lilian to stay, although she found her so trying she sent
her home again soon after his visit. It seems that her friendship with
Florence was at an end. Possibly she had understood how blind
she had been to the relationship between Florence and her husband.

Emma's new maid Dolly, only fourteen years old, was the
kindest presence in her life now. Dolly's tasks included brushing
her mistress's hair to soothe the eczema on her head and fetching
her large doses of painkiller from the chemist in Dorchester. She
carried her breakfast and lunch upstairs. Emma usually came down
for dinner. Hardy said later that she sometimes complained of her
heart during the autumn, but she would not have the doctor. He
was always busy. In late October he was sitting on a Grand Jury at
the Dorchester Assizes. But he did notice that one day she sat
down at the piano and played through her repertoire of favourite
songs, then closed the instrument and announced she would never
play again. It suggests she had some idea that her life had not long
to run.[33] Knowing your own death is approaching is a test of
character under any circumstances. To be in her position, with no
one you feel you can talk to, no sister or child, and no one to
comfort you or show you affection, must have been bitter beyond
most people's endurance. Emma had many faults, but her courage
was unflinching and she remained stoic.

On 19 November the Dorchester Dramatic Society was opening
a staged version of *The Trumpet-Major*. Rebekah Owen and her
sister had travelled from their house in the Lake District to Dorchester to be present, and Florence, avoiding Max Gate, was in
Weymouth for the same purpose. Emma does not appear to have
attended any performance. She hired a car one day around this
date to visit friends, the Wood Homers, who lived at Bardolf
Manor near Puddletown. The car was draughty and uncomfortable, and on her return she felt very ill with back ache. She refused
to call the doctor, but stopped eating and kept entirely to her
room. There she was writing poetry. One poem, 'Winter', was in
praise of moss, which survives all weathers with its 'happy lowly
ways'. Another looked back to her childhood:

Oh! would I were a dancing child!
Oh! would I were again
Dancing in the grass of Spring,
Dancing in the rain.
Leaping with the birds a-wing
Singing with the birds that sing.[34]

Her birthday on Sunday, 24 November, passed without notice
or incident, but the following day the Owen sisters called and sent
messages upstairs in their peremptory way, insisting that she should
come down for tea. She did so with obvious difficulty. They
were sympathetic, but decided she was suffering from nerves and
depression. She was still unwilling to see a doctor. On the 26th
she at last allowed the doctor to visit but not to examine her, and
he thought she might be making herself ill by her fasting. She
made her way slowly and painfully upstairs, and Hardy went out
to see the play performed in Dorchester in the evening. On the
morning of the 27th her maid Dolly went to her room as usual at
eight and found her dying. Although she did not remember doing
so, Dolly may have called the cook before fetching the master,
because, according to Rebekah Owen's letter written that day,
Emma died 'in the Cook's arms, who was trying to lift her'.[35] But
none of those who crowded up the narrow stairs and into the small
room could do anything for Emma by then.

The doctor gave the cause of death as heart failure and impacted
gallstones, and told Hardy he suspected some 'internal perforation'.
The back pain suggests an enlarged and leaking aortic artery as the
cause of death.[36] 'Poor thing, poor thing. I am crying for her now,'
Miss Owen went on. 'They had been married 38 years. It must be
a great shock to him. I believe his fidelity to her to have been
perfect.'

21. Satires of Circumstance

This is the point at which this book began, with a grieving Hardy inspired by Emma's death to begin his incomparable series of elegiac poems. No one who knew him expected it, or could have expected it without understanding the width of the gap between his imaginative life and the day-to-day events going on around him. He considered taking Emma's body to Cornwall but decided that, since he wished to be buried in the same grave, it was more sensible to make it at Stinsford. That meant putting her alongside his mother, her old enemy: no matter. Mary explained to friends that the grave 'is deep as Tom would like to rest on her there. Poor dear soul she was very trying to live with, but perhaps she could not help it, and she did her best to prepare for the life to come.'[1] The funeral took place three days after Emma's death, and Mary did not attend it. Emma's niece Lilian arrived after the ceremony, and Florence kept away. Henry and Kate Hardy were there, and so was Rebekah Owen, who was touched by the scene, 'the lonely Churchyard, the pale November sunlight, the very few who were there – Mr Hardy, his brother and sister, a deputation from some Dorchester society, a very few villagers'.[2] Hardy laid a wreath inscribed 'From her Lonely Husband, with the Old Affection'.[3]

The practical matters of the funeral were not the only ones to be dealt with. Who was to run Max Gate and give orders to the cook, the maids and the gardener? Three women with conflicting agendas were soon in the house. Kate Hardy moved in to take charge until a housekeeper could be found; she and Mary knew of a possible one, the daughter of a Lower Bockhampton boot-maker, who had experience of being in service, and they thought she would be most suitable.[4] Hardy had other ideas. He had written immediately to Florence, asking her to come, and she did. Lilian Gifford invited herself, gathered up her late aunt's clothes and took them to London to sell, then returned, declaring her intention of remaining to look after her 'daddy-uncle'. Kate was the oldest of the three women and had no wish to leave her own comfortable home, whereas Florence and Lilian, both in their mid thirties, faced dismal prospects. Kate and Florence were united in their detestation of Lilian, who insulted Florence to her face: 'I don't think a day ever passes but I get some gibe or sneer' or a reminder that while her Aunt Emma had been a lady, Florence was not. But she pleased Hardy by talking to him about Emma. Emma's cook Jane, who had respected her late mistress, remained in charge of the kitchen and also despised Florence for not being a lady.[5] Hardy worried that Dorchester would gossip about Florence's position in his house, with reason, the gossip being fuelled by Lilian's and the servants' tales. He told Florence not to go out and decreed that they could not visit Aldeburgh together. At the same time, when she went home to Enfield after Christmas he wrote to her, 'If I once get you here again won't I clutch you tight: you shall stay till spring.' Florence was back with him early in February, and the Max Gate circus continued, no one certain of the outcome.[6]

Mary Hardy wrote to her cousin Nat Sparks in February about Emma's death: 'She was strange in her head and did not improve as she grew older. A niece of hers who was brought up at Max Gate lives with Tom as he feels he can't have a stranger there now he is old. She and her brother will have what he has to give I suppose when his end comes.'[7] Nobody expected the end of a widower in his seventies to be very distant. In the spring both Lilian and Gordon were duly at Max Gate, Gordon for the Easter weekend and Lilian showing every sign of installing herself for good. They believed that they were to inherit the house.

Meanwhile Hardy had found Emma's diaries, with their angry and contemptuous accounts of his behaviour. Sensibly enough, he decided they were largely the product of a mind subject to delusions and refused to allow them to spoil his renewed vision of her as the love of his life. Some of her accusations may even have seemed justified. None of this in any way diminished his present need for Florence, but in March he left her at Max Gate while he travelled to Cornwall, a journey he had not made for forty years, to revisit the scenes of his first meeting with Emma and their courtship. Here there was fresh inspiration for poems. The intensity of the experience exhilarated him. His brother Henry, least troubling or intrusive of companions, went with him to Cornwall, and while they were there Hardy made arrangements for a memorial tablet to Emma to be prepared for the church at St Juliot. Then he returned to the problems at Max Gate. In his absence Florence had been keeping a loaded revolver in her bedroom, presumably intended for intruders rather than Giffords, but in any case a sign of her overwrought state.[8] When Mrs Henniker invited her to stay with her in April at Southwold, she accepted eagerly, Aldeburgh now being forbidden to her.

Hardy was not yet ready to make any decisions about the future. Part of him was ecstatically absorbed in recalling Emma and their early love, another part sorrowing for his neglect and unkindness to her. He wanted to keep hold of Florence but was fearful of scandal. He also wanted to look after Lilian, preferably at Max Gate. He had no one to turn to for advice. Gosse knew too little of his circumstances, Clodd too much. His sisters and brother were sympathetic but in no position to do anything. Mrs Henniker could be relied on for sympathy but could not solve his problems. So he struggled with them alone, and a black comedy continued to be played out at Max Gate.

On top of this there were all the usual accretions to a literary career to distract and keep him busy throughout 1913. He was preparing a last collection of stories – 'mostly bad', he told a friend – as well as the new poems, which were to make a section in his third volume of poetry.[9] He was asked to allow some of his work to be put into Braille, and agreed. He gave assistance to Hermann Lea with his *Thomas Hardy's Wessex*, suggesting that his American publishers might like to use Lea's photographs as illustrations to a new edition of his novels, which they did. He corresponded with Elgar about the possibility of collaborating on an opera and said that *A Pair of Blue Eyes* would be 'good for music . . . and has a distinct and central heroine, with a wild background of cliffs and sea. Two poets, Tennyson and Patmore, were attracted by the novel.'[10] Elgar promised to reread some of Hardy's books again with music in mind, but nothing came of the plan, which would have needed an English Boito to write the libretto. Meanwhile a film was being made of *Far from the Madding Crowd* and an option was taken out for *The Mayor of Casterbridge*. *Tess*, already filmed, was on at a picture-palace near Marble Arch, and Hardy made a special day trip to London for a showing in October. 'You would be amused to see an Americanized Wessex Dairy,' he told a friend.[11]

In the summer Florence went to Southwold, and Southwold is close to Aldeburgh. Hardy turned up at the Swan Hotel in Southwold for a few days and then moved on to stay with Clodd. Both he and Mrs Henniker were sympathetic to Florence, which may have encouraged Hardy to take action. By the summer there was an understanding between them that they would marry – a secret understanding, although she gave away the secret to Clodd in July. However pleased Hardy was with the engagement, his thoughts were not all with Florence, and in August he wrote two more poems about Emma. The brilliance of the 'Poems of 1912–13' was beginning to fade, but the impulse to set down all the phases of his grief stayed with him. In one her ghost comes to claim him:

> Something tapped on the pane of my room
>   When there was never a trace
> Of wind or rain, and I saw in the gloom
>   My weary Belovéd's face.
>
> 'O I am tired of waiting,' she said,
>   'Night, morn, noon, afternoon;
> So cold it is in my lonely bed,
>   And I thought you would join me soon!'
>
> I rose and neared the window-glass,
>   But vanished thence had she:
> Only a pallid moth, alas,
>   Tapped at the pane for me.[12]

The other is both stronger and more ambivalent:

> That day when oats were reaped, and wheat was ripe, and barley
>   ripening,
>   The road-dust hot, and the bleaching grasses dry,
>   I walked along and said,
>   While looking just ahead to where some silent people lie:

> 'I wounded one who's there, and now know well I wounded her;
>   But, ah, she does not know that she wounded me!'
>   And not an air stirred,
>   Nor a bill of any bird; and no response accorded she.[13]

The problem of who was to live at Max Gate apart from ghosts remained. In December 1913 Hardy wrote to Mrs Henniker that 'My niece [Lilian] & Miss Dugdale are here, ministering to my wants: I don't know what I should do without them, and I am sorry to say that just now Florence has a bad cold. I want her to stay in bed, but cannot get her to.'[14] Florence was not going to leave the field to Lilian, and Lilian was still in fighting form. Florence wrote to Clodd, 'She runs about Dorchester telling tales to all the idle gossiping women in the place . . . She does *nothing* in the house . . . she says she is "not a servant".'[15] But Florence, who had endured a terrible Max Gate Christmas before, was determined to stay on her feet throughout another. She knew she had the support of Henry, Mary and Kate against any Giffords. There had been a putsch, surely organized by Florence, to get rid of all Emma's cats, and she was awaiting the arrival of the dog Hardy had helped her choose.[16] The house was being redecorated, removing almost all traces of its former mistress, and a conservatory added to the drawing room. Rooms in the attic were still crammed with Emma's things, but the doors were simply shut and locked on them. At the end of the year Florence delivered an ultimatum to Hardy: either Lilian went back to her mother and went for good, or she would not marry him. 'If the niece is to remain here *permanently* as one of the family then I will not enter into that compact of which I spoke to you last summer. This must be decided in a week and if it is settled that she stays, I return to my own home, and *remain* there,' Florence wrote to Clodd.[17]

Hardy gave way at last. He remained very fond of Lilian, and arranged for an allowance and an annuity for her, but he told her she must go home to her mother. Florence wrote to Clodd, 'Of course her brother is an imbecile – one of them at least – and an uncle died in an asylum, and her grandfather was mad at times, so I ought to be profoundly sorry for her – but I *can't* be that.'[18] As Lilian departed, Florence's dog arrived: Wessex, a rough-haired terrier, white with brown ears and a brown splotch above his tail. Already a biter, he was soon known to one visitor as 'Florence's unspeakable dog "Wessie" '.[19] Neither Florence nor Hardy would ever attempt to discipline him: 'all of his kind are fighters,' she said, as though to justify his attacks. They doted on him together, ignoring the fear he inspired in postmen, maids and visitors alike, as well as repeated demands from local people that he should be put down. He was fed from their own plates at table, and sometimes on the table. Hardy laid an eiderdown on the floor of his study for him to sleep on during the day and kissed him goodnight at bedtime.[20] They indulged him in every way, like a delicate, delinquent child, and he behaved accordingly.

☙

Florence returned briefly to Enfield in January. Hardy visited her there at the end of the month and went to the Dugdales' parish church, St Andrew's, for Sunday service with the whole family. On 6 February 1914 he obtained a marriage licence. Four days later, at eight in the morning, he and Florence were married in the same church, accompanied only by Henry Hardy, Florence's father and her youngest sister, Marjorie. Florence wore a dark costume and felt hat: 'there never was a more unbridal dress and hat than mine, both atrociously ugly,' she wrote.[21] After a quick breakfast at the Dugdales', the newly married couple walked to the station and started on their journey back to Dorchester. It was even bleaker than Hardy's first wedding, and he was so frightened of publicity that they had told none of their friends about it. Soon after they left Enfield, reporters arrived at the Dugdale house, and that afternoon the story was in the papers. It was all over the next morning's press. Hardy and Florence had to spend the day writing to their closest friends to announce their marriage. 'We thought it the wisest thing to do, seeing what a right hand Florence has become to me, & there is a sort of continuity in it, and not a break, she having known my first wife so very well,' he told one friend. To Clodd he wrote, 'I am going to put over my study door, "Business as usual during alterations." '[22] All the same, he now had a sexually compliant wife, and this must have made life much more cheerful for him, even if it was only a matter of duty for her.[23]

Business as usual did not prevent them spending a few days on the Devon coast or visiting Cambridge together in April, where Benson thought that Hardy seemed 'very spruce and gay' and 'they seemed happy together.'[24] After this there were two celebratory dinners in London, one given by Frederick Macmillan, the other by Hardy's old friend Lady Jeune, now transformed into Lady St Helier by her husband's ennoblement and still an indefatigable hostess. Mrs Winston Churchill, placed next to Hardy, impressed him by telling him she had made her husband promise not to go up in an aeroplane – he was training for a pilot's licence – until she had given birth to the child she was expecting. In July they went for a weekend to Stourhead, the magnificent country place of the banker Sir Samuel Hoare, and Lady Hoare, an effusive admirer of Hardy's work. Meanwhile in June the Archduke Franz Ferdinand was assassinated at Sarajevo, and on 4 August Britain declared war on Germany. Hardy observed that all the nations were praying to the same God.[25]

The effects of the war erupted at once even into quiet Dorset. Several hundred German mechant seamen were soon held prisoner in the Dorchester barracks, the streets were full of drunken English soldiers, and every householder was told to expect to have men billetted on him, although the Hardys never did. At the beginning of September he was summoned at the behest of the Cabinet along with a large group of eminent literary men to a meeting in London intended to encourage them to make public statements on the strength of the British case for war; Hardy dutifully produced 'Men

who March Away', adopting the required tone and asserting the
confidence of the British soldier in the justice of his cause:

> In our heart of hearts believing
>> Victory crowns the just,
>> And that braggarts must
>> Surely bite the dust . . .

It was printed in *The Times*, *The Times Literary Supplement* and the
New York Times, and was enormously popular. Then Granville-
Barker asked if he might put on a shortened version of *The Dynasts*
as a form of highbrow patriotic entertainment, and Hardy gave
what help he could to the production, contributing a special prologue and epilogue. It attracted distinguished audiences, including
the Prime Minister, Asquith, and ran for seventy-two performances
at the Kingsway Theatre.

While the world was changing around him his mind was still
taken up with his new collection of poems. In July he had told
Macmillan he hoped to send it off at the end of the month. At the
same time he wrote to Mrs Henniker, 'Some of them I rather
shrink from printing – those I wrote just after Emma died, when
I looked back at her as she had originally been, and when I felt
miserable lest I had not treated her considerately in her latter life.
However I shall publish them as the only amends I can make, if it
were so.'[26] Hesitating again in August, he wrote to Macmillan, 'I
am not anxious to issue them at all, and perhaps they might be
brought out in paper covers.'[27] After war was declared he asked
Macmillan once more if they wanted the poems, and, when they
said they did, he insisted there was no hurry, and publication might
wait 'until people get tired of the war', but at the same time he
wrote to a friend that what he most cared about was that 'the
poems should be brought out by the Macmillans at some time or
other'.[28]

He did not show the poems to Florence or, it seems, discuss
them with her. Indeed he seems to have let no one see them but
his publisher. The volume in which they appeared was published
in November 1914 and named *Satires of Circumstance* after another

section of short, harsh poems, vignettes describing people behaving badly – rather appropriately, as it turned out, since Florence was bitterly offended by the section devoted to Emma, 'Poems of 1912–13', which she saw as parading his love for his first wife, both falsely and insultingly to her. In Florence's mind Emma had become a figure half mad and wholly dislikable, and she now saw her rising up as a permanent rival. To be jealous of a former love, and a dead one, might seem another form of madness, but, as Emma had once resented Hardy's failure to acknowledge her help and dedicate books to her, so Florence resented still more furiously his writing about Emma. Her teeth were set on edge, and she was not mollified by Hardy giving her a copy inscribed 'in all affection'. Having married the world-famous writer, the least she expected was to be celebrated as his muse. Instead she felt a humiliation from which she seems never to have recovered.

If Florence was oblivious to the power and beauty of the 'Poems of 1912–13', which she read only with pain and 'terrible fascination', the reviewers failed to notice them at all.[29] *Satires of Circumstance* could hardly have appeared at a more unpropitious time, in the first winter of the war, and the few critics who wrote about it gave their attention to other parts of the collection. Hardy inscribed a copy to Gosse, 'the mixture as before, of unstable fancies, conjectures, and contradictions', hardly expecting him to fathom what had gone into the poems, and indeed Gosse later described the volume as being the 'most dispensable' of all Hardy's poetry. To Mrs Henniker he wrote, after some reviews had appeared, that 'My own favourites, that include all those in memory of Emma, have been mentioned little . . . I am so glad you like, "When I set out for Lyonnesse". It is exactly what happened 44 years ago.'[30]

In January 1915 Virginia Woolf sent a letter thanking him for the sonnet on her father Leslie Stephen included in the collection, going on to say that she considered it to be 'the most remarkable book to appear in my lifetime'. Her singularly enthusiastic tribute has to be put into context: a few days after writing she was overtaken by an acute mental breakdown and became incoherent.[31] Hardy's personal confidence in the poems was made plain when he published his *Selected Poems*, made at the request of Macmillan, in 1916, in which ten of the eighteen 'Poems of 1912–13' appear alongside others relating to Emma from *Satires of Circumstance*: 'When I set out for Lyonnesse', 'Wives in the Sere' and 'Under the Waterfall'. J. C. Squire, writing in the *New Statesman*, singled out these poems for praise and quoted the closing lines from the end of 'The Phantom Horsewoman'.[32] In Hardy's *Collected Poems* of 1925 he added three more poems to the group. Very slowly they began to be seen for what they are.

Hardy was still 'in flower' as a poet, composing more rapidly and fluently than he had ever done. Between 1913 and 1916 he wrote something like 150 new poems. It was a heroic enterprise, and it must have taken the best of his time and energy, leaving Florence more solitary than a newly wedded wife expected to be. 'He says that when the wheels are going round it is a mistake to stop them ... He is working practically all day until after dinner ... and yesterday feeling very much inclined for work he did not even go for the daily walk,' Florence wrote in August 1916, adding, 'I am going to make a tremendous fight for a few days holiday.'[33] Poetry and marriage are not always easy to reconcile, and he was easily able to abstract himself from Florence's feelings of loneliness, resentment and jealousy, and pursue his own mental and imaginative course single-mindedly.

The results of this intensive labour appeared in a further volume, *Moments of Vision and Miscellaneous Verses*, published at the end of November 1917. It is Hardy's largest collection, made up of rich, varied, confidently written and intensely personal poems. In it he relives parts of his life and rethinks various aspects of it. The opening image in the first poem is of a mirror that 'throws our mind back on us, and our heart', and the poem also evokes 'night hours of ache', giving a picture of a sleepless man brooding painfully over the past. The last poem is in direct contrast, the tranquil 'Afterwards', in which he sums himself up as a man who watches birds, protects small animals, glories in the constellations of the winter sky and notices the details of country life, for instance the way a cross-wind cuts the sound of church bells, making a pause in the ringing. So the first and last poems span the contradictions always present in Hardy, between the vulnerable, doomstruck man and the serene inhabitant of the natural world.

Between these two are personal memories going back to his first school, where he sees himself as an unfledged bird, 'Pink, tiny, crisp-curled, / My pinions yet furled'. In 'Old Furniture' he thinks of the women of his family who had polished it over the years, leaving in the shining wood the image of 'Hands behind hands, growing paler and paler'. A field gate hung with drops of February rain takes him back half a century to the bonneted girls who did their courting at the same gate while they brought in the harvest. A poem about Shakespeare, son of a provincial nobody, is also of course about himself:

> – 'Ah, one of the tradesman's sons, I now recall . . .
>   Witty, I've heard . . .
> We did not know him . . . Well, good-day. Death comes to all.'[34]

The poems are not ordered chronologically or by subject – they appear to have been placed at random – but the outline of an autobiography is there.[35] At the centre of the story of his past was always Emma in her many different incarnations. Some thirty-six poems allude to her, and they run from minutely specific incidents of their wooing in Cornwall to his sad imaginings at Max Gate, where he persistently sees her in the garden as he walks there, and even fancies her head and hat moving towards him above the low-lying fog in the lane. There was plenty to upset Florence, and it seemed to her a fresh outrage, as she made clear in a letter to a friend when it was published in December: 'I expect the idea of the general reader will be that T.H.'s second marriage is a most disastrous one and that his sole wish is to find refuge in the grave with her with whom he found happiness. Well – all things end somewhere.'[36]

There are tender evocations of their life together at Sturminster Newton, where he took Florence for a day in June 1916.[37] There is the sour memory of a Bournemouth hotel and a quarrel, a grim one of Tooting, and sorrowful ones of her singing at the piano, and of the time she declared she would play no more. There is also something new in the poems that shows he has been considering the idea, prompted by her hostile diaries, that there must have been a strain of madness in her. 'The Interloper' imagines an invisible presence haunting her from the beginning, one 'Who ought not to be there', and its epigraph, 'And I saw the figure and visage of Madness seeking for a home', makes his meaning unequivocal. Yet, even if he had decided she was partly insane, it made no difference to his regrets or his love for her. Her family might all be quite mad too, but their history figures in 'During Wind and Rain', a surreal and lyrical lament for the Giffords, calling up scenes at their Plymouth home described by Emma: how they had to leave it, and how the years brought everything bright to an end for them, as they do for everyone. The last verse goes,

> They change to a high new house,
> He, she, all of them – aye,
> Clocks and carpets and chairs
>   On the lawn all day,
> And brightest things that are theirs . . .
>   Ah, no; the years, the years;
> Down their carved names the rain-drop ploughs.

Hardy is thinking through the past and feeling for new ways of looking at it, as in 'The Change', in which he asks himself whether he understood what really went on at St Juliot – 'who was the mocker and who the mocked when two felt all was well?' – and what happened between them and changed Emma's love:

> O the doom by someone spoken,
> O the heart by someone broken,
> The heart whose sweet reverberances are all time leaves to me.

His own death was also in his mind now, and in 'Who's in the Next Room?' he catches sight of it:

'Who's in the next room? – who?
        I seemed to see
Somebody in the dawning passing through,
        Unknown to me.'
'Nay: you saw nought. He passed invisibly.' . . .

        'Who's in the next room? – who?
            A figure wan
With a message to one in there of something due?
            Shall I know him anon?'
'Yea he; and he brought such; and you'll know him anon.'

    The collection presents the essence of Hardy's life during the years in which he wrote them, an old man with a lively brain and a transforming imagination at work. Great stores of intellectual and emotional vitality are required to be able to write like this, and Hardy put all his seven decades of experience to work. In almost every poem, as Philip Larkin said, 'there is a little spinal cord of thought and each has a little tune of its own'.[38] Here is the short, sharp 'Heredity', pared of any superfluous word and pointing out something no one else had seen:

I am the family face;
Flesh perishes, I live on,
Projecting trait and trace
Through time to times anon,
And leaping from place to place
Over oblivion.

The years-heired feature that can
In curve and voice and eye
Despise the human span
Of durance – that is I;
The eternal thing in man,
That heeds no call to die.

'The Oxen' is Hardy's musing at Christmas on his lack of faith and his regret for it, a poem even the most hardened unbeliever is likely to respond to. Entirely unlike any other in the collection, 'In a Waiting Room' goes into a scene so modern that we are reminded that Hardy was a contemporary of D. H. Lawrence. It describes a dirty railway waiting room with flyblown pictures of ocean liners on the wall and on the table a New Testament in which someone has scribbled his petty accounts in the margins. A soldier and his haggard wife come in, clearly to say their farewells. Rain is clattering on the skylight. Enter into this gloom the couple's two children, who laugh and point to the pictures of the 'lovely ships that we, / Mother, are by and by going to see!' They are confident that 'the band will play, and the sun will shine!' The children's words are enough to 'spread a glory through the gloom'. That is it – we are left with the glory. These are, incidentally, some of the very few joyful children in Hardy, on their way to Australia, it seems, for a new life. Did Hardy hope to have a child of his own even now? It is possible, since he told Florence years later that he would have welcomed one then.[39]

His old friend Gosse had reservations about the marriage to Florence. 'What distresses me is that he should so soon experience the misfortunes of an old man who marries a young and ambitious wife,' he wrote to another friend.[40] He might have had more confidence in Hardy's ability to put his work as a poet before everything else.

22. A Friend from Cambridge

The war meant that they now rarely went to London, there being no Season, little entertaining and small chance of seeing Mrs Henniker, Lady St Helier or Gosse. Then, because Hardy wanted their visits to Aldeburgh during Emma's lifetime to be effaced from the record, he decreed that there were to be no more, even when they were married; when he heard that Clodd was writing his memoirs, he made Florence warn him off any mention of their visits and threatened retaliatory measures if he did.[1] Clodd revealed nothing, but, not surprisingly, the friendship faded. There were no other holidays, which could be blamed on the war; but the fact was Hardy no longer wanted to go away.

The gaps left in his life – and in Florence's – were filled by a new friend, the ebullient Sydney Cockerell, director of the Fitzwilliam Museum in Cambridge. Cockerell had a tigerish energy in pursuing men and women he admired, and was also an obsessive collector. He had started with shells as a boy and progressed to medieval manuscripts, books and paintings. He had to leave school and go into the family coal business, rather than to a university, but kept up his intellectual interests. Bouncing his way into the affections of Octavia Hill, he helped her with her housing projects for the poor, then set his sights on John Ruskin, charmed him and was invited to travel with him in France. Then he took on William Morris, whose assistant he was for many years, acting as Secretary to the Kelmscott Press, becoming virtually part of the Morris family and after the death of Morris giving unstinted support to Mrs Morris and her daughters.[2] He took friendship seriously. As a young man he was a socialist, and all his life an atheist. He was also an obsessive diarist, writing down in unvarying thin green notebooks the activities and encounters of each day, although he lacked any gift of characterization or self-presentation, so that the description of him as 'a blameless Pepys' is sadly astray.[3] You long for him to expand his narrative but have to be grateful for what you get, and, since he was Hardy's friend for seventeen years and visited Max Gate many times, he does give an impression of its atmosphere and routines, and every now and then something unexpected and even precious is jotted down, between the precisely noted weather and train times.

Cockerell had been appointed director of the Fitzwilliam in 1908 at the age of forty. By his own account, 'I found it a pigstye; I turned it into a palace.' He had to overcome opposition, especially as he was not a Cambridge man, but he quickly became one of the most active and influential figures in the university. He brought in Sunday opening, prevailed on the King and the Duke of Devonshire to lend prints from their collections on a regular basis, started the 'Friends of the Fitzwilliam' scheme (the first of its kind in Britain) and began to acquire modern literary manuscripts. It was in the hope of persuading Hardy to let him have a manuscript that he wrote to him in 1911. Amazingly, he confessed after Hardy's death that he had read none of his novels at the time, 'though I read them all later'.[4] This makes him seem more like a bounder than a scholar, and there were always two sides to Cockerell, the red-hot enthusiast and the cool fixer.

In spite of his ignorance of Hardy's work he made such a good impression on his first visit to Max Gate that Hardy got out almost all the manuscripts he could lay his hands on and agreed with him immediately on a plan to divide the spoils among the British Museum, Cambridge, Oxford, Aberdeen (which had given him a degree), Birmingham, Manchester, Dorchester, Windsor and Boston or New York. Cockerell felt that Hardy was shy about writing to curators and librarians, so volunteered to do so on his behalf. In gratitude, Hardy presented him with the manuscript of 'The Three Strangers', one of his best stories, a valuable gift.[5] Cockerell made sure too that the manuscript of *Jude the Obscure*, the most famous of his novels, went to the Fitzwilliam. It was an astounding transaction between a successful writer and a man he was meeting for the first time, but Cockerell knew how to charm and how to pitch his demands, and Hardy was unaware of the value of what he was giving away, and not apparently interested.

It seems odd in a man who dealt sharply with publishers in his
financial dealings with them, but he had already given Clement
Shorter the manuscript of *The Return of the Native* as a way of
thanking him for getting his manuscripts bound, and he never
showed any sign of regretting what he had done – not even when
he found he could sell the manuscript of *The Woodlanders* for
£1,000 to an American collector in the early 1920s.[6] He also told
Gosse that, having no children and enough money for his wants,
he did not regard the value of the manuscripts.[7]

Cockerell did not meet Emma on this first visit, and he had
nothing to say about her on the second, in June 1912, when he
brought his wife, Kate, with him, beyond that both Hardys were
very nice, and he especially unassuming, and that Hardy expressed
his admiration for Shaw's plays, and for Synge's *Playboy of the
Western World*.[8] At the end of the year he noted again in his diary
that they had spent 'a delightful afternoon with Thomas Hardy
and his wife' – adding, with characteristic brevity, '(since dead)'.[9]

Cockerell's enthusiasm and air of authority, his knowledge of
libraries and museums, and his years with Morris all went to win
Hardy's trust. There was also his position at Cambridge, which
opened up the possibility of connections with the university Hardy
had once thought of applying to. And indeed Cockerell soon
repaid Hardy's generosity by putting forward his name for an
honorary degree at Cambridge. He seems to have tried and failed
in 1912, but within months of Emma's death, in February 1913,
the offer came. The Vice-Chancellor who tended the invitation
was the Revd Alexander Donaldson, an evangelical Christian who
had taught at Eton for thirty years and was now Master of
Magdalene, but there is no doubt that Cockerell was the man
responsible.[10] Hardy was asked to come to Cambridge to receive
his doctorate in June. His sister Mary, remembering he had thought
of applying to study at Cambridge in the 1860s, wrote to congratulate him: 'Now you have accomplished it all with greater honour
than if you had gone along the road you then saw before you.'[11]

The Cockerells put him up, and Sydney, who loved to arrange
such things, prepared a programme of pleasures. There was dinner
at Jesus, where he was a Fellow, and to which he had invited A. E.

Housman at Hardy's request. After dinner they went to see an undergraduate production of *The Importance of Being Earnest*, with the all-male cast expected at Cambridge, although possibly not by Hardy, who spoke of 'that man Oscar Wilde' and delighted in pretty actresses.[12] The next day there was lunch at Magdalene. 'Hardy chattered away very gaily ... and seemed in a chirpy mood,' wrote Benson, who had contributed a pallid appreciation of his writing to the *Cambridge Magazine* without mentioning his poetry.[13] At the degree ceremony Hardy received a great ovation, and in the evening they dined at Trinity, where the Master spoke fittingly of Hardy. There was a reception at Trinity Lodge lasting late into the evening, at the end of which Cockerell escorted his very happy guest back to his house.[14] The third day took in the Fitzwilliam and lunch at Peterhouse. Hardy's simplicity and charm was generally admired in Cambridge and the whole visit judged a great success.[15]

A week later both Sydney and Kate Cockerell took up Hardy's invitation to stay at Max Gate, where they found that 'Miss Florence Dugdale, Thomas Hardy's very nice secretary and kins-woman, had assisted him in preparing everything for our comfort, and we were very kindly received.'[16] Their fellow guest was the artist William Strang, a high-spirited man with a fund of good stories to tell. Hardy responded with stories of his own, and there was laughter all evening. It seems to have been the jolliest weekend ever recorded at Max Gate. No one wanted to go to church on Sunday, and they walked to see the grave of William Barnes and then across the water meadows to Stinsford. In the evening there was laughter again, Hardy and Strang exchanging more stories. On Monday, Florence took them to see Hardy's birthplace at Bockhampton. They left with a copy of *The Dynasts* and spent the next few days reading it respectfully and visiting sites associated with *Tess*.

If Cockerell records more hilarity than most visitors to Max Gate, it was perhaps because he helped to provoke it. He had given Hardy one part of his heart's desire at Cambridge, and Hardy's high opinion of him never wavered. Nor did Cockerell's assiduity. He worked at the friendship, writing and visiting Max

Gate often, always delighted by Hardy's conversation and sending presents of books chosen to interest him, among them biographies of Morris and of an earlier Thomas Hardy, the radical shoemaker of the 1790s. In November, Hardy was invited to Cambridge for a second celebration when Magdalene College made him an honorary Fellow. There had been some anxiety about his being described in the *Cambridge Magazine* as 'the celebrated Atheist' by a young Fellow of the college, 'that ass Ogden' (Benson's description of C. K. Ogden, editor of the magazine), because the Master had planned a religious service, but everything went smoothly, and it was during this visit that Hardy told Benson about the poems he had written following Emma's death.[17] Benson in turn showed Hardy the new college building he was responsible for, intended for his own use and then for the college after his death. It was just being finished and had a private dining room with a minstrels' gallery, stained glass brought from Austria and fine stone work. The young I. A. Richards, then an undergraduate, remembered Hardy's reaction to the building: while others admired, he went up and put his hand on the stone work and then smelt it – the gesture of a stonemason, thought Richards.[18]

Cockerell wanted to turn Hardy's thoughts to writing his memoirs, and he began to press him at least to give him a list of important dates in his life, to which Hardy responded by setting Florence to type diary entries from his notebooks, as well as Emma's recollections of her girlhood as she set them down in 1911. Florence wrote to Cockerell to tell him about the 'longish manuscript which Mr Hardy wants to send you – an account of Mrs Hardy's early life, together with extracts from Mr Hardy's own diary note-books'.[19] Hardy's next visit to Cambridge was made in May 1914. By now he and Florence were married, and this time she went with him. They stayed at the University Arms, Cockerell again took charge of everything, and there was another round of feasts for the men, while, this being Cambridge, 'Mrs H supped with Kate.'[20] Hardy saw Housman again and met Lowes Dickinson. Florence was, however, invited to lunch at Magdalene and subjected to Benson's scrutiny. He saw 'a shy, rather comely, youngish woman but with very ugly hands and feet . . . Hardy was very spruce & gay & had enjoyed himself here – he said it was wonderfully delightful to find himself really at home in a little academical body. They seemed happy together – I lent him the car for the afternoon.'[21] They took the car to Girton, where they had tea with the Mistress, E. E. Constance Jones, a philosopher about to publish *The Three Great Questions (An Outline of Private and Public Duty)*. Miss Jones had learnt her Greek from Coleridge's granddaughter Edith, a link which must have delighted Hardy.[22]

His remark about being at home in a little academical body clearly came from his heart, the courtesy, ceremony, friendship and conversation offered in Cambridge being enjoyable in themselves but also supplying a balm for all the years in which he had felt isolated and slighted. Benson saw that he greatly appreciated 'being one of a society', and it seemed likely he would become a regular visitor. In August 1914 any chance of that was knocked out. The war put an end to all feasting and celebrations in the universities, as their young men went off to fight, and when peace came Hardy was nearly eighty and no longer inclined to travel. This time fate defeated him conclusively, and he never made another visit to Cambridge.

He did, however, subscribe to the *Cambridge Magazine*, the remarkable publication edited by 'that ass Ogden', which ran throughout the war, raising its circulation to over 20,000 readers by allocating half its space to reports from the foreign press, not all of them sympathetic to the British. In 1916 he allowed Ogden to publish an advertisement in *The Times* quoting Hardy's praise: 'I read the *Magazine* every week, and turn first to the extracts from Foreign Newspapers, which transport one to the Continent and enable one to see England bare and unadorned – her chances in the struggle freed from distortion by the glamour of patriotism.'[23] And when the magazine's policy got it into trouble, Hardy joined Gilbert Murray, Quiller-Couch, Arnold Bennett, Jane Harrison and others in a letter of support.[24] The *Cambridge Magazine* continued publication, and Hardy made plain his dislike of narrow, simple-minded nationalism.

The war settled into its long and hideous pattern, devouring the young men all over Europe. Hardy expected it to drag on. As early as the spring of 1915 he wrote to Mrs Henniker that he thought it most probable 'that it will last till one of the combatants is exhausted and sues for peace without being beaten, or till one or more country is bankrupt, or starved, or till there is a revolution in Germany . . . I hardly think it will end by the sheer victory of one side or the other in the field.' He believed that England was 'innocent for once . . . the war began because the Germans wanted to fight.'[25] By now there were between 2,000 and 3,000 German prisoners held in the Dorchester camp. He noticed with amusement that the Kaiser was being moved at Madame Tussaud's 'from the Royal group to the Chamber of Horrors'.[26] He also wrote 'The Pity of It', about how the English and the Germans were 'kin folk kin tongued':

> I walked in loamy Wessex lanes, afar
> From rail-track and from highway, and I heard
> In field and farmstead many an ancient word
> Of local lineage like 'Thu bist', 'Er war',
>
> 'Ich woll', 'Er sholl', and by-talk similar,
> Nigh as they speak who in this month's moon gird
> At England's very loins, thereunto spurred
> By gangs whose glory threats and slaughter are.[27]

'I cannot do patriotic poems very well – seeing the other side too much,' he told John Galsworthy.[28] Another poem that went far beyond patriotism was 'In Time of "The Breaking of Nations"', dug out of the past from a memory of the summer of 1870 when he was in Cornwall with Emma during the Franco-Prussian War, and contrasting the immemorial life of the countryside with the sound and fury of battle.[29]

In August 1915 a second cousin, Frank George, a lawyer by profession, likeable and intelligent, was killed at Gallipoli. Hardy had thought of making him his heir and pulled strings to get him a commission, and he sorrowed for his death. He looked with interest and pity too at the German prisoners in the big camp now holding 5,000 men outside Dorchester. He had visited them in the spring, sent them German books from his shelves and on one occasion sat with a wounded prisoner, 'in much pain, who died whilst I was with him – to my great relief, and his own. – Men lie helpless here from wounds: in the hospital a hundred yards off other men, English, lie helpless from wounds – each scene of suffering caused by the other!'[30] In the autumn he asked the authorities if some of the German prisoners could do paid work in his garden. He kept up his interest throughout the war, telling Cockerell later,

We are having some trees rooted, so as to enlarge the kitchen garden for more potatoes, and the Commandant of the prison camp here has sent me out some prisoners for the job with guards, rifles, interpreter and all complete. Nothing has made me more sad about the war than the sight of these amiable young Germans in such a position through the machinations of some vile war-gang or other. Nevertheless they seem perfectly happy (though they get only 1d an hour each of the 6d each that I pay).[31]

Some of the Germans inscribed their names on a shed door in the garden, and Hardy used to point these out to visitors years later.[32]

He refused an invitation from Gosse in November 1915 to a dinner with the Prime Minister, Asquith, excusing himself with 'between ourselves my dining-out days are nearly over.' But he and Florence happily joined a November house party given by Lady Ilchester at Melbury, the great mansion of his mother's childhood. They stayed for four or five days, returning to Max Gate on the 20th to find that Mary was dying at Talbothays, where she had moved with Kate and Henry. She had been ill for some time – and she died of emphysema on the 24th, almost exactly three years after Emma. While Hardy grieved for the loss of his sister, Florence was appalled by Kate's insistence that she should kiss Mary's corpse, not once but many times. There was a quarrel when Hardy said he did not want to go back to Talbothays after the funeral. Florence thought he dreaded meeting the relatives who would be there, but he braced himself and went.

In the same letter in which Florence wrote to a woman friend about Mary's funeral, she described Lady Ilchester's charm as a hostess.

She is most unceremonious and by no means 'dressy' . . . Her evening dresses were quite simple – black and black and white. But she wore her famous pearl necklace and lovely diamond ear-rings. She spent all the time with us – showing us the house the park and the villages and motoring us about. There was nobody there of much importance – some of the Digbys, her relatives – a Miss Sonia Keppell.[33]

One of the villages they were shown was certainly Melbury Osmond, where Hardy's mother was born and married. The irony of their being driven there as Mary lay on her deathbed must have struck Hardy painfully afterwards, the more so because, although he was devoted to his sister, his devotion to her had always been in the style of accepting her love rather than demonstrating his. He had made very little effort to involve her in his life, even before the falling out with Emma, and there was a wistfulness in her awareness that he had moved into another world while she remained in the old one. She murmured once that she was not asked to dinner or treated like a lady by anyone except the Locks, the family of her solicitors in Dorchester.[34] Mary lived like a hermit, Hardy said, and would not even stay overnight in London when she went up to see the summer show at the Royal Academy each year, insisting on returning to Dorchester on the evening train.[35] She made one trip to the Lake District after the death of her mother, alone, fulfilling a lifelong ambition inspired by her love of Wordsworth.[36] She was well read, a gifted painter and a good cook; also kind, for example sending small sums of money to her cousin Nat Sparks when his wife Annie, her old friend from the training college, was ill. But, as Hardy said, she scarcely made a mark on the world. Her pupils were simple Dorset girls with no aspirations themselves, and she was isolated by her position as a headmistress in a small country town, and by her culturally divided family. No one fell in love with her or asked for her in marriage. Instead she mothered Kate. Kate and Henry learnt to ride bicycles;

Mary never did. She became deaf as she aged, and her world closed in around her. Although she had savings, and a friendly solicitor, she did not even write a will. Hardy told Cockerell that he had very little in common with either Kate or Henry; in practice he shared almost nothing with Mary either.[37] Yet he missed her and wrote a handful of small, sad poems in her memory. In the best of them he looks at a log of apple wood burning on the fire and remembers the tree it came from and how he climbed it as a child with her:

> My fellow-climber rises dim
> From her chilly grave –
> Just as she was, her foot near mine on the bending limb,
> Laughing, her young brown hand awave.[38]

The young brown hand, the laughter and the tomboyish climbing suggest a Mary who might have made more of her life. Instead, she was trapped as a spinster schoolteacher, tied to the childhood home and her mother's dominance, and she never belonged anywhere else.

After her death Hardy fell into gloom and kept his door shut even on Kate when she came to see him. Neither would he have Cockerell to stay when he proposed himself during the winter vacation, Florence complained, any more than he would let her accept invitations to go to friends in town or visit her own sick father.[39] Cockerell wrote urging Hardy to write his memoirs: 'write down something about yourself – and especially about that youthful figure whose photograph I have got, and of whom you told me that you could think with almost complete detachment.'[40] When Hardy's old friend George Douglas wrote with the same suggestion, Hardy answered, 'My reminiscences: no, never!'[41]

Yet Mary's death had forced him to think of his own and about the arrangements he needed to make. He decided to ask Cockerell to become his literary executor in partnership with Florence. It was a sensible decision, given Cockerell's experience in looking after Morris's affairs, and he was willing. From now on Cockerell corresponded far more intensively with Florence than with

Hardy.[42] She sometimes praised him for being like a son to Hardy, sometimes confided in him and at other times complained about him, but she depended on his friendship, and he was attentive to her, inviting her to Cambridge on her own and taking her to the theatre in London.[43] He made five visits to Max Gate during 1916, scarcely leaving himself time to fit in moving house with his wife and children in June, a move made necessary because Kate Cockerell had developed multiple sclerosis and walking was difficult for her. When Hardy heard this bad news, he at once offered to send Emma's bath chair, which was, he said, 'of the very best make and appearance', and it was duly shipped off to Cambridge for Kate. Her life became tragically confined, but Sydney never even considered changing his habits, and he continued his frequent visits to Max Gate on his own.

In February he found both Hardys welcoming. Florence told him that Hardy had spent much of the past two months in bed with a cold caught at Mary's funeral, but he was now on the mend, and clearly pleased to have Cockerell to talk to again. He told him something of Horace Moule, how he had been his early friend and adviser, and the tragedy of his suicide in Cambridge. He also gave him a set of the Wessex Edition of his books, and they discussed literary copyrights.[44] During his April visit Hardy explained that his family would become extinct with his generation, and they settled the final details of the executorship. Florence entertained Cockerell and herself by summoning Hermann Lea's car and taking him to meet neighbours, the Sheridans, who brought out the manuscripts of *The School for Scandal* and *The Critic*. In July they were all invited to lunch at Kingston Maurward House and walked there across the water meadows, pausing to visit the Hardy graves in Stinsford churchyard – now known to Cockerell by its fictional name of 'Mellstock'. In September they went to Weymouth for tea, and the next morning Florence seized her moment to tell Cockerell her version of the truth about her predecessor. 'Went for a short walk with Mrs Hardy who told me what a complete failure TH's first marriage had been and that when the first Mrs Hardy died they were in the midst of a bitter quarrel and even about to separate. All the poems about her are a fiction, but a fiction in which their author has come to believe!'[45] Cockerell wrote her words down carefully and without comment. In the afternoon there was a tea party, a stroll and 'TH exceedingly cordial.' The two men spent Monday morning talking happily, until it was time for Cockerell to go for his train. He was back in December, when J. M. Barrie was a fellow guest, and they dined at Kingston Maurward House and went to see a performance of the Wessex scenes from *The Dynasts* at the Corn Exchange in Dorchester, leaving Hardy in bed with a cold. Cockerell was now so much part of the family that in the morning he was invited to sit with Hardy in his bedroom for their talk.

He was there again during 1917, when Hardy was working on the proofs of *Moments of Vision*, and Cockerell volunteered to look over them. It is not clear from his diary whether he appreciated the privilege since he makes no comment about the poems, merely saying he talked about them with Hardy over breakfast. There were plenty of outings, people coming to call, lunches and dinners out, even though the war was at its grimmest. On 1 January 1918 Florence told him Hardy contemplated living into his nineties, 'and there seems to be no reason why he shouldn't.' In September he offered to rehang the pictures in the repapered drawing room at Max Gate, staying for five days to get the job done and enjoying himself thoroughly as he worked.

During 1917 Hardy had embarked on another large literary project. This one needed Florence's help from start to finish, typing out his notes and narrative as he compiled material for what was to be his own life story. He was giving way to Cockerell's urging that he should write his memoirs, if not in quite the style expected. His system was to go through his accumulation of old notebooks, diaries and letters, copy what he wanted preserved and then destroy the original documents, giving him complete control over what was quoted or told. It was to be written in the third person and its authorship assigned to Florence. There is nothing very unusual in writers seeking to control what is said about them, and Hardy simply went a stage further than most. It was a deception but not a very serious one. Florence was open with Macmillan as well as Cockerell about Hardy's intense involvement in every stage of the process of compiling the 'biography', and it was obvious that all the information came from him and that no further research was done. Work on this absorbed them both to the end of the war and beyond.

She kept Cockerell informed of progress on the book, and in June 1920, soon after Hardy's eightieth birthday, she showed him the work she had done, and Cockerell had the impression that, after much labour, it was now finished, which was far from the truth. That evening he and Florence were invited to dine with the Ilchesters in their great house at Melbury, to which they were driven along lanes in midsummer flower.[46] Hardy had stayed at home, and when they arrived back at ten they found him 'looking out for us. Talking about his family he said that he would have called his book Tess of the Hardys if it had not seemed too personal.' Cockerell was naturally intrigued by this, and the next morning, as he and Hardy walked into Dorchester together, 'I asked him about his wonderful mother.' If he was hoping for a revelation that Jemima had been the original for Tess, he was disappointed. 'He said she was short, with a fine head that looked a bit too big for her body. She had wonderful vitality.' Tess's history is impossible to match with what is known of any of the women of Hardy's family, so either Hardy knew what no one else does or he was teasing Cockerell.[47]

Florence was being hopeful when she described the *Life* as finished in 1920, because she was still taking Hardy's corrections and insertions six years later, warning his publishers that there seemed to be no prospect of the work being completed. It was only his death that brought an end to his revisions, and he left further instructions allowing her to cut out anything 'indiscreet, belittling, monotonous, trivial, provocative, or in any other way unadvisable'.[48] She took this as a licence to reduce the references to Emma, but she made a good job of the publication, and the two volumes are indispensable reading for anyone interested in Hardy, whatever is missing from them. They are idiosyncratic, sometimes entertainingly, sometimes infuriatingly, but the voice is unmistakably that of Hardy.[49]

23. The Wizard

When the war ended Hardy was seventy-eight. He still walked with the vigour of a young man, quickening his pace on an up-hill slope, and could bicycle the mile to his brother's house and back. His days and weeks were run to a pattern: every Monday morning he wound up the three grandfather clocks in the house, one in the hall, one in the drawing room and one in the passage to the kitchen. *The Times* was still his daily paper, and he break-fasted at eight thirty or nine – accounts differ – drinking tea and sprinkling brown sugar on his bacon. He liked to walk to his front gate after breakfast to see what the weather promised, looking south to the monument to Admiral Hardy on Blackdown in the distance. Punctually at ten he was in his study. It was at the side of the house, with an east-facing window, and it was always dusty because he would not allow the housemaids to touch his papers or books.[1] The walls were a faded pinkish red, and he had hung his violin on the wall and put his cello in the corner, a reminder of how the musical instruments were kept at Bock-hampton.[2] Round the fireplace were hung a framed sketch of Thackeray and prints of Tennyson and Meredith, and on his plain writing table was an inkwell given to him by Mrs Henniker and a perpetual calendar fixed on Monday, 7 March, marking his first meeting with Emma.[3] Most of the day was spent at this table, thinking, writing, thinking again. The best of his writing, he said, was done between tea and dinner. His poetry continued the process of mythologizing his life, and although the high sense of excitement and adventure that had driven the 'Poems of 1912–13' had dim-med, his imagination was still quick with memories and themes to be taken up.

He liked to work in old clothes, particularly a pair of trousers that went back to the turn of the century and that he mended himself with string. He also kept an ancient shawl, crocheted from fawn or beige wool, to put over his shoulders, and sometimes his head too, against the cold: it could have been his mother's work, or Emma's. There was an open fire, laid by the maid but not lit, because he liked to get it going himself. No other heat, since neither gas nor electricity had reached Max Gate, and light was provided by oil lamps. No telephone, although one was installed downstairs in 1920 which he refused to answer. In the same year the house acquired a wireless set, of which Wessex became so passionately fond that Hardy sometimes got up early and went down in his long nightshirt and short dressing gown to turn it on for him. He slept in an unheated bedroom and had his hot water brought up in jugs. Florence would join him for early morning tea at 7.45, coming through the dressing room between their rooms.

Florence dealt with much of his correspondence as well as working on the memoirs, and from 1923 a poetry-loving young woman, May O'Rourke, came for three mornings a week. If there was more to be done than usual, she stayed on for the afternoon, and she observed that, when Hardy was thinking about his work, he 'would be present at luncheon, but only corporeally'.[4] In good weather he might potter round the garden in the afternoon, seeing Emma out of the corner of his eye. The maid had strict instructions to put out food for the birds she had loved. He might take Wessie for a walk, with his overcoat flapping open, walking stick in hand, with or without Florence. Regular visitors and close friends such as Cockerell were accompanied on walks – to Stinsford Church, to the heath, over the water meadows – and driven further afield. In April 1919 he and Florence drove in Lea's car with Cockerell through Bridport, stopping to look at the church Hardy had helped Hicks 'restore' and enlarge in the 1860s, and on to Seatown for lunch at the Anchor Inn. It stood beside a few cottages in a bay flanked by high cliffs. That afternoon mackerel came into the bay, and to Cockerell's great joy he was allowed to help haul in the nets.[5] You can see why Hardy liked a man who could turn from running a museum to working with the fishermen and think it a treat.

When they were at home in the afternoon, tea was served by Florence in the drawing room, elegantly, with thin bread and butter and home-made cake on silver cake stands. Hardy would put on more formal clothes if he came down, entering quietly and invariably taking a straight-backed chair. There might be local friends, but increasingly there were visitors from further afield, because Thomas Hardy was now one of the sights of England. Pilgrimages were made to Max Gate, each pilgrim hoping to take away his own little impression or anecdote. It could be trying, but there was also a steady stream of men and women he was pleased to know, and real friendships were formed, remarkably for a man of his age. He especially enjoyed talking about poetry with young writers. One was Siegfried Sassoon, who made his name with fierce poems about the reality of the war, in which he fought in the trenches and against which he protested. In 1917 Sassoon dedicated a volume of verse to Hardy, and they met in November 1918. Sassoon was an attractive figure who had grown up in a privileged world and suffered not only from the war but from knowing himself to be a homosexual, and obliged to hide it. Sassoon thought Hardy would be shocked if he knew, and was probably right.[6] Both the Hardys were charmed by him, and he in turn felt a profound respect for Hardy, seeing in him a wizard who concealed his magic behind a deliberately ordinary appearance and behaviour. There were quarrels, because each enjoyed the other's attention and praise for his poetry, and sometimes it fell short, but these clouds passed.

Charlotte Mew came to their notice through Cockerell. Although Hardy found her shyness difficult, he admired her poetry, invited her to stay, and did what he could to encourage and assist her by getting her a small pension; Florence also corresponded warmly with her. Edmund Blunden, war poet and friend of Sassoon, introduced himself with a volume of his verse and came for weekends. So did Walter de la Mare, who had pleased Hardy first with a review of *The Dynasts* and then with his mysterious poem 'The Listeners'. Another friend of Sassoon, Robert Graves, wrote to Hardy on being demobbed: 'I must confess with shame that I have just read "Jude" for the *first* time only. What an amazing book!"[7] He was running a magazine and asked for poems, then brought his young wife Nancy Nicholson – the Nicholsons were friends of Cockerell – in the summer of 1920. Hardy told him he did not like to make more than four drafts of a poem for fear of it losing its freshness: a remarkable confidence, suggesting how well the spinal cords of the poems were laid down in his mind before he wrote anything down.[8]

His poetic output remained prodigious. Macmillan published a *Collected Poems* in 1919, far too soon, because there were three more volumes to come, containing 408 new poems in all. In 1922 *Late Lyrics and Earlier* was ready, the proofs read by Cockerell. Hardy wrote a prefatory 'Apology' in February 1922, in which he expressed his fear that the effect of the war might be to send the world into a new Dark Age. Yet he refused to be labelled as a pessimist. He was an 'evolutionary meliorist', he insisted, who believed that the world needed both religion and rationality, and that they might be reconciled and interfused through poetry. His theories are less interesting than his poetry, and *Late Lyrics* is not read for its ideas. It starts with 'Weathers' ('This is the weather the cuckoo likes'), which might be called an Elizabethan song – four and a half centuries late. 'The Fallow Deer at the Lonely House' magically incorporates a visual trick or puzzle:

> One without looks in to-night
>   Through the curtain-chink
> From the sheet of glistening white;
> One without looks in to-night
>   As we sit and think
>   By the fender-brink.
>
> We do not discern those eyes
>   Watching in the snow;
> Lit by lamps of rosy dyes
> We do not discern those eyes
>   Wondering, aglow,
>   Fourfooted, tiptoe.

The trick is that the person speaking the poem from inside the house cannot see what the reader is allowed to see, the animal outside in the snow, surprised by the light gleaming out. It makes it more mysterious, because nobody knows it is there except the reader, who is not there.

Another short, mysterious poem, 'Without, Not Within Her', seems to be about Mrs Henniker and credits her with a sanity that was able to drive out Hardy's demons:

> It was that strange freshness you carried
>> Into a soul
> Whereon no thought of yours tarried
>> Two moments at all.
>
> And out from his spirit flew death,
>> And bale, and ban,
> Like the corn-chaff under the breath
>> Of the winnowing-fan.[9]

Hardy wrote to Mrs Henniker after the publication of *Late Lyrics*: 'I ought to have sent you a copy of the Poems. But I don't send books to women nowadays – not because I despise the sex, far from it! but because I fear they will not like something or other I have written, and will be in the awkward position of having to pretend they do.'[10] She came to Dorset at midsummer, and the Hardys drove with her through the Blackmore Vale and to Sherborne. It was their last time together. Nine months later she died, in April 1923, 'After a friendship of thirty years!' wrote Hardy, needing to say no more. He had loved her, and she had acted as a muse. Some of his letters she had discreetly destroyed, the remainder she bequeathed, with perfect tact, to Florence, who preserved them and refused to let Hardy destroy or cut them further. They are among his best.

Half the 'new' poems in *Late Lyrics* were in fact old ones. He went back to 1867 for 'A Young Man's Exhortation', with its Yeatsian conclusion about 'the passing preciousness of dreams'.[11] Something like twenty-five are concerned with Emma, moving backwards and forwards in time. 'On a Discovered Curl of Hair' recalls how she gave him the curl before they were married, 'to abate the misery of absentness', and muses sadly on how it has kept its 'bright brown' through the years that turned the hair on her head grey. In 'Penance' he takes responsibility for his failings, answering his own questions about his past refusal to listen to Emma playing at her keyboard, and finds the grisly image for remorse quoted earlier, 'the chill old keys, / Like a skull's brown teeth / Loose in their sheath'.[12]

The collection ends with a poem of general contrition in which Hardy sits by the fire and listens to his own voice accusing him of arrogance and failure to love, using the language of the Bible:

> *'You slighted her that endureth all,'*
>   Said my own voice talking to me;
> *'Vaunteth not, trusteth hopefully;*
> *That suffereth long and is kind withal,'*
>   Said my own voice talking to me.
>
> *'You taught not that which you set about,'*
>   Said my own voice talking to me;
> *'That the greatest of things is Charity . . .'*
> – And the sticks burnt low, and the fire went out,
>   And my voice ceased talking to me.

His relationship with the Christian faith was a puzzle, but what poet can resist the words of the King James Bible? Florence gives a good example of his tipping further to the 'churchy, conservative' side as he aged in a letter to Cockerell:

We had another tea-party, of a kind you would *not* appreciate. The Rector of West Stafford and his wife, the Vicar of Stinsford and his wife, an elderly and religious peer, Lord Ellenborough, and our neighbours at Syward Lodge – all good Conservatives and staunch Anglicans. T.H. declares that he understands that type of person better than any other, and he prefers to know the rather narrow, churchy, conservative country person to the brilliant young writer who is always popping in and out of the divorce court. An interesting statement from the author of 'Jude'.[13]

He enjoyed his old man's privilege of making contradictory pronouncements and showing a different face to different people. If he went to church, he explained that it was not 'because he believed in it, which he did not, but because it was good for the people to get clean and come together once a week – like discipline in the army'.[14] And, while he listened to Florence read him Jane Austen and compared himself happily to Mr Woodhouse in the winter of 1919, in 1920 he was poring over the most modern of poets, Ezra Pound, and corresponding with him. E. M. Forster found him 'a very vain, conventional, uninteresting old gentleman . . . but perhaps at 82 one rots a little. His great pride is that the county families ask him to tea.'[15] Yet a young postman who delivered mail to Max Gate in the 1920s and told Hardy he liked reading was invited in to borrow two books, and when he brought them back Hardy made time to sit down and talk about them with him, and lent him another two.[16] He told Florence he had seen a ghost in Stinsford churchyard on Christmas Eve 1919, as he put holly on his father's grave; they exchanged words about it being a green Christmas; he followed it into the church and found no one there. He bought himself Einstein's *Relativity: The Special and General Theory. A Popular Exposition* in the 1920s, read and pondered over it, and took it to confirm what he believed, 'that neither chance nor purpose governs the universe, but necessity'. *Einstein and the Universe* by Charles Nordmann, published in 1922, was listed among other books he meant to acquire. In June 1923, thinking about Relativity again, he wrote in his notebook, 'Relativity. That things and events always were, are, and will be (e.g. E.M.F. etc. are living still in the past).'[17] And, in spite of his liking for the narrow, churchy and conservative, in 1924 he publicly attacked the Dean of Westminster for refusing to allow a memorial to Byron in Poets' Corner. 'Whatever Byron's bad qualities he was a poet, and a hater of cant.'[18]

Florence did a good deed in 1919, when there was news that the
detested Lilian Gifford was in a London County Council mental
hospital in Essex. Rather than triumphing over this evidence of
more madness in the Gifford family, she made the journey to visit
her, discussed her case with the doctors and decided she should be
rescued. Hardy was talked out of any idea that they should have
Lilian at Max Gate, and Florence helped to make other arrangements for her. These inevitably included more financial help from
him, which he was happy to give and could easily afford. Money
meant little to him: he spent a mere £600 a year out of an income
of over £2,000. He was silently accumulating a fortune. The only
extravagances of his life had been taking Emma on holiday abroad
and renting smart London houses for the Season in the 1890s.
Florence would have liked him to spend more freely, and in
Dorchester he had the reputation of being mean. It had not helped
that, sitting on the bench during the war, he had imposed fines on
local tradesmen for profiteering. Florence complained in 1918, 'I
shall soon be unable to enter a shop in Dorchester. The last was
our own grocer!'[19]

Oxford caught up with Cambridge in 1920 when he was given
an honorary D. Litt. there, and later an honorary fellowship at
Queen's College. In the same year he made his last trip to London
to attend the wedding of Harold Macmillan to Lady Dorothy
Cavendish, and was asked to be one of the witnesses. The bridegroom, grandson of a founder of the publishing firm, was about
to leave it for a career in politics, and in the 1950s he became a
liberal Conservative Prime Minister, which might have won
Hardy's approval. In June his eightieth birthday brought telegrams
from the King, the Prime Minister and the Vice-Chancellor of
Cambridge, and he wrote some 'Birthday Notes', expressing the
view that civilization might be at risk: 'it makes one feel he would
rather be old than young.' Yet his best friends now were younger
ones, not only Cockerell and Sassoon but T. E. Lawrence, who
asked Graves for an introduction and called on Hardy from his
nearby cottage at Clouds Hill in 1923. Lawrence, archaeologist
and writer, soldier and strategist, statesman and spokesman for the
Arabs in their fight against the Turks, was a legendary figure before

he was thirty, achieving fame and power and then fleeing from both, changing his name and enlisting as a common soldier. What he was seeking has never been entirely clear, but appears to have been some sort of moral cleansing. He was drawn at once to Hardy's 'dignity and ripeness' and to the simplicity of life at Max Gate; and both the Hardys responded to his friendliness and good humour, and read his book *The Seven Pillars of Wisdom* with admiration. He took to coming over on alternate Sundays, and, since he and Cockerell were already friends, they formed a congenial circle when he was also visiting.

In 1923 Hardy finished *The Famous Tragedy of the Queen of Cornwall*, a short and violent verse drama about the last hours of Tristan and Iseult, culminating in two murders and the suicide of Queen Iseult, who stabs her husband and jumps from the castle parapet into the sea below. Hardy said he had tried to avoid 'turning the rude personages of, say, the fifth century into respectable Victorians', but much of the language is archaic, and even the usually admiring Cockerell commented on 'a good many inversions and old words which may make it difficult to follow when acted'.[20] It is heavy going, and the most curious feature is the speech given to the second Iseult, which Hardy based closely on the words of Elfride, his heroine of *A Pair of Blue Eyes*, as she begs for forgiveness; whether this was writer's thrift or had some private significance is impossible to tell. He had planned the play in 1870, seeing Emma as Queen Iseult, and started it in 1916 when he visited Tintagel with Florence, then set it aside again, perhaps thinking a drama of marital jealousy inappropriate. It is the only work to which he put a dedication: to Emma, her sister Helen and brother-in-law Cadell Holder, with Florence's name tactfully added to the list. It was published and acted in Dorchester that winter, and soon afterwards the composer Rutland Boughton asked if he might make it into an opera. Boughton had achieved a wild success with his musical drama *The Immortal Hour*, opened at the first Glastonbury Festival in 1914, and his intention at Glastonbury was to bring art to ordinary people. He was a serious communist and did his best to establish a commune in Somerset. He found Hardy modest and generous, and Hardy took to him, listened to his communist ideas with interest, 'though he could not share them,' and went to Glastonbury to hear the musical version. It was no more successful than the commune, although Broughton's music still has admirers.[21] But it shows Hardy's continuing interest in the theatre and belief that it mattered to try to reach a wide audience. In March 1925 he put his signature to an appeal for funds to rebuild the Shakespeare Memorial Theatre in Stratford after a fire: Shakespeare, and a country theatre, were both good causes to him.[22]

In July 1923 the Prince of Wales was due to make a short tour of Somerset, Dorset and Wiltshire, to meet tenants on his estates, and also to show himself to the people of Bath and Dorchester. Lord Shaftesbury persuaded him to open a Drill Hall for the Dorset Territorials in Dorchester, and someone had the bright idea that the visit might be more entertaining if he combined it with lunch at Thomas Hardy's house. The Prince had never read a line of his work, but he was made aware that he was a very old and famous Dorset writer, and that some of his books were in the royal collection. Florence was thrown into panic by the idea of having to entertain the Prince and his considerable retinue, but Hardy, she noticed with surprise, was *pleased*.[23]

She sought the ever helpful Cockerell's advice and dashed to town to meet him. His diary for Wednesday, 11 July, describes how he met her at the New Century Club in Hay Hill, finding her in a state of agitation about the visit of the Prince, who would be coming with Lord Shaftesbury, equerries and chauffeurs, all needing to be fed. Cockerell cheered her up with tea and ice cream at Gunter's, helped her choose some glassware for her lunch table and introduced her to the worldly wife of a friend, who gave good advice about dealing with the Prince – 'much on the lines of my own', he noted with satisfaction. He then saw her to Liverpool Street on her way to her mother in Enfield for the night.[24]

The Prince's visit was scheduled for 20 July. Hardy offered his sister Kate the chance of being installed in 'the bedroom behind the jessamine – you would then see him come, and go: we could probably send you up a snack.' She refused, but Henry put up a Union Jack on a flagpole at Talbothays, and neighbours rallied round to lend anything needed at Max Gate.[25] Someone had the sense to lock up Wessie. A police cordon was set up round the house. It was a day of scorching heat. Hardy drove to the Drill Hall and was introduced to the Prince on the platform; then they drove together through Dorchester in an open car, to cheers and photographers. The Prince was taken up to a bedroom with his valet, his secretary waiting on the landing, Florence hovering downstairs. By her account a balled-up waistcoat flew out of the bedroom at the secretary, and the Prince came down to lunch under the trees in the garden, very sensibly minus his waistcoat.

A retinue of thirteen, mostly Duchy officials, had to be fed in the house, not counting the chauffeurs, while the grandees, who included Lord Shaftesbury and the gallant Admiral Sir Lionel Halsey, now an equerry to the Prince, ate in the shade of the trees. The Prince did not pretend to have read anything by his host, whereas Hardy knew that the Prince, as Duke of Cornwall, owned most of the land round Dorchester. It was after all from his grandfather that he had purchased the plot on which Max Gate was built, and only a month before Florence had applied to the Duchy to buy a further half acre, saying she wanted to build a cottage for her gardener on it.[26] So the conversation is likely to have turned on rural matters, rather than on literature, and indeed one of the maids believed that 'Mr Hardy spoke to the prince about a piece of land we called The Paddock, that he would like to have it for a kitchen garden . . . and Mr Hardy had the extra ground' – although it is highly unlikely that the Prince had anything to do with the negotiations over the land, which were in any case already proceeding smoothly.[27] Florence managed the arrangements for the lunch party well and hit exactly the right note with her principal guest. 'I didn't fuss around him, and I think he was grateful. He made himself very much at home . . . He grew rather gay and jocular during lunch . . . I had been told he ate nothing. He made an excellent lunch, and asked for a second helping of ham, and finished up with a glass of 40 year old sherry and one of the cigars.' When it was time for official photographs, she tried to avoid being included, but he insisted on her being in all of them: ' "Oh yes, you must be photographed too. Come along." So I did.' And with her big white hat and dark eyes she looks charming.

The Prince departed to visit his farm tenants around Dorchester, the police left, Wessex was let out, and ordinary life resumed. The next day the Hardys had themselves driven to Portland Bill to visit a new friend, Marie Stopes, who had settled in a lighthouse tower there. She found him boyish and twinkling, ready to talk indiscreetly of the lunch party, and eager to climb to the top of her tower and out on to the roof to see the circular view. Everyone found their own version of Hardy. To Lawrence he seemed 'so pale, so quiet, so refined into an essence'.[28] Yet Florence told Marie Stopes later that he was 'far more nervous and highly strung than appears to anyone outside the household', and her account of how difficult he could be when she planned to be away for two days in London suggests he could panic and bully.[29] He announced that he felt ill just as she was about to leave. 'He began to put his papers in order and told me he was doing it lest he should die suddenly . . . By this time I began to think it would be wrong to leave him and so I . . . cancelled all my engagements . . . whereupon he suddenly became quite well,' she told Cockerell, adding forgivingly, 'Perhaps it is that the prospect of being left really does alarm him and make him feel ill.'[30]

There is no doubt that he wanted her to be there all the time, but, looking at the fourteen years they spent together as man and wife, you notice how silent he was about her, while she experienced and presented her life as a series of discontents and dramas. One long-running drama revolved around her health. In 1915 she was in a London nursing home having surgery on her nose for 'nasal catarrh'. A year later her friendly specialist told her she was severely run down – she suffered from depression and sleeplessness – and needed a three-week holiday, but, because it was wartime and Hardy was opposed to holidays, nothing happened. In 1917 she was persuaded to have a series of expensive 'inoculations' which even her sister Eva, a nurse, thought useless. Florence grumbled, 'Were I a Gifford of course all this would be paid for me,' but Hardy let her pay for herself.[31] She had frequent X-rays and many discussions with her doctors about operations that might become necessary. In 1919 she was seeing a London surgeon about a 'displaced toe'.[32] In 1921 she told Cockerell she suffered from 'almost intolerable pains' as long as she was at Max Gate, which cleared up as soon as she got away.[33] In 1923 a swollen gland appeared in her neck which her surgeon was in two minds about. She consulted E. M. Forster, who recommended another specialist early in 1924, and he advised her against surgical intervention, as it was in any case getting smaller.[34] Hardy was fearful of her undergoing surgery, but she made up her mind to have it removed in any case, and alarmed Cockerell greatly by describing the swelling to him as a tumour. She was booked into a nursing home in Fitzroy Square on 30 September, and he was in London on the 29th to see her before the operation, and travelled up again from Cambridge on the next day. He made two visits on 1 October, writing to Hardy after each, and returned to the nursing home on the 2nd, 3rd, 6th and 7th.[35] She had other visitors, among them Sassoon, bearing a bunch of violets, Charlotte Mew and Virginia Woolf – something of a salon assembled around her bed.[36] But the most devoted and attentive was Cockerell. Florence now began to call him Sydney and confided to him 'how she dreaded the winter in Max Gate, its dismalness, and how she hated most of the furniture there'.[37] Afterwards she told him that 'the days in the nursing home remain as a happy memory.'[38] Her symptoms look more like an expression of her need to get away from Max Gate and a yearning for attention, sympathy and warmth than like anything clinically serious. You can feel sorry for her and at the same time believe Hardy was right to be sceptical about the various treatments she sought. The last operation at least roused him to arrange the luxury of a car to fetch her home from London, and to send his brother to escort her. He wrote a poem about his wait for her arrival – 'Nobody Comes'. Too late, too little, poetically, to please Florence, and more about his anxiety than about her:

A car comes up, with lamps full-glare,
That flash upon a tree:
It has nothing to do with me,
And whangs along in a world of its own,
Leaving a blacker air;
And mute by the gate I stand again alone,
And nobody pulls up there.[39]

There were lesser dramas over bringing modern technology to
Max Gate. Hardy was happy to go on living with hip baths in the
bedrooms, oil lamps and candles to light the house and no main
drainage, and Florence had to fight to have a bathroom and hot
water installed in 1920, and in the same year the telephone (Dorchester 43) and wireless. She was right to do this, of course, and
guests and maids must have been as pleased with the improvements
as she was, but the master was too old to change his ways, and for
him water was still carried up and down stairs. It was habit, but it
was also a way of remaining true to the early experience that was
so important to him.

The clash of past and present and Florence's sensitivity sometimes made her feel she was a usurper in the house. She told
Sassoon that she disliked being called Mrs Hardy because she felt
the name belonged to 'someone else, whom I knew for several
years, and I am oppressed by the thought that I am living in *her*
house, using *her* things – and, worst of all, have even stolen her
name.'[40] It is a pathetic confession.

Her feeling herself a usurper may have been what made her fearful
of being usurped in turn. Otherwise it is hard to explain her
behaviour over Gertrude Bugler. This was the biggest drama of
her marriage, centred round a Dorset girl who took part in productions put on by the amateur players active in Dorchester from
1908 specializing in adaptations of Hardy's novels. In 1913, when
Gertrude was sixteen, she played Marty in a production of *The*

Woodlanders, and in 1918 she, her parents and her sister Eileen were all in a revival of *The Mellstock Quire*. Hardy lent his father's working smocks to the boys in the *Mellstock* cast and also addressed the company about the origins of the story.[41] For him these were delightful occasions in which he saw his novels brought to life. Two years later Gertrude was Eustacia in *The Return of the Native*, and she also appeared at Max Gate at Christmas with a group of Mummers. Gertrude was a beauty, dark, lush, gentle, large-eyed, and a naturally talented actress. Florence joked to Cockerell, 'T H has lost his heart to [Gertrude] entirely, but as she is soon getting married I don't let that cast me down too much.'[42] And indeed in 1921 she married her cousin, Captain Ernest Bugler, MC, a war hero and a farmer, and they settled in Beaminster and began a family. Perhaps this too aroused Florence's jealousy: here was a girl whose beauty appealed to Hardy, and who was now married to a young husband and expecting a baby – whereas Florence's beauty had departed, her husband was old, and she had no children.

In the summer of 1922 Gertrude was pregnant. A production of *Desperate Remedies* was planned for the winter, and under the circumstances it would not be possible for her to appear in it. Hardy had told her to come over to Max Gate whenever she liked, but when she called and asked for him she was coldly received and sent away by Florence, who followed this up with an incredible letter of reproach, suggesting she had no manners and telling her that a lady did not call on a gentleman: 'As you must know this is a most extraordinary thing to do. In the first place, all invitations to Max Gate naturally come from me ... and again it is not usual in our station of life for any lady to call upon a gentleman. It is simply "not done".' Florence had either forgotten or perhaps remembered all too clearly her own first approach to Hardy.

A letter to Cockerell telling him about the production of *Desperate Remedies* shows the tone she took about her imagined rival: 'Poor Gertrude Bugler seems to have suffered agonies at being cut out by a rival leading lady ... and the tragic climax is that she had a still-born son on the day of performance. What a gossip I am.'[43] Happily Gertrude gave birth the next year to a healthy daughter, and in 1924 she appeared on stage in Dorchester again, this time

as Tess. It was Hardy's own adaptation, and he involved himself
in the production. He found Gertrude intelligent, and seeing and
hearing her in the part of his favourite heroine moved him deeply
– enough perhaps for her to become his 'well-beloved', according
to his own theories.[44] He was eighty-four, she was married and
the mother of a small baby, and the love was all in his mind, but
Florence reacted with jealous fury. She wrote to Cockerell to tell
him that Gertrude 'twitters affectedly in the tragic parts' and that
'she's so satisfied with her performance that I'm afraid she is not
going to be the gigantic success that is anticipated.'[45] Cockerell
saw the performance quite otherwise when he attended it in
November. He praised the reserve, pathos and charm of Mrs
Bugler's performance as Tess, saying she took the part to the life,
so much so that you could overlook the bad acting of the men
playing Clare and Alec.[46] He enjoyed the matinée so much that
he returned for the evening performance.

Bugler's performance was generally agreed to be outstanding.
J. M. Barrie wrote that she had delighted him 'beyond most
actresses'. A theatre manager was now eager to take her to London
in a production of Tess. As this was being set up, in January
1925, Cockerell returned to Max Gate to find Florence hysterical,
convinced that Hardy was so besotted with Gertrude that everyone
in Dorchester was laughing about it. There was some gossip, but
Cockerell urged her to see the situation as a comedy, given Hardy's
age. She said she was trying to, but that he spoke roughly to her
and showed her that she was in the way. She may have remembered how she had once heard him speak to Emma. In spite of
this she, Hardy and Cockerell went for a stroll together with Wessie
after lunch and, according to the diarist, had a very agreeable talk.
During the rest of the day he saw no sign of any trouble or quarrel.
But in the morning Florence again sought him out alone, told him
she had spent the night thinking she was going mad and begged
him to stay, since the theatre manager and Mrs Bugler were coming
over to discuss the plans for Tess being played at the Haymarket in
April. He complied and wrote of Gertrude afterwards that he could
not see her as presenting much danger to anyone.

Indeed there was no harm in Gertrude Bugler, who was naturally proud to have the approval and affection of a celebrated writer. Neither Cockerell nor Hardy knew the full extent of Florence's rage and bad behaviour. In February she sent a telegram to Gertrude to say she was coming to see her and arrived on her doorstep 'terribly upset and agitated, and said at once that her husband must not know of her visit to me. Then I listened with incredulous amazement to what she had to say.' She begged Gertrude to withdraw from the play, telling her that if she went to London Hardy would follow her there and that it would be bad for his health and lead to damaging publicity; and that he had been writing poems to her in which he spoke of running away with her – poems Florence had destroyed. Gertrude was taken aback by all this; she was also aware of her own husband's lack of enthusiasm about her going to London and anxious herself about the effect on their child. She therefore agreed to give up the part. 'So I wrote to Thomas Hardy and to Frederick Harrison to that effect. I never saw Hardy again.'[47]

Not satisfied with stopping Gertrude's chance of becoming a professional actress, Florence determined to bring an end to the amateur dramatics in Dorchester: 'if I can manage it the Hardy plays will stop now. I cannot go through another experience like that, and it would be bad for him also.'[48] She succeeded, and prevented Gertrude even from reciting one of Hardy's poems at a dinner for Dorsetmen; and she continued to complain about Hardy's infatuation.[49] Even after his death, in 1929, she explained her absence from the first night of a London production of *Tess* in which Bugler was to appear briefly by saying she thought 'my husband's heart was weakened by excitements connected with the production here in Dorset, & had it not been for that I think he might have been alive now.'[50] The suggestion is absurd and acts as a reminder of Florence's long-established habit of inventing stories to produce the effect she wanted. We shall never know whether she also invented the poems she said Hardy had written about Gertrude, but to have invented them would be easier to forgive than to have destroyed them.

Hardy himself remained silent and calm. He had given Gertrude inscribed copies of *The Return of the Native* and *Tess*, and written her a few simple letters signed 'Sincerely yours' and 'Your affectionate friend'. When she wrote to tell him she was giving up the London production, he answered, 'Although you fancy otherwise, I do not believe that any London actress will represent Tess so nearly as I imagined her as you did.'[51] Gertrude saw that Florence was driven by jealousy, and she remembered Hardy with affection. His last words to her, she said, were spoken when he saw her off as she left Max Gate in January 1923: 'If anyone asks you if you knew Thomas Hardy, say, "Yes, he was my friend." '[52]

To arouse an emotional storm between two women at the age of eighty-three is not given to many men. If Hardy was in any sense in love with Gertrude, it was because she embodied his most intimately imagined heroine, 'My Tess', so well.[53] If Florence could have understood that it was the dream of Tess he loved, she might have been more understanding. And he was wholly bound to Florence as his wife, depending on her for her affection and care in seeing to his needs and comfort.

He was pleased to find one of his own theories of love taken up by Marcel Proust, who believed that the lover creates an image of the beloved in his mind that may bear little resemblance to the real person. 'It appears that The Theory exhibited in "The Well-Beloved" in 1892 has since been developed by Proust still further,' he wrote in his notebook, followed by a quotation from *À l'ombre des jeunes filles en fleurs*:

Peu de personnes comprennent le caractère purement subjective du phénomène qu'est l'amour, et la sorte de création que c'est d'une personne supplémentaire, distincte de celle qui porte le même nom dans le monde, et dont la plupart des éléments sont tirés de nous-même . . . Le désir s'élève, se satisfait, disparait – et c'est tout. Ainsi, la jeune fille qu'on épouse n'est pas celle dont on est tombé amoureux.[54] (Few people understand the subjective nature of love and the way it creates another being, different from the actual person bearing the same name, and endowed with characteristics for the most part imagined by the lover . . . Desire arises, satisfies itself and disappears – that's all there is to it. So the young woman you marry is not the person you fell in love with.)

Hardy already understood this perfectly and had demonstrated its truth many times, in telling the story of Clym and Eustacia, of Bathsheba and Troy, and of Angel and Tess.

In the autumn of 1923 he sat for Augustus John. The portrait in oils and the preparatory sketch are both exceptionally fine, showing a man who has come to terms with old age, his face carved, seamed and furrowed by a long, reflective life. Two comments are attributed to Hardy, the earlier a jocular, 'Well, if I look like that the sooner I am under the ground the better.' The second, made several years later, has him saying, 'I don't know whether that is how I look or not – but that is how I *feel*.'[55] Within weeks of its being finished, Cockerell noted in his diary, 'Having heard from Augustus John that he would take £500 for his portrait of Hardy I went up to London by the 1 pm to see him and secured it, though I may have to raise the money.'[56] Cockerell never failed to raise the money when he was determined on a purchase, and the portrait was soon displayed among the treasures of the Fitzwilliam Museum in Cambridge.

24. Winter Words

What kept him going in these late years – eighty-four, eighty-five, eighty-six, eighty-seven – was the simple daily habit of picking up his pen. 'I never let a day go without using a pen. Just holding it sets me off; in fact I can't think without it. It's important not to wait for the right mood. If you do it will come less and less,' he told a visitor.[1] Dramatized versions of his work delighted him still, but his gaze turned increasingly inward, and not only because his eyes were tired. There were still drafts of old poems to be reworked, and memories of places, ghosts and loves to be summoned up yet again. Cockerell read the proofs of the 152 poems Hardy was proposing for a new collection and suggested changes, about half of which Hardy accepted. It is a pity they left no record of this collaborative process between poet and friend without an ounce of poetry in his soul. It began when Hardy read some aloud to him in March 1925. Cockerell went through them later by himself, and made up his mind they were good. In November of the same year the new volume was published, *Human Shows, Far Phantasies, Songs and Trifles*. The first edition of 5,000 copies almost sold out before publication. Hardy had become a popular poet. There were two more printings before the end of the year, and Macmillan put out a trade edition in America, where his poetry had not appeared in volume form since 1898.

As in any large collection there is weak material, but enough strong and original to carry the volume. 'Snow in the Suburbs' dates back to the freezing winter of his illness in Tooting in 1880, trimmed into a 1920s imagist shape with the crispness of a black-and-white print:

> Every branch big with it,
> Bent every twig with it;
> Every fork like a white web-foot;

Every street and pavement mute:
Some flakes have lost their way, and grope back upward, when
Meeting those meandering down they turn and descend again.
The palings are glued together like a wall,
And there is no waft of wind with the fleecy fall.

A sparrow enters the tree,
Whereupon immediately
A snow-lump thrice his own slight size
Descends on him and showers his head and eyes,
And overturns him,
And near inurns him,
And lights on a nether twig, when its brush
Starts off a volley of other lodging lumps with a rush.

The steps are a blanched slope,
Up which, with feeble hope,
A black cat comes, wide-eyed and thin;
And we take him in.[2]

There are many autumn poems, one the terrific 'Night-Time in
Mid-Fall', about bad weather, rain and the sort of wind that lets
you hear from inside your house the sound of tree roots being
wrenched underground outside, where conditions resemble a
storm scene in Shakespeare:

The streams are muddy and swollen; eels migrate
To a new abode;
Even cross, 'tis said, the turnpike-road;
(Men's feet have felt their crawl, home-coming late):
The westward fronts of towers are saturate,
Church-timbers crack, and witches ride abroad.

There is the poem about Moule's burial place, 'Before My Friend
Arrived'.[3] There are again many Emma poems, including the
ultra-romantic 'She Opened the Door', dated 1913. 'Days to
Recollect' has the memorable image of the 'Winged thistle-seeds'

rising in the air as her petticoat brushes them, the second image being the day of her death, when she 'lay by the window whence you had gazed / So many times when blamed or praised, / Morning or noon, through years and years'. 'Midnight on Beechen' goes back to their Bath holiday before they were married. 'The Frozen Greenhouse' is a memory of St Juliot, and 'Once at Swanage' is self-explanatory: 'And there we two stood, hands clasped; / I and she!' It is not all romance: he includes 'A Second Attempt', about his failure to revive his love for her in 1900.[4] As you read, you see that his memories of her are his own story too, which he continually unfolds and turns about like a much consulted map, alighting on familiar and half-forgotten spots which suddenly become vivid to him.

In December 1924, during the time when *Tess* was playing and Florence suffering, Hardy wrote to Canon Cowley, rector of Stinsford, formally establishing his allegiance to his local church and his wish to be buried in its churchyard: 'Regard me as a Parishioner certainly. I hope to be still more one when I am in a supine position some day.'[5] On Boxing Day there was a letter to Benson in Cambridge: 'We have been as cheerful as may be this Christmas.'[6] Six months later Benson died, and it happened by chance that Hardy's connection with Cambridge University was celebrated the next day, 18 June, when a group of undergraduates came to Max Gate to sing in his honour a programme of Purcell, Arne, Gibbons, Mozart and Haydn. Cockerell had organized and come with them for the occasion, and Lawrence came over to hear them.[7] Soon after this the University of Bristol sent a deputation to award him an honorary doctorate; it was his fifth. Oxford undergraduates, the Balliol Players, came several times to entertain him with Greek plays on the lawn, in 1924, 1926 and 1927. Hardy was always interested to hear what plans the young men had for their lives, how they hoped to succeed in the future and what new paths they might follow. His own notebook and other people's letters and memories reveal a steady stream of visitors coming to Max Gate. He kept faithfully in touch with Dorothy Allhusen,

whom he had known since she was a small child and he became
'Uncle Tom' when he visited her mother Mary Jeune in Harley
Street. When Dorothy was widowed, and two of her children
died, she turned to him for comfort, and he gave it.

In the autumn of 1925 two letters came from children of his
cousin Emma Sparks, whom he had visited in Somerset in 1861,
before she emigrated to Australia in the 1870s. The first was from
a daughter in Brisbane, 'M. M. Allen', who had read about the
visit of the Prince of Wales and described herself as one of a family
of teachers. Then her elder brother, James Sparks Cary, living in
New South Wales, wrote, 'Dear Cousin, My beloved Mother was
Emma Sparks of Piddletown I think they changed it to Puddle . . .
My grandmother's name was Maria Hand before marriage and
grandfather's name James Sparks. Mother's sisters were named
Rebecca, Martha and Tryfina and brothers James and Nathaniel.
She often spoke of you as Tom, and that you were in London,
and also of her Aunt Hardy.' He said he had been born and bred
in the village of Faulkland in Somerset and just remembered being
taken to Bockhampton as a five-year-old, and meeting Harry and
Kate but not Tom, who was away. After this the family set off for
Queensland to join Aunt Martha Duffield. 'She is dead and gone
now poor soul. She said she knew you well. Her husband was a
real nice man . . . but he's gone now.' He explained in a PS that
he was sixty-four, childless and 'I only had a village education.'[8]
Whatever memories of the past these letters stirred in Hardy, there
is no sign that he reacted or replied to them, and perhaps he had
left that part of the past too far behind to be able to revisit it.

He was in any case withdrawing from the world. He knew it had
changed and must change more, but he was too old to be involved
or stirred by the changes. He turned his back on politics, public
events and foreign affairs, almost as though the war had burnt out
any further interest in them. To a local visitor who noticed a
photograph of Lloyd George in the house, signed and with a
tribute to Hardy, he said he credited Lloyd George with much of
the country's success in the Great War, adding quickly, 'I never

talk politics.'⁹ Not a word came from him when Emma's cause triumphed in 1918 and women were given the vote.¹⁰ We know from Florence that he voted for the Conservatives in the local elections of 1922 because there was no Liberal candidate and he would not support Labour. (She took her own stance, and when she was made a JP she amazed the chairman of the Dorchester magistrates by declaring herself 'Labour'.¹¹) Hardy had nothing at all to say about the general elections, the fall of Lloyd George, the formation of the first Labour government in 1924 or the next election that brought back the Conservatives, which figures in his letters only as a possible problem in the setting up of the Dorchester Players' production of *Tess*. The economic collapse of Germany in 1923 goes without comment, and the rise of Mussolini in Italy, and the formation of the USSR. In 1926 he refused to let Sassoon have a manuscript poem to auction to help the miners in their six-month strike, Florence explaining that 'he will not do anything to give the impression that he approves of the strike. He thinks the miners are misled.'¹²

In July 1926 the daughter of his old editor Leslie Stephen invited herself to tea with her husband, Leonard Woolf. They came from London by train, taking the train back again after tea, and Virginia wrote a long account of the afternoon in her diary. After some preliminary talk with Florence about her dog, 'who is evidently the real centre of her thoughts', Hardy came in, 'dressed in rough grey with a striped tie', and sat on a three-cornered chair. 'He was extremely affable and aware of his duties. He did not let the talk stop or disdain making talk. He talked of father – said he had seen me, or it might have been my sister but he thought was me, in my cradle.' She tried to get him to talk about his novels, but he would not. He told her a friend had begged him not to give up poetry, and he had replied, 'I'm afraid poetry is giving up me.' She went on, 'The truth is he is a very kind man, and sees anyone who wants to see him. He has 16 people for the day sometimes . . . Do you think one can't write poetry if one sees people? I asked. "One might be able to – I dont see why not. Its a question of physical strength" said Hardy. But clearly he preferred solitude himself. Always however he said something sensible and sincere.'

'I forgot to say that he offered L. whisky and water, wh. struck me that he was competent as a host, and in every way. / So we got up and signed Mrs H's visitors books; and Hardy took my L[ife's] Little Ironies off, and trotted back with it signed, and Woolf spelt Wolff, wh. I daresay had given him some anxiety.' This made it clear that Hardy had read nothing of hers although she had published several novels, most recently *Mrs Dalloway*; and also that she was not vain enough to mind. 'But he no longer reads novels. / The whole thing – literature, novels &c – all seemed to him an amusement, far away, too, scarcely to be taken seriously. Yet he had sympathy and pity for those still engaged in it.'

'What impressed me was his freedom, ease and vitality. He seemed very "Great Victorian" doing the whole thing with a sweep of his hand (they are ordinary smallish, curled up hands) and setting no great stock by literature but immensely interested in facts; incidents; and somehow, one could imagine, naturally swept off into imagining and creating without a thought of its being difficult or remarkable; becoming obsessed; and living in imagination.'[13]

The Woolfs departed, Leonard taking with him an admiration for Hardy about which he wrote eighteen months later. He saw him as a novelist at the end of a great line stretching back to Fielding, 'in the full English tradition, solid works built about a story, in which, on the face of it, character, humour, description of scenery, criticism of life, philosophy, all have their place, but to which they are accessory': a tradition now ended, so that the novels were undervalued. He conceded that Hardy did not 'write well' and that only when you finished one and looked back on it as a whole did you see that it was 'a great novel and a great work of art'. He went on to say something of the man:

This impression of simplicity and of something which is almost the opposite of simplicity was the strongest impression which I got from Hardy personally. At first sight, and when he began to talk to you, you might have thought that he was merely one of many men born in English villages. But he is one of the few people who have left upon me the personal impression of greatness. I saw him last spring [in fact July] in the house which he had built for himself at Dorchester, and which, with its sombre growth of trees, seemed to have been created by him as if it were one of his poems translated into brick, furniture and vegetation. He talked about his poems, and London as he had known it in his youth, and about his dog 'Wessex', all with great charm and extraordinary simplicity. He was a human being, not 'the great man'.[14]

That autumn Hardy made what turned out to be his last visit to his birthplace, now standing empty, and looked at the trees and the fencing, anxious to have the garden tidy and the house better secluded.[15] Florence thought he was disappointed not to get the Nobel Prize when it went to Shaw in November: 'Between ourselves the award of the Nobel prize to GBS was rather a blow to him I thought. He had not counted on it exactly, but had always had the feeling that he had been passed over for some unjust reason.'[16] In the same month Lawrence was posted to India and came to say his farewell. It was a raw afternoon. Hardy came out to see him off on his motor-bike and hurried back into the house for a shawl against the cold, and while he was gone Lawrence quickly rode off to spare him the chill. This upset Hardy – missing the last word with his friend – and both men knew they were unlikely to meet again. Hardy refused an invitation to a dinner in London with the explanation, 'I am getting more and more like a vegetable that will not bear transplanting.'[17]

Two days after Christmas, Wessex had to be put to sleep, for which purpose a doctor was called in rather than a vet. There was much sorrow over this. Florence confided in Cockerell, telling him how '*thousands* (actually thousands) of afternoons and evenings I would have been alone but for him, and had always him to speak to.'[18] Hardy told the Granville-Barkers, 'Our devoted (and masterful) dog Wessex died on the 27th, and last night had his bed outside the house under the trees for the first time for 13 years.'[19] Death, as he saw it, was moving your bed from inside the house to outside. Bertie Stephens the gardener, who had mixed feelings about Wessex, buried him, and a gravestone was put up, inscribed 'Faithful, Unflinching'.[20] Florence bought a cat to cheer Hardy, but it was not the same.

The new year brought him a £5,000 royalty cheque from Macmillan. Cockerell gallantly came down for Florence's birthday in January. Hardy kept working. In June he told Cockerell he had got up in the night to see an eclipse. Gosse visited him in the same month and wondered at his being 'without a deficiency of sight, hearing, mind or conversation. Very tiny and fragile, but full of spirit and a gaiety.'[21] When Florence, thinking him gloomy on his eighty-seventh birthday, tried to cheer him by talking about the various festivities she planned for his ninetieth, 'with a flash of gaiety he replied that he intended to spend that day in bed.'[22] In August his fellow poet John Squire brought over a friendly singer, John Goss, for an afternoon of folk songs. The three of them gathered round Emma's old piano. Hardy joined in the refrains and beat time in the air with his hand, now laughing with pleasure and now with tears in his eyes as certain favourites came up; and he rooted out old music books with the Victorian ballads he associated with his mother and Emma. Squire marvelled at 'the unexhausted old man' and his fresh responses, and we are reminded of how as a child he danced ecstatically to his father's playing, and some tunes brought tears to his eyes.[23]

There was a trip to Bath and a drive to Puddletown with Gustav Holst, who came seeking permission to dedicate his tone poem *Egdon Heath* to Hardy.[24] But the small notebook in which he jotted down such visits and trips had its last entry on 19 September. Among a list of things to be done at the other end of the notebook was 'Get Mr Lamb, or other, to make sketch from photo of Emma, to match Strang's of F. (for N.P.G.)' – Lamb being the artist Henry Lamb and the NPG the National Portrait Gallery.[25] He wanted his portrait to hang between his wives just as he personally wanted to lie between them in Stinsford churchyard.

At the beginning of November he and Florence visited the Stinsford graves and went to Talbothays together. It was the last such trip. The end of the month was the time to wear a black hat and carry a black walking stick that had belonged to Emma when he went out of doors, to mark his mourning at the fifteenth anniversary of her death and the twelfth of Mary's. He planned to publish *Winter Words* on his eighty-eighth birthday, in June 1928, and he was working on it in his study until 10 December 1927. There are some quirky, vivid poems scattered through its pages. 'The Lodging-House Fuchsias' describes the landlady who lets her fuchsias grow and spread gloriously over the front path until they have to be cut back to let her coffin pass. 'A Countenance' is about an attractive woman whose laugh was 'not in the middle of her mouth quite'. 'Proud Songsters' is about the life-cycle of the garden birds, and how they sing 'As if all Time were theirs'. 'So Various' describes a man made up of contradictions, highly strung but also stiff and cold; a faithful lover but fickle too; pleased with his own cleverness but easily put down; always sad but cheerful company; cool to friends yet eager to please – all of course versions of himself. In 'Lying Awake' he visualizes the world outside from his bed:

> You, Meadow, are white with your counterpane cover of dew,
>   I see it as if I were there;
> You, Churchyard, are lightening faint from the shade of the yew,
>   The names creeping out everywhere.

On 11 December, Hardy went to his study as usual, sat at his writing table and found he could not work. He said it was the first time that such a thing had happened to him, and took to his bed. Florence called Dr Mann, a new local man, who diagnosed a weakness of the heart: this she told Gosse in a letter on the 15th. Hardy was still coming downstairs for a few hours each day, and he asked her to send off a poem he had prepared to *The Times*. He had begun it in 1905 and finished it in 1926, he said, and in it he imagined the figures of the gods as they appear in the Elgin Marbles, grumbling at being kept in a sunless room by the Christians who had ended their reign. It was called 'Christmas in the Elgin Room', and he was pleased when it appeared on Christmas Eve.

On Christmas Day he pencilled a line to Gosse, joking about his relief at not having to eat the traditional pudding. On the same day Florence wrote to Cockerell saying he had been in bed for three weeks – in fact, it was two – and now lacked the strength even to pencil a line, that he could not follow her reading aloud and did not want to talk to anyone. 'I asked the doctor what really was the matter, and he said "Old age".'²⁶ This was the last day he came downstairs. Sir Henry Head, an eminent medical man who lived near by, kept an eye on things with Dr Mann.

Now Hardy lay in bed, without visitors but talking to Florence and still thinking clearly and deciding what he wanted her to read to him. On Boxing Day he asked for the Gospel account of the birth of Christ and the massacre of the innocents, and also the entries in the *Encyclopaedia Biblica*, remarking when she had finished that there was not a grain of evidence that the Gospel was true. Outside there was snow on the ground. He was growing weaker, although on 30 December he enjoyed pheasant and champagne for lunch. But when Florence opened the window of the dressing room towards midnight on the last night of the year to let him hear the bells, he took no notice. Her sister Eva arrived to help. On 4 January he was better, and another doctor called in from Bournemouth said his arteries were like those of a man of sixty. On the 6th the digitalis for his heart was stopped, and he ate and slept better, but on the 8th he had fluid in his lungs, and the next morning Florence summoned Cockerell by telegram. She warned him that Hardy must not know of his presence at Max Gate.

Cockerell travelled all day and arrived at tea-time.

TH had had disturbing symptoms yesterday and they thought he was soon to die, but today they have abated and Dr Mann, whom I saw after his evening visit, declared that he had good hope of his recovery. My chief fear is that Florence will break down as she is too unselfish to conserve her strength – although I went to the King's Arms [the Dorchester hotel] as I found that I could not be helpful in the house.

At the King's Arms Cockerell talked on the telephone at length to a man at *The Times* about the reporting of Hardy's expected death and arrangements to be made. At Max Gate the next day he was told that Hardy had suffered a disturbed night but was a little better in the morning, and had even written a cheque for his subscription to the Society of Authors. It was the last he wrote. Barrie made a flying visit in the afternoon and urged Cockerell to stay on in Dorset as the two men walked together to the station. Some years later Barrie told Florence that during the walk to the station Cockerell urged him to agree to the idea that Hardy should be buried in Poets' Corner in Westminster Abbey rather than at Stinsford, as he requested in his will.[27]

Neither Cockerell nor Barrie was allowed to see Hardy. That evening Hardy asked Florence to read him 'Rabbi ben Ezra', Browning's poem in which he gives a voice to the twelfth-century scholar poet: 'Grow old along with me! / The best is yet to be, / The last of life, for which the first was made.' He listened intently to the whole of it and had a better night. In the morning of 11 January, Cockerell arrived to find a much more cheerful atmosphere in the house and a belief that Hardy was doing better. He was weak, but he had eaten his breakfast with pleasure.[28]

Nellie, the maid who had served Hardy for six years, was with him in his bedroom that morning, and he asked her to make him the foods of his childhood, kettle-broth and bacon grilled on the fire as his mother had cooked it.

Mr Hardy's last meal before he died was kettle-broth, of which he was very fond. He always asked for it when out-of-sorts. Kettle-broth was made from finely chopped parsley, onions and bread cooked in hot water. He had specially asked me for this on the morning of his death-day. He preferred my preparation, as I chopped the ingredients smaller than cook. He also asked for a rasher of bacon to be cooked in front of him in the flame of his bedroom coal-fire. While I cooked the bacon he quietly watched from his bed. He drank the broth, but could not eat the rasher. He only picked at that.[29]

Those who saw him thought he seemed stronger, except for his sister Kate, who called and thought 'he is not going to be here long. He looks like father and altogether I cannot blind myself to what is coming.'[30] He ate some grapes from a large bunch sent from London and said gaily 'I'm going on with these.' Then he dictated to Florence two rough and rude epitaphs on disliked contemporaries. One was George Moore, who had attacked him and was now accused of conceit. The other, ungrammatical but clear in its intentions, went for G. K. Chesterton:

> The literary contortionist
> Who prove and never turn a hair
> That Darwin's theories were a snare . . .
> And if one with him could not see
> He'd shout his choice word 'Blasphemy'.

It was his final word against Church doctrine and in favour of rational thinking, exemplified by Darwin – a magnificent blast from the sickbed.

As the afternoon darkened to dusk he fell silent, then asked Florence to read a verse from FitzGerald's *Omar Khayyám*:

> Oh, Thou, who Man of baser Earth didst make
> And who with Eden didst devise the Snake;
> For all the Sin wherewith the Face of Man
> Is blacken'd, Man's Forgiveness give – and take!

Dr Mann came as usual at 7.30 and Hardy talked to him cheerfully about recovering. After he had left, towards nine o'clock, Hardy had a heart attack. Eva was in the room with him as it happened. He spoke some confused words and, when she tried to take his pulse, asked, 'Eva, what is this?' It was death, coming to him as she held his hand in hers. His long life, which had begun early on a June morning, ended in the darkness of midwinter, when it is easiest to die.

Epilogue

Hardy's wish, expressed in his will, was to be buried in the church-yard at Stinsford. There his parents, his grandparents, his sister and Emma lay, in a green and peaceful place he had known from his earliest childhood and which over the years took on a sacred significance for him – sacred to memory, to family, to tradition and to love. Friends who visited it with him saw how he lingered there, reluctant to leave, discussing the gravestones and sometimes pointing to where his own body was to lie.

Sydney Cockerell had other ideas altogether. They came out of his conviction that Thomas Hardy, as a great English writer for whom he was particularly responsible as friend and literary executor, should be buried in Westminster Abbey. He was a man to whom the public realm meant more than private sensitivity, and words like 'he belongs to the nation' were brought out to justify his actions. His intentions were good, but what came out of them was a muddle which might have been comic had it not been hideous and false.

Dr Mann was not in the room at the moment of Hardy's death, and it is not certain that Florence was, but Nellie was in the dressing room and heard his last question to Eva.[1] The doctor was summoned back, and, after he had arrived and assured himself that Hardy was dead, Cockerell was told, and went into the kitchen to tell the cook and the maids. This done, he went with Dr Mann in his car into Dorchester and telephoned Barrie and *The Times*, evidently unwilling to use the Max Gate telephone. He returned to comfort 'the brave unselfish widow', sat up with her into the small hours and then attempted to sleep in a chair in the dining room.

Henry and Kate Hardy learnt of their brother's death only in the morning. They had been telephoned the night before, but they kept early hours and did not answer calls once they had gone to bed. As soon as they heard, from Nellie, who bicycled over, they came to Max Gate and saw their brother's body, with its 'triumphant look'.[2] By then Cockerell, in spite of his uncomfortable night, had already studied the will, agreed with Barrie that Hardy's written wishes should be ignored and set in train the arrangements for a funeral at Westminster Abbey. He had gone early to the King's Arms to resume his telephoning, and also talked to several journalists who turned up there. Then, returning to Max Gate, he had to argue with Henry Hardy, who became very upset when he heard of the Westminster Abbey plan and strongly opposed it. Kate was easier to talk round; and in any case the arrangements were all now under way. Cockerell helped Eva Dugdale wrap Hardy in his scarlet Cambridge Doctor's gown, observing that his expression was 'noble, majestic and serene, that of The Happy Warrior'.

A further problem arose when the Abbey indicated that it was not prepared for a ceremony such as had taken place for Dickens or Tennyson, whose bodies were buried under the floor, but that Hardy's body must be cremated first, so that they need give space only to a small urn containing his ashes. The idea of cremation had never been entertained by Hardy or his family, and this caused further distress.

On Friday telegrams of condolence arrived from King George and the Prince of Wales. The Prime Minister, Baldwin, the editor of *The Times* and the Dean of Westminster were now all in agreement about an Abbey funeral and Poets' Corner, and Florence was swept along by Cockerell's insistence that Hardy belonged to the nation as well as to his family. Worse followed. The vicar of Stinsford called to express his sympathy, and came up with the gruesome suggestion that Hardy's heart should be cut out and buried where he had asked to be laid. Incredibly, this was accepted by Florence, although she later denied that she had consented to it; but she was distressed and confused.

Cockerell's diary for Friday, 13 January, is silent on this part of the plan, but contains the surprising information that journalists were allowed in to view Hardy's body – something Florence later told T. E. Lawrence was 'without my knowledge or consent'.[3] It reads:

Another very busy morning seeing the undertaker, seeing journalists, five of them came to see the body, and telephoning to London about arrangements. Mrs Hardy full of doubt as to the decision to bury in the Abbey, instead of at Stinsford, but confesses that her doubts would have been equally great if the decision had been the other way about.

Cockerell was on the midday train to London and went straight to Macmillan's to make further arrangements for the service at the Abbey. After this he went to the crematorium to choose an urn for Hardy's ashes and decide on the inscription.

On the evening of the 13th Dr Mann came with the local surgeon, Nash-Wortham, and Mary Eastment, the young operating theatre Sister from Dorchester hospital, reluctantly giving up her off-duty time and unimpressed by the occasion. Hardy's heart was extracted from his chest and wrapped in a small towel. They had no container, so a biscuit tin was brought up from the kitchen. It was taken away by Mann to his house – why, nobody knows – and brought back to Max Gate, still in the biscuit tin, the following day, to be moved into a 'burial casket'. A persistent story that the doctor's cat had knocked the tin off the mantelpiece and attacked the heart was denied by Dr Mann; it may have originated in the pubs of Dorchester, where macabre jokes were no doubt appreciated. In any case the tin was back at Max Gate the next day and its contents transferred into the burial casket.[4] Gosse, when he heard what had been done, called it 'medieval butchery', but tactfully made no public comment.[5]

Cockerell went to Barrie's London flat that night, intending to return to Dorchester, where he had left his black suit, and to travel with Hardy's body to Woking Crematorium. It seems that no one else was expected to accompany the body there. On Saturday morning, however, Cockerell had a telegram from his invalid wife summoning him home to Cambridge, where he found her suffering from severe and exhausting pain. He remained in Cambridge and organized two nurses to come from London to look after her, while Barrie went to Dorchester in his place, with instructions to bring back Cockerell's black clothes with him. Early the next morning Barrie went with the first hearse to Woking, attended the cremation and travelled on to London with Hardy's ashes in the urn chosen by Cockerell, delivering it to those in charge at the Abbey. He kept with him a small wreath of lilies entrusted to him by Florence when he left Max Gate, which he carried into the Abbey two days later.

All this time there were journalists hanging about Dorchester. One managed to interview Hardy's 84-year-old cousin Theresa at Bockhampton and report her disapproval not only of the Abbey burial, away from his own people, but of his having taken up writing in the first place. On Monday, the day of the two funerals, there were dozens of press men and photographers gathered outside Max Gate early in the morning, and when the second hearse came for the heart they followed it up to the house. Bertie the gardener told them to leave the grounds, and they retreated, but when the undertaker came out to lay narcissi in the hearse, followed by the bearers with the casket, and by Florence, the photographers advanced again and she felt she had to hide in the porch.[6] Once the hearse had gone, she set off with Kate Hardy and Dr Mann for the London train. At Waterloo, Cockerell met them and drove with them to Dean's Yard, where they were given sandwiches and coffee before going into the Abbey. The service began at two.

Henry had stayed in Dorset to attend the burial of his brother's heart at Stinsford, also attended by Gertrude Bugler. There were crowds of curious local people and some friendly neighbours, and the sun shone, while in London rain poured down on the crowds outside the Abbey.

Inside, the floor of Poets' Corner was covered with a white-edged purple carpet with a small oblong hole in the centre, also edged in white, where the urn was to go. Ten pallbearers were assembled, the Prime Minister, Baldwin, and the leader of the opposition, Ramsay MacDonald, the heads of Magdalene College, Cambridge, and Queen's College, Oxford, and six writers: Housman, Kipling, Shaw, Barrie, Galsworthy and Gosse. To make sense of such a procession, the urn had been placed inside a coffin-like container covered with a white satin cloth and laid on a bier, beside which the 'elderly gentlemen, rather red and stiff' processed.[7] Kipling and Shaw had never met and were introduced to one another by Gosse in the Abbey: it was probably their only meeting. Charlotte Shaw described the occasion in a letter to T. E. Lawrence in India:

I went 35 minutes early and found nearly all the places filled up, but got a seat almost in the middle of the south transept. The burial was at the south end of the south transept . . . It seemed absurd to have an immense bier and a great and splendid pall, white, embroidered with royal crowns and many other emblems, to enclose one small casket, but it made its effect.

The service was very beautifully sung, and I have never heard anything better read than the lesson 'Let us now praise famous men'. When the procession came down the south transept they all passed quite near me. I was curiously impressed by Baldwin. I had never seen him before; he is far stronger than I thought. He was the only one who looked entirely unimpressed. I almost fancied he looked amused. I was terribly afraid GBS would act: but no. He did it perfectly. Kipling I thought sinister.

The clergy came first and shocked me. All except one looked full of worldly pomp and disdain; self-conscious jacks-in-the-box – but that one, young, appeared wrapped from the world. Then came the catafalque, and after some men friends and finally Mrs Hardy with Mr Cockerell. The first time they passed she looked sweet and calm, but was so completely swathed in crape that her face was invisible; as she passed [again?] she was hanging on Mr Cockerell's arm, and seemed completely broken. The service at the grave must have been terribly trying for her. All the rest of the time, they tell me, she was hidden in some recess; but there, of course, she had to stand out prominently. Mr Cockerell was splendid: a rock of strength and most dignified. He gives the impression (sometimes) of restrained emotion, but I don't think he feels anything very deeply really . . .

Then a wonderful thing came. On that glorious organ an almost divine organist played the Dead March from 'Saul'. I say advisedly that was among the most splendid things of my life. He began very low and soft and gradually opened out, making one's whole being thrill to each great phrase up to a most marvellous burst of great chords – confident, assertive, triumphant. Ah! it takes Handel to say the last word.[8]

Her husband, GBS, was less impressed. He remembered chiefly that, 'As we marched, pretending to carry the ashes of whatever part of Hardy was buried in the Abbey, Kipling, who fidgeted continually and was next in front of me, kept changing his step. Every time he did so I nearly fell over him.'[9]

So Hardy was treated to two religious burials, neither of them what he had wanted. Florence and Kate were given what Kate described as 'another crumb and a taste of tea' at Barrie's flat and put smartly on the 4.30 train back to Dorchester. It had been an exhausting day for them and one in which they had been denied any part in the arrangements. Mrs Woolf spent the evening with Bloomsbury friends, listening to Lytton Strachey blacken Hardy's reputation, his novels 'the poorest of poor stuff', etc.[10] On the day of the funeral the Dean of Westminster wrote to the vicar of Fordington, the Revd R. G. Bartelot, Emma's old friend and ally, to inquire about Hardy's spiritual status:

My permission to bury T. Hardy in Wr Abbey has given rise to a great deal of controversy. I am receiving every day furious protests on the ground that his teaching was antichristian: that he himself was not a Christian (!): that his moral standard was low etc. etc. etc. I should take no notice of wild talk of this kind: but today I have received a letter from the head of a great religious body – which I must answer. I knew little of T.H. beyond his writings, but a mutual friend of his and mine has a very high opinion of his essential Christianity and went so far as to describe him to me as a 'determined Churchman'.

Can you tell me what the truth really is – as to his own faith and practice and as to his moral standards.

I have no qualms about allowing his burial in Wr Abbey myself but I want material with which to confute his assailants.[11]

Bartelot wrote back at once testifying to Hardy's having been 'at heart a Christian and a Churchman', although he had not actually attended his church once in twenty-one years. His grounds for saying so were that he gave donations to church funds, had been observed joining in the Lord's Prayer and the Creed on occasion, had never formally recanted the Christianity conferred by christening and had lived a life of absolute moral rectitude. The testimonial would have made Hardy smile.

William Rothenstein, who had made a sketch of the pallbearers standing together in the Abbey, showed it to Gosse and to Florence, who were keen for him to make a proper record of the scene. The Prime Minister was easily persuaded to sit, but Housman and Barrie both made difficulties and after much negotiation Rothenstein gave up the project as too troublesome and tiresome, to Gosse's indignation and Florence's disappointment.[12] Henry Hardy, who hoped to build a memorial tower of his own design for his brother, did not achieve it and died at the end of the year.

Hardy's will caused a stir when it was published because no one had expected him to have an estate of nearly £100,000. He made small bequests to animal charities but nothing to any Dorchester ones. Like many people who live longer than they expect to, he had failed to bring his will up to date, so that his brother and sister, both old and childless, were left with much more money than they needed. To Florence went all his royalties, an annuity of £600 a year and Max Gate with everything in it; a clause, standard in rich men's wills and supposed to deter fortune hunters who prey on widows, halved her annuity should she marry again. Five months after the funeral, on 14 June, she told Cockerell that she and Barrie were to be married the following year. Cockerell put an exclamation mark after the entry in his diary and wrote 'A secret'.[13] In the autumn she took a flat close to Barrie's at Adelphi Terrace, and they saw a great deal of one another. Presently he managed to withdraw from his proposal, and Florence, humiliated, returned to Max Gate; although the friendship survived, it was not the same. With Cockerell the situation quickly became disastrous. He and Florence, joint literary executors, disagreed about memorials and publications; she thought him overbearing, and he found her devious. Within two years of Hardy's death they had quarrelled so badly that they were barely able to communicate, even by letter.

They had at least managed to bring out Hardy's last collection of poetry, *Winter Words*, which appeared in October and went into a second impression. She also published both volumes of the biographical work she and Hardy had prepared, *The Early Life of Thomas Hardy* in November 1928 and *The Later Years* in 1930, under her own name as agreed with him. They were respectfully received but did not arouse much interest or sell well.[14]

In 1930 a novel by Somerset Maugham appeared, *Cakes and Ale*, cruelly entertaining about the literary world and construed by many to be a portrait of Hardy and a mockery of his second wife. It became a bestseller, and, although the central figure is nothing like Hardy, it caused Florence intense distress, especially as she suspected supposed friends such as Sassoon of supplying Maugham with information about her. Bruised and sad, she devoted herself to good works in Dorchester and remained at Max Gate, the house she had always hated. A dull statue of Hardy was put up in Dorchester in 1931. The deaths of T. E. Lawrence in an accident in 1935 and of Barrie two years later were further blows to Florence. By then she was ill with cancer of the bowel, and she too died, a few months after Barrie, aged only fifty-eight. She had survived her old husband by less than ten years, a woman of many sorrows who had devoted herself to him and served him well but found no joy in her life.

The world was sliding into war again. Max Gate was put on the market, and Kate Hardy, the last of the family, bought it. When she died in 1940, she left it to the National Trust, and in 1948 the National Trust was able to acquire Hardy's birthplace. Max Gate is now at the edge of town with busy roads close by, but Higher Bockhampton still seems remote. Visitors come from all over the world to see the two houses, and the meadows, woods, rivers and lanes that were Hardy's home territory, and to walk the territory of his novels.

The wrongness of the two funerals and the wretchedness of Florence's later years bring a sombre end to any account of Hardy. They are also a reminder of how much awkwardness there was in his life. To rise out of a poor country family to a high place in literature and society took fierce willpower and intensive effort over many years, and had he not been a solitary and inward-looking boy, and remained so as a man, he might not have achieved it. It may also be that his powerful mother's warning to her children not to marry was good advice, because, although he felt the romance of love, wanted a wife, and twice married women he desired and valued, he did not know how to be an easily companionable and loving husband. He and they suffered also from having no children, and both wives grew lonely and bitter. Even when he fell in love with Florence Henniker, he could not find a way to win her. So, while he explored the dream of love in his writing, he lived more of its disappointments and frustrations.

Always his inner life took precedence over everything else. And from the inner life came the great panorama of the novels – books not perfectly written or plotted but full of curious and arresting perceptions, sublime moments, wilful and tragic men and women who impose themselves by their originality and their vivid human presence. There is Henry Knight hanging on to the cliff by his fingernails, while Elfride strips off her clothes in the rain to make a rope to rescue him. There is Viviette cutting a curl from the head of the sleeping boy she desires. There are the London servants leaping over the furniture in the drawing room in a silent game of cat-and-mice as their master and mistress dine with guests below. Gabriel watches the stars in the winter sky and feels the earth turn, Giles carries his apple tree like a god from the ancient world. Bathsheba appears in her red jacket and astride her horse, bending herself right back with her feet on the horse's shoulders to avoid the low branches as she rides under the trees. There is Mrs Yeobright seeing the sunset flight of the heron before she dies, and Henchard looking at his own drowned body in the mill pool. Tess with her arms cool from the curds in the dairy, and Jude giving a voice to the despair of the working man who hears only 'You shan't' when he tries for something better than what he has.

From the inner life also came the poems with which this book began, and which make an essential part of the narrative of his life. His voice as a poet is as individual as a fingerprint, but his sense of history, his curiosity and powers of observation make him at home with a vast range of subjects, and surprises spring off the page when you look through any of his volumes. He will write about the noise of a passing car or about a station waiting room as well as about his perpetual delight in the natural world of plants growing and decaying, of weather, birds, insects, wind, moonlight, sunshine and starlight. He describes what he sees from his window, and what he fears might come into his room, and what he cannot see except in his mind's eye, like the woman who knows that the outline of her son remains on the wall even after it has been whitewashed over. So he shows us the snails crushed under the wheels of the gun carriages at Waterloo, the southern stars above the grave of the drummer boy, the spirits of the village dead joking together, and the ghost-girl-rider he once knew and still loves.

The poems also act as a long-running conversation with himself, in which he can ponder, argue and joke, whether about Einstein's theories, the wit of a country girl who becomes a London prostitute or how his own death will release his wife from his old man's querulousness:

> It will be much better when
> I am under the bough;
> I shall be more myself, Dear, then,
> Than I am now.[15]

He did not take an exalted view of himself as a writer and did not mind writing occasional pieces to order, or saying that he hoped that some of his poems would earn a place in anthologies (as many have). He had, after all, learnt a great deal about poetry and how it might be written and enjoyed from the *Golden Treasury* presented to him when he was twenty-two by his friend Horace Moule. His modesty did not make him hesitate to take on the central themes of human experience, time, memory, loss, love, fear, grief, anger, uncertainty, death. He knew the past like a man who has lived more than one span of life, and he understood how difficult it is to cast aside the beliefs of your forebears. At the same time he faced his own extinction with no wish to be comforted and no hope of immortality. He wrote honest poems, almost every one shaped and structured with its own thought and its own music.

They remind us that he was a fiddler's son, with music in his blood and bone, who danced to his father's playing before he learnt to write. This is how I like to think of him, a boy dancing on the stone cottage floor, outside time, oblivious, ecstatic, with his future greatness as unimaginable as the sorrows that came with it.

Abbreviations

Biography Revisited	*Thomas Hardy: A Biography Revisited*, Michael Millgate (2004)
DCM	Dorset County Museum
DCRO	Dorset County Record Office
Interviews and Recollections	*Thomas Hardy: Interviews and Recollections*, ed. James Gibson (1999)
Letters	*The Collected Letters of Thomas Hardy*, ed. R. L. Purdy and Michael Millgate (7 vols., 1978–88)
Letters of E & F Hardy	*The Letters of Emma and Florence Hardy*, ed. Michael Millgate (1996)
Life	*The Life and Work of Thomas Hardy*, Thomas Hardy, ed. Michael Millgate (1984)
The Older TH	*The Older Hardy*, Robert Gittings (1978)
Variorum Poems	*The Variorum Edition of the Complete Poems of Thomas Hardy*, ed. James Gibson (1979)
The Young TH	*Young Thomas Hardy*, Robert Gittings (1975)

Notes

Prologue

1. 'Dolly' Gale of Piddlehinton, a wheelwright's daughter and one of twelve children, was born in 1897, left school in 1911, saw an advertisement for a job as a maid with the Hardys, wrote off and bicycled over to be interviewed. She immediately liked Mrs Hardy and found her 'considerate and kindly'. She disliked him. She said she never saw or heard them speak to each other in the year she spent there. She worked for them for about a year, leaving after Mrs Hardy's death. She married and moved to Canada, where she was known as Alice Harvey, and she gave her recollections to J. Stevens Cox, who interviewed her in Ontario and wrote up the interview in *The Thomas Hardy Year Book* (St Peter Port, 1973–4). It must be remembered with this, as with other interviews given decades after the events described, that few people have perfect recall.

2. The placing of the coffin in his bedroom is described by Dolly Gale, ibid.

3. TH to Edward Clodd, 13 Dec. 1912, *Letters*, IV, 239.

4. *Life*, Chapter 32. Hardy explains that he has adopted the description of being 'in flower' as a poet from Walpole's description of Gray.

5. 'At Castle Boterel'. On the MS he first wrote 'Boscastle: Cornwall'.

6. All of these quotes are from 'Poems of 1912–13'. Hardy changed the 'clodded' to 'jailing' – I prefer the first version.

7. TH to Florence Henniker, 17 July 1914, *Letters*, V, 37–8.

8. The words are taken from the *Aeneid*, Book IV, line 23, where Dido explains that the love she once felt for her husband, now dead, will revive for Aeneas. In Book VI Aeneas, who has betrayed Dido's love by abandoning her, so that she kills herself, encounters her silent ghost on his visit to Hades. J. Hillis Miller points out that the silence of Dido's ghost is echoed in Hardy making the ghost of Emma 'voiceless' in 'After a Journey': see *Thomas Hardy: Distance*

and Desire (1970), 248–9. There were originally eighteen poems, to which Hardy added three more in later editions.

9. There is also a faint echo of Donne's 'Twicknam Garden' ('Blasted with sighs and surrounded with tears / Hither I come to seek the spring') in the line 'Hereto I come to view a voiceless ghost.' Edmund Gosse had given Hardy an edition of the poems of John Donne for his birthday in the summer of 1908. See his letter of thanks, 24 July 1908, 'The Donne has arrived and is just the type for my eyes . . . 1000 thanks.' *Letters*, III, 326.

10. *Letters of Ezra Pound*, ed. D. D. Page (1950), 386, Pound writing to John Lackay Brown [n.d. but Apr. 1937], about Hardy's *Collected Poems*.

11. Sydney Cockerell noted Florence Hardy's remark to him in his diary for 24 Sept. 1916. British Library Add. MSS 52653.

12. From the unpublished diary kept by Arthur Benson, Nov. 1913, by permission of the Master and Fellows of Magdalene College, Cambridge.

13. TH to Florence Henniker, 23 Dec. 1914, *Letters*, V, 70–71. 'When I Set Out for Lyonnesse' is in *Satires of Circumstance* but not among the 'Poems of 1912–13'; nor is 'Under the Waterfall', based on Emma's own account of losing their picnic glass in the summer of 1870. 'Lost Love' and 'My Spirit Will Not Haunt the Mound' are also about Emma.

14. *New Statesman*, 23 Dec. 1914.

15. 'Days to Recollect', first published in *Human Shows, Far Phantasies, Songs and Trifles*, 1925. 'On a Discovered Curl of Hair' was written in Feb. 1913 but not published until 1922 in *Late Lyrics and Earlier*.

16. This is from 'Penance', first published in 1922 in *Late Lyrics and Earlier*.

PART ONE   1840–1867

1. Mother

1. *Life*, Chapter 1, first section. A surgeon is mentioned, but that is likely to be an embellishment, as cottage deliveries at this time were rarely presided over by doctors or surgeons. *Life* was written in the third person, since the author was ostensibly Hardy's widow.

2. ibid.

3. ibid.

4. Hardy told Sydney Cockerell on 23 Aug. 1925 that 'his mother had wished to call him Christopher, and that he wished he had had that name as there were so many Thomas Hardys.' Cockerell's diary for 1925, British Library Add. MSS 52662.

5. The 1801 census for Melbury Osmond is in the DCRO and shows Elizabeth Swetman, 'Spinner', living with her father, who was in Agricultural Husbandry, mother not working, and brother John employed like his father. See also *Life*, first section of Chapter 1.

6. The 1801 census shows 'George Hann', with some doubt about the spelling, in the household of the Revd Jenkins (DCRO).

7. Betty Hand to her daughter Mary, letter 17 Jan. 1842, in which she complains of her poverty separating her from her children, worries about her son Christopher's brutal treatment of his pregnant wife and expresses her love for her grandson 'Tomey', i.e., little Thomas Hardy. DCM, Kate Hardy and Lock Collection.

8. TH to Frederic Harrison, 20 June 1918, *Letters*, V, 269.

9. Even if she went to school, as a girl she would have been made to concentrate on knitting, sewing and mending. A school founded in Dorchester in 1813 did not allow girls to learn either writing or ciphering (arithmetic) until they were ten and could already knit stockings, read the Bible fluently, repeat the Catechism and do 'all sorts of common plain work'.

10. Personal communication from John Antell, great-grandson of Jemima's younger sister Mary Hand and her husband, John Antell of Puddletown.

11. Kate Hardy to cousin Jim Sparks, 2 Dec. 1902, Sparks Archive, Hardy Collection, Eton College.

12. E.g., to her sister Martha after she emigrated to Canada. In July 1870 TH's first cousin Louisa Sharpe, daughter of Jemima's sister Martha, wrote to Jemima from Canada recalling how TH had written for his mother on 11 Jan. 1858: 'a letter from you written by my cousin Thomas dated Jan. 11 1858'. DCM, H. 1975.316.30.

13. Henry Moule was appointed to Fordington, a village with a rough population, so close to Dorchester that it had become part of it. He had seven sons, of whom Horace particularly was Hardy's friend.

16. TH to Lytton Strachey, 20 Apr. 1921, thanking him for the gift of his book on Queen Victoria. *Letters*, VI, 84.

15. Caroline Leonora Murray married Lord Ilchester in 1812 and died in childbirth at Melbury House in January 1819, her death recorded in the diary of Lady Susan O'Brien, her husband's aunt, according to her sister Amelia Matilda Murray's *Recollections, from 1803 to 1837* (1868).

16. Amelia Matilda Murray, *Recollections*. Miss Murray lived from 1795 to 1884 and was the fourth daughter of Lord George Murray (1761–1803), Bishop of St David's, who invented and organized the first telegraphic communication. In acknowledgement of this, Pitt gave a pension to his widow after his early death, and a dowry of £70 to each of his daughters.

17. She seems to have gone with her previous employer too, but she specified the time of her last visit when she went through London with her son in 1849. See *Life*, Chapter 1, section 'A Journey': 'Mrs Hardy had not been to London since she had lived there for some months twelve years earlier.'

18. *Life*, first section of Chapter 1: 'She resolved to be a cook in a London club-house; but her plans in this direction were ended by her meeting her future husband, and being married to him at the age of five-and-twenty.' (In fact, she was twenty-six when she married.)

19. It happens that Hardy drew a plan of Stinsford House in his architectural notebook, and it shows that the library was one of the largest rooms. A facsimile of Hardy's architectural notebook in the DCM

was published in 1966 with notes by C. J. Beatty. The plan of Stinsford House is on p. 44.

20. Dr F. B. Fisher, quoted in *Life in Thomas Hardy's Dorchester 1888–1908*, (Beaminster, 1965), 21.

21. Handley Moule, *Memories of a Vicarage* (1913), 67.

22. Jo Draper's booklet *Regency, Riot and Reform* (2000) gives a useful summary.

23. Entry dated 30 Oct. 1870, *The Personal Notebooks of Thomas Hardy*, ed. Richard H. Taylor (1978), 'Memoranda, I', 6–7.

24. He died in 1852.

25. Celia Barclay suggests in her study of Thomas Hardy's cousin, *Nathaniel Sparks: Memoirs of Thomas Hardy's Cousin the Engraver* (1994), 30, that Jemima went back to the Maiden Newton vicarage after Murray moved to London and worked as a cook for 'Hon. William Scott MA', and the information must have come through the Sparks family, i.e., her sister Maria, brother-in-law James and their children.

26. *Life*, Chapter 20, taken from diary entry for 14 Aug. 1892.

27. Census for 1841. Shirley kept four servants. He married later.

28. Robert Gittings in *The Young TH* suggests Kingston Maurward House, 7.

29. The 1841 Census gives Herbert Williams, banker, aged thirty-four, with wife, Marie, aged thirty-five, and seven servants.

30. See Celia Barclay, *op. cit.*, 30–31.

31. *Life*, Chapter 20, entry for 4 Aug. 1892.

32. *Life*, first section of Chapter 1, for her wanting to be a cook in London. For her remark about rustic and quaint country neighbours, May O'Rourke reports Hardy telling her this about his mother, *Hardyana* (1966), 8–12.

33. Hardy told this to Edmund Blunden in July 1922, as he related in *The Great Victorians*, 'Notes on Visits to Thomas Hardy', cited in *Interviews and Recollections*, 171.

34. *Life*, Chapter 35, reporting a speech made by Hardy on opening Bockhampton Reading Room and Club on 2 Dec. 1919. He also spoke of there having been a water mill, homes for parish paupers, predating the workhouse system, and old Elizabethan houses of stone, with mullioned windows, near the withy bed.

35. Hardy pointed out the pit to Sydney Cockerell on Wednesday, 30 June 1926, telling him that his father had helped the smugglers. British Library Add. MSS 52663.

36. The story, set in the 1830s, was first published in 1879 in the *New Quarterly Magazine* and in America in *Harper's Weekly*. It was collected in *Wessex Tales*.

37. See Robert Gittings *The Older TH*, 55–6. He found in the parish register that Hardy's great-grandmother had an illegitimate son who died in infancy, and that in 1796 a girl was born to a Mary Head and a John Reed, baptized seven years later, in 1803, as Georgiana Reed at St Mary's, Reading, and presumably given up by Mary Head, who then moved south to Dorset, where she met her future husband, Thomas Hardy. Other parts of Gittings's research which appeared to link Mary Head's story with that of *Tess* have been shown by Michael Millgate to be inaccurate.

38. Fanny Robin is the maid whom Sergeant Troy deserts to marry her mistress, Bathsheba, in *Far from the Madding Crowd*. Tess is the heroine of *Tess of the D'Urbervilles*, seduced by her 'cousin' Alec. She calls her baby 'Sorrow' and baptizes him herself before he dies.

39. TH to Florence Henniker, 27 Oct. 1918, *Letters*, V, 283.

2.   Child

1. He would certainly have learnt later that, although in Christian imagery the snake is a symbol of evil, in Greek mythology it signifies fertility and wisdom.

2. Opening words of *Life*. The census lists twenty-two children in Higher Bockhampton alone, with many more in the surrounding area.

3. *Hardyana* (1969), 229. Interview with Harold Voss.

4. He told Sydney Cockerell about hearing his parents on 12 Jan. 1927. British Library Add. MSS 52664.

5. *Life*, Chapter 38, section 'Notes by F. E. H.'.

6. TH made the handkerchief rabbit for Middleton Murry's daughter in the 1920s, and said he had not done it or seen it done for seventy-five years. *Interviews and Recollections*, 159.

7. Timothy Hands, *Thomas Hardy: Distracted Preacher?* (1989), 5 and note. Stinsford Church accounts for 1842 to 1871 show that Hardy's father was paid sums of up to £15 a year for work he did for the church.

8. J. Stevens Cox in *Hardyana* (1964), 56, on apples grown at Bockhampton. On 12 June 1913 Mary Hardy wrote to TH saying their brother Henry's garden was like their father's, listing the vegetables in order: large beds of carrots, onions and parsnips, a patch of broad beans, a line of peas and potatoes recently hoed up. DCM, H.1975.316.22.

9. *Life*, Chapter 38, section 'Notes by F. E. H.'.

10. *Life*, Chapter 1, first section.

11. Michael Millgate, *Thomas Hardy: A Biography* (1982), 38, Note 34, gives a reference to G. H. Moule, *Stinsford Church and Parish* (Dorchester, 1940), 27–8.

12. Sydney Cockerell noted Hardy's words about the skull on 30 June 1926 when they drove to Stinsford and Bockhampton and past his first school. British Library Add. MSS 52663. It is a grisly one.

13. *Life*, Chapter 1, first section.

14. *Life*, Chapter 16, passage from journal dated 15–21 Oct. 1888.

15. Both stories in *Life*, Chapter 1.

16. Hardy told this to the publisher Newman Flower in his seventies. *Interviews and Recollections*, 176.

17. Hardy told T. E. Lawrence this story in 1925. *Interviews and Recollections*, 184.

18. *Life*, Chapter 1.

19. TH to William Archer in interview of 1901, *Interviews and Recollections*, 68. Hardy also said, in a speech made in 1910 on accepting the freedom of Dorchester, that he had seen a man in the stocks in Dorchester 'in the back part of this very building'.

20. *Life*, Chapter 1, section 'Birth and Boyhood 1849–50'.

21. 'The Roman Road' in *Time's Laughingstocks and Other Verses* (1909).

22. *Life*, Chapter 1, section 'Birth and Boyhood 1849–50'.

23. 'Childhood among the Ferns' was first printed in the *Daily Telegraph* on 29 Mar. 1928 and collected in *Winter Words in Various Moods and Metres* (1928).

24. *Life*, Chapter 1, first section.
25. Celia Barclay, *Nathaniel Sparks: Memoirs of Thomas Hardy's Cousin the Engraver* (1994), 32.
26. The MS letter signed 'Mary', dated Hitchin, 11 Dec. 1846, begins 'My dear Mother'. DCM.
27. He lived from 1816 to 1878, had four children and became an alcoholic. By family tradition he was one of the inspirations for Jude.
28. They were a couple, John and Martha Horsman, according to the 1851 Census. The attractive school building is still standing, but is now a private house and somewhat changed.
29. Contributory evidence to the supposition that Jemima was not a confident writer.
30. *Life*, Chapter 7. Hardy cancelled the passage, but it has been restored in later editions.
31. Hardy's words in *Life*, Chapter 1, section 'A Journey'.
32. The third-class fare on the London and South Western Railway in 1850 was 3 s. for an excursion train, which meant travelling in open carriages.
33. So he told Stewart M. Ellis in 1913, who described the conversation in an article in the *Fortnightly Review*, Mar. 1928, just after Hardy's death. Cited in *Interviews and Recollections*, 110.
34. TH letter to Florence Dugdale, 18 Nov. 1909, about the actress playing Bathsheba in a production of *Far from the Madding Crowd*: 'she gave the real B. quite startlingly to me, seeming just like my handsome aunt from whom I drew her.' *Letters*, IV, 58.
35. *Life*, Chapter 1, 'A Journey'.
36. In the DCM.
37. *Life*, Chapter 1, section 'Birth and Boyhood 1849–50'.
38. The census for 1851, taken in June, shows that Kingston Maurward House was empty.

3.   The Bookish Boy

1. We don't know where his Bockhampton cousins, the children of his uncle James Hardy, were educated, but one of them, Augustus,

a year older than Thomas, left Dorset, settled in Twickenham and raised his children there. One of his sons, Henry, became an Anglican clergyman, and *his* son Basil Augustus went to Oxford and became head of the choir school of Chester Cathedral. Augustus died in 1916, and Hardy wrote a letter of condolence to the eldest son, Albert; and there is a sparse occasional exchange of letters, initiated by the Revd Henry, who invited Hardy to visit him in Fifeshire in 1906 when he went to Aberdeen – Hardy declined – and sent a card for his seventy-second birthday. See *Letters*, V, 151.

Uncle James's eldest son married a local girl and the second, Walter, died as a child in 1844. The girl, Theresa, born in 1843, remained all her life at Bockhampton, eccentric, reclusive and disliked by Thomas Hardy's family.

Uncle James is known to have given violin lessons as well as being a builder. He lived until 1880, but the two families were not on close terms.

2. See, for instance, the history of Joseph Arch, whom Hardy knew and admired later when he was a trades union organizer and MP. Arch was born in Warwickshire in 1826. His father owned his own cottage, and his mother was a strong-willed, intelligent woman – she had been a nurse and laundress at Warwick Castle – but Arch got only three years of schooling and went to work when he was nine, scaring crows in the fields for a farmer twelve hours a day for fourpence (the experience Hardy gave to Jude). The best his mother could do for him was to encourage him to read in the evening, and she died early. He worked his way up as a ploughboy and hedge-cutter. He wrote his own *Life* (1898).

3. James Savage, *History of Dorchester* (1832) gives the time of the arrival of the London post and the name of the local paper, *Dorset County Chronicle and Somersetshire Gazette*, in full, founded in 1821.

4. Savage, *op. cit.* The theatre was put up in Back West Street in 1828 by the theatre manager Henry Lee.

5. Captain Frederick Hovenden, in charge of defence measures during risings of 1830, to the Home Office, from Barbara Kerr, *Bound to the Soil: A Social History of Dorset 1750–1918* (1968).

6. For Hardy pulling the carriage, *Life*, 50, giving Florence Hardy as

source, in conversation with R. L. Purdy and written down by him in his private notes, 1931. A search of the electoral registers shows that Hardy's father acquired a vote only in 1885.

7. *Life*, Chapter 38, Florence Hardy's notes made after drive with TH, 4 Nov. 1927.

8. *Far from the Madding Crowd*, Chapter 39, 'On Casterbridge Highway', and Chapter 6, 'The Fair; the Journey; the Fire'.

9. *Life*, Chapter 38, Florence Hardy's notes dated 27 Oct. 1927.

10. ibid. This is Florence Hardy's rendering of his words. Robert Gittings suggests the men were smugglers sitting on their casks, although it may seem unlikely that they would hide them from a small boy. Another possibility is that they were strolling actors.

11. *A Pair of Blue Eyes*, Vol. II, Chapter 9.

12. *The Mayor of Casterbridge*, Chapter 43. *The Return of the Native*, Book 4, Chapter 5.

13. Florence Hardy to Sydney Cockerell, 14 Oct. 1917: 'My husband says he did not like going to school as a boy.' *Letters of E & F Hardy*, 133.

14. Anonymous article 'My Famous Schoolfellows' in *Sunday at Home*, 1915, reprinted in *Interviews and Recollections*, 1. Author P. claimed to have been at school with Hardy and sometimes walked home with him. Jemima Hardy described her husband and father-in-law as having curly hair in her description of their appearance when she first knew them, given to Hardy 14 Aug. 1892: see *Life*, Chapter 20.

15. Farmer Locke, talking in 1931 to Llewelyn Powys at the unveiling of the statue of Hardy in Dorchester; given in *Interviews and Recollections*, 4.

16. According to George (Dadie) Rylands, who wrote to James Gibson on 9 Nov. 1990, 'my Great Grandfather was Rector of West Stafford (next parish to Stinsford) for 60 years. He had a large family – contemporary with Hardy: who as a boy on his way to Dorchester School had a glass of milk at the Rectory and later became a close friend. One son, Bosworth, a Master at Harrow, knew him best.' True, although West Stafford was not on the direct way from Bockhampton to Dorchester. He goes on to describe his own visit to Hardy: 'It was clear that he had very warm memories of the

Stafford children in early days; I have a Golden Treasury given by one Great Uncle in memory of another to his sister Mary.' This letter is in an archive given to me by the late James Gibson.

17. Julia Green née Harding, cited in *Interviews and Recollections*, 3.

18. TH to James Murray, 9 July 1903, *Letters*, III, 70.

19. Interview with William Archer, Apr. 1901, printed in *Interviews and Recollections*, 67 (from Archer's *Real Conversations*).

20. TH to William Rothenstein, who had sent him *The Village Labourer: 1760–1832. A Study in the Government of England before the Reform Bill* (1911), by John Lawrence and Barbara Bradby Hammond, 11 Mar. 1912, *Letters*, IV, 206. Hardy said this happened soon after his return from Hatfield, i.e., in 1850, when he was nine or ten.

21. *Dorset County Chronicle*, 22 May 1834. Cited by Jo Draper in *Regency, Riot and Reform* (2000).

22. *Life*, Chapter 1, section '1852'.

23. *Biography Revisited*, 49 and note, attributes this story to Nathaniel Sparks.

24. Handley Moule recalls, in his *Memories of a Vicarage* (1913), how his father, the rector of Fordington, took him and two of his brothers by train to see the Exhibition.

25. Hardy was well informed about the trains. See his story of 1893 'The Fiddler of the Reels', in which he describes the arrival of the heroine on an 1851 excursion train from Dorchester, having travelled with her little girl in just such an open carriage. It is early summer, and they are wearing cotton dresses; both are chilled and wet through. He tells us that some of the men travelled without hats, and the women put their skirts over their heads to protect themselves from the rain, getting their hips wet and cold in the process.

26. It was suggested by Lois Deacon and Terry Coleman in *Providence and Mr Hardy* (1966), that Tryphena was Rebecca's illegitimate child, brought up as her younger sister. It is possible, but unproven in their book, and not likely to be proven or disproved at this date.

27. Lord Salisbury gave £50 towards the Sharpes' passage. I am indebted to Robin Harcourt Williams, archivist at Hatfield House, for this information.

28. Hardy told Sydney Cockerell that he had 'very little in common'

with Henry. Cockerell's diary, 17 Apr. 1916, British Library Add. MSS 52653.

29. It was supported by the British and Foreign Bible Society, a Nonconformist body, and also by the considerable Congregationalist community in and around Dorchester.

30. Hardy describes a village confirmation in Chapter 24 of *Two on a Tower*, his young hero being an unenthusiastic candidate. In Chapter 22 the villagers comment that there has not been a confirmation for twenty years in the parish, and that in the past 'The Bishops didn't lay it on so strong then as they do now. Now-a-days, yer Bishop gies both hands to every Jack-rag and Tom-straw that drops the knee afore him; but 'twas six chaps to one blessing when we was boys.' In a letter of 8 May 1923 to Arthur Benson he recalls that he was confirmed by the Bishop of Salisbury, *Letters*, VI, 194.

31. In the *Life*, Chapter 1, penultimate paragraph, Hardy says the original girl 'was by no means a model of virtue in her love-affairs', but Marian is not so characterized. She takes to alcohol when working conditions are harsh, but otherwise she is trustworthy and loyal and tries to help Tess. Her chief bond is with her friend Izzy, who becomes her companion in their travels as itinerant labourers.

32. 'Lizbie Browne' was written for the gamekeeper's daughter, Elizabeth Bishop, a lively poem with a dancing rhythm, published in his first collection, *Wessex Poems and Other Verses*. It calls up her red hair, her gaiety and bright glance, regrets his failure to woo her, being too young, says she married someone else and was happy and had no reason to remember him. 'The Passer-By' (in *Late Lyrics and Earlier*) gives Louisa a voice to describe a young man – presumably Hardy – who passed her window and blushed at the sight of her, until she came to love him but too late – he stopped passing by. 'Louie', written in July 1913 (in *Human Shows, Far Phantasies, Songs and Trifles*), raises the phantom of 'Louie the buoyant' but says 'She will never thrust the foremost figure out of view!' (the foremost figure being that of his first wife, Emma), rather a backhanded compliment. Finally 'To Louisa in the Lane', a short, late poem in *Winter Words in Various Moods and Metres*, imagines meeting her ghost in the lane where they had passed one another when young. The real Louisa never married and lived out her life in Dorchester,

but as far as we know they had no contact in later life. It was the memory of the young Louisa he cherished.

33. TH to Edmund Gosse, 22 Jan. 1920, *Letters*, VI, 3.

34. This is from Florence Hardy's letter of 3 Apr. 1937 to Morris Parish about Joshua J. Foster, a few years younger than Hardy, son of the Dorchester bookseller James Foster, listed in the 1861 Census as bookseller and printer. Florence reported that 'JJF told me this himself, and he was the only person I ever spoke to who remembered T.H. at that early age.' *Letters of E & F Hardy*, 346.

35. *Life*, Chapter 2, first paragraph.

36. ibid.: 'he had sometimes . . . wished to enter the Church.'

37. The present John Antell told me that it was well known in the family that Jemima Hardy disapproved of large families and had not wanted one herself.

38. He told his second wife, Florence, and she passed it on to R. L. Purdy in 1933. Timothy Hands has questioned whether Shirley was likely to have preached in this way, saying that both his character and the ethics of Tractarianism made it unlikely (*Thomas Hardy: Distracted Preacher?*, 1989, 10). But it seems unlikely that Hardy would have imagined it, and there is plenty of evidence of clergymen objecting to village people getting above themselves – see, for example, Joseph Arch's *Life*.

39. James Criswick, *Walks Round Dorchester* (1820).

40. TH to Lady Pinney, 20 Jan. 1926, *Letters*, VII, 5. Robert Gittings suggests in *The Young TH*, 34, that Hardy's response to the hanging 'supplied at least part of the emotional power of his best-known novel'. Gittings also accuses him of finding some sort of sexual meaning in hanged women. His ideas have been taken up by other writers, e.g., Howard Jacobson in his novel *Peeping Tom*.

41. *Household Words*, 30 Oct. 1852, cited in Philip Collins's *Dickens and Crime* (1994).

42. TH to W. Stebbing, Oct. 1926, *Letters*, VII, 46.

43. *Life*, Chapter 2, section 'July 1856'.

4. Friends and Brothers

1. Barnes, born in 1801 in north Dorset, had published poems both in English and in the dialect. He was now a widower and his school was failing. It closed in 1862, when he was given a 'Literary Pension' of £30 a year by the government, and a living at Winterborne Came, three miles from Dorset, where he settled in the parsonage.

2. According to Hardy's great-nephew John Antell the Hardy family spoke what he calls 'old Dorset', in which pronunciation, grammatical construction and some vocabulary would all differ from standard English. Hardy said they did not speak the local dialect at home, only with the men who worked for his father, but 'old Dorset' and the dialect would certainly have shaded into one another.

3. Swithin St Cleeve's Granny Martin in *Two on a Tower*, written in 1881–2, Chapter 2. Swithin's father was a clergyman who married beneath him, his mother a village girl who was not accepted by the local gentry. Both parents die young, and Swithin, brought up by his maternal grandmother, is a very clever boy and has been sent to the grammar school.

4. In his novel *A Laodicean*.

5. He become curator of the Dorset County Museum in 1883.

6. This was in 1833. Handley Moule, *Memories of a Vicarage* (1913), 56–7.

7. In 1854 there was an outbreak of cholera in the Millbank Prison in London, where 700 convicts were held, and the Home Secretary, learning that the Dorchester barracks were empty, simply packed off all the prisoners and their warders to Dorset. In Moule's parish the women were used to taking in washing from the barracks to earn money, and within days of the prisoners' arrival two women had arranged to do washing for them. In another few days there were cases of cholera in Fordington, and people began to die. The disease was not yet understood, and those who could fled, but Moule stayed. Fires in the streets were thought to purify the air, and he made such bonfires, using them to burn linen and bedding and to heat cauldrons to disinfect. He held open-air services. He hardly expected to survive himself but worked steadily, visiting,

comforting, burning, boiling and praying. His school was closed, but he sent two of his sons out on ponies to millers in the area, asking them to release river waters to wash out the local ponds. He aimed to confine the outbreak to Fordington, and he succeeded.

8. Meanwhile Dr John Snow was establishing how it travelled through an infected water pump in London and a parcel of infected clothes in Yorkshire, but he had not yet published his findings, and the disease was still a mystery, like the plague. It killed quickly and spread through bacteria, for which water and soiled clothing were ideal agents.

9. Handley Moule, *Memories of a Vicarage*, 62

10. Information from Handley Moule's *Memories of a Vicarage* and J. B. Harford's *Biography of Bishop Moule* (1922).

11. Information from *The Memory of the Just is Blessed: A Brief Memorial of Mrs Moule of Fordington* (1877), 56, quoting a letter of 20 Apr. 1871 which mentions Horace writing to her 'almost every year' about the death of the fifteen-month-old baby.

12. From 'The Muffled Peel', 1858:

> Flow gently, sweet Frome, under Grey's gleaming arches,
> Where shines the white moon on thy cold sparkling waves;
> Flow gently tonight, while time silently marches
> Fast hastening to lay the Old Year in her grave.

13. See H. and H. Moule, *Fordington Times Society* (1859), privately printed.

14. Bastow went first to London and then Tasmania, where he practised as an architect. His letters are in the DCM. None of Hardy's has survived, and the correspondence dwindled away within a few years.

15. Timothy Hands, *Thomas Hardy: Distracted Preacher?* (1989), 14.

16. A manuscript in his hand adds a note, '[T. Hardy's [first *del*] earliest known production in verse] (originally written between 1857 and 1860 this being a copy some years later.)' See *Variorum Poems*, 3.

17. *Life*, Chapter 2, section 'Student and Architect 1860–61'.

18. The story about Martha comes from the family of her brother Nathaniel Sparks. For Mary Waight, the only evidence is the word of a granddaughter who was five years old when her grandmother

died: see *Thomas Hardy Proposes to Mary Waight* (Beaminster, 1964), a leaflet reporting Constance M. Oliver's words to J. Stevens Cox in 1963. Mary Waight was born in 1833. She worked in a Dorchester shop selling mantles, i.e., coats. She married George Oliver in 1865, bore a son the same year, and her husband emigrated alone to the US almost at once. She kept a lodging house at 1 West Walks in Dorchester and died in Jan. 1915. She never spoke about Hardy, and the story was told by her daughter-in-law, who said there had been a signed photograph of Hardy in her possession but which had disappeared.

19. Asked about his boyhood by a journalist, Hardy, in his forties, described it as 'uneventful and solitary', which may have been simply a way of dealing with the journalist; but the 'solitary' invites a question about Mary, so close to him in age and so little mentioned in his own accounts of his life. TH to William Henry Rideing, journalist compiling collection 'The Boyhood of Living Authors', *Letters*, I, 13 Dec. 1886, 158.

20. *Life*, end of Chapter 37, his own note dated 23 Dec. 1925.

21. All the other students at Salisbury were Queen's Scholars at this time. There was a government grant to cover this, and it was highly unusual for any students to be paid for by their families. Teacher training colleges for young women were first set up in England in the 1840s by two competing religious groups, the Church of England and the Nonconformist British and Foreign Bible Society. Both were supported by the government, which gave them grants to cover the costs of non-paying students. They were known as 'Queen's Scholars', and most had been pupil teachers in their schools. Mary had not, which may be why she was not taken as a scholar at first. The Salisbury college was one of the first, founded in 1841 (it closed in 1978). A similar college for young men at Winchester was founded in 1840.

22. From an anonymous account by a student of the 1850s printed in Clare Conybeare's *Short History of the King's House, Salisbury* [1987], 10.

23. *Jude the Obscure*, Part III, Chapter 3.

24. *Jude the Obscure*, Part III, Chapter 1. This is Sue speaking to Jude when he visits her. 'She told him about the school as it was at that

date, and the rough living, and the mixed character of her fellow-students, gathered together from all parts of the diocese.'

25. Frederick Maurice in his 'Lectures to Ladies on Practical Subjects' in 1855, cited by Ray Strachey in *The Cause* (1928), 168.

26. The first women's colleges in Oxford and Cambridge were started in the 1870s. Mill's *The Subjection of Women* appeared in 1869. Florence Nightingale became a public heroine by her work during the Crimean War and set up her School of Nursing in 1861 at St Thomas's Hospital.

27. *Under the Greenwood Tree*, Part IV, Chapter 2.

28. Diary of Wynne Alfred Bankes, pupil of Moule, cited in *Biography Revisited*, 60, from DCRO.

5. The Londoner

1. *Life*, Chapter 4, section '1869'. The rest of the information in this paragraph comes from the *Life*, from his letters to his sister Mary, from later letters (on hearing Mill, see below note 26) and from poems dated by him to the 1860s. Some is inferred from his other writing, e.g., going into Rotten Row, which he described in both his first unpublished novel, as we know from the comments of a publisher, and in *A Pair of Blue Eyes*.

2. In *Life*, Chapter 14, he writes 'In evening to bookstalls in Holywell Street known to me so many years ago.'

3. So Hardy told Sydney Cockerell on 26 July 1917, standing on Adelphi Terrace. Cockerell diary for 1917, British Library Add. MSS 52654.

4. *Life*, Chapter 4, section '1869'.

5. Celia Barclay, *Nathaniel Sparks: Memoirs of Thomas Hardy's Cousin the Engraver* (1994), 32, for information about James and Nat in London.

6. This is Picotee arriving in Feb., in *The Hand of Ethelberta*.

7. TH to Mary Hardy, 19 Feb. 1863, *Letters*, I, 3–4.

8. *The Hand of Ethelberta*, Chapter 32.

9. TH to Florence Henniker, 21 Apr. 1912, *Letters*, IV, 211.

10. See Leon Edel's *Henry James: The Untried Years* (1953), 288–91, with

quotations from his letters to his family on his arrival in London in Mar. 1869.

11. *Life*, Chapter 3, section 'A New Start'.

12. For reference: Hardy's salary was better than Gosse's starting pay of £100 a year at the British Museum, less than the £250 Eliza Lynn Linton earned by journalism in a year, and a great deal less than the £400 a year allowed to the young Swinburne by his father.

13. TH to Mary Hardy, 17 Aug. 1862, *Life*, Chapter 3.

14. TH to Mary Hardy, 19 Feb. 1863, *Letters*, I, 4; TH to Mary Hardy, 19 Dec. 1863, *Letters*, I, 5; TH to Mary Hardy, 5 Oct. 1865, *Letters*, I, 5. Information from Christian Wolmar's *The Subterranean Railway* (2004), 39, 41, 81.

15. Horace Moule to TH, 2 Mar. 1863, DCM H. 4469.

16. George Somes Layard, *Mrs Lynn Linton: Her Life, Letters and Opinions* (1901), chapter on the 1850s, when she arrived in London.

17. *Life*, Chapter 3, section 'At Blomfield's'.

18. This house is still standing. Clarence Place in Kilburn has gone.

19. Eliza Nicholls (1840–1914) is a shadowy figure. R. L. Purdy heard about her from her niece in the 1950s, who said Hardy had given her his photograph, which she produced, and a ring, and said they were engaged for several years, and that she was the original for Cytherea in *Desperate Remedies*, which seems particularly far-fetched. She was the daughter of a coastguard official who worked at Kimmeridge in Dorset until 1861, when he moved to Findon in Sussex and ran a pub there. Millgate believes that there was an 'understanding' between them from 1863, when she left London, which lasted until 1867, and it is true that Hardy visited Findon in 1866, when he drew the church. It is possible, but not certain, that she inspired the 'She, to Him' sonnets. She never married and is said to have called on Hardy after the death of his first wife. Caution is necessary with stories given by descendants because well-known men attract claims of this kind.

20. See Chapter 4, p. 57 and Note 18.

21. Note dated in *Life*, Chapter 3, section 'At Blomfield's'.

22. There were probably more than four sonnets in the sequence originally, but these were the ones he thought worth saving and published in his first collection, *Wessex Poems and Other Verses*, in 1898.

23. Printed in *Poems of the Past and the Present*, published 1901, the poem has a note at the end reading 'Westbourne Park Villas 1866'.

24. An obvious exception is George Eliot, who triumphed over the disadvantages of being female, low-born, provincial, denied university education and irregular in her sexual life, by having a brain so large and a personality so strong that she imposed herself on Victorian society through her writing as no one else did.

25. This is Sol Chickerel, one of two brothers, country-born carpenters working in London, in *The Hand of Ethelberta*. Other remarks are made to his sister, who has bettered herself: 'you keep to your class, and we'll keep to ours' and 'you'd better not bide here, talking to we rough ones.' And she says, 'My brother . . . represents the respectable British workman in his entirety, and a touchy individual he is . . . on points of dignity, after imbibing a few town ideas from his leaders.' Robert Gittings believes that Hardy based Sol, 'a carpenter of radical tendencies', on his cousin James, and in *The Young TH*, 103, quotes from a letter from the younger brother, Nat, about James, describing him as 'a real loyal Rad'. Gittings does not give a date for the letter but says that James was then working at Windsor, hence the 'loyal' – possibly satirical? I have not been able to trace the letter.

26. The description was written in a letter to *The Times*, 20 May 1906, reprinted in Chapter 28 of *Life*. Either Hardy was using old diary notes or his memory was phenomenal.

27. A search of the register of electors for Bockhampton and Dorchester in 1851/2 shows that Thomas Hardy's name was not entered. Nor was it entered for 1866/7.

28. Gittings describes in *The Young TH*, 79, this annotation in Hardy's copy of *Queen Mab and Other Poems*, bought and inscribed by Hardy in 1866. *The Revolt of Islam* is a political epic in twelve cantos, originally written under the title 'Laon and Cythna; or, The Revolution in the Golden City, A Vision of The Nineteenth Century'. It alludes to the French Revolution but transposes the action to the East. The revolution is set off by an incestuous brother and sister, both ardent feminists.

29. Park Honan, *Matthew Arnold* (1981), 240–41.

30. *Life*, Chapter 3, section 'At Blomfield's'.

31. See Delmore Schwartz's 'Poetry and Belief in Thomas Hardy', on which I draw here, printed in *Hardy: A Collection of Critical Essays*, ed. Albert Guerard (1963).

32. Horace Moule to TH, 2 July 1863, from Dorchester, DCM, H. 4470.

33. Horace Moule to TH, 21 Feb. 1864, DCM, H. 4471.

34. So Hardy says in the *Life*, Chapters 3 and 19. Note however that Arthur Benson, in a conversation about Newman with Hardy in 1904, thought he heard him say 'I joined the RC Church for a time, but it has left no impression.' See Chapter 19 below, p. 284.

35. According to his poem 'A Confession to a Friend in Trouble', dated 1866.

36. Diary of Wynne Albert Bankes in DCRO, quoted in *Biography Revisited*, 68. Millgate also quotes from R. L. Purdy's notes of a conversation with Florence Hardy in 1933 giving the story of Moule having an affair with a Mixen Lane Dorchester girl who went to Australia, adding the gruesome extra that the son of the girl was hanged. *Thomas Hardy: A Biography* (1982), 154.

37. Horace Moule to TH [fragment undated but probably June 1867], DCM, H.4472.

38. First printed in *Time's Laughingstocks and Other Verses* in 1909, placed and dated '16 W.P.V. 1866'.

39. MS title 'An Exhortation'. First printed as 'A Young Man's Exhortation' in *Late Lyrics and Earlier* in 1922, fifty-five years after he wrote it, dated and given its place of composition as Westbourne Park Villas.

40. They also represent his withdrawn state. This is roughly what T. S. Eliot described years later as an objective correlative. First printed in *Wessex Poems* and dated 1867.

41. In *Wessex Poems*.

42. It lasted long enough for Sydney Cockerell to have it handsomely bound in 1917, but Hardy later burnt it. See Florence Hardy to Sydney Cockerell, 10 Feb. 1917, and note, *Friends of a Lifetime: Letters to Sydney Carlyle Cockerell*, ed. V. Meynell (1940), 295.

PART TWO 1867–1874

6. The Clever Lad's Dream

1. Hardy's own description in *Life*, Chapter 4, section 'End of Summer 1867'.
2. Used at the end of *Under the Greenwood Tree*: 'Tippiwit! swe-e-et! ki-ki-ki!'
3. Hardy says in *Life*, Chapter 4, section '1869', that the manuscript was read by only three people, Macmillan, Morley and Meredith, and he told Cockerell that he was the fourth person to read it, but this is clearly wrong because it must have been read by Chapman's reader and Tinsley, and it seems unlikely that Moule would write a letter of recommendation without having read it.
4. ibid.
5. TH to Alexander Macmillan, 10 Sept. 1868, *Collected Letters*, I, 8.
6. Information from Hardy's published letters and from *Life*, Chapter 4, section '1869'.
7. Emma Gifford, who became his first wife, remembered it as yellowish in 1870.
8. A description from Chapter 3 of *Desperate Remedies*.
9. The note on the boat trip is from Hardy's 'Poetical Matter' notebook, cited by Millgate, *Thomas Hardy: A Biography* (1982), 112. Catherine Pole (1845–91) was the daughter of James Pole, the butler at West Stafford House, not far from Bockhampton. She went to London with her mistress Emily Fellowes when the latter married in 1872, and herself married a Londoner, landlord of a pub in Shepherd's Market, and died young.
10. Hardy's first cousin Nat Sparks left London at about the same time that he did and went to work in Somerset, becoming a restorer of violins and other musical instruments. He married Mary Hardy's college friend Annie Lanham in 1877 and settled in Bristol. His son, confusingly also named Nat Sparks, became a fine artist. He disliked Thomas Hardy and resented what he felt were the superior airs of the Hardy family. In fact, Mary and Kate Hardy kept up friendly relations with the Sparkses – there are letters to show this – but

Hardy himself did become distant and formal towards them. Nat talked and wrote about Hardy at various times – e.g., in letters cited by Robert Gittings, *The Young TH*, 115 and Note 17, where he claimed that Hardy had wanted to marry his aunt Martha. More of his views appear in Celia Barclay's *Nathaniel Sparks: Memoirs of Thomas Hardy's Cousin the Engraver* (1994). Lois Deacon took up the idea of a love affair between Hardy and Tryphena and expanded it into a book written with Terry Coleman, *Providence and Mr Hardy* (1966), which takes off into fantasy.

11. The story of a love affair between Hardy and Tryphena, with the birth of an illegitimate son, caused a stir, but no hard evidence has ever been produced to support it. Tryphena attended Stockwell Training College on a scholarship from Jan. 1870 to Dec. 1871, did very well and was immediately appointed headmistress of a small girls' school in Plymouth at a salary of £100 a year. Her sister Rebecca went to live with her. After six years she resigned her post in order to marry a local publican, Charles Gale. There were four children, and she died young of cancer in 1890. Hardy wrote his poem 'Thoughts of Phena' in memory of her.

12. There was some communication between them later. In 1902 Hardy told his sister Mary he had heard from Martha, announcing the coming visit to England of two members of her family, May and Ethel. A letter from Kate Hardy to her cousin Jim Sparks, 2 Dec. 1902, confirms that a grandson of Martha was brought to see him and was christened in Puddletown Church (Sparks Archive, Hardy Collection, Eton College). Martha died in 1916. According to Emma Cary's son James, many of the Cary family became schoolteachers in Queensland. Letter from James Cary to TH, 11 Sept. 1925, DCM, B5.

13. *The Mystery of Edwin Drood* did not begin to be serialized until the spring of 1870.

14. Robert Gittings speculated that his cousin Martha Sparks might be his source, perhaps the most likely, although it could have been another of the several maids he knew well.

7. Lyonnesse

1. One of the first reviews of *Desperate Remedies* was in the *Athenaeum*, 1 Apr. 1871, 398–9, and praised a character as 'really almost worthy of George Eliot'. When *Far from the Madding Crowd* began to be serialized, the *Spectator* guessed that Eliot was the author. The comparison with French novelists comes from an unsigned article in the *Saturday Review*, 2 Aug. 1873, 36, 158–9.

2. Henry Holt of Holt & Williams in New York was quick to acquire Hardy's work. In June 1873 they started with *Under the Greenwood Tree* and went on to *A Pair of Blue Eyes* in July, then *Desperate Remedies* the following Mar. *Far from the Madding Crowd* would follow in Nov. 1874.

3. Emma described herself as the fair sister, Helen being the dark one, and because of *A Pair of Blue Eyes* people expected her to have blue eyes like the heroine. When she described herself in 1892, however, she said her eyes were dark.

4. Most likely a slightly dislocated hip that went untreated.

5. Emma Hardy to Lady Grove, 23 Jan. 1906, *Letters of E & F Hardy*, 32.

6. Rawle (1812–89) was consecrated Bishop of Trinidad in June 1872 and returned to the West Indies, where he remained until his death.

7. By then it had become important to him to fix every detail of their life together, but the poem is a plod: 'Green slates – seen high on roofs, or lower / In waggon, truck or lorry – / Cry out: "Our home was where you saw her / Standing in the quarry!"' In another version of his visit, given to Eden Philpotts in a letter of 24 Oct. 1915, he was taken back to the manager's house and given gin and hot water at the end of his visit. Perhaps there were two visits?

8. Her remarks in this paragraph are from her own writing published after her death as *Some Recollections of Emma Hardy*, ed. Evelyn Hardy and Robert Gittings (1961), as are her remarks about neighbours.

9. The four phrases come from Coleridge's 'Kubla Khan', Keats's 'La Belle Dame sans Merci', Wordsworth's 'Phantom of Delight' and Shelley's 'Song': 'Rarely, rarely, comest thou / Spirit of Delight!'

10. The poem clearly describes the end of his first visit, although he

suggests it might have been the second in *Life*, Chapter 5. The dark dawn, alley of bare boughs overhead in the garden, clammy lawn, candlelight in the house, all point to Mar., not Aug.

11. He gave them to Henry Knight in *A Pair of Blue Eyes*, according to his own testimony in *Life*, Chapter 5.

12. Louisa Sharpe was acting as mother to a brood of younger siblings. As the years went by, she is likely to have heard something of cousin Tom and his work, but she did not try to contact him again. She outlived him by many years, reaching the noble age of ninety-seven and dying in 1941.

13. *Life*, Chapter 5.

14. *Some Recollections*, 35.

15. Millgate points out in *Biography Revisited*, 119 and note, that there is a pencilled note of a scene something like this by Hardy in the endpapers of a German prose textbook in R. L. Purdy's private collection, reading: 'Sc. rusty harrow – behind that rooks – behind them, 2 men hoeing mangel, with bowed backs, behind that a heap of couch smoking, behind these horse & cart doing nothing in field – then the ground rising to plantn.' So there were no other lovers in view.

16. All three are in the DCM.

17. Lyonesse was the name given to a mythical land between Land's End and the Scilly Isles from which came King Arthur and Tristram: 'that sweet land of Lyonesse', according to Spenser in the *Faerie Queene*; it was 'Lyones' in Milton's *Paradise Regained*.

8.   The True Vocation

1. This is from the Hardys' friendly but objective neighbour Evangeline Smith. See Michael Rabiger's account of the papers of Harold Hoffman in *The Thomas Hardy Year Book* (St Peter Port, 1981). Hoffman interviewed Evangeline Smith in 1939 and noted what she said about Jemima's complaints. Hoffman's papers are held at Miami University of Ohio. This is the only record of her views, given long after Mrs Hardy's death, and uncheckable, but likely to be true.

2. From *Hardy's Notebooks*, ed. Evelyn Hardy (1955), 31, quoting from a letter by Emma dated Oct. or Nov. 1870.

3. *Biography Revisited*, 122 and note. The Shakespeare is in the DCM.

4. The quotation is from Scott's 1830 introduction to his novel *The Monastery*, first published in 1820, in which he apologizes for its clumsy construction.

5. Simon Gatrell gives a full and clear account of these striking additions and changes, based on his study of the manuscript, in *Hardy the Creator: A Textual Biography* (1988).

6. Tim Dolin, in his introduction to the 1998 Penguin Classics edition, on p. xxiii, writes of Hardy disowning the first published version as 'the careless work of his youth'. He also suggests, on p. xxiv, that 'The dominant love romance of 1872 was a paltry confection for subscribers to circulating libraries, he implied.' See also Hardy's remark in a letter to Florence Henniker that 'the "Mellstock" choir' consisted of 'the characters that I like best in my own novels'. 30 Dec. 1896, *Letters*, II, 141.

7. *Under the Greenwood Tree*, Part I, Chapter 8.

8. 'Great Things', first printed in 1917, lists cider, dancing and love as three great things for him, and associates the last two.

9. Denys Kay-Robinson, *The First Mrs Thomas Hardy* (1979), 104, 'Because of her lameness it is improbable that she could walk much, or dance.'

10. *Under the Greenwood Tree*, Part II, Chapter 7.

11. ibid., Part V, Chapter 2.

12. ibid., Chapter 1.

13. The unsigned article was written by Charles Kegan Paul, who had been a clergyman in Dorset. He lost his faith and became a publisher and writer, and a friend of Hardy. See Michael Millgate, *Thomas Hardy: His Career as a Novelist* (1971), 121.

14. In *Life*, Hardy says what he felt as a rejection from Macmillan came in Aug., and that Emma wrote to him urging him to stick to his writing, but Macmillan's letter is dated Oct., when Hardy was with Emma in Cornwall.

15. Hardy's second wife, Florence, put forward suggestions that Hardy was pressurized into marrying Emma by the Holders, but this does not fit with Hardy's own account of the sequence of events.

16. In 1920 Vere H. Collins asked him about his poem 'I Rose and Went to Rou'tor Town', which clearly alludes to this visit, and what the evil mentioned in it was. Hardy replied 'Slander, or something of the sort'. *Talks with Thomas Hardy at Max Gate 1920–1922* (New York, 1928; reprinted St Peter Port, 1971), 26.

17. TH to Florence Hardy, 9 Mar. 1913, from Boscastle where he was staying, a propos the ritualistic services now held in the church at St Juliot.

18. *Some Recollections of Emma Hardy*, ed. Evelyn Hardy and Robert Gittings (1961), 20.

19. Her letter to Hardy is quoted in *Hardy's Notebooks*, 31, written apparently in late Oct.

20. *Some Recollections*, 18–19.

21. Horace Moule to TH [n.d. but 21 May 1873], DCM. Moule's point about Hardy understanding the woman better than the lady was echoed by Virginia Woolf, who complained that he could not draw a lady. Moule may have made amends in an anonymous piece in the *Saturday Review* praising Hardy as 'a writer who to a singular purity of thought and intention unites great power of imagination . . . without resorting to mere surprises or descending to what is ignoble'. Moule had earlier reviewed *Desperate Remedies* and *Under the Greenwood Tree* in the same journal, always anonymously. This one is dated 2 Aug. 1873, 36, 158–9.

22. *Life*, Chapter 6, last page. Part of the entry at least was clearly written later. The Backs are the wide grassy grounds stretching between the colleges and the river.

23. 'Midnight on Beechen, 187–' It is of course 1873.

9.　Easy to Die

1. *Life*, Chapter 7, and interview with Frank Hedgcock in 1910, cited in *Interviews and Recollections*, 93.

2. James reviewed *Far from the Madding Crowd* in the *Nation*, 24 Dec. 1874, Lang in the *Academy*, 2 Jan. 1875.

3. *Far from the Madding Crowd*, Chapter 50 and Chapter 4.

4. ibid., Chapter 8.

5. ibid., Chapter 3. We have been told in Chapter 2 that she is not using a side saddle: 'I can ride on the other: trust me,' she tells her aunt. Hardy's graphic and detailed description of her riding feats prompts the question as to whether he ever saw Emma ride without her habit and side saddle, enjoying herself in the same way.

6. ibid., Chapter 15.

7. Henery Fray describing Bathsheba's sacking of her dishonest bailiff in Chapter 8.

8. *Far from the Madding Crowd*, Chapter 12.

9. Lang's review appeared in the *Academy* on 2 Jan. 1875 and is partly reprinted in R. G. Cox's *Thomas Hardy: The Critical Heritage* (1995). This passage, 35.

10. Joseph Arch, *Life* (1898), 110.

11. Hardy himself said he heard Arch speak in his essay 'The Dorsetshire Farm Labourer' (1883).

12. Joseph Arch, *Life*, 35.

13. *Far from the Madding Crowd*, Chapter 41.

14. TH to Smith, Elder, 4 Dec. 1873. Hardy did not know at this stage who would be illustrating the book.

15. *Far from the Madding Crowd*, Chapter 2.

16. ibid., Chapter 11.

17. J. M. Barrie, 'Thomas Hardy: The Historian of Wessex' in the *Contemporary Review*, 56, 57 (1889), printed in R. G. Cox, *Thomas Hardy: The Critical Heritage*, 156–66.

18. *Life*, Chapter 7.

19. F. W. Maitland, *The Life and Letters of Leslie Stephen* (1906), 273. Neither Stephen nor Hardy explained who the other Leslie Stephen was.

20. ibid.

21. Minny Stephen to Anny Thackeray [n.d. but 1874], cited in Henrietta Garnett, *Anny: A Life of Anne Isobella Thackeray Ritchie* (2004), the source given as 'MS to AIT' from Eton Ritchie Papers at Eton College Library.

22. F. W. Maitland, *The Life and Letters of Leslie Stephen*, 266.

23. Leslie Stephen to TH, 12 Mar. 1874, printed in R. L. Purdy, *Thomas Hardy: A Bibliographical Study* (1954), 338–9.

24. ibid., 13 Apr. 1874.

25. *Life*, Chapter 7.
26. From his *Essays on Free Thinking and Plain Speaking* (1873).
27. TH to Leslie Stephen, 18 Feb. 1874, *Life*, Chapter 7.
28. Emma Gifford to TH, July 1874, printed in *The Personal Notebooks of Thomas Hardy*, ed. Richard H. Taylor (1978), 17.
29. TH to Geneviève Smith, 6 Jan. 1874, *Letters*, I, 26.
30. He was Basil Montagu, an illegitimate but acknowledged son of the fourth Earl of Sandwich by Martha Ray, brought up at Hinching-brooke and sent to Cambridge.
31. A story was put about by Hardy's second wife that Emma travelled to Bockhampton to speak to Hardy's parents, or so Henry Reed told Michael Millgate. Reed said that Florence Hardy told him Emma travelled to Bockhampton before her marriage in an unannounced visit intended to make the Hardy family accept her, with disastrous results. There is no other source for the story, nothing written down, Florence Hardy was hostile to Emma, and everything she said about her has to be taken with caution. It seems unlikely that Emma would have considered making such a difficult journey alone across country to seek out people she did not know. She had no money and no friends in Dorset. Her own family would not have approved, and what could she have said to the Hardys? She would not have done it without Hardy's agreement, and she had no need to ask for their approval once she had decided to do without her own parents' – she and Hardy were in the same boat and planning to start their lives in splendid isolation. *Biography Revisited*, 134, Note 19.
32. *Far from the Madding Crowd*, Chapter 56.
33. Hamilton Gifford to TH, 4 Sept. 1874, DCM, H.2587.
34. ibid., 12 Sept. 1874, DCM, H.2588.

10. A Short Visit to the Continent

1. *Some Recollections of Emma Hardy*, ed. Evelyn Hardy and Robert Gittings (1961), 60, and *The Emma Hardy Diaries*, ed. Richard H. Taylor (1985). All quotations are taken from this facsimile edition.
2. The church did not last very long but was pulled down and replaced

a hundred years later, between 1974 and 1977, by a modern complex of buildings, a low church-cum-hall, day centre, sheltered housing and vicarage. Pevsner finds the fine old plane tree preserved on the site more interesting than the buildings, which might have pleased Hardy.

3. Queen's Road was renamed Queensway later.

4. TH to Henry Hardy, Friday [18 Sept. 1874], *Letters*, I, 31.

5. *Life*, Chapter 7.

6. The house is no longer there. It stood just south of the junction of Hook Road with Ditton Road. See Mark Davison's booklet *Hook Remembered Again* (2001), 11. Davison believes that a Francis Honeywell, who grew up in Weymouth before moving to Kingston upon Thames and knew Hardy, found the lodgings for him. Emma's diary entry 'Annie & the Retriever playing in the garden with Papa' has been misinterpreted to mean that her own father, Mr Gifford, called on them, which of course he did not – the Papa was Mr Hughes.

7. Tinsley to TH, 5 Jan. 1875, printed in R. L. Purdy, *Thomas Hardy: A Bibliographical Study* (1954), 335.

8. The first edition was of 1,000 copies, the second of 500.

9. Purdy, *op. cit.*, 18.

10. See Raymond Williams, 'Wessex and the Border' in *The Country and the City* (1973), 197.

11. Hardy quotes this remark in the *Life*, Chapter 7.

12. Leslie Stephen to TH, 13 May 1875, F. W. Maitland, *The Life and Letters of Leslie Stephen* (1906), 276.

13. The evidence of Emma's dislike rests on what she said to an American friend, Rebekah Owen, in 1892, when they visited Swanage together. Asked about *Ethelberta*, which was partly written there, Emma said she disliked talking about it because it had 'too much about servants' in it. See Denys Kay-Robinson's *The First Mrs Hardy* (1979), 94 (taken from Carl Weber's *Hardy and the Lady from Madison Square*, 1952).

14. Noel Annan, *Leslie Stephen: The Godless Victorian* (1984), 2.

15. *The Hand of Ethelberta*, Chapter 23.

16. For Katie's pupil teaching, see records of Salisbury Teacher Training College for 1876, with summary of previous experience of scholars.

Martha and her husband and children emigrated in May 1876. Hardy does not mention seeing her after her marriage, but you would expect them to have kept up some contact as long as she was in London.

17. *The Hand of Ethelberta*, Chapter 29.

18. ibid., Chapter 9.

19. ibid., Chapter 7.

20. ibid., Chapter 42.

21. ibid., Chapter 25.

22. ibid., Chapter 46.

23. ibid., final chapter, headed 'Sequel'.

24. Leslie Stephen to TH, Aug. 1875, F. W. Maitland, *The Life and Letters of Leslie Stephen*, 276.

25. ibid., 263–4.

26. It is in *Moments of Vision and Miscellaneous Verses*, published in 1917.

27. This is from Sir George Douglas's recollections, printed in *Interviews and Recollections*, 32–3. It was written much later, but Sir George first met the Hardys in 1881, six years into their marriage, and saw it as a happy one.

28. Again, Rebekah Owen's account, in Denys Kay-Robinson's *The First Mrs Hardy*.

29. All these quotations from Emma's diary for 13 Sept. 1875, 65–7 in Richard H. Taylor's edition.

30. At this stage it was called 'The Fire at Tranter Sweatley's'.

31. TH to William Minto, 4 Nov. 1875, *Letters*, I, 41.

32. The house, 7 Peter Street, is no longer there; its site is now covered by a car park.

33. F. W. Maitland, *The Life and Letters of Leslie Stephen*, 290.

34. The typescript, made much later by Florence Dugdale, is held at the DCM, H.6213. It is subtitled 'A story of fair passions, and bountiful pities, and loves without stain'. The original manuscript is no longer extant, but there are a few notes relevant to the novel in Emma's diary.

35. *Life*, Chapter 8.

36. She has a passage in *The Maid on the Shore* about 'poor little rustic Rosabelle' who had 'never breathed the dear smokiness of London

life and was ... a mere country maiden, sweet and pure, gently nurtured it is true, but bearing the signs of complete rusticity', which looks like an allusion to her own situation.

37. Hardy, however, told Virginia Woolf in 1926 that he had seen her mother when he visited Leslie Stephen at his friends, the Lushingtons, in Kensington Square: 'She used to come in and out when I was talking to your father.' Also that he saw a Stephen baby in a cradle whom he thought was Virginia, born in 1882, but may have been Vanessa, born in 1879. This from *The Diary of Virginia Woolf*, III (1979), 99, 97.

PART THREE   1875–1905

11.   Dreaming the Heath

1. The mansion is said to have been the home of Robert Young (1811–1908), a Dorset dialect poet who took the pseudonym 'Rabin Hill'. He was a friend of William Barnes, but there is no evidence that Hardy knew him.

2. *Life*, Chapter 8, note from Nov. 1877.

3. *Life*, Chapter 8.

4. Especially since Annie Lanham, Mary's friend, was already pregnant and Nat needed some persuading to marry her. See Celia Barclay, *Nathaniel Sparks: Memoirs of Thomas Hardy's Cousin the Engraver* (1994), 37. The Sparks family built up strong resentments against Hardy for his stand-offishness, a good deal of it chronicled in Barclay.

5. 13 Nov. 1876, *Emma Hardy Diaries*, ed. Richard H. Taylor (1985), 103.

6. Michael Millgate suggests she may have been the 'Jenny Phillips' whose name appears in one of Hardy's song books, and he thinks her family may have been descended from the ancient Phelips family of Corfe Mullen. He also argues that she is a model for Tess, which in certain respects is plausible.

7. The poem first appeared in 1922 in *Late Lyrics and Earlier*, undated. The manuscript from which it was printed bears no signs of revision, but that does not mean it had not been worked over.

8. He means Eustacia, of course. Book IV, Chapter 3. A 'reddleman' is one who deals in red dye, used for marking sheep.

9. *The Return of the Native*, Book I, Chapter 1.

10. ibid., Book V, Chapter 5.

11. ibid., Book IV, Chapter 1.

12. Simon Gatrell, *Hardy the Creator: A Textual Biography* (1988), 42.

13. ibid., 41.

14. Frank Hedgcock's 'Reminiscences of Thomas Hardy', published in the *National and English Review* in 1951, relating to two interviews in July 1910.

15. *The Return of the Native*, Book IV, Chapter 2. They sound like Lulworth Skippers, butterflies that favour 'arid localities and steppes' outside England (*A Field Guide to Butterflies and Moths* by Ivo Novak, 1980) and in England are found only around Swanage and the coast from Swanage to Devon, according to Charles Knight and Margaret Brooks's *Complete Pocket Guide to British Butterflies* (1982).

16. *The Return of the Native*, Book I, Chapter 6.

17. ibid., Chapter 5.

18. ibid., Book IV, Chapter 5.

19. ibid., Chapter 6.

20. TH to George Smith, 5 Feb. 1877, *Letters*, I, 47.

21. TH to John Blackwood, 13 Feb. 1877, *Letters*, I, 47.

22. Blackwood's comments given by Simon Gatrell in *Hardy the Creator*, 33, 43.

23. Stephen's remark cited by John Paterson, *The Making of 'The Return of the Native'* (1960). Also given by F. W. Maitland for 1877 in *The Life and Letters of Leslie Stephen* (1906).

24. George Smith of Smith, Elder did publish it, in three volumes, in Nov. 1878.

25. *Life*, Chapter 9, dated note.

26. This and the reviews cited by R. G. Cox in his *Thomas Hardy: The Critical Heritage* (1995).

27. See unpublished letter from Emma Dashwood to Emma Hardy, 1883, DCM, H.6252.7. 'I hope your stories will emerge one after the other and pleasantly astonish the literary world, they have been concocting in your brain long enough and should now see the light.'

28. Described in 'The Musical Box': 'the dusky house that stood apart,

/ And her, white-muslined, waiting there / In the porch with high-expectant heart'. Hardy himself says this poem refers to their time at Sturminster Newton in *Life*, Chapter 8.

29. 'On Sturminster Foot-Bridge', dated 1877 in the MS.
30. She was Julia Duckworth, and their four children were Toby, Vanessa, Virginia and Adrian.
31. *Life*, Chapter 8, dated notebook entry.
32. Millgate, in *Thomas Hardy: A Biography* (1982), 191, suggests she was the Jane Phillips who registered the baby in Nov.
33. My transcription of unpublished letter, TH Snr to Kate Hardy, 13 Nov. 1877. DCM, Kate Hardy and Lock Collection, A2 and H.2003.453.
34. The house is now 172 Trinity Road.

12.   Hardy Joins a Club

1. *Life*, Chapter 8.
2. Garrett Anderson, *Hang Your Halo in the Hall: A History of the Savile Club* (1993), 52. The Irving evening is mentioned on p. 53.
3. *Life*, Chapter 10, and TH to Walter Besant, 17 Mar. 1879, *Letters*, I, 63. Hardy had received a flattering letter from Besant [7 Mar. 1879] praising *The Return of the Native* as 'the most original the most virile and most humorous of all modern novels' – a curious description but likely to make Hardy look favourably on joining Besant's club. Besant's letter cited in *Biography Revisited*, 194.
4. TH to Charles Kegan Paul, 21 June 1878, *Letters*, I, 57.
5. Cited in *Biography Revisited*, 182.
6. Leslie Stephen to Charles Eliot Norton, 5 Aug. 1880, F. W. Maitland, *The Life and Letters of Leslie Stephen* (1906), 341.
7. *Life*, Chapter 10.
8. ibid. She told Hardy about Henry James's proposal, which he doubted, but James himself told his mother about it. It was a gesture that clearly gave both parties pleasure without either taking it seriously. See Leon Edel, *Henry James: The Conquest of London* (1962), 355. James went to her funeral in 1888, with Browning, who had been encouraged as a young writer by her husband.

9. *Interviews and Recollections* gives this, 12–13, taken from E. McCluny Fleming's *R. R. Bowker: Militant Liberal* (1952), 146.

10. *Life*, Chapter 10.

11. *Life*, Chapter 9.

12. Hardy's essay 'The Dorsetshire Farm Labourer' was published in *Longman's Magazine* in July 1883. He describes improvements in their lives but laments the breakdown of rural communities and says they have 'lost touch with their environment'.

13. All this from *Life*, Chapter 10.

14. For Leslie Stephen, Smith, Elder records, *Life*, Chapter 9; for Blackwood, TH to John Blackwood, 9 June 1879, *Letters*, I, 64–5.

15. The US serialization was in *Demorest's Monthly Magazine*.

16. It was remaindered in 1882.

17. *Life*, Chapter 9.

18. TH to Henry Hardy, 20 Apr. 1880, *Letters*, I, 73.

19. Cited in *Biography Revisited*, 190–91; from 'Poetical Matter' notebook, dated 19 Jan. 1879.

20. TH to Edmund Gosse, 14 Feb. 1922, *Letters*, VI, 115.

21. A note made in Jan. 1881, printed in *Life*, Chapter 11.

22. Mary Hardy, writing from her headmistress's house in Bell Street, to Emma Hardy, 28 Jan. 1881, DCM, H.6302.

23. All from *Life*, Chapter 11.

13.   The Tower

1. TH to George Greenhill, a mathematician, Professor at the Royal Artillery College in Woolwich, 6 Apr. 1881, *Letters*, I, 88.

2. I assume this is because he recommended the King's Arms in Dorchester as 'fairly comfortable' two years later to an American visitor, Brander Matthews. You can still stay there.

3. A letter from Hardy dated 4 June 1881 gives Dorchester but asks for his proofs to be sent to Tooting. His next letter, dated 22 June, is from Tooting, announcing the imminent move to Wimborne.

4. *Life*, Chapter 11.

5. Astronomers had travelled all over the world in 1769 and arrived at

a good result, which they hoped to improve in 1882 and succeeded in doing. Transits come in pairs, eight years apart, but then do not happen again for about a century. The 1882 transit had been preceded by one in 1874.

6. He said he had other towers in mind also, one being the brick obelisk set up in the eighteenth century over an Iron Age hillfort known as Weatherby Castle, at Milborne St Andrew; the other, Horton, north of Wimborne, is described by Pevsner as 'a megalomaniac folly, called "observatory" in 1765, when it must have been quite new'. It is a six-storey brick tower, hexagonal, with pointed windows and domed turrets. But Charborough is clearly the chief inspiration. It is still not open to the public.

7. Hardy did visit Charborough House but not until 1927, when he was invited to lunch.

8. *Two on a Tower*, Chapter 1.

9. From Hardy's 1895 preface to the book.

10. The German physicist Rudolf Clausius formulated the basis of the Second Law in 1850, but only in 1863 did he express it in the familiar form, 'Heat cannot of its own accord move from a colder to a hotter body.'

11. *Two on a Tower*, Chapter 4.

12. ibid., Chapter 11.

13. Hardy calls Swithin 'the Adonis-astronomer' in Chapter 8 – the manuscript shows he inserted the 'Adonis' as an afterthought, on folio 64.

14. *Two on a Tower*, Chapter 14.

15. ibid., Chapter 8.

16. ibid., Chapter 7.

17. ibid., Chapter 36.

18. TH to Henry Massingham, 31 Dec. 1891, *Letters*, I, 250. Ibsen's *A Doll's House* was put on for the first time under that name in England in 1889, although there had been performances earlier in the 1880s under other titles such as *Nora*.

19. See Chapter 4 for an account of Hardy's grandmother as the original for Gammer Martin.

20. The story was 'Benighted Travellers', which appeared in England

and the US, and was collected in *A Group of Noble Dames* as 'The
Honourable Laura'. *A Laodicean* was published in the US in Nov.,
in England in Dec. 1881.

21. *Life*, Chapter 11.

22. As it happens, he did jot down some notes about writing fiction at
    this time, but they are thin and unilluminating, and he soon set
    them aside. They are given in Chapter 11 of *Life*.

23. Hardy adapted *Far from the Madding Crowd* for theatrical performance
    in 1879, while living in Tooting, passed it on for further work to
    Comyns Carr and submitted it to the St James's Theatre. It was
    turned down, but Mrs Kendal, who had read it, described it to
    Pinero, from which he wrote his own play, *The Squire*, with a
    strikingly similar plot. Hardy objected in letters to *The Times* and
    other papers in Jan. 1882, and his own, or partly his own, version,
    with melodramatic additions, was put on as a result. It ran for over
    100 performances in London but was disliked by the critics, and by
    Hardy himself. No script survives among his papers.

24. *Life*, Chapter 12.

25. Hardy's wording for the advertisement placed in the *Athenaeum*, 2
    Dec. 1882, cited by R. L. Purdy, *Thomas Hardy: A Bibliographical
    Study* (1954), 44.

26. Havelock Ellis's review is printed in R. G. Cox, *Hardy: The Critical
    Heritage* (1995), 103–32.

27. *Two on a Tower*, Chapter 7.

28. ibid., Chapter 14.

29. ibid., Chapter 3.

30. Emma Hardy to Mary Haweis, 13 Nov. 1894: 'He understands only
    the women he *invents* – the others not at all.' *Letters of E & F Hardy*,
    6.

31. TH to Edmund Gosse, 21 Jan. 1883, *Letters*, I, 114.

32. *Life*, Chapter 13.

33. Quoted in *Interviews and Recollections*, 16–17.

34. Helen Holder to Emma Hardy [13 or 15 Aug. ?], 1881, DCM,
    H.3605.

35. Helen Holder to Emma Hardy, 28 Nov. 1882, DCM, H.6306.

36. 'The Romantic Adventures of a Milkmaid' is poor stuff, which he
    regretted. 'Our Exploits at West Poley' is an excellent and exciting

children's story with a theme along the lines of Pagnol's *Manon des Sources.*

37. TH to Joseph Eldridge, declining to nominate the Liberal candidate for South Dorset, 8 June 1892: 'I am & have always been compelled to forego [*sic*] all participation in active politics, by reason of the neutrality of my own pursuits, which would be stultified to a great extent if I could not approach all classes of thinkers from an absolutely unpledged point – the point of "men, not measures" – exactly the reverse of the true politician's.' *Letters*, I, 272.

38. TH to Percy Bunting, editor of the *Contemporary Review*, 12 Oct. and 5 Nov. 1883, *Letters*, I, 121, 123.

14.   The Conformers

1. Hardy describes the touring players admirably in a note dated 14 Aug. 1884, printed in *Life*, Chapter 13.

2. *Life*, Chapter 13.

3. *Biography Revisited*, 228, for details of the lease.

4. This was Virginia Woolf's description when she visited Max Gate in 1926.

5. *The Woodlanders*, Chapter 8. He also wrote a poem, 'The Pine Planters (Marty South's Reveries)', printed in *Time's Laughingstocks and Other Verses*. Marty goes further here and makes the trees' sighing signify grief that they have not remained undeveloped seeds, safe from storm and drought.

6. 'Some Romano-British Relics Found at Max Gate, Dorchester', text of speech read by Hardy at Dorchester meeting of the Dorset Natural History and Antiquarian Field Club in 1884. Printed in *Thomas Hardy's Personal Writings*, ed. H. Orel (1990).

7. So Hardy told William Archer when he interviewed him in 1901. *Interviews and Recollections*, 69.

8. So he told John Middleton Murry in 1921, adding that 'nothing had happened' to bear out his fear. Cited in ibid., 154, taken from J. M. Murry, *Katherine Mansfield and Other Literary Portraits* (1949).

9. *Life*, Chapter 20, in a passage contrasting the gaieties of the London Season with his home life.

10. ibid., Chapter 14.
11. Details of Wilde's lecture taken from Richard Ellmann, *Oscar Wilde* (1987), 184.
12. TH interview with Frank Hedgcock in 1910, *Interviews and Recollections*, 95.
13. Hardy reported by John Middleton Murry, *Interviews and Recollections*, 156.
14. The phrase is from his paper 'Memories of Church Restoration', given in 1906 and partly printed in 'Thomas Hardy and Anti-Scrape', *The Times Literary Supplement*, 23 Feb. 1928.
15. *The Mayor of Casterbridge*, Chapter 7.
16. ibid., Chapter 45.
17. ibid., Chapter 9; ibid., Chapter 14. Auden's essay on Hardy is from the *Southern Review*, 1940, 6.
18. *Life*, Chapter 29: '*The Mayor of Casterbridge* was issued complete about the end of May [1886]. It was a story which Hardy fancied he had damaged more recklessly as an artistic whole, in the interest of the newspaper in which it appeared serially, than perhaps any other of his novels, his aiming to get an incident into almost every week's part causing him in his own judgment to add events to the narrative somewhat too freely. However, as at this time he called his novel-writing "mere journey-work" he cared little about it as art, though it must be said in favour of the plot, as he admitted later, that it was quite coherent and organic, in spite of its complication.'

    See also TH to W. D. Howells, 9 Nov. 1886: 'Accept my best thanks for your kindly notice of *The M of C* . . . It is what the book would probably have deserved if the story had been written as it existed in my mind, but, alas, was never put on paper. / I ought to have improved it much – for the greater part was finished in 1884 – a year & half nearly before publication. But I could not get thoroughly into it after the interval.' *Letters*, I, 156. The interval was presumably the period in June and July spent in London for the Season that year, followed by his trip to Jersey with Henry in Aug.
19. *The Mayor of Casterbridge*, Chapter 7.
20. ibid., Chapter 20. This is a slight preview of Tess's suffering when Angel rejects her.

21. ibid., Chapter 44.

22. Mabel Robinson (1858–1954), who wrote a long letter answering questions from Florence Hardy's executrix, Irene Cooper Willis, 17 Dec. 1937, DCM. She met the Hardys in London in the 1880s and stayed with them at Max Gate.

23. I have taken this idea from Lawrence Lerner's excellent *Thomas Hardy's 'The Mayor of Casterbridge': Tragedy or Social History?* (1975), 72.

24. Information about Abel Whittle of Maiden Newton from the Census and with kind help from David Smith. The 1871 Census does not give Whittle, who was presumably dead by then.

25. TH to Edmund Gosse, 30 Aug. 1887, *Letters*, I, 167.

26. All three quotations from *Life*, Chapter 14.

27. Written to Edmund Gosse many years later, in a year when he did not get to London, 13 Dec. 1916, *Letters*, V, 190.

28. *Life*, Chapter 14.

29. ibid., Chapters 13 and 19.

30. TH note, 15 Mar. 1890, in *Life*, Chapter 18 – after attending a crush at the Jeunes'.

31. This is what he wrote on the subject of shooting for pleasure, from a notebook kept at Wimborne, DCM fragment H.1958.57: 'I meet with a keeper – tells me that one day this season they shot – (3 guns) 700 pheasants in the day – a *battue* – driving the birds into one corner of the plantation – when they get there they will not run across the open ground – rise on the wing – then are shot wholesale – they pick up all that have fallen – night comes on – the wounded birds that have hidden or risen into some thick tree, fall and lie on the ground in their agony – next day the keepers come and look for them. (They found 150 on the above occasion, next day.) Can see that night scene – moon – fluttering and gasping birds as hours go on – the place being now deserted of human kind.'

32. *Biography Revisited*, 227, citing a letter from her uncle Archdeacon Gifford to Emma Hardy, 6 Apr. 1885, letter in DCM.

33. Her marriage to John Stanley meant she was Bertrand Russell's aunt – Stanley's sister Kate married Frank Amberley, son of Lord John Russell. Both the Amberleys were admirers of John Stuart Mill, and Kate was a remarkable young woman with advanced ideas, an atheist

and feminist who would have interested Hardy. Sadly, she and her husband both died young in the mid 1870s.

34. Edith Wharton, *A Backward Glance* (1934), 213.

35. *Life*, Chapter 18, note dated 8 Dec. 1890.

36. *Biography Revisited*, 251, citing Purdy's report of a conversation with Dorothy Allhusen (*née* Stanley) in 1931 in which she said, 'We all hated her.'

37. *Life*, Chapter 12.

38. Edmund Gosse to his wife, 22 July 1883, cited in Edmund Gosse, *Portraits from Life*, ed. Ann Thwaite (1991).

39. The population remained below 10,000 into the twentieth century. Fordington Field began to be enclosed in the 1870s.

40. Emma Dashwood to Emma Hardy, 1883, DCM, H.6252.7.

41. The *'Facts' Notebook* has been usefully edited by William Greenslade (2004).

42. He dated it when he printed it in 1909 in *Time's Laughingstocks and Other Verses*.

43. 'The Conformers' is not dated. The section in which it appears, close to 'He Abjures Love', is rather oddly headed 'Love Lyrics'.

15.   The Blighted Star

1. *The Mayor of Casterbridge*, Chapter 44.

2. One modern critic, Lawrence Lerner, calls it 'the most unsatisfactory ending of all Hardy's novels', describes him as writing against the grain, not wanting to renounce or modify his pessimism 'under the pressure of a happy ending'. *Thomas Hardy's 'The Mayor of Casterbridge': Tragedy or Social History?* (1975), 64.

3. R. H. Hutton in the *Spectator*, 26 Mar. 1887.

4. Irving Howe, *Thomas Hardy* (1985 ed.), 91.

5. *Life*, Chapter 17, note dated under 15–21 Oct. 1888.

6. TH to Florence Dugdale, 22 Apr. 1912, *Letters*, IV, 212.

7. Cited by David Lodge in his essay '*The Woodlanders*: A Darwinian Pastoral Elegy' in *Working with Structuralism: Essays and Reviews on Nineteenth and Twentieth Century Literature* (1981), 79–94.

8. He told J. A. Symonds he thought *The Woodlanders* 'rather a failure towards the end'. 14 Apr. 1889, *Letters*, I, 191.

9. *Life*, Chapter 20.

10. *Jude the Obscure*, Part I, Chapter 4.

11. Edmund Gosse in *Cosmopolis*, 1 (Jan. 1896), 60–69, reprinted in R. G. Cox, *Thomas Hardy: The Critical Heritage* (1995), 269.

12. The research of Charles Booth and Beatrice Webb showed that about a third of the population lived in poverty and that there was bitter class hatred. The English translation of Marx's *Das Capital* appeared in 1884, and there were riots in the West End in Feb. 1886 and Nov. 1887.

13. T H to J. A. Symonds, 14 Apr. 1889, *Letters*, I, 190.

14. ibid.

15. Harrison's article was in the *Fortnightly*, Feb. 1920. Hardy's response is described in *Biography Revisited*, 488 and note, based on Florence Hardy's letter of 24 Feb. to Sydney Cockerell, and her later conversation in 1933 with R. L. Purdy, in whose collection the letter is.

16. *Life*, Chapter 14, note dated May 1886.

17. This was in answer to a review of his poems by Alfred Noyes, who alleged that Hardy believed in a malign force in charge of the universe. 20 Dec. 1920, *Letters*, VI, 54.

18. 'God's Education' was printed in *Time's Laughingstocks and Other Verses* and originally called 'His Education'.

19. *Life*, Chapter 27, note dated 7 Apr. 1889.

20. TH to H. Rider Haggard [n.d. but the Haggards' son died in Feb.], *Letters*, I, 135.

21. The ballad-style poem is about a mother who procures an abortion for her daughter which kills her. Hardy wrote it in 1904 and later told Galsworthy he had wanted to make 'a tragic play' of the subject and shaped some scenes before realizing it would never be put on.

22. *Life*, Chapter 16.

23. The poem is dated 1896 on the manuscript.

24. TH to Thomas Macquoid, 29 Oct. 1891, *Letters*, I, 245.

25. TH interview with Frank Hedgcock in 1910, *Interviews and Recollections*, 92; TH to George Douglas, 30 Dec. 1891, *Letters*, I, 249.

26. *Tess of the D'Urbervilles*, last words of Chapter 15.

27. From Hardy's 1892 preface to the fifth edition.

28. *Tess of the D'Urbervilles*, Chapter 15.

29. Already cited in Chapter 13, TH to Henry Massingham, 31 Dec. 1891, *Letters*, I, 250.

30. *Life*, Chapter 18.

31. See interesting arguments in Linda M. Shire's essay 'The Radical Aesthetic of *Tess of the D'Urbervilles*' in *The Cambridge Companion to Thomas Hardy*, ed. Dale Kramer (1999).

32. D. F. Hannigan in the *Westminster Review*, Dec. 1892, reprinted in R. G. Cox, *Thomas Hardy: The Critical Heritage*, 244–8.

33. The first English edition of 1,000 copies was in three volumes, published by Osgood, McIlvaine on 29 Nov. 1891. Harper & Bros published the first American edition in Jan. 1892.

34. W. P. Trent in the first issue of the *Sewanee Review*, Nov. 1892, reprinted in R. G. Cox, *Thomas Hardy: The Critical Heritage*, 221–37.

35. Robert Louis Stevenson from Samoa to Henry James, 5 Dec. 1892. Henry James to Robert Louis Stevenson, 17 Feb. 1893, both from P. Horne, *Henry James: A Life in Letters* (1999), note on 249. *Tess* has always had its detractors. Someone complained to me recently of 'Tess's violet eyes', suggesting this was a novelettish touch. In fact, Hardy says her eyes are 'neither black nor blue nor gray nor violet'.

36. Irving Howe, *Thomas Hardy*, 131.

37. TH to Mrs Fawcett, 14 Apr. 1892, *Letters*, I, 264.

38. *Life*, Chapter 21.

39. *The Well-Beloved* appeared in 1897, and, although it has never been popular, it was admired by Proust, who gives his narrator a little educational speech about Hardy to Albertine in 'La Prisonnière', Vol. XII of *À la recherche du temps perdu*. The sculptor hero falls in love regularly from the age of nine, each time with a girl who seems to embody his dream of a 'well-beloved', but only temporarily. Each soon loses what he thought he saw in her and she becomes 'a corpse' to him. The chief charm of the book lies in the descriptions of the Isle of Portland (renamed the Isle of Slingers), home of the hero and the three generations of women he falls in love with. See below, Chapter 18.

40. Collected in *Life's Little Ironies* (1894).

16. Tom and Em

1. There was a third, Randall, mentioned in Walter Gifford's letters to Emma, who was considered an unsuitable visitor and seems to have suffered from some disability.
2. TH to Elspeth Grahame, 31 Aug. 1907, *Letters*, III, 270.
3. TH to Florence Henniker, 23 Aug. 1899, *Letters*, II, 227, and *Life*, Chapter 25.
4. Frank Hedgcock reported in 1951 his visit in 1910, when she talked about her little emendations and referred to 'our books'. *Interviews and Recollections*, 92.
5. Alfred Pretor to Emma Hardy, letter dated 1899, DCM, cited in Denys Kay-Robinson, *The First Mrs Hardy* (1979), 174.
6. Raymond Blathwayt's interview in *Black and White*, 27 Aug. 1892.
7. It was sold to Howard Bliss in 1924, and he found that 106 pages were partly or wholly in Emma's hand. He insisted that he found this interesting, but when he got into financial difficulties later he sold it back to the Hardys. See Florence Hardy to Howard Bliss, 14 Dec. 1924, *Letters of E & F Hardy*, 217.
8. Mabel Robinson to Irene Cooper Willis, 17 Dec. 1937, DCM.
9. F. Stevenson to S. Colvin, Sept. 1885, and to D. Norton Williams, also 1885, both cited in *Biography Revisited*, 250.
10. Cited from a Gissing letter of 22 Sept. 1895 in *Interviews and Recollections*, 50.
11. Gertrude Atherton's *Adventures of a Novelist*, 258, given in *Interviews and Recollections*, 26.
12. It appeared May 1895 in the *Ladies' Home Journal* and is cited in *Interviews and Recollections*, 41.
13. Emma Hardy to Revd Bartelot, 3 July 1912, cited in Denys Kay-Robinson, *The First Mrs Hardy*, 6–7.
14. Emma Hardy, *Alleys, and Spaces. Poems and Religious Effusions* (1966 ed., first published privately by F. G. Longman of Dorchester in 1912).
15. 'An Old Likeness (*Recalling R. T.*)' was published in 1922 in *Late Lyrics and Earlier*. Rosamund Tomson had died in 1911.
16. TH to Florence Henniker, 16 July 1893, *Letters*, II, 24. His last surviving letter to her is dated Dec. 1891.

17. These three words set off a search for evidence of a love affair, and Lois Deacon devoted years to trying to prove that Tryphena bore Hardy a child. The book she wrote with Terry Coleman, *Providence and Mr Hardy* (1966), was taken seriously by many before Robert Gittings disproved most of it in his *The Young TH* in 1975, and Michael Millgate concurred in his 1982 *Thomas Hardy: A Biography*, where he said no evidence 'capable of withstanding scholarly or even common-sensical scrutiny' had been produced by Deacon.

18. In a letter of 30 Aug. 1898 he told Mrs Henniker, 'I have not yet been to Exeter, though I had hoped to get there this summer,' and in Sept. he announces he is going, on his bicycle, and chiefly to see the cathedral. *Letters*, II, 199, 201.

19. *Interviews and Recollections*, 228, citing Lady Tweedsmuir's recollection of what she had been told by Margaret Newbolt.

20. Since Hardy destroyed these diaries, there is no certainty about their dates or contents, but Florence Hardy saw them and told Edward Clodd in a letter of 16 Jan. 1913 that Emma's 'bitter denunciations' of Hardy began 'about 1891' and continued 'until within a day or two of her death'. *Letters of E & F Hardy*, 75.

21. Hardy said he shaved off his beard in 1890, but it is still there in photographs of 1891. Sydney Cockerell claimed that he persuaded Hardy to stop waxing his moustache, which must have been after 1911.

22. Note dated 17 Sept. 1892, given in *Life*, Chapter 20.

23. Note dated 28 Apr. 1888, given in *Life*, Chapter 26.

24. This from his preface, where Tryphena is simply 'a woman' recently dead.

25. Note dated Oct. 1892, *Life*, Chapter 20.

26. *Letters*, I, 287.

17.   The Terra-cotta Dress

1. Quoted from a letter from Swinburne to Monckton Milnes dated 27 Dec. 1862, in James Pope Hennessy's *Monckton Milnes: The Flight of Youth 1851–1885* (1951), 143. I am indebted to Mark Bostridge for pointing this out.

2. MS Houghton 43/18, Trinity College, Cambridge, kindly sent to me by the librarian, David McKitterick. Mrs Henniker's brother kept some of her 'squibs' in his diary for 1872. The word 'airified' is applied to someone who gives himself airs.

3. TH to Florence Henniker, 13 July 1893, *Letters*, II, 23.

4. TH to Florence Henniker, 2 July 1893, *Letters*, II, 20.

5. First printed in 1914 in *Satires of Circumstance, Lyrics and Reveries*.

6. So Hardy told his friend Edward Clodd, according to his diary for 18 July 1896. Information from *Biography Revisited*, 313, and note on 581.

7. According to R. L. Purdy in *Thomas Hardy: A Bibliographical Study* (1954), 113. He gives no source, but he must have had it from Florence Hardy, and she from Hardy himself, or possibly Mrs Henniker, whom she came to know well. The poem was printed in *Poems of the Past and the Present* in 1901. 'Time-torn' was originally 'soul-sad'. Florence Henniker kept a bundle of manuscript poems given to her by Hardy, which have sadly disappeared.

8. TH to Florence Henniker, 6 Sept. 1893, *Letters*, II, 29. 'I should call the book "The Statesman's Love-Lapse, & other stories namely . . ."'

9. TH to Florence Henniker, 16 Sept. 1893, *Letters*, II, 32.

10. TH to Florence Henniker, 28 Oct. 1893, *Letters*, II, 40. For details of their joint authorship, see R. L. Purdy, *Thomas Hardy: A Bibliographical Study*, Appendix IV, 346–8.

11. So Hardy told Mrs Henniker. TH to Florence Henniker, 16 Sept. 1893, *Letters*, II, 32.

12. Review quoted by R. L. Purdy in *Thomas Hardy: A Bibliographical Study*, Appendix IV, 348.

13. Clement Shorter of the *Sketch*. Letter dated 25 Apr. 1894, *Letters*, II, 55.

14. Emma Hardy to Mary Haweis, 13 Nov. 1894, *Letters of E & F Hardy*, 6.

15. This was the belief of her nephew Gordon Gifford, who stayed with them a good deal at the time. He wrote a letter to the *TLS*, 1 Jan. 1944, claiming that *Jude* 'was the first of the Hardy novels in which she had not assisted by her counsel, copious notes for reference and mutual discussion'.

16. TH to Florence Henniker, 10 Nov. 1895, *Letters*, II, 94.

17. Mrs Henniker left instructions before her death in 1923 that all of Hardy's letters that she had kept – she destroyed a good number – should be given after her death to his second wife, whom she knew well and liked. The second Mrs Hardy considered publishing them, but decided against. She preserved them carefully, however, and left them to the DCM, and they were published in 1972.

18. TH to Arthur Henniker, 19 Oct. 1899, *Letters*, II, 233. Request for photograph, TH to Florence Henniker, 9 Nov. 1899, *Letters*, II, 236.

19. According to his poem 'Concerning Agnes', written after her death in Dec. 1926.

20. First printed in *Wessex Poems and Other Verses*, his first collection, in 1898.

21. *Jude the Obscure*, Part VI, Chapter 2.

22. Hardy mentions this in his preface to the 1912 edition of *Jude*.

23. TH to Florence Henniker, 10 Nov. 1895, *Letters*, II, 94.

24. *Jude the Obscure*, Part I, Chapter 11.

25. ibid., Part III, Chapter 9.

26. ibid., Part IV, Chapter 2.

27. Information given by Florence Hardy to R. L. Purdy in 1933, cited in *Biography Revisited*, 25–6 and note.

28. 'humanity' replaces 'morality', which he wrote first.

29. TH to Edmund Gosse, 10 Nov. 1894, *Letters*, II, 93.

30. See second paragraph of *Life*, Chapter 24. Arthur Benson records Hardy's remark in his diary for Nov. 1913, Magdalene College, Cambridge.

31. *Jude the Obscure*, Part I, Chapter 2; cf. passage in Chapter 1 of *Life*.

32. Hardy could have learnt about his accidental conception and the reluctance of both his parents to marry from his Sparks cousins. I think it slightly more likely he realized it when dealing with his father's papers after his death. Since he never alludes to it, we do not know whether he ever discussed it with his mother, but he must have asked himself how welcome he was to her at birth, and even possibly whether she had tried to get rid of the pregnancy.

33. Alfred Sutro, *Celebrities and Simple Souls* (1933), 58, described lunch at Max Gate in 1895, at which he praised the newly published *Jude*.

'Mrs Hardy was far from sharing my enthusiasm. It was the first novel of his, she told me, that he had published without first letting her read the manuscript; had she read it, she added firmly, it would *not* have been published, or at least, not without considerable emendations.'

34. W. D. Howells's review in the Dec. 1895 issue of *Harper's Weekly* is reprinted in R. G. Cox, *Thomas Hardy: The Critical Heritage* (1995), 253–6.

35. Cited in R. G. Cox, *Thomas Hardy: The Critical Heritage*, 283.

36. Hardy printed the letter in *Life*, Chapter 22.

37. TH told this to James Milne in 1905, *Interviews and Recollections*, 81, from *The Memoirs of a Bookman* (1934). Hardy recalled the Gosse incident in a letter to him of 14 July 1909, *Letters*, IV, 33. Another admirer of Hardy's work, George Gissing, wrote privately to a friend of his view of *Jude*: 'Jude I shall never be able to read again. It is powerful, yes; but its horribleness does not, I feel, faithfully represent the life it pretends to depict . . . But I greatly admire Hardy and am very sorry he will write no more fiction. His verse (a volume or two recently published) has but small value.' Gissing to Eduard Bertz, 16 Nov. 1902, *The Letters of George Gissing to Eduard Bertz*, ed. A. C. Young (1960), 314.

38. For his statement, see *Life*, Chapter 24. He also made the curious claim here that he was worried 'whether he might not be driven to society novels' and that for this reason he had felt he must keep a record of his experiences 'in upper social life, though doing it had always been a drudgery to him'. In fact, *Jude* was not the last novel he published, *The Well-Beloved* appearing in volume form in 1897.

39. *Life*, Chapter 23, mentions his 'quick sense of humour . . . which could not help seeing a ludicrous side to his troubles over *Jude*'.

40. He first called them 'De Profundis', later changed to 'In Tenebris', presumably because of Oscar Wilde's *De Profundis*, published posthumously in 1905.

41. TH replying to the question about 'Methods of Authors' for an American newspaper, published in 1894, cited by Michael Millgate in his edition of *Thomas Hardy's Public Voice* (2001), 131.

18.   A Witch and a Wife

1. TH to Florence Henniker, 30 Nov. 1895, *Life*, Chapter 23.
2. TH to Grant Allen, 7 Jan. 1896, *Letters*, II, 106.
3. R. L. Purdy, *Thomas Hardy: A Bibliographical Study* (1954), 77. It was reworked for America by Lorimer Stoddard and put on in Mar. 1897 under his name, successfully. Mrs Campbell never played Tess. Hardy revised his own version in 1924 for the amateur production in Dorchester, and this version was played in London in 1925 and 1929.
4. Mrs P. Campbell to Mrs S. Coleridge, 12 Jan. 1896, letter in DCM, quoted in *Interviews and Recollections*, 52.
5. *Life*, Chapter 23.
6. ibid. This was in 1896.
7. All this information from his letters of Feb. 1896, *Letters*, II, 108–12.
8. Emma Hardy to Mary Hardy, 22 Feb. 1896, printed in *Letters of E & F Hardy*, 7–8.
9. In 1902 Mary Hardy told her cousin Jim Sparks in a letter, à propos Max Gate, that 'we never visit there.' Mary Hardy to Jim Sparks, 1 July 1902, Sparks Archive, Hardy Collection, Eton College.
10. Hardy's own account, although given in the third person in *Life*, Chapter 23.
11. TH to Florence Henniker, 1 June 1896, *Letters*, II, 122.
12. *Life*, Chapter 23.
13. TH to Florence Henniker, 17 Mar. 1903, *Letters*, III, 55–6.
14. She mentions the Rousseau and the Tolstoy in letters to Rebekah Owen, 14 Feb. 1899 and May 1900, *Letters of E & F Hardy*, 13, 21.
15. Emma Hardy to Rebekah Owen, 31 Dec. 1900, cited in *Biography Revisited*, 376.
16. Walter Gifford to Emma Hardy, 7 Sept. 1898, DCM, H.6286.
17. Walter Gifford to Emma Hardy, 24 Oct. 1898, DCM, H.6288.
18. Emma Hardy to Rebekah Owen, 27 Dec. 1899, *Letters of E & F Hardy*, 18.
19. Florence Dugdale to Edward Clodd, 16 Jan. 1913, *Letters of E & F Hardy*, 75: 'voluminous diaries that Mrs H has kept from the time

of their marriage . . . bitter denunciations beginning about 1891 & continuing until within a day or two of her death'.

20. Hardy noted their attendance in the Bible Emma gave him in 1899, marking their initials against the text from Jeremiah read by the Canon of Salisbury on this occasion. *The Older TH*, 97.

21. TH to Winifred Thomson, 31 Oct. 1897, *Letters*, II, 181.

22. TH to Thackeray Turner, 12 Oct. 1897, *Letters*, II, 179.

23. TH told Henry Nevinson in 1906 about the Kipling episode, *Interviews and Recollections*, 79.

24. See Chapter 15, p. 232.

25. *The Well-Beloved*, Part I, Chapter 2.

26. The epigraph, 'one shape of many names', is taken from Shelley's *The Revolt of Islam*.

27. *The Well-Beloved*, Part II, Chapter 1.

28. ibid., Part III, Chapter 2.

29. ibid., Part II, Chapter 3.

30. Emma Hardy to Elspeth Grahame, 20 Aug. 1899, *Letters of E & F Hardy*, 15–16.

31. The Grahames' only child, a son, was an unhappy boy who committed suicide at Oxford – an awful echo of Little Father Time and 'the coming will not to live'.

32. Emma Hardy to Rebekah Owen, 24 Apr. 1899, *Letters of E & F Hardy*, 19.

33. Emma's MS plan for a story, dated 1900, is in the DCM, H.6216. Hardy's poem was published in the *Tatler* in July 1901 and in *Poems of the Past and the Present*, also 1901, and included in *Selected Poems* of 1916, chosen by himself as one of his favourites.

34. TH to Florence Henniker, 25 Feb. 1900, *Letters*, II, 248.

35. Hardy told Mrs Henniker in a letter 25 Feb. 1900, *Letters*, II, 248.

36. Emma Hardy to Rebekah Owen, 27 Dec. 1899, *Letters of E & F Hardy*, 19.

37. First printed in *Literature*, 25 Nov. 1899, 513, with a note added to the title: 'One of the Drummers killed was a native of a village near Casterbridge.' It then appeared in *Poems of the Past and the Present* in 1901. Later, Hardy changed the name of the poem to 'Drummer Hodge'. The idea may have helped to inspire Rupert Brooke's

famous sonnet: 'If I should die, think only this of me, / That there's some corner of a foreign field / That is forever England.'

38. Bertha Newcombe to Mrs Edmund Gosse, 5 Mar. 1900, cited in *Emma Hardy Diaries*, ed. Richard H. Taylor (1985), 10, and Denys Kay-Robinson, *The First Mrs Hardy* (1979), 183, from Brotherton Library Collection, Leeds.

39. He did not publish it until 1925, in *Human Shows, Far Phantasies, Songs and Trifles*, dating it 'about 1900'.

40. TH to Emma Hardy, 11 Dec. 1900 and 23 Dec. 1900, *Letters*, II, 276, 270.

41. When printed in *Poems of the Past and the Present* in 1901.

42. Barbara Hardy makes the connection in her *Thomas Hardy* (2001), 200.

19. Cat, Bird, Eagle, Sphinx

1. TH to Edward Clodd, fragment of letter, May 1902, *Letters*, III, 20.

2. Figures taken from Michael Millgate's article on Macmillan & Co. in *The Oxford Reader's Companion to Hardy* (2000), 250.

3. Hardy told Henry Nevinson about the young women who wrote to him asking for advice on settling in Wessex. *Interviews and Recollections*, 77–8.

4. Published by Harper Brothers in London in the autumn of 1898, and in New York in 1899.

5. See above, Chapter 5, pp. 81–2.

6. See above, Chapter 17, pp. 247–9.

7. See above, Chapter 17, p. 253.

8. From Gosse's *Portraits from Life*, cited in *Interviews and Recollections*, 109.

9. Wells's remark was reported by many, among them R. E. Zachrisson, the Swedish writer, who visited Max Gate in 1920 and thought Wells's description reasonable, but insisted on Hardy's 'wonderful light blue eyes'. Cited in *Interviews and Recollections*, 132.

10. Archer's interview was printed in the *Pall Mall Magazine* in Apr. 1901, reprinted in his *Real Conversations* (1904).

11. From Desmond MacCarthy's *Memories* (1953).

12. William Rothenstein visited Hardy in 1897; his remarks are in *Men and Memories: Recollections 1872–1938*, given in *Interviews and Recollections*, 53–4.

13. Frank Hedgcock in 1910, struck by Hardy's 'simplicity and modesty'. 'The great dome-like forehead spoke of power and his eyes, though tired, were dreamy and imaginative. His nose, which seemed slightly bent, was beak-like.' 'Reminiscences of Thomas Hardy' in *National and English Review*, Oct. and Nov. 1951, cited in *Interviews and Recollections*, 91.

14. Winifred Fortescue, *There's Rosemary . . . There's Rue* (1939). This was in 1908. Keeping up the bird imagery, in 1926 another visitor, Virginia Woolf, likened him to a pouter pigeon.

15. Diary of Arthur Benson for 30 Apr. 1904, Magdalene College, Cambridge. If Benson heard Hardy's remark about joining the Catholic Church correctly, it casts a new light on his London years and his friendship with Moule, whose interest in Newman and Roman Catholicism he mentions in the *Life* – but with no suggestion that he shared it at any point. It is an intriguing piece of information, but hung on a slender thread.

16. Details of Hardy's visit from Martin Ray's 'Thomas Hardy in Aberdeen', *Aberdeen University Review*, 56 (1995), 58–69. This was kindly brought to my attention by Myrrdin Jones.

17. TH to Florence Henniker, 2 June 1901, *Letters*, II, 288; TH to George Douglas, 3 Apr. 1901, *Letters*, II, 282; and Emma Hardy to Rebekah Owen, 4 Apr. 1901, *Letters of E & H Hardy*, 23.

18. According to Christine Wood Homer in *Thomas Hardy and His Two Wives* (1964), 48.

19. Described in a passage written into the *Life*, Chapter 26, by Florence Hardy on the advice of J. M. Barrie, who had the details from Hardy.

20. Lillie May Farris, granddaughter of Jemima's brother William. 'Memoirs of the Hardy and Hand Families', *Hardyana* (1968–73), 65.

21. TH to Edward Clodd, 12 Apr. 1904, *Letters*, III, 119.

22. First published in 1909 in *Time's Laughingstocks and Other Verses*.

23. Hardy quotes this entry from her diary in the *Life*, Chapter 28.

24. Cited in *Interviews and Recollections*, 108, from an undated text by Gosse given in Ann Thwaite's edition of *Portraits from Life* (1991).

25. Jacques Blanche, *Mes Modèles* (1928), 84.

26. TH to Edward Clodd, 1 May 1909, *Letters*, IV, 21.

27. The letter is so well written and coherent that Michael Millgate has suggested that it was 'polished' at the *Nation. Letters of E & F Hardy*, p. xii.

28. *Life*, Chapter 1.

29. *The Dynasts*, Part III, Act VI, Scene viii. Hardy's tramps over the field of Waterloo had stirred his imagination, and, as it turned out, he was predicting what would happen all over northern France in the coming war of 1914–18.

30. *The Dynasts*, Part III, Act I, Scene i.

31. Beerbohm was reviewing Part I only, in the *Saturday Review*, 30 Jan. 1904.

32. Harold Child in the *TLS*, 27 Feb. 1908, and unsigned review in *Edinburgh Review*, Apr. 1908.

33. I see that my own copy was bought in 1953 from Blackwell's in Oxford for 8/6d. It is the 1910 first complete edition but bears no signs of having belonged to a previous owner.

34. This striking tribute is told in *Interviews and Recollections*, 181–2.

PART FOUR   1905–1928

20.   Convergence

1. TH to Florence Dugdale, 10 Aug. 1905, *Letters*, III, 179.

2. Florence Dugdale to Rebekah Owen, 1 Dec. 1914, *Letters of E & F Hardy*, 101–2.

3. This is what she told R. L. Purdy in 1935 – see *Biography Revisited*, 409–10.

4. Michael Millgate gives these various accounts in his *Thomas Hardy: His Career as a Novelist* (1971), 446–7. In his *Biography Revisited* he settles for the version she gave Purdy, about visiting with Mrs Henniker, which seems wholly implausible.

5. From Dorothy Meech's monograph *Memories of Mr and Mrs Thomas Hardy* (Beaminster, 1963). Dorothy Meech did typing work over a period of time at Max Gate for Florence Hardy after Hardy's death.

She liked her, and they often talked together. It must be remembered that such accounts, made over thirty years after the conversations described, are not necessarily accurate. It seems unlikely, for example, that Florence would have said she met the Hardys on holiday in Wareham. The point about this account is to convey that her friendship with Emma began at the same time as that with Hardy. All this information on p. 5 of the monograph.

6. 'After the Visit' was first printed in the *Spectator*, 13 Aug. 1910. It was then included in *Satires of Circumstance, Lyrics and Reveries* (1914) after Emma's death, with the additional '*(To F.E.D.)*' under the title.

7. Dorothy Meech, *Memories of Mr and Mrs Thomas Hardy*, 5. Even given Hardy's reluctance to spend money, this is hard to believe.

8. TH to Reginald Smith, 26 Sept. 1907, *Letters*, III, 274.

9. For instance, he thanked her for a box at the Court Theatre, saying his wife could not be there, but he would bring 'a young cousin' – meaning Florence. TH to Lady Gregory, 7 June 1910, *Letters*, IV, 95.

10. According to Edward Clodd's diary, 5 July 1909, cited in *Biography Revisited*, 424.

11. Robert Gittings and Jo Manton, *The Second Mrs Hardy* (1979), 46.

12. Edward Clodd to Clement Shorter, 27 Aug. 1909, cited in ibid., 50.

13. *The Oxford Reader's Companion to Hardy* (2000), 416.

14. This was also in 1909. Netta Syrett, *The Sheltering Tree*, cited in *Interviews and Recollections*, 86.

15. From TH's contribution to the symposium 'How Shall We Solve the Divorce Problem?' in *Nash's Magazine*, 5 Mar. 1912, cited in *Thomas Hardy's Public Voice*, ed. Michael Millgate (2001), 332.

16. TH to Austin Harrison, 9 May 1910, *Letters*, IV, 87.

17. TH to Agnes Grove, 13 May 1910, *Letters*, IV, 89.

18. Emma Handy to Lady Hoare, 24 Apr. 1910, *Letters of E & F Hardy*, 48.

19. Florence Dugdale to Edward Clodd, 11 Nov. 1910, ibid., 66.

20. See Florence's letters to Edward Clodd, 8 and 19 Nov. 1910, ibid., 65, 68. The amateur theatrical group became 'The Hardy Players' and caused much distress to Florence later; see Chapter 23, below.

21. Florence Dugdale to Edward Clodd, 19 Nov. 1910, ibid., 68.

22. Florence Dugdale to Sydney Cockerell, 25 Dec. 1925, ibid., 234.

23. As Pamela Dalziel demonstrates in *Thomas Hardy: The Excluded and Collaborative Stories* (1992), 336–55.

24. TH to Florence Henniker, 3 May 1911, *Letters*, IV, 150.

25. Florence Dugdale to Edward Clodd, 11 Dec. 1911, cited by Robert Gitting and Jo Manton, *The Second Mrs Hardy*, 64.

26. So he told Sassoon in 1921. Siegfried Sassoon's diary for 22 Feb., quoted in *Interviews and Recollections*, 128.

27. Donald Davie, *Thomas Hardy and British Poetry* (1973), 17.

28. The *Titanic* sank on 15 Apr. 1912 and Hardy's poem was completed and first printed on 24 Apr. in a programme for a Covent Garden matinée in aid of a disaster fund. A final version was printed in *Satires of Circumstance* in 1914.

29. From *The Later Life and Letters of Sir Henry Newbolt*, cited in *Interviews and Recollections*, 99–100.

30. TH to Arthur Benson, 30 July 1892, *Letters*, I, 280.

31. Benson's diary for Saturday, 22 Apr. 1905, Magdalene College, Cambridge.

32. Benson's diary for Thursday, 5 Sept. 1912, Magdalene College, Cambridge.

33. *Life*, Chapter 31.

34. Both poems are in MS, held at the Berg Collection. The first poem is MS 64B7402 and is signed 'E. L. Hardy' and dated Max Gate, 22 Nov. 1912. The second is MS 64B7433, with pencilled words by Hardy, 'Written by Mrs (Emma) Hardy 22 Nov. 1912: 5 days before her death'.

35. Rebekah Owen to a Mrs Fauty, presumably her housekeeper in the Lake District, 28 Nov. 1912, quoted in Carl Weber's *Thomas Hardy and the Lady from Madison Square* (1952), 162–4. Owen was quite capable of questioning servants to extract information.

36. Dr Alan Frizzell writes, 'Impacted gallstones could produce a fatal outcome, but I would not expect the pain of gallstones to be felt in the back. Mrs Hardy may have had gallstones, but I doubt if she died of them. The back pain suggests a retroperitoneal problem, and the course of her final illness is typical of a leaking abdominal aortic aneurysm. In the course of my career I came across more than one

unfortunate patient who went to bed with the observation "My back is bad tonight", to be found expired the next day from that cause.'

21.   Satires of Circumstance

1. Mary Hardy to Mr and Mrs Hull [28 Nov. 1912?], DCM, H.1987.227.

2. Rebekah Owen to Mrs Fauty [n.d.], cited in Carl Weber, *Thomas Hardy and the Lady from Madison Square* (1952), 165.

3. Reported in the *Dorset County Chronicle*, 5 Dec. 1912.

4. See Florence Hardy's letter to Lady Hoare, 22 July 1914, *Letters of E & F Hardy*, 98.

5. So Robert Gittings and Jo Manton allege in *The Second Mrs Hardy* (1979), 79. They also say on p. 93 that Jane Riggs stayed until 1917, when Florence alienated her further by taking cooking lessons herself.

6. So Florence reported to Edward Clodd in a letter of 30 Jan. 1913, *Letters of E & F Hardy*, 77.

7. Mary Hardy to Nat Sparks, 15 Feb. 1913, Sparks Archive, Hardy Collection, Eton College.

8. Florence Dugdale to Edward Clodd, Max Gate, 7 Mar. 1913, *Letters of E & F Hardy*, 78–9.

9. The volume of stories was *A Changed Man and Other Tales*, published 24 Oct. 1913 and simultaneously by Harper's in the US.

10. TH to Edward Elgar, 28 July 1913, *Letters*, IV, 291.

11. TH to Edward Clodd, 10 Dec. 1913, ibid., 327–8.

12. First printed in *Moments of Vision and Miscellaneous Verses* (1917), where it is dated Aug. 1913.

13. 'When Oats Were Reaped' is also dated Aug. 1913, but Hardy did not print it until 1925, in *Human Shows, Far Phantasies, Songs and Trifles*.

14. TH to Florence Henniker, 21 Dec. 1913, *Letters*, IV, 330.

15. Florence Dugdale to Edward Clodd, 3 Dec. 1913, *Letters of E & F Hardy*, 87.

16. In the *Life* Hardy describes this period in these words: 'The autumn

glided on . . . In the muddle of Hardy's unmistressed housekeeping, animal pets of his late wife died, strayed, or were killed, much to Hardy's regret.'

17. Florence Dugdale to Edward Clodd, 1 Jan. 1914, *Letters of E & F Hardy*, 92.

18. Florence Dugdale to Edward Clodd, 3 Dec. 1913, *Letters E & F Hardy*, 86. The 'imbecile' must be Randolph, mentioned in Walter Gifford's letters to Emma.

19. See Wilfrid Blunt's *Cockerell* (1964), 214.

20. Florence Dugdale to Rebekah Owen, 18 Jan. 1916, *Letters of E & F Hardy*, 114.

21. Florence Hardy to Rebekah Owen, 20 Sept. 1915, cited by Robert Gittings and Jo Manton, *The Second Mrs Hardy*, 72.

22. TH to Sydney Cockerell, 11 Feb. 1914, *Letters*, V, 9; TH to Edward Clodd, 11 Feb. 1914, *Letters*, V, 9.

23. Hardy told Edmund Blunden that he was capable of sexual intercourse until he was eighty-four, i.e., until 1924, ten years after he married Florence. This was told by Blunden to Martin Seymour-Smith, who gives it in his *Hardy* (1994), 728. Florence would certainly have understood that the duty of a wife was to submit to her husband's embraces, but there is nothing to suggest that she took any pleasure in them, and a good deal to suggest she did not – her depression and hypochondria and her perpetual longing to get away from Max Gate.

24. Diary of Arthur Benson, Friday, 8 May 1914, Magdalene College, Cambridge.

25. TH to Sydney Cockerell, 9 Aug. 1914, *Letters*, V, 41.

26. TH to Florence Henniker, 17 July 1914, *Letters*, V, 37.

27. TH to Maurice Macmillan, 6 Aug. 1913, *Letters*, IV, 293.

28. TH to George Macmillan, 10 Aug. 1914, *Letters*, V, 41, and TH to Sydney Cockerell, 28 Aug. 1914, *Letters*, V, 45.

29. Florence Dugdale to Lady Hoare, 6 Dec. 1914, *Letters of E & F Hardy*, 104.

30. TH to Florence Henniker, 23 Dec. 1914, *Letters*, V, 70.

31. Virginia Woolf to TH, 17 Jan. 1915, *The Letters of Virginia Woolf*, II (1976), 58. On 23 Feb. she became ill and was out of action throughout the summer.

32. 'Books in General', *New Statesman*, 4 Nov. 1916. Squire wrote under his pseudonym 'Solomon Eagle'. A week later Robert Lynd attacked the poems in the *Nation* for being ugly, prosaic and exaggerated.

33. Florence Hardy to Sydney Cockerell, 12 Aug. 1916, *Letters of E & F Hardy*, 118.

34. 'To Shakespeare', one of the few poems that had already appeared in print, first in *A Book of Homage to Shakespeare* edited by Israel Gollancz for the 300th anniversary of his death, then in the *Fortnightly Review* for June 1916. Florence Hardy then printed it as a separate pamphlet with the help of Sydney Cockerell in July 1916.

35. The apparently random order of the poems is mysterious. Hardy must have realized that such personal work would be scanned for what it tells about his life, and that jumbling would not prevent this. Indeed he says himself in a letter of early Nov. 1919, 'there is more autobiography in a hundred lines of Mr Hardy's poetry than in all the novels.' This is from a draft in Florence Hardy's hand, to Archie Whitfield, a critic who had suggested that *Jude* might be autobiographical. *Letters*, VII, 161. So, given that he did put the 'Poems of 1912–13' and his war poems into clear, separate sections, why did he not arrange other poems by subject, or put them in chronological order? I am unable to suggest any explanation.

36. Florence Hardy to Sydney Cockerell, 8 Dec. 1917, cited in *Biography Revisited*, 474, Yale.

37. These are discussed in Chapter 11, above.

38. From an edited version of a Radio 4 conversation between Vernon Scannell and Philip Larkin, printed in the *Listener* as 'A Man who Noted Things', 25 July 1968.

39. A letter from Florence Hardy to Marie Stopes in Sept. 1923 reads: 'I find on talking to him [Hardy] that the idea of my having a child at his age fills him with terror . . . He said he would have welcomed a child when we married first, ten years ago, but now it would kill him with anxiety to have to father one.'

40. Quoted by Ann Thwaite in *Edmund Gosse: A Literary Landscape* (1984), 461.

22.   A Friend from Cambridge

1. See Florence Hardy's account of this to Rebekah Owen, 18 Jan. 1916, *Letters of E & F Hardy*, 113–114.

2. Cockerell also worked for Wilfrid Scawen Blunt in Egypt and was shipwrecked with him in the Gulf of Suez. He visited Tolstoy at Yasnaya Polyana in 1903, and Tolstoy spoke to him of his admiration for Dickens: 'All his characters are my personal friends ... What a spirit there was in all he wrote!' and his dislike of Shakespeare, who 'had no feeling for the peasants. He never introduces a "clown" except to make fun of him. That is why I cannot read him with pleasure.' These notes from *Friends of a Lifetime: Letters to Sydney Carlyle Cockerell*, ed. V. Meynell (1940), 81, 83–4.

3. This was Charlotte Mew and her sister Anne's name for him, according to Penelope Fitzgerald, *Charlotte Mew and Her Friends* (1984), 176, which gives a good account of Cockerell.

4. *Cockerell* (1964) by Wilfrid Blunt, 269, given as a direct quotation but without a source.

5. Cockerell's diaries are unpublished and held in the British Library. For 1911, Add. MSS 52648.

6. Howard Bliss, who sold it back when he got into financial difficulties. See *Letters of E & F Hardy*, 175–6, 217.

7. The remark is in Benson's long diary entry describing the visit to Max Gate with Gosse in 1912. Hardy did give Florence the MS of *Under the Greenwood Tree*, as she informed Cockerell firmly in 1916: 'We have been looking at "Under the Greenwood Tree" (which belongs to me now).' Florence Hardy to Sydney Cockerell, 12 Aug. 1916, *Letters of E & F Hardy*, 118.

8. Cockerell's diary for 1912, British Library Add. MSS 52649. Hardy was on friendly terms with Shaw and saw his *Man and Superman* performed. He does not mention Synge in the *Life*.

9. ibid., summary of year at beginning of diary.

10. See Note 15 below.

11. Mary Hardy to TH, 12 June 1913, DCM, also cited in *Biography Revisited*, 454.

12. The performance was given by the ADC, the Amateur Dramatic

Club of Cambridge. At that date none of the Newnham or Girton students could belong. The *Cambridge Magazine* critic remarked on A. E. Moorsom, who played Gwendolen, having 'just that doll's beauty which fits with the Comedy', otherwise regretting 'what it means to give women's parts to men: angular shapes and solid voices to the daintiness of feminine dress'. Siegfried Sassoon noted Hardy's reference to 'that man Wilde' and his innocence about homosexuality in his diary for 28 June 1922, passage given in *Interviews and Recollections*, 130.

13. Diary of Arthur Benson, Wednesday, 11 June 1913, Magdalene College, Cambridge. His appreciation of Hardy is in the issue of 6 June 1913.

14. Sydney Cockerell's diary for 1913, British Library Add. MSS 52650 for this and further quotes in this paragraph.

15. Cockerell wrote a memo in his diary explaining that 'At my original suggestion, backed by Dr Verrall & all who stand for English Literature in Cambridge, Thomas Hardy received Doctor's degree with great applause on June 11 and stayed with us at Wayside [SC's house] for the purpose.'

16. All quotes and information in this paragraph from Sydney Cockerell's diary for 1913, British Library Add. MSS 52650.

17. Arthur Benson's diary, November 1913, notes: 'That ass Ogden, in the Cambridge Magazine, said that Thomas Hardy "the celebrated Atheist" had been elected an Hon. Fellow. He meant it he said as a compliment to the Dons; but I wrote sharply to him to say that the word was simply an insulting word, both to Hardy & to us.' C. K. Ogden founded the *Cambridge Magazine* in 1912 and an undergraduate association 'The Heretics'. In 1923 he wrote *The Meaning of Meaning* with I. A. Richards and went on to invent and promote the idea of Basic English as an international language.

18. Alan Rusbridger was told this by I. A. Richards and kindly passed it on to me. Richard Luckett, friend and executor of Richards, believes it must have been the Benson building, finished in 1913, and tells me that Benson's diary shows that he knew and liked the young Richards.

19. Florence Dugdale to Sydney Cockerell, 30 Nov. 1913, *Letters of E & F Hardy*, 85.

20. Sydney Cockerell's diary for 5 May 1914, British Library Add. MSS 52651.

21. Arthur Benson's diary for Friday, 8 May 1914, Magdalene College, Cambridge.

22. Information about Emily Elizabeth Constance Jones, Mistress of Girton from 1903 to 1916, kindly provided by Kate Perry, Archivist of Girton College.

23. Quoted in Michael Millgate's edition of *Thomas Hardy's Public Voice* (2001), 374. Bernard Shaw, Sassoon, Masefield, I. A. Richards (later co-editor) and the young historian Eileen Power were among contributors to the English part of the magazine.

24. This was in Mar. 1917. Hardy always took care with group letters and suggested changes because this one seemed to be attacking the whole of the British press, 'which would have the effect of setting it all against you, which I am sure you do not wish to do'. His emendation was accepted, and the letter appeared in the *Morning Post* and in the *Cambridge Magazine* itself. See *Letters*, V, 207–8.

25. TH to Florence Henniker, 23 Mar. 1915, *Letters*, V, 86.

26. TH to Florence Hardy, 28 May 1915, *Letters*, V, 101.

27. Printed in *Moments of Vision and Miscellaneous Verses* (1917), in a small section of war poems at the end.

28. TH to John Galsworthy, 15 Aug. 1918, *Letters*, V, 275.

29. See Chapter 7, above, for genesis of this poem, which was first published in the *Saturday Review*, 29 Jan. 1916.

30. *Life*, Chapter 33.

31. TH to Sydney Cockerell, 23 Feb. 1917, *Letters*, V, 203.

32. He showed them and talked about them to John Squire in Aug. 1927 as part of the history of the garden, along with the Roman remains. From his *Sunday Mornings*, quoted in *Interviews and Recollections*, 234.

33. Florence Hardy to Rebekah Owen, 3 Dec. 1915, *Letters of E & F Hardy*, 111.

34. Made in a letter to Emma, 28 Jan. 1881, after the Lock family had invited her to dinner. DCM, H.6302.

35. Vere H. Collins, *Talks with Thomas Hardy at Max Gate 1920–1922* (New York, 1928; reprinted St Peter Port, 1971), 58, a conversation held on 29 Oct. 1921. Florence added that Mary collapsed at the station the last time she went.

36. Mary Hardy to older Nat Sparks, 16 Jan. 1905, Sparks Archive, Hardy Collection, Eton College.

37. Diary of Sydney Cockerell, 17 Apr. 1916: 'He told me that his surviving brother and sister (born eleven years or so after him and his favourite sister who died at the end of last year) are wholly without interest in art and letters, and that he has very little in common with them – with them the family becomes extinct.' British Library Add. MSS 52663.

38. 'Logs on the Hearth (A Memory of a Sister)', dated Dec. 1915, published in *Moments of Vision*.

39. Florence Hardy to Rebekah Owen, 18 Jan. 1916, *Letters of E & F Hardy*, 113.

40. Sydney Cockerell to TH, 7 Dec. 1915, DCM, given in Michael Millgate, *Testamentary Acts* (1992), 123.

41. TH to Gertrude Bugler, 7 Dec. 1915, *Letters*, V, 137.

42. His diary shows that he sent her forty letters in 1916 alone, and he kept up a tremendous volume of correspondence with her for many years, rarely writing less than once a fortnight except when he was abroad.

43. For example, he suggested she come and hear Quiller-Couch lecture in Cambridge in Feb. 1918, but she felt it her duty to stay with Hardy: Florence Hardy to Sydney Cockerell, 2 Feb. 1918, *Letters of E & F Hardy*, 137. He took her to Shaw's *St Joan* with his wife and saw her off on the Dorchester train on 4 June 1924. Diary of Sydney Cockerell, British Library Add. MSS 52661.

44. Diary of Sydney Cockerell, 19 Feb. 1916, British Library Add. MSS 52653, as are all entries for 1916.

45. Diary of Sydney Cockerell, Sunday, 24 Sept. 1916, British Library Add. MSS 52653.

46. Diary of Sydney Cockerell for 1920, British Library Add. MSS 52657, for this and all other quotations in this paragraph.

47. Robert Gittings made a bold attempt to claim that Hardy's grandmother Mary Hardy, née Head, born in 1772, was the original for Tess, and he did discover that she had almost certainly given birth to an illegitimate child some years before her marriage, but that isn't enough to make her Tess. There are too many discrepancies, starting with her not being a Dorset girl, and going on to her happy marriage

to his grandfather and long life with more children and grand-children at Bockhampton. It is extremely tempting to try to make out a case for Jemima having had some of Tess's experiences before her marriage – a rich lover, a lost child – but there is no evidence at all to support it.

48. 'Private Memorandum/Information for Mrs Hardy in the prep-aration of a biography' in DCM, quoted in Millgate's introduction to his 1984 edition of the *Life*, p. xix.

49. They were published as her work, she died in 1937, and by the 1950s the truth of their composition had emerged. R. L. Purdy's *Bibliographical Study* of 1954 gave the true facts and described the process by which the *Life*, originally in two volumes published in 1928 and 1929, was put together from Hardy's manuscript, which was then destroyed, along with most of the source materials. Michael Millgate's edition is outstanding, combining the two volumes as *The Life and Work of Thomas Hardy*, with notes and index, first published 1984 and revised 1989.

23. The Wizard

1. It was his third study at Max Gate, to which he moved after he had given up writing novels.

2. Hardy bought the cello from his cousin Nathaniel Sparks of Bristol, a restorer of musical instruments, in 1902. See *Letters*, III, 38, TH to Nathaniel Sparks, 'No doubt the old viol has many a score time accompanied such tunes as "Lydia" or "Eaton" – (the latter was the tune with which they used nearly to lift off the roof of Goddard's chapel of a Sunday evening).' This was a Dissenting chapel in Puddle-town, obviously well known to them both from their childhood.

3. Cynthia Asquith visited Max Gate in May 1921 and published her account in 1954 (in *Portrait of Barrie*, whose secretary she was, 105–10). She thought there were no pictures hanging in the study except for a framed 'wage-sheet' from Hardy's father's or grandfather's papers, on the shelf over the fireplace. She also gave her view that the study, 'bare, simple, workmanlike and pleasantly shabby, was the only room in the house that had any character at all'. On the

other hand Florence Hardy pointed out to R. L. Purdy in 1929 (after Hardy's death) family photographs, portraits of Shelley and George Eliot, and illustrations to *Tess* and *Jude*, all hanging on the walls. It is of course perfectly possible that things changed between 1921 and 1928, and memories are fallible.

4. May O'Rourke's reminiscences are in the monograph *Thomas Hardy: His Secretary Remembers* (1965), reproduced in *Interviews and Recollections*, 188–91.

5. Diary of Sydney Cockerell for 1919, British Library Add. MSS 52656.

6. See Note 12 to Chapter 22, above. Sassoon described Hardy as the 'Wessex wizard' in his poem 'At Max Gate'.

7. Robert Graves to TH, 9 Jan. 1919, DCM, H.2633.

8. Article by Graves in the *Sphere*, 28 Jan. 1928, reprinted in *Interviews and Recollections*, 135.

9. These are the second and third stanzas. Bale means evil, suffering, injury, infliction of death; ban signifies a curse or malediction.

10. TH to Florence Henniker, 29 May 1922, *Letters*, VI, 132.

11. See Chapter 5, p. 81.

12. See Prologue, p. xxv.

13. Florence Hardy to Sydney Cockerell, 6 Feb. 1919, *Letters of E & F Hardy*, 157.

14. Elliott Felkin, 'Days with Thomas Hardy: From a 1918–1919 Diary', *Encounter*, 18, Apr. 1962, 27–33. Felkin was a young officer on the staff of the prisoner-of-war camp at Dorchester at the end of the war and afterwards, introduced to the Hardys by the Cambridge don Lowes Dickinson and welcomed by them. He kept a diary recording his visits to them between Oct. 1918 and Aug. 1919.

15. This is from Virginia Woolf's report of Forster describing a visit to Max Gate, in a letter to Janet Case, 23 Sept. 1922, *The Letters of Virginia Woolf*, II (1976), 559.

16. This was Harry Bentley, a young Dorchester man with a liking for books but denied secondary education by his parents' poverty. Personal information from Anne Blandamer, wife of his nephew, who talked at length with Mr Bentley in 1978 and saw the pictures of Hardy and William Barnes he put up in his house.

17. The book is in the DCM, from Hardy's library. His remark comes

from *Life*, last words of Chapter 28. Notebook entry, *The Personal Notebooks of Thomas Hardy*, ed. Richard H. Taylor (1978), 71. The listing of the Nordmann book is on p. 99, at the back of the notebook.

18. TH to Sir Rennell Rodd, 27 June 1924, *Letters*, VI, 262.

19. Florence Hardy to Louise Yearsley, 10 Nov. 1918, *Letters of E & F Hardy*, 151.

20. Hardy's account of his intentions are in a letter to the music critic Harold Child, 11 Nov. 1923, *Letters*, VI, 221. Diary of Sydney Cockerell, 11 Aug. 1923, British Library Add. MSS 52660.

21. *Life*, Chapter 37. Boughton's account of their venture appeared in the *Musical News and Herald*, 15 Feb. 1928, 73, 33–44, and ends, 'His work is not a refuge from the woe of the world, but the battle-plain of a courageous spirit.'

22. Hardy, when invited in 1917 to support a proposal for a memorial to Shakespeare to be put up in Rome after the war, had agreed, but insisted it should not be characterized as pertaining to 'Christian civilization', saying 'I for one could not subscribe to a manifesto which did not keep silence on that point.' TH to Richard Bagot, 7 June 1917, *Letters*, V, 218.

23. Florence Hardy to Sydney Cockerell, 30 June 1923, *Letters of E & F Hardy*, 197.

24. Diary of Sydney Cockerell for 1923, British Library Add. MSS 52660.

25. TH to Kate Hardy, 18 July 1923, *Letters*, VI, 204–5 and note.

26. On 26 June the Council of the Duchy noted in their minutes that 'Mrs Hardy is the wife of the celebrated novelist, Thomas Hardy O. M.' The Duchy records say nothing about what prompted the Prince's advisers to suggest his visit to Max Gate, but it seems just possible that the negotiations for the little plot of land gave them the idea, since the Prince's visit was primarily to visit his tenants.

Neither Hardy nor Florence appears to have explained why they wanted the extra land, or why it was negotiated for in her name, nor is it clear which of them actually paid for it, but the Duchy dealt only with her, mostly through the Hardys' solicitors, Lock, Reed & Lock. In Sept. the £100 asked by the Duchy was paid through the lawyers, and in Oct. the land was pegged out and

Florence formally took possession of it, but no gardener's cottage was ever built on it.

27. 'Afterthoughts of Max Gate' by Ellen Titterington, *Hardyana* (1969), 342.

28. Description of Hardy in T. E. Lawrence's letter to Robert Graves, 8 Sept. 1923, cited in *Interviews and Recollections*, 182.

29. Florence Hardy to Marie Stopes, 14 Sept. 1923, *Letters of E & F Hardy*, 203.

30. Florence Hardy to Sydney Cockerell, 3 Jan. 1922, ibid., 179.

31. Letter quoted by Robert Gittings and Jo Manton in *The Second Mrs Hardy* (1979), 87, no source but attributed to 1917.

32. See letter from TH to Lady St Helier, 25 Sept. 1919, *Letters*, V, 325.

33. Florence Hardy to Sydney Cockerell, 31 Jan. 1921, *Letters of E & F Hardy*, 173.

34. Florence Hardy to E. M. Forster, 6 Jan. 1924, ibid., 206.

35. Diary of Sydney Cockerell for 1924, British Library Add. MSS 52661.

36. Virginia Woolf, who was just finishing writing *Mrs Dalloway*, noted in her diary for 17 Oct. 1924 her musing about her own predicted fame:

> . . . very likely this time next year I shall be one of those people who are, so father said, in the little circle of London Society which represents the Apostles [exclusive Cambridge club] . . . on a larger scale . . . To know everyone worth knowing. I can just see what he means; just imagine being in that position – if women can be. Lytton is: Maynard; Ld Balfour; not perhaps Hardy. Which reminds me I ought to dash in Mrs Hardy in nursing home, having had her tumour cut out with Miss Charlotte Mew. Nothing very exciting, even as a boast not very exciting now. H. remembers your father: did not like many people, but was fond of him; talks of him often. Would like to know you. But I cant easily fit into that relation; the daughter grateful for old compliments to her father. Yet I should like to see him; to hear him – say something. But what? One or two words about a flower, or a view, or a garden chair, perhaps.

No doubt this led to her visit to the Hardys in 1926.

37. Diary of Sydney Cockerell for 1924, British Library Add. MSS

52661. Florence Hardy mentions Virginia Woolf's visit in a letter to her, 31 May 1925, *Letters of E & F Hardy*, 225. Woolf put a post-script to her letter to V. Sackville-West, 9 Nov. 1924, 'I have met Mrs Thomas Hardy, Charlotte Mew . . . Siegfried Sassoon . . .', all evidently at the nursing home. *The Letters of Virginia Woolf*, III (1977), 140.

38. Florence Hardy to Sydney Cockerell, *Letters of E & F Hardy*, 213.

39. This is the second of two stanzas. The poem is dated 9 Oct. 1924 and was first printed in *Human Shows, Far Phantasies, Songs and Trifles* (1925). The word 'whangs', meaning to make a noise while moving along, is unusual and comes from northern and Scottish dialect, but it was used by Browning and also by Masefield in 1912, 'the organ whangs, the giddy horses reel', where Hardy is likely to have read it.

40. Florence Hardy to Siegfried Sassoon, 30 June 1922, Eton College Archive, cited in *Letters of E & F Hardy*, p. xxii.

41. This was in Jan. 1918. The production, a revival of one performed in 1910, was based on *Under the Greenwood Tree*. Information from W. G. L. Parsons, '*A Mellstock Quire*' *Boy's Recollections of Thomas Hardy* (St Peter Port, 1967).

42. Florence Hardy to Sydney Cockerell, 26 Dec. 1920, *Letters of E & F Hardy*, 171. Hardy must have known that Gertrude Bugler's mother had grown up at Higher Bockhampton and worked in a dairy, like Tess. She married a Dorchester confectioner, and their children were brought up in South Street. Gertrude chose to be married in Stinsford Church.

43. Florence Hardy to Sydney Cockerell, 26 Nov. 1922, ibid., 193.

44. Hardy wrote to Florence in London on 5 Oct. 1924 about 'Gertrude B.', saying she was rather dismayed at the bigness of her part '& says she does not like the Tess of the play as well as the Tess of the book (which is intelligent criticism)'. *Letters*, VI, 279.

45. Florence Hardy to Sydney Cockerell, 22 Oct. 1924, *Letters of E & F Hardy*, 213.

46. Diary of Sydney Cockerell, 27 Nov. 1924, British Library Add. MSS 52661.

47. Gertrude Bugler's letter of 18 Feb. 1964 to Cockerell's biographer, Wilfrid Blunt, *Cockerell* (1964), 216.

48. Florence Hardy to Sydney Cockerell, 10 Mar. 1925, *Letters of E & F Hardy*, 220–21.

49. For Florence preventing her from reciting a Hardy poem at a recital at a Dorsetmen's dinner in London, see Florence Hardy to Gertrude Bugler, 7 Feb. 1925, ibid., 219. Cockerell's diary shows that in Aug. 1925 he was still doing his best to allay her uneasiness by pointing out that Gertrude lived at Beaminster, a considerable distance from Max Gate, and that she and Hardy did not even correspond with one another.

50. Florence Hardy to Sir Arthur Pinero, 1 Aug. 1929, ibid., 297.

51. TH to Gertrude Bugler, 7 Feb. 1924, *Letters*, VI, 308.

52. As Note 47, above.

53. Marjorie Lilly reports him telling her in the 1920s that 'Tess was his favourite heroine; "my Tess" he called her.' 'The Hardy I Knew', *Hardy Society Review*, 1, 4 (1978), 100–103.

54. From *À la recherche du temps perdu*. Hardy's note dated July 1926 suggests that someone drew his attention to this passage, because he does not appear to have read Proust otherwise. *The Personal Notebooks of Thomas Hardy*, ed. Richard H. Taylor (1978), 92.

55. Michael Millgate gives the first in *Biography Revisited*, 510, its source a letter from Florence Hardy to Sydney Cockerell in 1924. The second is in the *Life*, Chapter 38, from Mrs Granville-Barker's description of Hardy's visit in 1927.

56. Diary of Sydney Cockerell for 19 Nov. 1923, British Library Add. MSS 52660.

24. Winter Words

1. Marjorie Lilly, 'The Hardy I Knew', *Thomas Hardy Society Review*, 1, 4 (1978), 100–103.

2. On the manuscript he wrote and erased 'Snow at Upper Tooting'.

3. Discussed above in Chapter 9.

4. Discussed above in Chapter 18.

5. TH to Revd H. G. B. Cowley, 16 Dec. 1924, *Letters*, VI, 298.

6. TH to Arthur Benson, 26 Dec. 1924, *Letters*, VI, 300.

7. Diary of Sydney Cockerell for 18 June 1925, British Library Add.

MSS 52662. During 1925 he visited Max Gate in Jan., Mar., June, Aug. and Sept. 21 June: 'TH extremely well, preparing a new volume of poems! TEL came to dinner and we were all in very good spirits.' On Sunday, 22 Mar., TH shows Cockerell 'some of his new poems' and Cockerell goes by car with Florence to spend an hour at T. E. Lawrence's cottage. In 1926 he visited in Apr. and June.

8. M. M. Allen to TH, 23 Aug. 1925, and James Sparks to TH, 11 Sept. 1925, headed 'Almora', Corowa, N.S.W. DCM, Kate Hardy and Lock Collection, B5.

9. H. A. Martin, Hon. Secretary of the Dorchester Dramatic and Debating Society, writing in the *Dorset County Chronicle*, 6 June 1940. Hardy also said that revolutionaries lacked historical knowledge and advised any local parliamentary candidate to stand at the Town Pump on market day and shake hands with as many farmers as possible.

10. Women of thirty and over until 1928, when, soon after his death, they achieved equal voting rights.

11. Florence Hardy to Rutland Boughton, 29 June 1924, *Letters of E & F Hardy*, 208.

12. Florence Hardy to Siegfried Sassoon, 5 July 1926, *Letters of E & F Hardy*, 241.

13. 25 July 1926, *The Diary of Virginia Woolf*, III (1979), 96–101.

14. Leonard Woolf, 'Thomas Hardy', *Athenaeum*, 21 Jan. 1928, 597–8.

15. 1 Nov. 1926, *Life*, Chapter 38.

16. Florence Hardy to Sydney Cockerell, 17 Nov. 1926, *Letters of E & F Hardy*, 245.

17. TH to Ernest Barker, 23 Nov. 1926, *Letters*, VII, 50.

18. Florence Hardy to Sydney Cockerell, 29 Dec. 1926, *Letters of E & F Hardy*, 247.

19. TH to the Granville-Barkers, 29 Dec. 1926, *Letters*, VII, 54.

20. Bertie Norman Stephens, *Hardy and His Gardener* (Beaminster, 1963).

21. Quoted in Ann Thwaite's *Edmund Gosse: A Literary Landscape* (1984), 507.

22. *Life*, Chapter 38.

23. J. C. Squire, *Sunday Mornings*, cited in *Interviews and Recollections*, 233–5.

24. Hardy never heard it. It was first performed early in 1928.

25. The NPG did not accept posthumous representations and would certainly not have considered either Florence or Emma Hardy eligible.

26. Florence Hardy to Sydney Cockerell, 25 Dec. 1927, *Letters of E & F Hardy*, 256.

27. According to Florence, at any rate, in a letter to Howard Bliss, 11 Mar. 1930, *Letters of E & F Hardy*, 304. In a postscript she writes, 'I did not intend to return to this painful topic, but I feel obliged – I asked J. M. Barrie whether he could recall the circumstances of the Abbey burial, and whether Cockerell was against it, as he now represents himself to have been. J. M. B.'s reply, as nearly as I can quote it was: "Why, he was the one who was all for it. I remember that he walked to the station with me the night before Hardy's death, and he was *urging it on me* all the way." Cockerell knew that I did not wish it.'

28. Diary of Sydney Cockerell for 1928, British Library Add. MSS 52666.

29. Ellen Titterington (1899–1977) was in service at Max Gate from 1921 to 1928. This and the quotation in the next paragraph are from her monograph *Hardy and His Parlour-Maid* (Beaminster, 1963).

30. Diary of Kate Hardy, cited in *Biography Revisited*, 531.

Epilogue

1. Dr Mann's account, given years later, was wrong about this and about details of the day of the funeral in London.

2. From Kate Hardy's diary in DCM, quoted in *Biography Revisited*, 533.

3. Florence Hardy to T. E. Lawrence, 5 Mar. 1928, *Letters of E & F Hardy*, 275.

4. Harry Bentley, the postman befriended by Hardy (see Chapter 23) who also delivered post to Dr Mann, believed the story. Bentley lived at 3 Rothesay Road, Dorchester, and died in 1985. He said the doctor called him in, saying, 'Come and look at this', and showed him the biscuit tin.

The theatre Sister Mary Eastment was only twenty-three. She was the daughter of a schoolmistress at Haselbury Plucknett and like many local people had no great admiration for Hardy. She told her daughter that Mr Nash-Wortham summoned her on her free afternoon with 'Sister, I have a job for you. We have to cut out Mr Hardy's heart.' All she could think of was how much she resented losing her free time, and she had no sense of making history. The job was done antiseptically, and she never heard the story of the cat. All this from Mrs A. Brock, her daughter.

5. Ann Thwaite, *Edmund Gosse: A Literary Landscape* (1984), 508.

6. From account by Bertie Norman Stephens, *Hardy and His Gardener* (Beaminster, 1963).

7. 17 Jan. 1928, *The Diary of Virginia Woolf*, III (1979), 173–4. Virginia Woolf was among the mourners and described the pallbearers. She thought the coffin 'like a stage coffin, covered with a white satin cloth'.

8. The late James Gibson showed me a copy of Mrs Shaw's letter to T. E. Lawrence.

9. Hesketh Pearson, *Bernard Shaw* (1961), 378.

10. *The Diary of Virginia Woolf*, III, Note 23.

11. Photocopy of the Dean's letter, clearly dated 16 Jan. 1928 (the day of the funeral), in file given to me by the late James Gibson, with Bartelot's reply. It would be nice to know who the head of the 'great religious body' was – could it have been the King? No member of the royal family attended the funeral, only aides representing them.

12. From William Rothenstein, *Since Fifty: Men and Memories 1922–1938* (1939), 99–104.

13. The diary of Sydney Cockerell, 14 June 1928, British Library Add. MSS 52666.

14. American editions were published at the same time.

15. 'When Dead', published in *Human Shows, Far Phantasies, Songs and Trifles* in 1925, headed 'To—'. The joke about Einstein comes in 'Drinking Song', published posthumously in *Winter Words in Various Moods and Metres* in 1928. 'The Ruined Maid' was written in the 1860s and first published in *Poems of the Past and the Present* in 1901.

Bibliography

UNPUBLISHED MATERIAL

Diary of Sydney Cockerell at the British Library
Diary of Arthur Benson and manuscript of *Moments of Vision* at the Pepys
    Library, Magdalene College, Cambridge
Manuscript of *Jude the Obscure* at the Fitzwilliam Museum, Cambridge
Hardy family letters held in the Dorset County Museum, Dorchester,
    together with manuscripts and other papers, drawings and photographs
Manuscripts, drawings and photographs in the Berg Collection, New
    York Public Library
Hardy and Sparks family letters held at Eton College Library

WORKS BY HARDY

Fiction

Desperate Remedies 1871
Under the Greenwood Tree 1872
A Pair of Blue Eyes 1873
Far from the Madding Crowd 1874
The Hand of Ethelberta 1876
The Return of the Native 1878
The Trumpet-Major 1880
A Laodicean 1881
Two on a Tower 1882
The Mayor of Casterbridge 1886
The Woodlanders 1887
Wessex Tales 1888
A Group of Noble Dames 1891
Tess of the D'Urbervilles 1891

Life's Little Ironies 1894
Jude the Obscure 1895
The Well-Beloved 1897
A Changed Man and Other Tales 1913

The novels have been published in innumerable editions. The old Macmillan pocket editions can be picked up in second-hand bookshops and are usefully small and light enough to go in a pocket or handbag. The Penguin Classics series, which prints from the first editions, annotated and with introductions, is excellent.

Poetry

Wessex Poems and Other Verses 1898
Poems of the Past and the Present 1901
The Dynasts. Part I 1904. Part II 1906. Part III 1908
Time's Laughingstocks and Other Verses 1909
Satires of Circumstance, Lyrics and Reveries 1914
Selected Poems 1916
Moments of Vision and Miscellaneous Verses 1917
Late Lyrics and Earlier with Many Other Verses 1922
The Famous Tragedy of the Queen of Cornwall 1923
Human Shows, Far Phantasies, Songs and Trifles 1925
Winter Words in Various Moods and Metres 1928
Chosen Poems 1929

The poetry, which was initially published in eight separate collections, also exists in many different editions and selections, including two made by Hardy himself: the *Selected Poems* of 1916 and the larger *Chosen Poems*, which he prepared shortly before his death and which was published in 1929. There are two variorum editions: one, edited by James Gibson, is a large single volume that appeared in 1978; the other, by Samuel Hynes, is in five volumes (1982–95) and includes *The Dynasts* and *The Famous Tragedy of the Queen of Cornwall*.

Biographical

What was published as Florence Hardy's two-volume life of Hardy, *The Early Life of Thomas Hardy* (1928) and *The Later Years of Thomas Hardy* (1930), is most conveniently read now in Michael Millgate's one-volume, annotated *The Life and Work of Thomas Hardy* by Thomas Hardy (1984).

The Collected Letters of Thomas Hardy, eds. Michael Millgate and R.L. Purdy. 7 vols. 1978–88

One Rare Fair Woman: Thomas Hardy's Letters to Florence Henniker, eds. Evelyn Hardy and F.B. Pinion 1972

The Architectural Notebook of Thomas Hardy, facsimile with Introduction by C.J.P. Beatty 1966

The Personal Notebooks of Thomas Hardy, ed. Richard H. Taylor 1978

Excluded and Collaborative Stories, ed. Pamela Dalziel 1992

Studies and Specimens Notebook of Thomas Hardy, eds. Michael Millgate and Pamela Dalziel 1994

Thomas Hardy's Public Voice, ed. Michael Millgate 2001

Thomas Hardy's 'Facts' Notebook, ed. William Greenslade 2004

TOPOGRAPHY AND BACKGROUND

Criswick, James, *Walks round Dorchester* 1820

Draper, Jo, *Regency, Riot and Reform* 2000 (Discover Dorset series)

Freeman, Michael, *Railways and the Victorian Imagination* 1999

Hurst, Alan, *Hardy: An Illustrated Dictionary* 1980

Jefferies, Richard, *Hodge and His Masters* 1880

—*Amaryllis at the Fair* 1887

Kerr, Barbara, *Bound to the Soil: A Social History of Dorset* 1968

Kilvert, Francis, *Diaries*. 3 vols. William Plomer ed. 1971

Lea, Hermann, *Thomas Hardy's Wessex* 1969

Lee, C. E., *Passenger Class Distinctions* 1946

Mitford, Mary, *Our Village* [no date but first pub. 1832]

Oakley, Mike, *Railway Stations* 2001 (Discover Dorset series)

O'Sullivan, Timothy, *Thomas Hardy: An Illustrated Biography* 1975

Pevsner, Nikolaus, and Newman, John, *Dorset* 1972 (The Buildings of England series)

Pitt-Rivers, Michael, *Dorset* 1966

Savage, James, *Dorchester and Its Environs* 1832

Wolmar, Christian, *The Subterranean Railway* 2004

BIOGRAPHICAL MATERIAL

Letters of Emma and Florence Hardy (a selection), ed. Michael Millgate 1996

Thomas Hardy: Interviews and Recollections, ed. James Gibson 1999

Hardyana, collected by James Stevens Cox 1966

Hardyana [2], a further collection by James Stevens Cox 1967–71

Collins, Vere H., *Talks with Thomas Hardy at Max Gate 1920–1922* 1971 (first pub. 1928)

Felkin, Elliott, 'Days with Thomas Hardy: From a 1918–19 Diary', *Encounter*, 18 Apr. 1962

Gatrell, Simon, *Hardy the Creator: A Textual Biography* 1988

—*Thomas Hardy's Vision of Wessex* 2003

Gibson, James, *Thomas Hardy: A Literary Life* 1996

Gittings, Robert, *The Young Thomas Hardy* 1975

—*The Older Hardy* 1978

—*The Second Mrs Hardy* 1979

Hands, Timothy, *A Hardy Chronology* 1992

Hardy, Emma, *Some Recollections*, eds. Evelyn Hardy and Robert Gittings 1961

Hedgcock, Frank, *Thomas Hardy: Penseur et Artiste* 1911

Kay-Robinson, Denys, *The First Mrs Thomas Hardy* 1979

Millgate, Michael, *Thomas Hardy: A Biography* 1982

—*Testamentary Acts* 1992

—*Thomas Hardy: A Biography Revisited* 2004

Purdy, R.L., *Thomas Hardy: A Bibliographical Study* 1954

Rabiger, Michael, 'The Hoffman Papers Discovered', *Thomas Hardy Yearbook*, No. 10

Seymour-Smith, Martin, *Hardy* 1994

Sutherland, John, 'Hardy and His Publishers' in *Victorian Novelists and Publishers* 1976

Weber, Carl, *Thomas Hardy and the Lady from Madison Square* 1952

FAMILY AND DORSET

Barclay, Celia, *Nathaniel Sparks: Memoirs of Thomas Hardy's Cousin the Engraver* 1994

Barnes, William, *Selected Poems of William Barnes*, ed. Andrew Motion 1994

—*William Barnes the Dorset Poet*, introduced and selected by Chris Wrigley 1984

Barter, Charles H.S., *Melbury Osmond: The Parish and Its People* 1996

Conybeare, Clare, *Short History of The King's House, Salisbury* 1987

Ginever, Edwin D., *History of Maiden Newton* 1965

Harford, J.B., *Biography of Bishop Moule* 1922

Moule, H. and H. *Fordington Times Society* 1859

Moule, H.C.G., *Memories of a Vicarage* 1913

Moule, Henry, *Scraps of Sacred Verse* 1846

—*Eight Letters to Prince Albert* 1855

Moule, Horace Mosley, *Roman Republic* 1860

Moule, Mary, *The Memory of the Just is Blessed: A Brief Memorial of Mrs Moule of Fordington* 1877

Murray, Amelia Matilda, *Recollections* 1868

Murray, Revd Edward, *Prayers and Collects* 1825

—*The Ethiopic Book of Enoch* 1836

LONDON, EARLY NOVELS AND MARRIAGE

Arch, Joseph, *The Life of Joseph Arch* 1898

Briggs, Asa, *Victorian People* 1965

Davison, Mark, *Hook Remembered Again* 2003

Edel, Leon, *Henry James: The Untried Years* 1953

—*The Middle Years* 1963

Garnett, Henrietta, *Anny: A Life of Anne Isabella Thackeray Ritchie* 2004

Hardy, Emma, *Diaries*, ed. Richard H. Taylor 1985

Humphrey, A.W., *Robert Applegarth* 1913

Layard, George Somes, *Mrs Lynn Linton: Her Life, Letters and Opinions* 1901

Maitland, F.W., *Life and Letters of Leslie Stephen* 1906

Morgan, Charles, *The House of Macmillan* 1944

Paul, Charles Kegan, *Memories* 1899

Tinsley, William, *The Random Recollections of an Old Publisher* 1900

Return of the Native, facsimile manuscript, introduced by Simon Gatrell 1986

LATER YEARS

Cambridge Magazine, ed. C. K. Ogden 1912–20

Blunt, Wilfrid, *Cockerell* 1964

Clodd, Edward, *Memoires* 1916

Cockerell, Sydney, *Friends of a Lifetime: Letters to Sydney Carlyle Cockerell*, ed. Viola Meynell 1940

Dugdale, Florence, 'The Apotheosis of the Minx', *Cornhill*, June 1908

Fortescue, Winifred, *There's Rosemary . . . There's Rue* 1939

Garrett, Anderson, *Hang Your Halo in the Hall: A History of the Savile Club* 1993

Gifford, Henry, 'Thomas Hardy and Emma' in *Essays and Studies* 1966

Gissing, George, *Letters of George Gissing to Edouard Bertz*, ed. A.C. Young 1960

Hardy, Emma, *Alleys, and Spaces* (poems and religious effusions) 1966

Henniker, Florence, *Outlines* 1894

—*In Scarlet and Grey* 1896

—*Contrasts* 1903

Lhombreaud, Roger, *Arthur Symons* 1963

McCabe, Joseph, *Edward Clodd: A Memoir* 1932

Nevill, Dorothy, *Reminiscences of Lady Nevill* 1906

St Helier, Lady, *Memories of Fifty Years* 1909

Sutro, Alfred, *Celebrities and Simple Souls* 1933
Thwaite, Ann, *Edmund Gosse: A Literary Landscape 1849–1928* 1984
Wharton, Edith, *A Backward Glance* 1934
Woolf, Virginia, *Diaries*, Vol. III, ed. Anne Olivier Bell 1980
—*Letters*, Vol. III, ed. Nigel Nicolson 1977

CRITICISM

Lawrence, D.H., *Essay on Thomas Hardy* 1914 (unpublished until 1936, in *Phoenix*)
Woolf, Virginia, 'The Novels of Thomas Hardy' in *Common Reader* (second series) 1932
Eliot, T.S., *After Strange Gods* 1934 (for his attack on Hardy, recanted in letter to Roy Morrell of 15 May 1964, held at Berg: 'The book in which I criticised Thomas Hardy severely is one which I have subsequently regretted, and I regret in particular what I said about Hardy. // I particularly admire *The Mayor of Casterbridge* and parts pf *Far from the Madding Crowd*. There are scenes in both which remain permanently in my memory, such as that when the Mayor of C looks over the bridge and sees his own effigy floating in the water.' Eliot went on to say he found some of the poems 'moving' but thought Hardy should have pruned down his collection.)
Auden, W.H., 'A Literary Transference', *Southern Review*, 1940
Schwartz, Delmore, 'Poetry and Belief in Thomas Hardy', *Southern Review*, 1940
Cecil, David, *Hardy the Novelist* 1943
Brown, Douglas, *Thomas Hardy* 1954
Paterson, John, *The Making of 'The Return of the Native'* 1960
Hardy: A Collection of Critical Essays, ed. Albert Guerard 1963
Lodge, David, *The Language of Fiction* 1966
—'*The Woodlanders*: A Darwinian Pastoral Elegy', Introduction to New Wessex ed. 1974
Howe, Irving, *Thomas Hardy* 1967 (revised 1985)
Miller, J. Hillis, *Thomas Hardy: Distance and Desire* 1970
Millgate, Michael, *Thomas Hardy: His Career as a Novelist* 1971
Williams, Merry, *Thomas Hardy and Rural England* 1972

Williams, Raymond, 'Wessex and the Border' in *The Country and the City* 1973

Ingham, Patricia, 'The Evolution of *Jude the Obscure*', *Review of English Studies*, new series, 27, 1976

Bayley, John, *An Essay on Hardy* 1978

King, Jeanette, *Tragedy in the Victorian Novel* 1978

Critical Approaches to the Fiction of Thomas Hardy, ed. Dale Kramer 1979

Thomas Hardy: The Critical Heritage, ed. R.G. Cox 1995 (first pub. 1979)

Morgan, Rosemarie, *Cancelled Words* 1992 (a study of the changes made to *Far from the Madding Crowd* under Leslie Stephen's editorial directions)

Wright, T.R., *Hardy and His Readers* 2003

Poetry

Richards, I.A., *Science and Poetry* 1926

Lucas, F.L., 'Truth and Compassion' in *Ten Victorian Poets* 1940, reprinted in *Thomas Hardy. Poems: A Casebook*, eds. James Gibson and Trevor Johnson 1979 (a valuable book – see below)

Letters of Ezra Pound, ed. D.D. Paige 1950

Larkin, Philip, 'A Poet's Teaching for Poets' (from a conversation with Vernon Scannell on Radio 4, printed in the *Listener*, 25 July 1968, reprinted in *Thomas Hardy. Poems: A Casebook*, eds. James Gibson and Trevor Johnson 1979)

Marsden, Kenneth, 'Hardy's Vocabulary' in *The Poems of Thomas Hardy* 1969, reprinted in *Thomas Hardy. Poems: A Casebook*, eds. James Gibson and Trevor Johnson 1979

Gunn, Thom, 'The Influence of Ballad-Forms', *Agenda*, 1972, reprinted in *Thomas Hardy. Poems: A Casebook*, eds. James Gibson and Trevor Johnson 1979

Davie, Donald, *Thomas Hardy and British Poetry* 1973

Lerner, Lawrence, *Thomas Hardy's 'The Mayor of Casterbridge': Tragedy or Social History?* 1975

Hynes, Samuel, Introduction to *Selected Poems of Thomas Hardy* 1984

Hardy, Barbara, *Imagining Imagination in Hardy's Poetry and Fiction* 2000

Beer, Gillian, 'Hardy: The After-Life and the Life Before' in *Thomas Hardy: Texts and Contexts*, ed. Phillip Mallet 2002

MISCELLANEOUS

Oxford Reader's Companion to Hardy, ed. Norman Page 2000
Cambridge Companion to Thomas Hardy, ed. Dale Kramer 1999
Maugham, Somerset, *Cakes and Ale* 1930

Text and Illustration Permissions

The publishers would like to thank the following individuals and organizations for their kind permission to reproduce copyright material in the book:

Text

Extracts from letters by Emma Dashwood, Mary Hardy, Helen Holder and Horace Moule, and from Thomas Hardy's 'Wimborne Notebook', are from the Thomas Hardy Collection, Dorset County Museum, Dorchester

Extracts from letters by James Sparks Cary and Thomas Hardy Snr are from the Kate Hardy and Lock Collection, Dorset County Museum, Dorchester

Extracts from the unpublished diaries of A. C. Benson are reproduced by permission of the Master and Fellows of Magdalene College, Cambridge

Illustrations

First Inset
1. The view of Dorchester that Hardy knew from his earliest years (The British Library)
2. Hardy's drawing of his birthplace at Higher Bockhampton, which shows it as it was in the 1890s (from *The Early Life of Thomas Hardy*, 1928)
3. and 4. Hardy's parents in old age (Dorset County Museum)
5. Melbury House, the seat of the Earls of Ilchester (Mary Evans Picture Library / Alamy)

6. Stinsford House, near Bockhampton (Dorset County Museum)

7. Hardy's first school at Lower Bockhampton (Dorset County Museum)

8. The Revd Moule and his family on the lawn in front of his Fordington vicarage (Dorset County Museum)

9. Horace Moule, Hardy's great friend and mentor (Dorset County Museum)

10. Hardy at nineteen, when he was an architectural pupil in Dorchester (National Portrait Gallery)

11. The garden terrace of the rectory at St Juliot, showing the Revd Cadell Holder, his wife, Helen, and her sister, Emma Gifford (Berg Collection, New York Public Library)

12. Emma Gifford (Dorset County Museum)

13. Hardy at thirty (National Portrait Gallery)

14. Hardy's sketch of Emma on her knees searching in the river (Dorset County Museum)

15. Emma's sketch of Hardy holding a flag (Dorset County Museum)

16. Emma's drawing of the summerhouse in the garden of the St Juliot rectory, where she and Hardy often sat together (Berg Collection, New York Public Library)

17. Emma's drawings of the Boscastle Valley and 'The Watercourse' of the Valency River (from *The Early Life of Thomas Hardy*, 1928)

18. A page of Emma's honeymoon diary (The British Library)

19. Riverside Villas, near Sturminster Newton, where Hardy and Emma enjoyed two happy years from 1876 (Rodney Legg / Hallsgrove)

20. The view of the Blackmore Vale from Hardy's upstairs study window at Riverside Villas, where he wrote *The Return of the Native* (Rodney Legg / Hallsgrove)

Second Inset

21. Hardy at thirty-four, looking the part of the successful Victorian literary man (Dorset County Museum)

22. Leslie Stephen, the editor of the *Cornhill*, who commissioned *Far from the Madding Crowd* (Mortimer Rare Book Room, Smith College)

23. The house in Tooting taken by the Hardys in 1878 (Dorset County Museum)

24. Max Gate, the house designed by Hardy and built by his brother. Hardy and Emma moved there in June 1885 (National Portrait Gallery)

25. The hall at Max Gate (Dorset County Museum)

26. Hardy dressed for the road, with his bicycle (Dorset County Museum)

27. Mrs Florence Henniker, with whom Hardy fell in love in 1893 (photo by Chancellor of Dublin, 1894)

28. Emma Hardy in her later years, dressed for one of her garden parties (Berg Collection, New York Public Library)

29. Drawing of Florence Dugdale by William Strang (National Portrait Gallery)

30. Florence Dugdale and Hardy on the beach at Aldeburgh in 1909 (Dorset County Museum)

31. Florence, Hardy and their dog Wessex (Bettman / Corbis)

32. Luncheon visit to the Hardys by the Prince of Wales in 1923 (Dorset County Museum)

33. Hardy in 1924: 'a human being, not "the great man" ' (Dorset County Museum)

34. Augustus John's 1923 portrait of Hardy (Fitzwilliam Museum, Cambridge © The Estate of the artist / Bridgeman Art Library)

Index